Black Republicans
and the Transformation of the GOP

POLITICS AND CULTURE IN MODERN AMERICA

Series Editors:
Margot Canaday, Glenda Gilmore, Michael Kazin, Stephen Pitti, Thomas J. Sugrue

Volumes in the series narrate and analyze political and social change in the broadest
dimensions from 1865 to the present, including ideas about the ways people have
sought and wielded power in the public sphere and the language and institutions
of politics at all levels—local, national, and transnational. The series is motivated
by a desire to reverse the fragmentation of modern U.S. history and to encourage
synthetic perspectives on social movements and the state, on gender, race, and labor,
and on intellectual history and popular culture.

BLACK REPUBLICANS

AND THE TRANSFORMATION OF THE GOP

Joshua D. Farrington

PENN

UNIVERSITY OF PENNSYLVANIA PRESS

PHILADELPHIA

Published by
University of Pennsylvania Press
Philadelphia, Pennsylvania 19104–4112
www.upenn.edu/pennpress

Printed in the United States of America
on acid-free paper
1 3 5 7 9 10 8 6 4 2

Library of Congress Cataloging-in-Publication Data
ISBN 978-0-8122-4852-4

To Dad

CONTENTS

We Negro-Americans, sing with all Americans . . .
Let freedom ring—From every mountain side, let
freedom ring! Not only from the Green Mountains
and White Mountains of Vermont and New
Hampshire; Not only from the Catskills of New
York; but from the Ozarks in Arkansas, from the
Stone Mountain in Georgia, from the Great Smokies
of Tennessee, and from the Blue Ridge Mountains
of Virginia . . . may the Republican Party, under
God, from every mountain side, Let Freedom Ring!"

—Archibald Carey, Jr., Floor Speech at the 1952
Republican National Convention

BLACK REPUBLICANS

AND THE TRANSFORMATION OF THE GOP

Introduction

In 1986, the Republican Party of Memphis, Tennessee, sent a form letter to residents of the city's African American neighborhoods promising to bring "economic growth" through tax cuts. Included among the recipients was Roberta Church, who once served on Tennessee's Republican State Executive Committee, held influential positions in the administrations of Presidents Dwight Eisenhower and Richard Nixon, and was the daughter of Robert Church, one of the most powerful black Republicans of the twentieth century. Scrawling her response on the back of the envelope, the third generation black Republican found it "very ironic" that the Republican Party of Memphis—a party that her father had single-handedly built decades earlier—had become a lily-white haven whose only effort to reach out to African Americans came via a generic letter tone-deaf to the needs of her community. She then lamented that "since the passing of Henry Cabot Lodge, Jacob Javits, Hugh Scott, and Nelson Rockefeller who tried to have the party live up to its founding principles," the party had become home to the conservative "Goldwater wing," advocating policies that had little room for moderates like herself.[1]

Most black Republican activists who joined Roberta Church inside the Grand Old Party (GOP) would no doubt have echoed her reply. These men and women spent decades of their lives fighting from within the Republican Party for civil rights and "first-class citizenship." During these transformative decades of the mid-twentieth century, black Republicans forged an alliance with white liberals and moderates in their party, and were constant lobbyists for a proactive civil rights agenda at the national, state, and municipal levels. They were spokesmen for their communities, untiring advocates for civil rights, and voices of conscience inside the party. While the GOP's relationship with African Americans changed dramatically from the New Deal to the 1970s, the many black Republicans who remained inside the party actively engaged in the struggle for civil rights in areas such as fair employment, housing, voting, and desegregation of schools and public accommodations. This book tells their story.

A 1973 survey of black Republican leaders in Chicago offers a particularly illuminating picture. The study found a "high incidence of participation in the civil rights movement," including "active involvement in protests, demonstrations, and sit-ins." One of the Republicans sampled, Genoa Washington, was a current state representative and had previously served as president of the Chicago branch of the National Association for the Advancement of Colored People (NAACP).[2] He was a powerbroker not only in the state capitol, but within the states' black establishment. Black Republicans like Washington were a constant voice for black equality inside the party's infrastructure, while also playing influential roles in civil rights organizations, including the NAACP, the Congress of Racial Equality (CORE), and the Southern Christian Leadership Conference (SCLC).

Unlike contemporary black Republicans of the twenty-first century, many of whom have a tenuous relationship with other African American leaders, black Republicans of the mid-twentieth century were recognized by their peers—including Democrats—for their contributions to the black freedom struggle. L. K. Jackson, whom Martin Luther King, Sr., called "the Daddy of the militant civil rights movement," was not only the leader of numerous direct action protests in Gary, Indiana, but was also one of the city's loudest supporters of the Republican Party. Benjamin Hooks, who headed the national NAACP from 1977 to 1992, often referenced his years as a Republican civil rights activist in Memphis, and claimed that his black Republican mentors spent their lives "beating the drum for equality." Two of the most well known black Republicans of the civil rights era, Edward W. Brooke and Jackie Robinson, joined Thurgood Marshall, Martin Luther King, Jr., Medgar Evers, and other civil rights leaders in receiving the NAACP's highest honor, the Spingarn Medal. The NAACP officially praised Samuel C. Jackson, one of the most powerful African Americans in the Nixon administration, for carrying "the cause of civil rights into the high echelons of the GOP." The Congressional Black Caucus recognized his colleague in the Nixon White House, Arthur Fletcher, in 2005 as "a true pioneer in the movement for racial and socioeconomic equality." These men, and many others, worked within their party to promote the aims of the civil rights movement.[3]

One would be hard pressed, however, to find substantive analysis of black Republicans in the historical literature on black politics, which has tended to portray the Democratic Party as the exclusive home of African Americans since the 1940s. Countless authors have written with an underlying assumption that black voters bid farewell to "the party of Lincoln" during the New

Deal era and never looked back. Typically ignored altogether, when mentioned black Republicans have too often been dismissed as accommodationists without community support or elderly partisans clutching to hallowed memories of Abraham Lincoln. As historian Richard Walter Thomas writes, black Republicans since the 1930s have been "relegated to the dust bin of black political history."[4]

Though this narrative of black partisanship remains popular in the accounts of many scholars and journalists, a number of recent studies point towards significant partisan fluidity among black voters in the midcentury U.S., and demonstrate that near monolithic black identification with the Democratic Party did not fully solidify until the 1960s.[5] Black voters from the 1930s through 1960s practiced a high degree of ticket splitting, with many casting their vote for Democratic presidents but Republican gubernatorial, senate, congressional, and municipal candidates. Indeed, it was on the local level, even in communities that voted reliably Democratic in presidential elections, where black and white Republican candidates repeatedly secured electoral victories in the mid-twentieth century's fluid political landscape. For this reason, this study takes a wide-angled view, examining Republican politics on the national, state, and local levels. As often as black Republicans may have been marginalized within the national establishment, they found powerful white allies on the state and local levels.

Deeming the political arena as the best avenue to achieve civil rights victories, black Republicans stressed that African Americans should actively work inside both parties, forcing each side to compete for the African American vote. This argument for bipartisanship (accompanied by nonpartisan independence) was well received by many within the middle class leadership of the civil rights establishment. Martin Luther King, Jr., A. Philip Randolph, and other black leaders shied away from committing their allegiance to a Democratic Party still dominated by race-baiting southerners devoted to preserving white supremacy. Indeed, the Democratic Party's primary advantage over Republicans prior to the early 1960s was its connection to the New Deal's labor and welfare state provisions, not a stronger commitment than the GOP to civil rights. Both Republicans and Democrats had relatively equal records on civil rights, and strategies promoting black participation in both parties were commonplace throughout the civil rights era. Martin Luther King and the NAACP's strategic stances of partisan independence would have been less effective had black voters not been willing to support state and local Republican candidates who embraced civil rights. This two-party strategy was a unifying force, connecting black Republicans to a larger network of nonpartisan activists. To black Republicans and their independent allies, the GOP offered African Americans an additional vehicle to pursue an active civil rights agenda, and provided them access to the power necessary to achieve political reform.

Their value to midcentury politics notwithstanding, black Republicans make few appearances in the plethora of books on the modern Republican Party, even those focused on issues of race. Some of these works give a great deal of attention to liberal and moderate Republican opposition to the rising tide of conservatism within the party, but the people they discuss are almost exclusively white elites.[6] In the few instances where black Republicans are mentioned, they are treated as victims caught off guard by a party turned racist, or are defined by extremists who fell far to the right of the black Republican mainstream.[7]

Black Republican activism in the South is particularly understudied.[8] So-called "Black-and-Tan" organizations, the name given by Democrats to integrated southern Republican parties with black leadership, play a prominent role in this book. African Americans held positions of power and harnessed black voters in Memphis, Louisville, Atlanta, and other cities across the South. Their activism, however, has been overlooked in contemporary studies of southern Republicanism.[9] Even scholars who mention the presence of southern black Republicans tend to write them off as marginal figures stuck in Reconstruction era politics.[10] Additional depictions of a Democratic "Solid South" devoid of Republicans similarly ignore Black-and-Tan organizations, and popular narratives of the "rise" of southern conservative Republicans implicitly ignore a parallel form of "Black-and-Tan" southern Republicanism characterized by its biracial leadership's commitment to black advancement. Though mostly confined to the major cities of the urban South, Black-and-Tan leaders like Robert Church of Memphis were important figures in southern black politics, wielding power and influence in both their communities and the national GOP.

Though African Americans have largely been left out of party narratives, there have been a number of biographies of individual black Republicans that emphasize their contributions to the civil rights movement.[11] Overreliance on biographies, though valuable sources, runs the risk of cordoning off black Republicans from a larger network of fellow black partisans. Additionally, a number of recent works have examined persistent strains of black social, cultural, and religious conservatism. These studies play an important role in expanding our knowledge of black political thought; however, they may serve to further obscure popular perceptions of black Republicans by focusing exclusively on the Right.[12] Rather than placing mainstream black Republicans of the mid-twentieth century within a middle class consensus that existed among most African Americans of the same socioeconomic status, many writers have incorrectly used the terms "black conservative" and "black Republican" interchangeably.[13] This book, on the other hand, examines the full ideological range of black Republicanism in the twentieth century, emphasizing their moderate and liberal stances on issues of social justice.

Paying particular attention to the voices and actions of black Republicans—most of whom openly objected to the ideals and strategies of the post-World War II conservative movement—this book treats them as savvy political operators who used their partisan affiliation to advance the goals of the civil rights movement. Rather than viewing black Republicans as pawns of a hopelessly lily-white party, or as out-of-touch relics, it argues that they were pragmatists who saw the potential benefits in two-party competition throughout the mid-twentieth century. From the presidential nominations of Wendell Willkie in 1940 to Richard Nixon in 1960, the Eastern Establishment dominated the party at the national level, running on platforms that rivaled or surpassed their Democratic counterparts in the field of civil rights. To black Republicans, this moderate establishment offered a viable alternative for black voters, and a means to pressure both parties to support civil rights legislation.

Even after the Right had assumed control of the Republican infrastructure by 1964, moderates and liberals remained an important voice in party affairs for more than a decade afterward. Although conservatives undeniably played a significant role in the Republican Party of the 1960s and 1970s, there existed an unresolved intraparty "political and ideological tug-of-war," where powerful liberals and moderates like Nelson Rockefeller, Hugh Scott, and John Sherman Cooper maintained a sizeable base—in which African Americans were a key constituency—and refused to concede to the conservative groundswell.[14] And though conservatives undeniably emerged as the dominant force within the party, their triumph was far from inevitable.[15] It was in this ideological contest for the future of the GOP that black Republicans in the civil rights era operated and maneuvered in their quest to form a feasible alternative to the Democratic Party.

Though important figures within the civil rights movement, most black Republicans possessed a distinctly middle- and upper-class brand of politics.

In contrast to the New Deal-inflected activism of other African Americans, black Republicans were not drawn to the labor and welfare oriented policies that were bread and butter to the Democratic base. Though a number of black Republican leaders did not oppose collective bargaining, there was never a strong tie between them and the labor movement, which was one of the strongest forces in the Democratic coalition. While this lack of ties to organized labor provided black Republicans more leeway to address union discrimination, the organizational and grassroots edge that unions, in their ability to reach millions of black voters, gave to Democrats was a perpetual obstacle for Republicans by the 1930s.

Secure in their own economic status, black Republicans also did not seek government welfare relief, nor view it as essential to the uplift of their communities. Rather, their conception of civil rights was dominated by a desire to promote economic advancement through black businesses and equal employment opportunities, and to achieve sociopolitical equality by ending de jure segregation. Thus, while they often diverged from black Democrats on economic policy, black Republicans converged with the black mainstream on pivotal civil rights issues, including fair employment, fair housing, equality in the voting booth, and the complete dismantling of Jim Crow. Their vision for black advancement was not just distinct from that of many black Democrats, whose political impulses also lent support for Roosevelt's New Deal and Lyndon Johnson's War on Poverty, but was also a vision much closer to the actual achievements of the civil rights movement. Prior to the passage of the major federal civil rights legislation of the 1960s, the differences between black Republicans and Democrats were masked by their shared desire to rid the nation of the scourge of legalized discrimination. By 1968, however, as the civil rights movement shifted to issues of economic inequality, the stark class-based ideological differences between black Republicans and Democrats were manifest in their conflicting views of economic progress.

William T. Coleman, Jr., typifies midcentury black Republican activism and ideology. An integral member of the NAACP Legal Defense Fund (where he would later serve as president), Coleman helped dismantle Jim Crow through his work on *Brown v. Board of Education* and other major civil rights cases. His objective was the eradication of "state-sanctioned racial discrimination," and the creation of "a fully integrated society." Once the legal impediments against African Americans were torn down, they could then "apply their God-given talents to reach their potential." While this goal was shared by many black leaders, Coleman departed from his contemporaries in criticizing "well-intended but ill-conceived" government welfare programs. He condemned Democrats for creating "a huge government-dependent constituency," believing that the Democrats' New Deal and War on Poverty amplified "dependence on the federal largess, deterring minorities from competing in the economic mainstream." Instead, Coleman advocated policies such as affirmative action and skills training that would lead to independence and self-sufficiency. It was not until the legal barriers of Jim Crow were torn down in the 1960s, however, that Coleman's economic ideas came to the fore.[16] Though his positions on welfare differed from those of many African Americans, Coleman was a major actor in the legal dismantling of Jim Crow in the 1940s through 1960s, and one of the GOP's loudest proponents of affirmative action from the 1970s onward. Like other black Republicans, Coleman was not a marginal figure, or an anomaly, in the African American freedom struggle.

Written chronologically, this book explores how black Republicans navigated the shifting currents of GOP politics from the 1930s through the 1970s. It begins with the historic relationship between African Americans and the Republican Party, and explores the continued presence of African Americans inside the party during the New Deal era. Drawn largely from the ranks of the black middle and upper classes, black Republicans were not attracted to the government relief provided by the Roosevelt administration, but instead intensified their protests for civil rights. Far from being an aberration in black communities during the 1930s and 1940s, black Republicans remained deeply entrenched in the political landscape. They led southern Black-and-Tan Republican organizations, ran competitive campaigns in municipal and state elections in the North, and agitated for fair employment, military desegregation, and civil rights legislation.

With the return of the party to the presidency under Dwight Eisenhower in the 1950s, black Republicans were the beneficiaries of high-ranking federal appointments and influential positions within the party, which remained a viable political alternative for many African Americans. From these relative positions of power, black Republicans continued to advocate their civil rights agenda. Despite their vocal criticisms of the administration, many black Republicans in the late 1950s remained loyal to the party they believed could surpass the Democrats in advancing the cause of racial equality. The political victories of Nelson Rockefeller and other liberals sustained this hope.

The 1960 election proved to be a decisive turning point in the GOP's relationship with black voters. As Richard Nixon's campaign unfolded, he reached

out to both African Americans and racially conservative southerners. Black
Republicans, like most African Americans, criticized this paradoxical strategy, and warned against an alliance with the burgeoning conservative movement. Following Nixon's defeat, Barry Goldwater and fellow conservatives
launched a revolution inside the GOP and assumed control of much of the
party's infrastructure. Though many black Republicans deserted the party
during this period, those who remained persisted in an increasingly uphill
battle to encourage the party to embrace civil rights and make sincere efforts
to court black voters. As participants in the civil rights movement, black Republicans also continued to fight for black equality as community leaders and
politicians. Like other Republican liberals, they found success in state and
local elections in places like Pennsylvania, New York, and Kentucky, but
found themselves on the outside of the national party's leadership. As the
GOP moved toward the right, black Republicans shifted their focus from recruiting African Americans to preventing their party from being taken over
by conservatives who were antagonistic to their vision of civil rights.

    After Goldwater's crushing defeat, conservatives, liberals, and moderates
contested the future direction of their disoriented party. Like other factions,
black Republicans sought to exploit this state of instability, and launched an
organized and aggressive effort to defeat the party's expanding conservatism.
Additionally, as liberal and moderate Republicans remained active inside
their party, politicians like Winthrop Rockefeller and George Romney continued to offer African Americans hope for the party's future.

    As the civil rights movement achieved its major legislative victories by the
late 1960s, it turned to economic and structural issues left unchanged by the
dismantling of Jim Crow. It was in these areas where black Republicans diverged from other civil rights leaders, but found allies among young black
nationalists drawn to their ideas of self-help and self-determination. As President Nixon sought to court these black nationalists in place of traditional
civil rights leaders, a new generation of black Republicans were drawn to the
GOP. Floyd McKissick of CORE and others found an ally in the president,
who offered black nationalists a "piece of the action" through his black capitalism initiatives. The Nixon era was both an exciting and trying time for
black Republicans. Black businessmen enjoyed massive federal support, but
many longstanding black Republicans who had previously allied with the
Eastern Establishment found themselves outside Nixon's circle, unable to stop
the administration from approaching civil rights with "benign neglect." Just
as the civil rights movement had become fractured and decentralized by the

1970s, so had black Republicanism splintered along ideological and strategic lines, as multiple leaders and organizations competed for the attention of their party's leadership.

This book, then, is the story not just of black Republicans, but of the Republican Party itself. Black Republicans were actors in a larger drama of a party seeking to find its way in the wake of the seismic political shift unleashed by the New Deal. The mid-twentieth-century battles for the future of the Republican Party between liberals, moderates, and conservatives not only provided an opportunity for black Republicans to forge alliances in their quest for civil rights, but also gave them a platform from which they could serve as the conscience of their party as they urged it to not forget its historic ties to African Americans.

Though they do not fit neatly into the traditional narratives of either the civil rights movement or Republican Party, black Republicans deserve overdue historical recognition. To exclude them is to deny them the place they rightfully earned in their decades' long fight to compel their nation—and their party—to address civil rights. As George W. Lee, who served as a powerful force inside the Tennessee Republican Party from the 1920s through 1960s, declared towards the end of his career, "long before the country paid any attention to legalized civil rights movements, before there was any civil rights laws, I was fighting for Negro freedom and first class citizenship."[17] Lee's fight, like the fight of black Republicans across the country in the mid-twentieth century, was against not only Jim Crow, but also for the future of his own party.

CHAPTER 1

Farewell to the Party of Lincoln?
Black Republicans in the New Deal Era

Frederick Douglass's well-known adage that "the Republican Party is the deck, all else is the sea" reflects the significance of the Party of Abraham Lincoln to black politics for more than five decades after the Civil War. Even by the 1930s, when the Grand Old Party lost millions of black voters to Franklin Roosevelt's Democratic Party, many African Americans still lingered on the GOP deck. Far from being an aberration in black communities during the 1930s and 1940s, Republicans remained deeply entrenched in the African American political landscape, leading southern "Black-and-Tan" organizations, running competitive campaigns in municipal and state elections, and lobbying for civil rights. As politicians, black Republican officials like Kentucky's Charles W. Anderson and Chicago's Archibald Carey, Jr., sponsored, and sometimes secured, passage of groundbreaking state and local civil rights legislation. Others, such as Robert Church, Jr., and Grant Reynolds, partnered with A. Philip Randolph and other independent black leaders in protest against racial discrimination. Though they were not members of Roosevelt's New Deal coalition, black Republicans remained integral figures inside communities across the nation, and their emphasis on eliminating Jim Crow and other blatant forms of institutional racism remained popular with their allies in the black middle class.[1]

In the Reconstruction years that followed the Civil War and the end of slavery, black Republican voters and politicians became fixtures of southern politics. During these transformative years of the late 1860s and 1870s, approximately 2,000 African Americans held public offices that ranged from county administrators to senators. Black Republican P. B. S. Pinchback served as governor of Louisiana, and U.S. senators Blanche Bruce and Hiram Revels represented Mississippi. Over half the politicians elected in South Carolina between 1867 and 1876 were black, including Representative Joseph Rainey and Senator Robert Smalls, who were joined in Washington, D.C., by African Americans representing southern states spanning from Virginia through the Deep South. These politicians, on both the federal and state levels, played instrumental roles in the passage of the south's and the nation's first civil rights laws and progressive reforms in education, orphanages, asylums, and economic development.[2]

Black Republicans were also the targets of systematic violence at the hands of ex-Confederates intent on restoring white supremacy in the up-ended South. In 1873, an estimated one hundred and fifty African Americans were killed by a mob of white Democrats in Colfax, Louisiana, following a contested election. Similar massacres occurred across the South from New Orleans to Wilmington, North Carolina, through the end of the century. Terrorist organizations such as the Ku Klux Klan served as Democratic proxies bent on ridding the South of black voters and their white Republican allies. By the 1890s, their campaign of violence and intimidation had paid off, as Democratic politicians swept into state offices, where they rolled back voting rights, instituted racial segregation, and turned a blind eye to murderous lynch mobs resolved to keep African Americans "in their place" of inferiority. This racially oppressive Jim Crow South, built and preserved by Democrats, would remain the defining characteristic of southern politics, society, and culture for the next half century.[3]

In the face of Democratic resurgence, the national Republican Party abandoned the South, and shifted its focus to northern businessmen and to industrial development. Despite this betrayal, the GOP remained one of the nation's only institutions for black political advancement. In the South, where many African Americans could not even vote, black elites still controlled the skeletal remains of Republican parties in many states throughout the early decades of the twentieth century. Among their primary roles was that of patronage dispenser during the administrations of the Republican presidents who governed all but eight years from 1897 to 1933. "Black-and-Tan" organizations, a name given to southern Republican parties by Democrats, supported the northeastern wing of the party as delegates to national conventions, and in return were rewarded with financial assistance and political appointments. They were often responsible for recommending federal marshals, attorneys, and judges in their respective states, and were even privately treated with deference by Democrats seeking federal jobs.[4]

While the influence of black Republicans within southern politics was limited to patronage, they had a modicum of power inside the national party infrastructure. As residents of rural states that elected few Republicans to national office, they held disproportionate representation within the Republican National Committee (RNC). According to GOP rules, regardless of population, each state was allotted two members on the committee, who set the party's agenda by planning the national convention, allocating state delegates, and running the party nominee's presidential campaign. As state representatives within the GOP infrastructure, some black southerners had connections that extended deep into the halls of Washington, D.C., and were among the few African Americans of the early twentieth century with the ability to leverage white politicians for a share of spoils and patronage. Though a nation shrouded in discrimination forced many Black-and-Tans to adopt a public stance that did not openly challenge white supremacy, members wheeled-and-dealed behind the scenes for piecemeal benefits on behalf of their communities.[5]

In Georgia, for example, Henry Lincoln Johnson and Benjamin J. Davis, Sr., controlled the allotment of federal patronage from the 1910s through the 1930s. Davis represented the state as a delegate to every Republican National Convention from 1908 until his death in 1945, and served as one of Georgia's two members on the national committee and as secretary of Georgia's Republican Executive Committee. Other African Americans in high-ranking positions included William Shaw, secretary of the Georgia Republican State Central Committee, and national committeewoman Mamie Williams. Supported by Atlanta's large population of middle-class African Americans, Georgia's Black-and-Tan leadership was among the most active in the South. Davis and Shaw made the black vote an important factor in Atlanta's municipal elections through intensive registration drives, and Davis, a founding member of the Atlanta branch of the National Association for the Advancement of Colored People (NAACP) and an occasional member of the Platform Committee, successfully pressed the national party to include anti-lynching legislation on party platforms.[6]

African Americans in other southern states possessed similar positions of influence within GOP ranks. Little Rock attorney Scipio Jones controlled federal patronage in Arkansas for almost three decades, and served as a delegate to national conventions into the 1940s. In South Carolina, N. J. Frederick served as Richland County (Columbia) commissioner and as a delegate to national conventions throughout the 1920s and 1930s. As secretary of the Republican State Central Committee and secretary of the Orleans Parish

Central Committee, Walter L. Cohen led the Louisiana Republican Party from 1898 until his death in 1930, and was appointed to one of the most valued federal posts in the South, comptroller of customs for the Port of New Orleans.[7]

Black control of southern Republican organizations did not always go unchallenged. Their opponents, self-professed "Lily-Whites," consisted mainly of southern industrialists who were skeptical of Democratic populist appeals, and sought to "purify" the GOP of African Americans in order to bring competitive two-party politics to the South. On issues of white supremacy, there were few differences between Lily-Whites and race-baiting Democrats. Though they assumed control of the GOP in some states, such as North Carolina, their ascendance was far from guaranteed, as the case of Mississippi demonstrates. Despite fierce Lily-White opposition in the Magnolia State, a delegation led by black attorney Perry W. Howard was seated at the 1924 Republican National Convention, and Howard was elected to represent the state alongside an African American woman, Mary Booze, on the national committee. Locally, S. D. Redmond, a black dentist from Jackson, became chairman of the state executive committee, a post he held until 1948. Though Lily-Whites would continue to challenge Howard's leadership, the victories of his Black-and-Tan faction in the mid-1920s solidified his power for the next three decades. Howard attended all but one national convention as a delegate from 1912 to 1960, and served as one of Mississippi's two members on the national committee until his death in 1961, the longest tenure of a committeeperson in party history.[8]

Despite being a fierce competitor of Lily-Whites, Howard was mostly silent on the issue of civil rights. In 1921, he became the highest paid black federal employee, when President Warren G. Harding appointed him special assistant to the attorney general. After moving to Washington, D.C., he rarely returned to Mississippi, and, unlike Benjamin Davis, Sr., of Georgia and other more race-conscious Black-and-Tans, Howard declined to challenge his party on issues of race, and even joined conservatives in opposing anti-lynch legislation. His accommodationism appealed to Mississippi's Democratic establishment, who defended him in 1928 after he was indicted on charges of selling federal jobs. Not only did Democrats receive over 90 percent of Howard's appointments, but they also enjoyed the presence of an allegedly corrupt black official as the head of the state's Republican Party.[9]

As much as Howard represented the most dubious example of Black-and-Tan politics, the Republican Party of neighboring Tennessee sustained the hope many African Americans placed in the GOP. The state's party was shared by traditionally Republican Appalachian counties in the east and Black-and-Tans in the west led by Robert R. Church, Jr., of Memphis. The son of one of the wealthiest black men in America, Church retired from the family-owned Solvent Savings Bank as a twenty-seven-year-old millionaire, and devoted his life to politics. He was first elected as a delegate to the 1912 Republican National Convention, and over the subsequent decades served on the state Republican Executive Committee and the Republican State Primary Board.[10]

His standing in the party was enhanced by his ability to finance a large share of southern and midwestern Republican campaigns with his own money, or money he raised via his family's extensive business network. Preferring to wield influence behind the scenes, and in spite of vehement opposition from state Democrats, Church secured patronage for major southern appointments, including several racially progressive federal judges and the U.S. attorney general for West Tennessee. He also recommended African Americans to positions inside his district and within the federal government. Because of Church, African Americans made up almost 80 percent of Memphis's mail carriers in the 1920s, who received the same salary and pension as their white coworkers. On the national level, he secured positions for Charles W. Anders as the internal revenue collector for New York's wealthiest district and James A. Cobb as judge of the Washington, D.C., municipal court. One of the South's most rabid segregationists, Alabama senator James Heflin, gave inadvertent homage to Church's influence when reciting a derogatory poem on the floor of the Senate in 1929: "Offices up a 'simmon tree / Bob Church on de ground / Bob Church say to de 'pointing power / Shake dem 'pointments down."[11]

In addition to securing federal posts for African Americans, Church was deeply concerned with issues of black social and political equality. A close friend of NAACP executive secretary James Weldon Johnson, Church served on the organization's national board of directors and contributed to its growing presence in the South by subsidizing nearly seventy branches in fourteen states. He also organized the Lincoln League of Memphis to ward off Lily-White opponents in February 1916. The league registered almost 10,000 voters by the fall, and black Republicans outnumbered Lily-Whites by a four-to-one margin, comprising almost one-third of Shelby County's total electorate.[12]

Three years later, Church expanded the league into a national organization comprised of some of the country's most influential African Americans.

Figure 1. Black-and-Tan leaders outside Robert Church, Jr.'s Solvent Savings Bank and
Trust in Memphis, Tennessee, circa 1920s. Left to right: Church, Henry Lincoln
Johnson, Roscoe Conkling Simmons, Walter L. Cohen, John T. Fisher, and Perry W.
Howard. M.S.0071.038087.001, Robert R. Church Family of Memphis Collection,
University Libraries Preservation and Special Collections, University of Memphis.

In February 1920, four hundred delegates attended the Lincoln League's first
national convention in Chicago, and demanded that the Republican National
Committee increase the presence of African Americans in the forthcoming
presidential campaign. RNC Chairman Will H. Hays responded by appointing five members of the league, Church, James Weldon Johnson, Roscoe Conkling Simmons, S. A. Furniss, and William H. Lewis, to the Advisory
Committee on Policies and Platforms. On election day, Church further
demonstrated his importance to the GOP when black voters helped secure
President Harding's victory in Tennessee, the only southern state to swing to
the Republican column.[13]

    As Church assumed a national role in the 1920s, his pupil, George W. Lee,
took control of duties in Memphis. A World War I veteran commissioned by
the Army as a lieutenant, Lee founded a successful insurance company in the

1920s. "Lt. Lee," as he referred to himself, secured the promotion of the county's first black rural mail carrier, post office station superintendent, and foreman, and the mid-South region's first assistant postal distribution officer. An active member of the Memphis NAACP and Urban League, Lee also drafted resolutions for the national Lincoln League demanding that the Republican Party increase federal appointments of African Americans, pass anti-lynch legislation, and reach out to black voters by combating Jim Crow. Like Church's, Lee's partisan affiliation was not based on sentimental attachment, but, in his own words, he sought to use "the machinery of the Republican Party to advance the cause of the Negro."[14]

African Americans in northern cities also found positions within Republican ranks. Black Republicans held influence in Seattle, Washington, which had a long history of progressive Republicanism that reached out to black voters, where they continued to obtain local and state patronage positions from the national party throughout the 1920s and 1930s. Well into the late 1930s, African Americans in Philadelphia remained a vital constituency of the city's Republican machine, whose black supporters included E. Washington Rhodes (a state legislator and publisher of the *Philadelphia Tribune*) and city magistrates J. Austin Norris and Edward Henry. Black Republicans also played a prominent role in Chicago, home to one of the largest GOP machines in the country. Roscoe Conkling Simmons, nephew of Booker T. Washington and president of the South Ward Republican Committee, politically organized waves of black immigrants fleeing the South, and procured licenses for black undertakers, barbers, and pharmacists. His work culminated in the 1928 election of black Republican Oscar DePriest to the U.S. House of Representatives.[15]

Though African Americans had a presence in the RNC and state parties in the 1920s, the decade's three Republican presidents did little to ease a growing frustration among rank-and-file black voters. Presidents Harding and Calvin Coolidge failed to reverse the policies of their Democratic predecessor, Woodrow Wilson, that segregated federal departments. Coolidge, one of the most hands-off presidents in U.S. history, could barely even denounce lynching or the Ku Klux Klan, let alone actively pursue a civil rights agenda. Most notably, despite Republican control of both houses of Congress and the White House throughout the decade, the party failed to pass a promised anti-lynching law. By the end of the decade, black voters in the North had already begun the process of realignment toward more sympathetic Democratic politicians.[16]

The national Democratic Party, however, was not a welcoming alternative, as it still had a large southern bloc and made few efforts to court African Americans. There were no black delegates at the 1928 Democratic National Convention in Houston, and black attendants were segregated behind humiliating chicken wire. By contrast, forty-nine black delegates attended the Republican convention in Kansas City, though the party's nominee was not much of an improvement over his lackluster predecessors. Herbert Hoover, a former U.S. secretary of commerce with few black contacts in his home state of Iowa, ignored black Republicans like Robert Church and instead courted southern Lily-Whites in order to secure his nomination. His supporters deleted phrasing from the platform that condemned Lily-White discrimination against Black-and-Tans, and a former Klansman was named his southern campaign manager.[17]

In spite of Hoover's nomination, many black Republicans remained loyal to the party. Robert Vann of the *Pittsburgh Courier* and Claude Barnett of the Associated Negro Press served as publicity directors of the RNC Colored Voters Division, and Nannie Burroughs and Daisy Lampkin of the National Association of Colored Women mobilized on behalf of the Women's Division. Some joined Robert Church in vocally criticizing Hoover's nomination. Near the end of the campaign, in response to growing fears of black desertion, Hoover met with Church, and promised that his administration would respect southern Black-and-Tan leadership. Church subsequently purchased a full page ad in the *Chicago Defender*, one of the nation's most widely circulated black newspapers, where he reluctantly endorsed Hoover. Though he was "not satisfied with some of Mr. Hoover's [Lily-White] company," Church argued that Al Smith, the Democratic nominee, would be politically indebted to white southerners despite his northern, progressive background, concluding, "the Republican Party offers us little. The Democratic Party offers us nothing."[18]

Following Church's endorsement, nineteen of the twenty-five largest black newspapers that had previously supported Smith changed their endorsements to Hoover. Though Smith made inroads within the black electorate in northern cities on election day, Hoover retained the majority of black voters. His political debt to African Americans, however, was overshadowed by victories in the upper and border South driven by record-setting white support. Though these southern gains were due in large part to anti-Catholic sentiment against his opponent, Hoover's southern success further enticed him to pursue policies that expanded his Lily-White base.[19]

Disregarding his campaign promise to Church, Hoover stripped many Black-and-Tans of patronage influence by doling out federal appointments to their Lily-White opponents. He sat idly by as Lily-Whites launched campaigns to unseat Black-and-Tans in Louisiana and Texas, and personally requested that the Republican Party of Georgia dismiss Benjamin Davis, Sr., because it "humiliated" whites to go through him for federal jobs. Cloaking himself in the mantle of reform, Hoover promised to end "corruption" in southern Republican parties and to replace current (black) leadership with the "highest type" of citizen. "It is time for the cream to rise to the top," he declared in a thinly veiled allusion to Lily-White ascendance.[20]

Hoover's most obvious gesture to white southerners was the Supreme Court nomination of a Lily-White Republican from North Carolina, John J. Parker, who once claimed, "participation of the Negro in politics is a source of evil." As a result of coordinated pressure from the NAACP and labor unions, the Senate rejected the nomination in what turned out to be a major turning point in black politics. At the time, it was the largest demonstration yet of black political independence, and in the following midterm elections black voters helped defeat pro-Parker Republican senators in Kansas and Ohio.[21]

Leading up to Hoover's 1932 reelection campaign, most black Republican leaders continued to give him begrudged support, but rank-and-file black voters were growing increasingly weary of the party. In addition to his support of Lily-Whites, Hoover failed to provide meaningful relief for Americans at the outbreak of the Great Depression, an economic disaster that especially devastated black workers. Many African Americans agreed with *Pittsburgh Courier* editor Robert Vann, who famously wrote that it was time to "turn Lincoln's picture to the wall," as the Democratic presidential nominee, New York Governor Franklin D. Roosevelt, emerged as a viable candidate. While cautious not to offend white southerners by endorsing racial equality, Roosevelt pledged federal action to combat the Depression and promised African Americans "as full a measure of citizenship in every detail of my administrative power, as accorded citizens of any other race or group." Hoover still won the majority of black voters on election day, but Roosevelt made considerable inroads among African Americans in northern cities. The tide was turning among black voters.[22]

Although President Roosevelt did not pursue a civil rights agenda, his New Deal provided impoverished black families with tangible benefits. By the spring of 1935, more than 20 percent of African Americans were on welfare provided by the Federal Emergency Relief Administration. In major cities, including Baltimore, Philadelphia, and St. Louis, more than 40 percent of African Americans received some form of federal relief, and the Works Progress Administration alone provided over one million African Americans with jobs. Its educational programs taught more than one million African Americans how to read, and other agencies poured millions of dollars into improving schools and public housing utilized by black families. Roosevelt also far outpaced his Republican predecessors in terms of black appointments, and named a number of white racial liberals to powerful cabinet posts. His wife, Eleanor, publicly identified with the struggles and aspirations of African Americans, and provided an unprecedented ally in the White House. And though the New Deal was rife with blatant discrimination—some of which enshrined structural racism into federal policy and widened the economic gap between whites and blacks for decades to come—still, to many poor African Americans, discriminatory relief was better than none at all.[23]

As members of the party out of power, black Republicans could no longer provide African Americans with patronage or access to the federal government, a fact that undermined their ability to court new voters. Black-and-Tans in the South focused much of their attention in the 1930s and 1940s on combating Lily-Whites for representation in the RNC and at national conventions, goals far removed from the Depression-era concerns of impoverished African Americans. Old Guard black Republicans who had been active for decades relied on outdated rhetoric that had little appeal to new generations of black voters. Roscoe Conkling Simmons, for example, told a crowd of African Americans during a 1930 congressional campaign, "If I had one word to the Negro in Chicago, it would be patience." This message failed to resonate with an increasingly assertive and politically aware black electorate. Similarly, though Congressman Oscar DePriest was the darling of black Chicago for three terms, he lost community support when he opposed New Deal legislation, and in 1934 narrowly lost his seat to a man who himself had been a Republican just four years earlier, Arthur Mitchell, the first African American Democrat elected to Congress.[24]

Like many black elites, DePriest embraced Booker T. Washington's message of individual responsibility and racial uplift through self-help. Just as self-sufficiency was one's personal duty, so too was it the responsibility of African Americans to collectively advance through racial solidarity and self-determination, not external reliance on "the dole system," as he described government assistance. To this end, DePriest opposed New Deal "handouts," but supported community-driven responses to the Great Depression. For instance, he mobilized the Third Ward Republican organization to provide 65,000 meals in the winter of 1930–1931, and picketed the Sopkin Apron factory alongside workers who demanded better wages and improved conditions. While opposing federal intervention in the economy, DePriest did believe it was the government's responsibility to protect civil rights. Unlike his Democratic successor in Congress, who rarely rocked the boat on issues of racial equality, DePriest consistently supported anti-lynching legislation and the integration of public facilities. He also wrote, and secured passage of, an anti-discrimination amendment that applied to the Civilian Conservation Corps, one of the New Deal's largest programs.[25]

To many black Republicans like DePriest, the New Deal was a step backward for racial progress. Grant Reynolds, one of the most active black Republicans of the mid-twentieth century, claimed that African Americans "got the shaft" from Roosevelt. Whereas landowning farmers were given buyouts that revolutionized American agriculture, and ethnic whites were appointed to some of the most powerful positions in the country, Reynolds argued, "blacks got an invitation to go on welfare. . . . The New Deal confined us to a period of dependency." Similarly, acclaimed author Zora Neale Hurston believed that the New Deal "was the biggest weapon ever placed in the hands of those who sought power and votes" by making African Americans "dependent upon the Government for their daily bread." Though out of step with most African Americans, black Republicans like Reynolds and Hurston did not oppose the New Deal out of callous disregard for the plight of the poor, but out of a genuine concern that accepting economic relief was not in the long-term interest of black advancement.[26]

Their opposition to the New Deal additionally did not mean black Republicans were not progressive when it came to civil rights. Betty Hill, a wealthy black Republican organizer from California, feared that Roosevelt had "fooled" many African Americans into settling for government scraps, but she was also a civil rights pioneer in the West who served seventeen years as chair of the Los Angeles NAACP and led the campaign to end discrimination against black nurses in state hospitals. Her activism, which included assuming the presidency of the California Republican Women's Committee, helped push California's GOP establishment, including Governor Earl Warren, into supporting an active civil rights agenda by the 1940s. Hill was not alone among Republicans in powerful positions within the NAACP, and, until her death in 1960, could count two of the national branch's chief representatives, Clarence Mitchell, Jr., and James Nabrit, Jr., as fellow Republicans-in-arms.[27]

While black Republicans like Hill were deeply skeptical of the New Deal, issues of economic policy were secondary to their focus on civil rights. Robert Church was leery of government relief, but his philosophical disagreements with federal expansion were rarely discussed in his public remarks or private correspondence. While this may have been a deliberate strategy not to alienate himself from poor blacks, his inattention to poverty also reflected the centrality of social and political equality to his vision of black progress. Indeed, as the GOP began to lose African American voters in the New Deal era, black Republicans like Church adopted even more militant positions on civil rights. Concede welfare to Democrats, they reasoned, but pressure the GOP to become the party of civil rights by supporting fair employment, open housing, desegregation of the military, and protection of voting rights. Though this was a daunting task in a party with constituencies that included corporate interests and western states with few black voters, black Republicans believed it was better than the alternative, as southern racists remained a dominant bloc within the Democratic establishment, preventing even liberals like Roosevelt from endorsing legislation as fundamental as an anti-lynching law.

Black Republicans' relationship with labor, a Democratic constituency that became intertwined with the civil rights movement during Roosevelt's presidency, was more complicated than their opposition to welfare. Because of their positions in and relationship with business management, black elites had a history of opposing collective bargaining. Perry Howard and other black Republicans worked as lawyers for the Pullman Company, for example, and vocally opposed A. Philip Randolph's Brotherhood of Sleeping Car Porters in the 1910s and 1920s. By the 1930s, however, more militant Republicans like Robert Church recognized the fusion between African Americans and labor. Church and other leading black Republicans endorsed the right of collective bargaining, even opposing the Republican-sponsored, anti-union, Taft-Hartley bill. Younger black Republicans saw unions, unlike welfare, as a positive force that ensured black jobs and promoted self-sufficiency. Though Church, Grant Reynolds, and other black Republicans would become close friends with independent labor leaders, particularly Randolph, rank-and-file black union members still looked skeptically at those whose loyalties linked them with a generally anti-labor party.[28]

As the presidential election of 1936 neared, both parties saw black voters as a valuable swing vote. For the first time in party history, Democrats sent black delegates to their national convention and invited an African American to speak on the floor. The Republican convention featured a marked increase in black delegates, who were given leading spots on the Credentials and Resolutions Committees. Black delegates on the Credentials Committee even succeeding in seating South Carolina's Black-and-Tan delegation over the state's Lily-White faction, concluding a multiyear dispute. Roscoe Conkling Simmons was given a high-profile spot on the floor to deliver a speech seconding the presidential nomination of Alf Landon, a racially progressive governor of Kansas who opposed Lily-Whites, condemned lynching, and called for an end to discrimination in federal employment.[29]

On the campaign trail, Republicans spent twice as much as Democrats in their efforts to woo black voters. Younger, more assertive African Americans like Francis E. Rivers were assigned prominent roles in the campaign. Light complexioned with blue eyes, Rivers had degrees from Yale and Columbia Law School, and was described by a peer as carrying himself "as one might imagine British nobility would." His daily lunch routine included ordering a "martini, made with Tanqueray gin, up, with a twist." Though distinctly upper crust, Rivers saw himself as a "New Negro," no longer drawn to Abraham Lincoln, and in the early1930s, Harlem voters elected him to the New York State Assembly on the basis of his unequivocal advocacy for civil rights. In 1936, Rivers was named director of the RNC's Colored Voters Division's eastern campaign, where he produced pro-Landon films featured in black theaters and sponsored a thirty-city tour of Jesse Owens, fresh from spectacular victories at the Berlin Olympics.[30]

The biggest hurdle Rivers faced among African Americans was his party's failure to offer a meaningful alternative to New Deal relief. Without their own program to sell, black Republicans focused on highlighting discrimination within Roosevelt's agencies. A well distributed statement signed by Rivers and sixty-five other black Republican leaders, including Roscoe Conkling Simmons, Oscar DePriest, Robert Church, and Perry Howard, provided a laundry list of examples of inequality within the New Deal, hoping that disgust over discrimination would outweigh support of its benefits. Some black Republicans also challenged the New Deal on ideological grounds. Rivers warned that Democrats sought to reduce the African American to "'an unemployable,' whom it will treat like the American Indian was treated, and confine the colored man on modern reservations of relief." Perry Howard proclaimed, "Capital is in the Republican Party. The Democratic Party is the poor man's party," a sentiment that served Democrats more than it did his own party.[31]

Despite one of the most aggressive campaigns among black voters in the party's history, the Republican message often fell on deaf ears. Though black Republican criticisms of discrimination within the New Deal may have been technically accurate, and in line with their broader attack on institutionalized racism, millions of African Americans viewed its programs as a source of jobs, food, and shelter. On election day, black voters moved solidly into the Democratic column, with over 70 percent nationwide casting their ballots for Roosevelt. However, the GOP still had a strong presence among middle- and upper-class African Americans, who cast a slight majority of their votes for Landon. Indeed, 70 percent of the men and women listed in the 1937 *Who's Who in Colored America*, a biographical anthology of black America's elite, still identified themselves as Republicans.[32]

It is important to note that widespread African American support for Roosevelt in 1936 did not reflect equivalent support of the Democratic Party. Many black voters could be accurately described as "Roosevelt Republicans," or those who, as the NAACP noted, "voted for Roosevelt, *in spite* of the Democratic party," whose prominent southern wing continued to protect Jim Crow. Indeed, the late 1930s and 1940s were a period of unparalleled black voting independence and fluidity. In his now classic treatise on race relations, *An American Dilemma* (1944), sociologist Gunnar Myrdal suggested that "it is not certain whether the Northern Negro vote will remain Democratic, but it is certain that it has become more flexible and will respond more readily to the policies of the two parties toward the Negro." Polls in the late 1930s and 1940s indicated that black registered voters were split 40-40 between the two parties, with the remaining 20 percent self-identified as independent. In the words of Florida's Progressive Voters' League, a black organization that endorsed both Republicans and Democrats, "We believe in the principle of 'men and measures,' rather than blind allegiance to any one political party."[33]

In this context, the period saw a considerable degree of black ticket splitting. African Americans in Cleveland, a city that gave Roosevelt some of his highest percentages of black support in 1932 and 1936, cast the majority of their votes for Republican candidates for senator, governor, and mayor in 1938 and 1939. African Americans similarly remained key supporters of local Republican machines in the GOP strongholds of Philadelphia and Seattle. In Kentucky, black voters were essential to the election of Republican governor Simeon Willis in 1943, and continued to vote overwhelmingly for the state's Republican candidates through the rest of the decade. So crucial were black voters to GOP success that party officials in Louisville formed a Negro Personnel Committee to guarantee black patronage.[34]

The Black-and-Tan organizations of Memphis and Atlanta continued to thrive in the 1940s. George W. Lee formed a political relationship with Representative B. Carroll Reece of eastern Tennessee, who voted for laws that guaranteed fair federal employment, banned lynching, and outlawed the poll tax. Benjamin Hooks, the future national executive director of the NAACP, recalled that "it was not difficult for me to join up with the Republican Party" on returning to Memphis after graduating from law school in 1948, and he partnered with Lee in organizing black voters. Vernon Jordan, who later became president of the National Urban League, recalled a similar story regarding his upbringing in Atlanta. As an eighth grader in 1948, Jordan attended a local Republican meeting led by a white lawyer, Elbert Tuttle, who later became one of the most important enforcers of civil rights on the federal bench. Accompanying Tuttle in the party's leadership were African Americans William Shaw, John Wesley Dobbs, and John H. Calhoun. The meeting had a profound impact on Jordan, who later remarked with pride that "Blacks played an active participatory role in the Republican Party in Georgia, and I have never forgotten that my first political meeting was an integrated occasion." In 1949, Dobbs and Calhoun partnered with black Democrats to form the Atlanta Negro Voters League, which spearheaded one of the most successful voter registration drives in the South. Though nominally bipartisan, the organization was practically an extension of the city's Republican establishment through the 1950s.[35]

Even in Roosevelt's 1936 sweep, nearly one-third of the black state legislators elected were Republican. Black Republican politicians in the New Deal era often found success in states that were evenly divided between the two parties. As such, both Democrats and Republicans had the incentive to slate African Americans in competitive elections, and to make sincere efforts to court black voters. Additionally, freed from the national politics of the New Deal, black Republican politicians, such as state legislators E. Washington Rhodes of Pennsylvania and J. Mercer Burrell of New Jersey, emphasized a civil rights agenda favored by most African Americans. In 1943, Francis Rivers ran on a joint Republican and American Labor Party ticket for a countywide judicial position on the New York City Civil Court. Winning the majority of the black vote, he won the post, which he retained through the 1950s. At the time, it was the highest judicial post held by an African American, and the best paid position of any black public official in the country. Even communist organizer Benjamin Davis, Jr., son of Atlanta's Black-and-Tan leader, called Rivers's election part of the "high-water mark" of the city's "progressive coalition." Elsewhere, Lawrence O. Payne, editor of Ohio's largest black newspaper, the *Call and Post*, was elected to multiple terms on the Cleveland City Council from 1929 through the 1930s, and was succeeded by his protégé William O. Walker, who represented African Americans on the city council through the 1940s.[36]

As fierce advocates of racial equality, Depression-era black Republican politicians led their states in passing meaningful civil rights legislation. After winning his 1934 bid for the state legislature, Philadelphia's Hobson Reynolds spearheaded the passage of the Pennsylvania Civil Rights Act of 1935, which banned discrimination in places of public accommodation. Cleveland attorney Chester K. Gillespie, who also served as president of the city's NAACP, represented black voters in Ohio's House of Representatives from 1933 to 1944, where he sponsored legislation that ended discrimination at Ohio State University and combated discrimination in state employment. Similarly, Richard McClain, a black dentist from Cincinnati, sponsored a 1935 bill that banned discrimination in employment in publicly contracted jobs.[37]

In the Midwest, Indianapolis NAACP attorney Robert Lee Brokenburr became Indiana's first black state senator, an office he held from 1940 to 1964. In the 1940s, he sponsored legislation that established a fair employment commission, banned discrimination in public accommodations and education, and prohibited race-based hate speech. Two additional black Republicans, William Fortune and Wilbur Grant, joined Brokenburr in the state legislature as the decade progressed, where they sponsored bills prohibiting segregation in all public schools and colleges. Republican Charles Jenkins represented black Chicagoans in the Illinois House of Representatives from 1930 to 1955, and coordinated with the NAACP to secure passage of fair employment legislation, amend riot laws to provide financial assistance to black victims of white mobs, and prohibit state funding of racially segregated schools.[38]

Even black Republicans in segregated Kentucky saw electoral success. In 1935, Charles W. Anderson, who had previously headed Louisville's NAACP, became the first African American to serve in the legislature of a southern state since Reconstruction. During his eleven-year tenure in the General Assembly, he successfully fought to expand educational opportunities by desegregating the state's graduate and nursing schools. His successor, Jesse Lawrence, helped pass additional legislation that further desegregated higher education in the state. In 1945, Eugene Clayton won his race for a seat on Louisville's Board of Aldermen, making him the first African American elected to a city council in the South since Reconstruction. Oneth M. Travis, a member of Kentucky's Republican State Central Committee from Lexington, and the first African American appointed to the State Board of Education, similarly used his position to narrow the salary gap between black and white teachers.[39]

As the nation headed toward World War II and slowly emerged from years of economic crisis, one of the primary goals of the Republican Party in the 1940 presidential election was to win back African Americans. Their nominee, Wendell Willkie, represented the party's burgeoning Eastern Establishment that would rise to power throughout the decade. Centered in the Northeast and Mid-Atlantic, and bolstered by moderate Republicans in other states with large African American populations, the Eastern Establishment sought to restore the GOP's progressive legacy and wrest control of the party from midwestern and western conservatives. Willing to support moderate government activism in economic policies, its leaders, including Willkie, also sought to win back African American voters through endorsing civil rights. Since the 1920s, Willkie had publicly fought against the rise of the Ku Klux Klan in his home state of Indiana, served as a trustee of the Hampton Institute, a historically black university, and supported the National Urban League. In a campaign speech at the NAACP's annual convention, an appearance that was itself groundbreaking, he employed the rhetoric of the country's most militant activists, declaring, "When we talk of freedom and opportunity for all nations, the mocking paradoxes of our own society become so clear they can no longer be ignored." After his death four years later, the NAACP named its renovated headquarters the Wendell Willkie Memorial Building.[40]

Prior to the election, the Republican Program Committee commissioned Howard University political scientist Ralph Bunche to write a report detailing how the GOP could regain black voters. Bunche argued that while the New Deal "has fallen far short of meeting adequately the minimal needs of the Negro," Republicans must formulate their own "constructive program for the economic and political betterment" of African Americans. Largely ignoring Bunche's suggestion on economic policy, black Republicans continued to argue that African Americans wanted, first and foremost, the eradication of legalized discrimination. Appearing before the Committee on Resolutions at the 1940 Republican National Convention, Robert Church was quiet on economic issues, but demanded that the party make efforts to eliminate black disfranchisement in the South and enact legislation banning segregation. Written by Francis Rivers, the "Negro plank" of the party platform was one of the strongest ever approved, pledging Republican support to end "discrimination in the civil service, the army, navy, and all other branches of the Government." On the subject of economics, however, the plank was less specific, simply claiming that African Americans "shall be given a square deal in the economic and political life of this nation."[41]

As they had in 1936, black Republicans played an active role in the campaign. Rivers oversaw the production of literature that promised an end to segregation in the armed forces and other branches of the federal government. Boxing legend Joe Louis toured the country on the party's behalf, and Robert Vann returned to GOP ranks, citing Willkie's forthright stance and Roosevelt's cowardice on civil rights. He joined Claude Barnett, director of the Associated Negro Press, and Chester Franklin, editor of *The Call* (Kansas City), as key members of the Non-Partisan Negro Citizens Committee for Willkie. Popular among the black publishing elite, Willkie earned the endorsement of some of the country's leading black newspapers by the end of the campaign, including Vann's *Pittsburgh Courier, Baltimore Afro-American, New York Age, Philadelphia Tribune*, and *Cleveland Gazette*.[42]

Despite these efforts, the election results were disappointing. Though Willkie increased the Republican majority among members of the black middle class, he made little headway among those who relied on New Deal programs. He did significantly better than Landon, winning, by some estimates, 40 to 50 percent of the total black vote, but the persistence of "Roosevelt Republicans" remained in the election outcomes. According to surveys conducted after the election, though Roosevelt won the majority of black votes, only 42 percent of African Americans who voted for him were registered Democrats. Indeed, depending on the geographic region, 50 to 80 percent of black professionals remained registered Republicans. Ralph Bunche remarked on this phenomenon in 1941, writing that while "the underprivileged Negro gives enthusiastic support to the Democratic party," among the middle class "it is still fashionable to be a Republican."[43]

In 1944, Robert Church founded the Republican American Committee (RAC) to lobby for fair employment and other civil rights measures. Five years earlier, the Democratic machine of Memphis seized his mansion, allegedly for failure to pay taxes, and burned it to the ground as part of a fire department "exercise." Undeterred by intimidation, Church moved to

Chicago and Washington, D.C., where he intensified his advocacy for civil rights. The RAC's first meeting in February 1944 drew two hundred black Republicans from across the country to Chicago. They named Church president, and elected Grace Evans, Edward Jourdain, Charles W. Anderson, and Lawrence O. Payne as vice presidents. All were representative of the party's more militant black leaders who identified with the Eastern Establishment. The organization issued a "Declaration by Negro Republican Workers" that condemned "the unholy and vicious alliance" between conservative Republicans and southern Democrats, "whose avowed objectives are to defeat progressive legislation and maintain 'so-called white supremacy.'" They urged their party to abolish discrimination in the armed forces, pass fair employment legislation, and end discrimination in federal housing aid.[44]

The Platform Committee of the 1944 Republican National Convention was sensitive to Church's demands. Representing the RAC, he appeared before the committee to emphasize the growing independence and importance of African Americans as one of the nation's largest swing votes, and stressed that the party had never won a presidential election without their support. The party's final platform offered an explicit pledge to support legislation for a national Fair Employment Practices Committee (FEPC) to enforce a federal ban on racial discrimination in employment. It also called for an end to segregation in the armed forces, and promised to pursue an amendment that would outlaw the poll tax. The RAC endorsed the platform, and NAACP head Walter White praised its FEPC plank as "unequivocal and excellent." The Democrats' civil rights plank, dismissed by White as a "splinter," was silent on fair employment and other major issues. The platform initially seemed to confirm the RAC's argument that civil rights could best be secured by working within the Republican Party.[45]

New York governor Thomas Dewey, the Republican presidential nominee, continued in this positive direction during the campaign. Criticizing the New Deal as corrupt and inefficient, Dewey offered a Republican alternative for the poor, supporting a moderate economic agenda that included unemployment insurance, disability pay, and increased funding of education. On issues of civil rights, he supported fair employment legislation and the eradication of discrimination within the federal government. He also had a proven track record with black voters, winning Harlem in 1942. By the fall of 1944, he had secured a number of major black endorsements, including one from the National Negro Council, whose director, Edgar G. Brown, declared that "the Governor's forceful and fearless public career has impressed the Negro deeply and has restored his long and earlier confidence in the Republican party."[46]

Throughout the fall of 1944, predictions of renewed African American support for the GOP filled national newspapers and magazines. The *New Republic* warned, "The Democratic Party is threatened with the loss of large segments of the important Negro vote," and *Harper's* claimed, "the Negro vote . . . is shifting back into the Republican column." The NAACP emphasized the independence of African Americans, declaring that their vote "no longer belongs to any one political party." Like Willkie, Dewey earned endorsements from major black newspapers, including the *Pittsburgh Courier, Baltimore Afro-American*, and *New York Amsterdam News*. Despite the governor's appeal, however, the GOP received its fourth straight loss to President Roosevelt on election day. Though Dewey connected with the black middle class's aspirations for civil rights reform, and won roughly 40 percent of the entire black vote, the draw of the New Deal, and the incumbent, again plagued his party among the working class.[47]

The Republican American Committee continued to lobby party leaders following Dewey's loss. In January 1945, Church demanded a greater role for African Americans in the RNC, and chairman Herbert Brownell (a member of Dewey's inner circle) responded by replacing the aged Colored Voters Division with a new Minorities Division. Inspired by Dewey's successful black outreach in New York, the division was headed by Valores ("Val") Washington, the former general manager of the *Chicago Defender*, who caught Brownell's eye after publishing a 1944 booklet touting the civil rights records of liberal Republican governors. During an August meeting in New York, the RAC issued another "Declaration to the Republican Party," demanding that the GOP's congressmen fulfill the FEPC pledge they made in their 1944 platform. Over the next two years, RAC members continued to promote the declaration to the national committee and Republican politicians as part of an intense lobbying campaign for federal and state FEPC legislation.[48]

By the mid-1940s, the passage of a federal fair employment law had become one of the primary objectives of black Republicans and the broader civil rights leadership. In addition to leading the RAC, Church partnered with A. Philip Randolph to form the National Council for a Permanent Fair Employment Practices Committee. Despite their differences on economic policy, Randolph recognized that Church "was a persona grata in the offices of Republican leaders of place and power . . . there was no other person of color in the country who could reach as many outstanding Republican spokesmen of power as he could." Working closely with NAACP lobbyist Clarence Mitchell, Jr., Church canvassed the halls of Congress, sometimes waiting up to five hours in politicians' offices. He touted fair employment as a potential Republican alternative to the New Deal, one that would open jobs to African Americans in places where they were previously barred and help them get off government relief and instead earn for themselves. In private letters to Republican leaders, Church argued, "FEPC is bread and butter, rent and fuel and clothing for millions of colored voters." Though Church's argument swayed some congressional Republicans to support an FEPC law, it failed to convince Ohio Senator Robert Taft to place fair employment above the "rights" of businesses. And as the leader of midwestern and conservative Republicans, Taft's opposition ensured the failure of any FEPC legislation in Congress through the decade.[49]

Though unsuccessful in Washington, D.C., black Republicans saw a groundswell of fair employment legislation on the state level. Nearly all of the eleven states that passed FEPC laws between 1945 and 1951 were controlled by Republican governors or Republican legislatures. Eight of the eleven victories were pushed through by both a Republican governor and legislature in states from New England to the Pacific Northwest. Republicans also sponsored municipal fair employment ordinances, such as Cleveland's extensive 1950 law that covered both public and private-sector jobs. Most of the FEPC measures passed during this period were modeled after New York's Ives-Quinn bill. Signed into law by Governor Dewey on March 12, 1945, the bill was promoted by powerful liberal Republicans Fiorello La Guardia and Irving Ives. It banned racial discrimination in employment and created a commission to investigate claims. Within a year after its passage, rail companies eliminated "colored only" sections on trains, unions eradicated white-only clauses, and many businesses hired their first black employees. Within two years, the number of black women employed in clerical and sales jobs more than quadrupled.[50]

Many black voters were drawn to pro-FEPC Republicans on the state level, and leading up to the 1946 midterm elections the RAC focused on promoting candidates who supported fair employment. The elections bore fruit: black voters played an essential role in the victories of liberal Republican senators and congressmen in Missouri, New York, Philadelphia, Detroit, and Chicago. In Kentucky, Senator John Sherman Cooper and Congressman Thruston Morton received an estimated 90 percent of the black vote, and black Republican Dennis Henderson was elected to the General Assembly.

The passage of FEPC laws under Republican governors and state legislatures, coupled with the 1945 death of Roosevelt and continued disillusionment with the prominent role of white southerners in the Democratic Party, had reversed the trend of black Democratic support that had begun ten years earlier. While some black Democrats simply chose to remain at home, an estimated 15 percent nationwide switched their support to the Republican Party, which assumed control of both houses of Congress for the first time since 1932.[51]

The 1946 elections also launched the political careers of two of the mid-century's most important black Republicans: Grant Reynolds and Archibald Carey, Jr. As an army chaplain during World War II, Reynolds was honorably discharged after his commanding officers grew tired of his complaints against racial discrimination. His continued activism after returning home to New York drew him into activist circles, and he listed Thurgood Marshall and Roy Wilkins among his friends. He was also an ally of Thomas Dewey, who helped pay for his education at Columbia Law School and appointed him state commissioner of corrections after he delivered a fiery 1944 campaign speech on the governor's behalf in Madison Square Garden. In 1946, Reynolds ran against Harlem's venerable Democratic congressman Adam Clayton Powell, campaigning on a liberal platform that called for a substantial rise in the national minimum wage, anti-poll tax legislation, a national FEPC, low-rent public housing, and an end to segregation in the military. Attacking "Part-time Powell's" notorious absentee record, he earned the support of some of Harlem's most recognized citizens, with boxer Joe Louis, author Zora Neale Hurston, singer-actress Etta Moten, and A. Philip Randolph's wife working in his campaign headquarters. His supporters argued that it was important for Harlem to be represented by a Republican who would work alongside liberals in the GOP to break the stranglehold of the Democratic South on civil rights legislation.[52]

As Powell did in all his elections, he ran in the Republican primary, and his loss to Reynolds that spring was the only electoral defeat of his entire career. Fearing another, more catastrophic upset, Democratic stars, including Eleanor Roosevelt, rallied to Powell's side, providing important financial support and campaign appearances. Though Harlem media advertised the race as "giant versus giant," and Reynolds pulled some of the strongest numbers of any Republican congressional candidate in Harlem before or since, the wildly popular Powell cruised to victory on election day. The relative strength of Reynolds's campaign, however, demonstrated to both parties the full emergence of black Republicans who were willing to challenge both parties to confront the existing racial status quo.[53]

Though Reynolds could not overcome the Powell juggernaut, militant black Republicans scored a major victory in Chicago with the election of Archibald Carey, Jr., to the Board of Aldermen. Fair-skinned, red-haired, and freckled, Carey came from an elite family entrenched in GOP politics, with his father serving as postmaster in Athens, Georgia, prior to becoming an advisor to Chicago mayor William Thompson. Carey, Jr., continued in his father's partisan footsteps, believing that southern Democrats would always hold back their party when it came to civil rights. As the pastor of Chicago's influential Woodlawn AME Church, he was also one of the country's leading black ministers. Through Carey's financial and institutional support, the Congress of Racial Equality (CORE), one of the most important organizations of the civil rights movement, was formed inside Woodlawn AME, with his personal office becoming its first headquarters. The church served as the host location of CORE's first national convention in 1943, and the organization's cofounder, James Farmer, described Carey as "CORE's patron saint." In his 1946 campaign, Carey challenged incumbent Old Guard Republican Oscar DePriest, who was elected alderman of Chicago's Third Ward in 1943. Running on a platform that emphasized his civil rights militancy, Carey won the Republican primary and the subsequent general election against venerable Democrat Roy Washington.[54]

Carey also served stints as vice president of the Chicago NAACP during his nine-year tenure on the Board of Aldermen, where he established himself as one of the city's most radical elected officials. He sponsored measures that expanded public housing, established the Chicago Council on Human Relations, and created a Division of Human Relations in the police department that offered courses "to teach police to protect minorities." In 1948, he sponsored an ordinance that banned discrimination in the sale or rental of housing and provided housing to residents displaced by "slum clearance" programs. The "Carey Ordinance" was met with a fury of opposition by the city's Democratic machine, with Mayor Martin Kennelly taking the floor in a board meeting for the only time of his entire term to voice opposition. Though the open housing law fell to defeat, Carey emerged, in the words of a subsequent profile in the New Republic, as one of the nation's "most vigorous fighters" for progressive urban reform.[55]

Following his defeat by Adam Clayton Powell, Grant Reynolds set his sights on military desegregation, forming the Committee Against Jim Crow in Military Service and Training with A. Philip Randolph. On March 22, 1948, Randolph and Reynolds met with President Harry Truman, and warned that African Americans would no longer settle for a segregated military. The duo appeared before the Senate Armed Services Committee the following week, and threatened to encourage African Americans to boycott the draft unless the military banned discrimination. Using his ties to Governor Dewey, Reynolds courted Republicans to join his crusade, and led efforts to include a platform plank at the Republican National Convention in June that called for an end to military segregation. Congressional Republicans followed suit. Even the conservative Senator Robert Taft allied with liberal Henry Cabot Lodge, Jr., in sponsoring anti-discrimination amendments to the 1948 draft bill. In the House, Speaker Joseph Martin and Jacob Javits joined black Democrats Adam Clayton Powell and William Dawson in offering similar amendments. Having secured Republican support, Reynolds and Randolph wrote a letter to Truman informing him that he must act, since there was now "a bipartisan mandate to end military segregation." On July 26, 1948, Truman yielded and issued an executive order integrating the armed forces.[56]

While Republicans in Congress embraced the opportunity to embarrass Truman on the issue of military desegregation, they were far less willing to fulfill their own promises from the 1946 campaign to pass a federal fair employment law, despite controlling Congress. Conservative Republicans joined with southern Democrats in opposing FEPC legislation, and in a rare moment of candor, Speaker of the House Joseph Martin, who had publicly endorsed the party's fair employment plank in 1944, told a group of black Republicans in 1947, "I'll be frank with you. We are not going to pass a FEPC bill," as the party's corporate donors "would stop their contributions if we passed a law." While he assured them with a vague promise that "we intend to do a lot for the Negroes," the damage had already been done in the party's refusal to actively pursue a permanent federal FEPC. Though liberal Republican congressmen like Irving Ives of New York and James Fulton of Pennsylvania sponsored legislation in 1947 and 1948, it quickly fizzled without significant support from either party's leadership.[57]

Recalling his endorsements of the GOP in 1944 and 1946, Edgar G. Brown of the National Negro Council described the Republican-controlled Congress as the "cruelest disillusionment" since Reconstruction. In October 1947, the Republican American Committee issued a statement claiming they were "deeply disturbed and justifiably apprehensive over the failure of the first Republican-controlled Congress in sixteen (16) years," and warned party

Figure 2. Grant Reynolds (left) and A. Philip Randolph (right) address the Senate Armed Services Committee on behalf of the Committee Against Jim Crow in Military Service and Training in 1948. LC-USZ62-128074, Library of Congress.

leaders "of the dangers which lie ahead if it continues its policy of inaction." Signed by some of the country's leading black Republicans, including Robert Church, Lawrence O. Payne, Charles W. Anderson, Archibald Carey, and George W. Lee, the document advised congressional Republicans they would no longer be content with promises, "but will demand . . . actual performance and fulfillment of platform pledges and campaign promises."[58]

Entering into the 1948 presidential election, the GOP again selected two of the party's prominent liberals, Thomas Dewey and Earl Warren, as their presidential and vice-presidential nominees. Since 1944, Dewey had burnished his reputation as the Republicans' leading supporter of civil rights through his signing of the Ives-Quinn Act, which was the first state law to prohibit discrimination in employment on the basis of race, and a law that

banned discrimination in higher education. The Republican platform repeated many of the same civil rights promises as in 1944, but this time was
silent on the issue of a national FEPC. In spite of this omission, Dewey's record again earned him the endorsements of the majority of the country's
black newspapers.[59]

Throughout the fall, polls indicated a sweeping Dewey victory, prompting
his campaign to avoid controversial issues, including civil rights. The NAACP
lamented that "Dewey made no move to exploit his excellent record on civil
rights," in his empty, clichéd speeches. On the other hand, Truman launched
an aggressive campaign to court black voters. Having already seemingly lost
the Deep South following the Dixiecrat revolt at the Democratic National
Convention, and facing even more dangerous opposition from the Progressive Party's Henry Wallace, Truman spent much of 1948 improving his civil
rights record. In addition to his executive order desegregating the military,
Truman created a Fair Employment Board to combat discrimination in the
civil services, and announced his support of anti-lynch and anti-poll tax legislation. The failure of the Republican-controlled Congress to pass a national
FEPC in 1947 and 1948, combined with Dewey's refusal to highlight his own
record in the face of Truman's vigorous campaigning, contributed to a Democratic landslide among black voters in one of the biggest upsets in presidential history. Receiving almost 80 percent of the black vote, a higher percentage
than Roosevelt ever received, Truman won tight races in California, Ohio,
Illinois, and Missouri. By ignoring the Deep South and actively courting
black voters, Truman surpassed Roosevelt in pushing the national Democratic Party into identifying not only with the black economic plight but also
with civil rights.[60]

In the spring of 1951, two figureheads of the black Republican Old Guard,
Roscoe Conkling Simmons and Oscar DePriest, passed away. *Ebony* magazine remarked that, to many young African Americans, the two were relics of
a bygone era who wooed "great masses of Negroes . . . like some Pied Piper
into the ranks of Republicanism without doubt or question." By the time of
their deaths, not only had the ranks of black voters been radically trans-
formed since the 1920s, but so had black Republican leadership. As a minority group in a minority party, black Republicans no longer wielded the
patronage powers of their predecessors, but by 1951 black Republican leadership included Robert Church, Grant Reynolds, Archibald Carey, Jr., and
scores of local politicians who were among the most vocal civil rights advocates of either party. They were central actors in the era's civil rights battles,

serving in leadership positions in the NAACP and CORE, sponsoring unprecedented legislation as elected officials, and partnering with independent
activists like A. Philip Randolph to combat discrimination in employment
and the military. They were also among the most vocal critics of their own
party, continually prodding its leaders to embrace issues of civil rights. In a
1951 letter, Robert Church reminded Massachusetts Senator Henry Cabot
Lodge, Jr., a key figure of the Eastern Establishment, that the GOP still could
surpass the Democrats on issues of black equality, writing, "The Republican
Party is above all the party of Civil Rights. We can never compromise on that
question." As Republicans finally found renewed electoral success under
Dwight Eisenhower's leadership in the 1950s, and as the civil rights movement intensified, black Republicans would redouble their efforts to steer the
GOP into advancing racial equality.[61]

CHAPTER 2

Flirting with Republicans:
Black Voters in the 1950s

The return of the Republican Party to the presidency in the 1950s initiated a decade of modest resurgence in black support for the GOP. During the administration of Dwight Eisenhower, black Republicans were the beneficiaries of high-ranking federal appointments and influential positions within the party, which remained a political option for southern and middle-class blacks. By the time of the 1956 election, strategists from both parties saw cracks in the New Deal coalition, as African Americans showed signs of breaking ranks with a Democratic Party that was home to southern racists. As black journalist James Hicks wrote after a strong Republican showing in 1956, African Americans had temporarily "divorced" the Democratic Party, and "the divorcee is carrying on a flirtation with a new friend," the GOP. Hicks's observation about black voters in the 1950s points to the continued flexibility of black politics during a decade when their partisan affiliation had been far from solidified by the New Deal.[1]

Eisenhower's moderate ideology aligned well with the Eastern Establishment, whose powerbrokers—Thomas Dewey, Henry Cabot Lodge, Jr., and Herbert Brownell, in particular—organized a "Draft Ike" movement early in 1952. Fearing that the conservative Robert Taft might win the party's nomination, they believed the popular World War II hero was the only candidate who could win both the nomination and the general election. He promised to preserve Social Security and other New Deal programs, and openly embraced America's new status as a world leader—positions the fiscally conservative and isolationist Taft derided as "me-tooism." His views on civil rights, however, were initially ambiguous. Though he called for troops "without regard to color" during the Battle of the Bulge, Eisenhower testified in 1948 against military desegregation. During his first official press conference in the Republican primaries, he emphasized that "we must abandon segregation" and endorsed state fair employment laws, but he refused to support a national Fair Employment Practices Commission, one of the most significant policy proposals among black Republicans. Despite this stance, Eisenhower assured Brownell that if elected he "would seek to eliminate discrimination against black citizens in every area under the jurisdiction of the federal government."[2]

Prior to the Republican National Convention, Eisenhower's nomination was not yet guaranteed, and he privately courted Harold C. Burton, a delegate from Harlem who, in the spring of 1952, had become one of the party's most vocal black Republicans after Robert Church, Jr., died in April. The meeting backfired as an angered Burton left, visibly upset by Eisenhower's refusal to support an FEPC plank on the party's platform. At the start of the July convention, Burton and another African American, Charles Hill, announced they would go against the rest of New York's delegation and oppose Eisenhower unless the party enacted a pro-FEPC plank. As Burton hoped, his defection was widely reported in the national media, and was a front page story in black newspapers. Seeking to avoid further embarrassment and negative attention, Eisenhower again met with Burton, and promised to "use my influence, if I am elected President, to see that the Negro and every other citizen of America get their rights." While not explicitly endorsing a federal FEPC, the final GOP platform promised to enact "Federal legislation to further just and equitable treatment in the area of discriminatory employment practices." Though not completely satisfied, Burton agreed to support Eisenhower, believing "those who would surround" him as president would be "liberal."[3]

With the convention held in Chicago, Illinois Republicans saw to it that their most important black ally, alderman Archibald Carey, Jr., was granted time for a floor speech. Given twenty-five uninterrupted, nationally broadcast minutes, Rev. Carey began by asserting that "the Democratic Party of late has been the party of promises. . . . As a Negro-American I have been sorely disappointed, and millions of freedom-loving people of every race have been disappointed with me." While President Truman had promised to end the poll tax, enact a federal FEPC, and pass an anti-lynch law, these failed to survive a Democratic Congress. Carey continued, claiming that while some Democrats may cry, " 'The Dixiecrats did it.' I answer—there is no Dixiecrat Party—only the Democrat." Turning inward, he reminded the audience that "the Republican Party has not occupied the White House since it lost the

Negro vote." He then delivered the best remembered verses of his long career—lines that scholars later argued directly influenced Martin Luther King, Jr.'s "I Have a Dream" speech. The cadence of his poetic words echoed through Chicago's International Amphitheater as he proclaimed, "some will say, 'The time is not ripe,'" but "we Negro-Americans, sing with all Americans . . . Let freedom ring!" His voice grew louder with each phrase:

> That's exactly what we mean, from every mountain side, let freedom ring! Not only from the Green Mountains of Vermont and the White Mountains of New Hampshire; not only from the Catskills of New York; but from the Ozarks in Arkansas, from the Stone Mountain in Georgia, from the Great Smokies of Tennessee, and from the Blue Ridge Mountains of Virginia . . . may the Republican Party, under God, from every mountain side, Let Freedom Ring![4]

Carey had powerfully laid out the black Republican vision of civil rights. When looking at American politics, he saw the Democratic Party not as the party of the working man, but as the party of the Jim Crow South. Though the GOP was admittedly not perfect, as Burton's fight for an FEPC plank demonstrated, to Carey it still offered a preferable alternative. His primary focus was the eradication of legal barriers against African Americans, believing that, once guaranteed equal opportunity, they would enter a color-blind society where they would succeed on their individual merits. These principles were shared not only by much of the GOP's Eastern Establishment, but also by civil rights activists like King, who dreamed of the day when African Americans would be judged "by the content of their character." While the New Deal-inflected activism of many black leaders was absent in Carey's message, which hoped to rally black voters behind a collective desire for civil rights, not economic policies benefiting the poor, his demands for "freedom"—essentially, the eradication of state-sanctioned discrimination—were shared by civil rights leaders across partisan lines. In the words of the president of a Texas NAACP branch, Carey "left no doubt in the minds of the Republican Party, the Democrats, the Americans, [and] the World as to what the American Negro wants."[5]

Winning the nomination with delegates from the East and West coasts, and the progressive midwestern states of Michigan, Minnesota, and Wisconsin, Eisenhower solidified his relationship with the Eastern Establishment. In an appeal to the party's broader base, he selected California Senator Richard

Nixon, one of the country's most rabid anti-Communists, as his vice presidential nominee. Despite his ruthless attacks on alleged Communists, the ever-calculating Nixon had carefully maintained a close relationship with influential party liberals, and generally supported most civil rights legislation in Congress. California's largest black newspaper, the *Los Angeles Sentinel*, had endorsed him in his 1950 Senate race against Helen Gahagan Douglas. Linking civil rights to the Cold War, Nixon believed that "we must be vigilant against the doctrines of [segregationists] . . . who are just as dangerous to the preservation of the American way of life on the one hand as are the Communists on the other." In many ways, Nixon and Eisenhower were similar in that they maintained close relations with eastern party leaders and supported moderate civil rights measures, though issues of black equality were never at the forefront of either's agenda.[6]

For their part, Democrats nominated Illinois Governor Adlai Stevenson, after President Truman declined to run for a second term. Like Eisenhower, Stevenson argued that fair-employment legislation should be left to the states, but was open to a federal law if states failed to act. Fearing another Dixiecrat revolt, the Democratic convention passed a weakened civil rights plank to appease southerners. Harlem Congressman Adam Clayton Powell called the plank "virtually nothing," and labeled Chicago's black Congressman, William Dawson, an "Uncle Tom" for helping write it. Stevenson's most blatant appeal to Dixiecrats was the selection of Alabama Senator John Sparkman as his running mate. Though one of the South's more moderate politicians, Sparkman supported segregation, once declaring, "I am against the Civil Rights proposals—always have been and always will be."[7]

Recognizing an easy target, Republicans were quick to attack Sparkman's nomination. One advisor called for the party to demand that Stevenson "again and again . . . repudiate Senator Sparkman, whose views on the Negro and civil rights represent a point of extreme vulnerability for the Democrats." Another strategist urged the campaign to "tie Sparkman completely around Stevenson's neck with the 'White Supremacy' label." Thomas Dewey did just that, publicly asserting, "so long as Senator Sparkman is on that ticket, this is a Jim Crow ticket." Republican advertisements in black newspapers featured the slogans, "Jim Crow Sparkman Would Be One Heartbeat from the White House" and "He Never Voted for You—Why Should You Vote for Him?"[8]

The anti-Sparkman theme was also hammered home in campaign speeches by Carey. The RNC Minorities Division, headed by Val Washington of the *Chicago Defender*, organized Carey's itinerary, making him one of the most active African Americans on the campaign trail for either party. By November, he had traveled over twenty thousand miles, with appearances in fourteen states. In Denver he was greeted with a "torchlight parade," and introduced by the governor before speaking to listeners on one of the state's largest radio stations. He also met privately with Eisenhower, who reassured him that he supported military integration "one hundred percent," and was "immensely sorry" for bowing to the "pressures of war" when he testified against it. The general further told Carey that he would consider signing a federal FEPC law if it was passed by Congress, and pledged commitment to "full freedom" for African Americans. During the final days of the campaign, Carey again met with Eisenhower, and the two traveled together from New York to Chicago, where they rode in an open car through black neighborhoods and placed a wreath on a monument honoring black soldiers. On the night of November 3, the two appeared together on a national television broadcast, where Carey delivered excerpts from his fiery convention speech.[9]

Val Washington also placed E. Frederic Morrow on Eisenhower's staff. Morrow had previously served twelve years as an NAACP field secretary, where he was twice almost murdered during his investigations of lynchings. He had also led the effort to integrate the New Jersey Young Republicans, after a series of petitions to state GOP leaders, becoming one of the organization's first black members and eventually its vice chairman. In 1952, he was approached by Washington, who wanted "strong, able Blacks" with proven militancy "in every echelon of the party structure during the campaign," so that they could "influence the leaders of the party and liberalize their thinking." Morrow accepted Washington's offer and was assigned by Eisenhower's staff to the official campaign train. Just ten days after being hired, he refused to ride the train "for token purposes" in "strategic areas," and threatened to quit unless he was used as more than just a stage prop. He was soon reassigned duties on the train as a speechwriter and drafted responses for the campaign's "Truth Squad." At a campaign stop in Morrow's home town of Hackensack, New Jersey, Eisenhower defended his aide after a group of local officials complained that his critiques of party leaders caused them "great embarrassment." According to Morrow, Eisenhower "gave them hell for intruding into his personal bailiwick," and during his public remarks mentioned Morrow by name and praised his service to the party.[10]

Eisenhower received the endorsement of some of the country's most prominent African Americans. Edward G. Brown's National Negro Council returned to GOP ranks and denounced the Stevenson-Sparkman ticket as "a

Democrat-Dixiecrat coalition." Bishop D. Ward Nichols, head of the African Methodist Episcopal Church, which at the time represented 1.6 million African Americans, told the press that he would "vigorously support" Eisenhower, after he privately promised to "take immediate steps" to desegregate Washington, D.C. Leading clubwomen also endorsed the Republican nominee, such as Jane Morrow Spaulding of the National Association of Colored Women, who served as cochair of the advisory committee of the Women's Division of Citizens for Eisenhower. Daisy Lampkin, national NAACP board member and cofounder of the National Council of Negro Women, left the Democratic Party to join the Republican campaign, declaring it "impossible . . . as a self-respecting American and an intelligent Negro" to support a ticket that included Sparkman.[11]

Privately, Lampkin feared that her Democratic colleagues in the NAACP, particularly Walter White and Roy Wilkins, were tempering their criticisms of Sparkman to help Stevenson. Believing the organization's national leadership was overly partisan, she warned White, "It would be tragic if the GOP wins with no Negro support. We would be in a very bad bargaining position." Similarly, as vice president of Chicago's NAACP, Archibald Carey privately told Wilkins that while "I still love you . . . you are horribly biased." Carey was livid over an NAACP report that criticized Sparkman and Nixon as equally unsatisfactory candidates, "leaving the unwary public believing that on civil rights their records were the same." He continued, "I think you honestly believe that all the Democratic talk for civil rights is genuine, whereas the Republican opposition represents an even deeper sinister and venal attitude." Carey could understand African American support for Truman, though he believed Truman was more "talk" than action, but it was difficult to comprehend why black leaders would support a ticket that included a southern segregationist. To black Republicans, Democrats were still the party of the South, as proven by Sparkman's nomination, and could never deliver on empty civil rights promises made by party liberals. White and Wilkins, however, were willing to overlook Sparkman in hopes that Stevenson would continue Truman's example of supporting both black civil rights and working-class interests.[12]

Eisenhower welcomed black endorsements, but civil rights were secondary to his emphasis on foreign policy and "honest government." He also believed he could use his enormous national appeal to make inroads among moderate whites in the South drawn to the GOP's support of the private sector. He was greeted by a Charlotte, North Carolina, crowd of forty thousand,

and his visit marked the first time a presidential nominee had campaigned in the city since 1896. A similar crowd welcomed him in Columbia, South Carolina, where he received the endorsement of the segregationist Democratic governor, James Byrnes, and professed his fondness for the minstrel song "Dixie." On the other hand, he did not shy away from civil rights, telling the crowd, "We will move forward rapidly to make equality of opportunity a living fact for every American." In another southern campaign stop, George W. Lee and Benjamin Hooks organized an Eisenhower tour of the heart of black Memphis, Beale Street, and the general made an "impromptu" stop at Lee's office. Additionally, Jesse Lawrence, Kentucky's black Republican state representative, joined the Eisenhower train as it moved through Indiana and Kentucky. In Louisville, GOP Congressional candidate John Robinson insisted that African Americans sit on stage with Eisenhower, who told a crowd of ten thousand that his administration would "be guided by one idea . . . there shall be no second-class citizenship among all Americans."[13]

On election day, despite support for Eisenhower among many in the black middle class, more than 80 percent of black voters remained loyal to the party of Franklin Roosevelt. The middle class made up only 10 to 13 percent of the black population in the 1950s, leaving the majority of African Americans impoverished or in the working class. While many prominent blacks were aghast at Sparkman's nomination, it would take more for most African Americans to leave a party that represented, in their minds, workers like themselves. Those in the middle class could focus on combating Jim Crow through the two-party system, but, in the words of E. Frederic Morrow, "civil rights is not the burning question" among the majority of black voters, many of whom feared "loss of jobs gained under Democrats." According to Morrow, "this powerful desire to hold on to the status quo was the most difficult problem for Republican campaigners," as many black workers felt uncomfortable deserting the Democrats after they "had prospered in a fashion never known before the 20 years prior to 1952." That a majority of black voters cast ballots for a presidential ticket that included an avowed segregationist from Alabama suggests the primacy of economics and New Deal-era government activism to many black voters. Among middle-class Republicans, many of whom were already skeptical of government relief, civil rights and pragmatic two-party politics were essential to their rationale for supporting Eisenhower, who they believed would join with liberals in the Eastern Establishment in combating institutional discrimination.[14]

Among black workers and the poor, Eisenhower faced the same problems as Wendell Willkie and Thomas Dewey had, in failing to shake the image of the GOP as the party of elites. As one Democratic organizer argued, black voters should not give up the "many basic gains for the common man" by supporting the party of "rich, privileged corporations." When only nuanced differences exited between the civil rights positions of Eisenhower and Stevenson, the legacy of Roosevelt and Truman outweighed any hypothetical promises Republicans could offer. James Nabrit, Jr., a Republican NAACP lawyer, noted, "as a member of the working class," most black voters in northern cities would only support candidates "which have as one of their major policies the welfare of workers." Political scientist Samuel Lubell similarly concluded in the 1950s that "Negro attachment to the Democratic party has been as much economic as racial in motivation. As the lowest-paid worker in our industrial society, the Negro is both class and race conscious." Thus far, aside from advocating for the creation of a national FEPC, black Republicans had no answer to the question of economic interest.[15]

Though the figures among black voters were disheartening, black Republicans saw Eisenhower's election as a boon to restoring their influence in federal patronage. E. Frederic Morrow advised Eisenhower's chief of staff, former New Hampshire governor Sherman Adams, to place "Negroes in positions of responsibility wherever the party has jurisdiction," and Adams later noted that the president himself "made a point of insisting that he wanted qualified Negroes to be considered." The Minorities Division became the party's central funnel for black appointees, and on Val Washington's watch Eisenhower far surpassed the appointment rates of Roosevelt and Truman. According to Washington, he and his assistant, Thalia Thomas, "cracked job barriers in many departments." Whenever they were informed of a "lily-white agency," they would immediately send "a letter prodding them" to hire blacks, and would also "ship a copy to the White House." Major black appointments included Jewell Stratford Rogers as assistant U.S. district attorney, L. B. Toomer as registrar of the U.S. Treasury, and Scovel Richardson as chairman of the Board of Parole. Robert Church, Jr.'s daughter, Roberta Church, became the highest ranking black woman in the federal government, given a policy-making position in the Department of Labor. Washington also helped secure a sub-cabinet post for J. Ernest Wilkins as assistant secretary of labor, one of the highest positions ever offered to an African American.[16]

To assist Washington's efforts in securing federal jobs for African Americans, Eisenhower created the President's Committee on Government

Employment Policy. He named Archibald Carey as vice-chairman, and by 1957 Carey had been promoted to chairman, making him the first African American head of a President's Committee. Through his efforts, the number of blacks employed in white-collar federal jobs nearly doubled, to more than 9,000 by 1960. Segregated offices in Atlanta and other southern cities were eliminated. In New Orleans, the number of black federal employees increased by almost 600 percent. Though some agencies in the Deep South still did not have any black employees, and many offices just hired tokens, Carey was proud of personally overseeing "a manifest rise" in thousands of jobs directed to African Americans.[17]

Eisenhower's most important appointment, however, was also one of his most bungled. Though Sherman Adams had promised E. Frederic Morrow a position in the new administration, Morrow approached Val Washington months after the inauguration without a job. Washington "probed and probed" the administration on its failure to appoint the outspoken Morrow, and the two deduced that an unnamed "someone of great prominence and power had blocked the appointment." According to Morrow, Washington launched a "relentless job campaign" that succeeded in "embarrassing the ad-ministration into looking for a job for me." He was eventually given a position in the Department of Commerce, and in 1955 was promoted to administra-tive officer for special projects on the president's staff, making him the first African American to have an office inside the White House. Though his office provided access to close confidants of the president, Morrow's official duties focused on the mundane, replying to letters to the president relating to issues of civil rights, and overseeing office and parking assignments.[18]

In addition to black appointments, Eisenhower amassed a positive record in other areas as well. In his first State of the Union address, he pledged to rid Washington, D.C., of segregation, a change that had long been a goal of black activists outraged by blatant discrimination in the nation's capital. Weeks earlier, Mary Church Terrell, a lifelong Republican, first president of the Na-tional Association of Colored Women, founding member of the NAACP, and sister of Robert Church, Jr., had led a series of boycotts, pickets, and sit-ins targeting D.C. businesses that refused to serve African Americans. Attorney General Herbert Brownell assisted Terrell in the legal campaign against the city's segregation laws, and argued alongside black lawyers when the case reached the Supreme Court in 1953. The court sided with the administra-tion, and the city was ordered to immediately desegregate places of public accommodation.[19]

Figure 3. E. Frederic Morrow is congratulated following his swearing-in ceremony at
the White House as administrative officer for special projects. Left to right: Bernard
Shanley, Val Washington, Morrow, and New Jersey Representative William Widnall,
July 11, 1955. National Park Service photo, 72-1447-3, Dwight D. Eisenhower
Presidential Library and Museum.

The president also fulfilled his campaign promise to rid vestiges of segregation from the armed forces. Though Truman had issued an executive order,
segregated facilities still existed in much of the South. In his first year in office, Eisenhower enlisted Maxwell Rabb, a white aide sympathetic to African
Americans, to ensure the desegregation of mess halls, lavatories, and drink-
ing fountains in Norfolk, Virginia, and Charleston, South Carolina. Additionally, he ordered forty-seven Veterans Administration hospitals to
integrate their facilities, and directed schools on southern military bases to
open their doors to black students. By the fall of 1954, the Department of
Defense formally announced that the military's last segregated unit had been
eliminated.[20]

Eisenhower's judicial appointments were his most lasting contribution to civil rights. Of particular importance were appointees to southern judicial circuits who later ensured that civil rights laws were enforced in the 1960s. Eisenhower's tendency to take Attorney General Brownell's advice regarding court nominees led to a steady stream of liberal appointments that included Elbert Tuttle, John Minor Wisdom, Frank M. Johnson, and other southern Republicans who had previously allied with Black-and-Tans. During his first year on the Fifth Circuit, Johnson made national headlines by ordering the desegregation of Montgomery's public buses after the successful black boycott. Even more important were Eisenhower's Supreme Court appointments, particularly Earl Warren, John Marshall Harlan II, and William Brennan, who played an active role in the court's progressive decisions of the 1950s and 1960s.[21]

The first major decision of Chief Justice Warren was *Brown v. Board of Education*, a case that Eisenhower's Justice Department had been involved with since his inauguration. Early in 1953, NAACP lawyer Thurgood Marshall met several times with Brownell, who submitted an *amicus* brief that called for the overturning of *Plessy v. Ferguson*, the legal backbone of Jim Crow, and the integration of public schools. In 1954, the Supreme Court ruled in favor of the NAACP and the Justice Department, paving the way for the legal dismantling of segregation. After the decision, Eisenhower told Walter White, "we had passed, in this year, a milestone of social advance in the U.S.," and claimed in his memoir that "there can be no question that the judgment of the Court was right." On the other hand, Eisenhower as president never publicly endorsed *Brown*, a failure that perhaps emboldened opponents of the decision. White House speechwriter Arthur Larson alleged that the president privately said, "I personally think the decision was wrong," and Earl Warren claimed the president told him that white southerners had legitimate concerns about their daughters attending school with "big overgrown Negroes."[22]

Regardless of Eisenhower's private beliefs, the RNC and black Republicans immediately attached the victory to his administration. Richard Tobin, a public relations specialist with the national committee, encouraged Republicans to tout their relationship with Warren, arguing that "in the context of the Supreme Court decisions under a Chief Justice appointed by President Eisenhower, decisions as historic as the Emancipation Proclamation of Lincoln, we have a wonderful story to tell." The Minorities Division issued a press release stating, "This administration can take pride in having thrown its full weight behind the vigorous presentation of this case to the Supreme Court by Attorney General Herbert Brownell, Jr." E. Frederic Morrow similarly declared before a Philadelphia audience that the case was "typical of the healthy climate-of-equality that prevails in the Eisenhower Administration."[23]

Because of his early administrative actions in the field of civil rights, by 1955 Eisenhower had received the most distinguished prize given by black journalists, the Russwurm Award, and the *Chicago Defender*'s Robert F. Abbott Memorial Award, given to the person who "did the most to extend democracy at home and abroad." Even the NAACP's Walter White and Roy Wilkins, whom black Republicans had criticized as Democratic partisans in 1952, praised Eisenhower's first years in office. In his 1954 "Report of the Executive Secretary," White argued, "we owe a debt of gratitude to President Eisenhower for his firm stand against racial segregation," and separately, Wilkins praised the president's "personal leadership where the executive can act." Iowa's largest black newspaper declared, "no president in our lifetime has struck such a blow against segregation."[24]

Seeing these gains, African Americans began to warm to the GOP in the 1950s, with 63 percent of blacks approving Eisenhower's overall performance by 1955. Polls conducted from 1952 to 1960 found that self-identified Republicans increased from approximately 10 percent of African Americans polled in 1952 to around 21 percent by 1960. Support for the Republican Party remained strong in southern cities with active Black-and-Tan organizations, especially Atlanta and Memphis. During the decade, the Republican leadership of the nominally bipartisan Atlanta Negro Voters League organized thousands of new black voters inside GOP ranks, and George W. Lee's Lincoln League added nearly fifty thousand African Americans to Memphis voting rolls.[25]

Republican support among black voters was also high in the border states of Maryland and Kentucky, both of which had a history of competition between moderate Republicans and southern-leaning Democrats. In Baltimore, 44 percent of black voters were registered Republican in 1957, and over 55 percent of that year's newly registered voters registered with the GOP. The city's Republican mayor during World War II, Theodore McKeldin, served as governor from 1951 to 1959, and his electoral coalition relied on black voters, whom he won by frequenting black churches and embracing civil rights. In Louisville, Kentucky, 64 percent of registered black voters were Republicans in 1952. They played a significant role in securing the U.S. Senate victory of John Sherman Cooper, who ran to the left of his Democratic opponent on issues of labor, economic relief for the poor, and civil rights.[26]

The GOP also remained popular within the black middle class. Polls taken during the 1950s found that 30 percent of northern middle-class African Americans were registered Republicans, with numbers potentially higher in under-analyzed rural and southern black communities. Of those who provided their political affiliation in the 1950 edition of *Who's Who in Colored America*, a volume that represented a cross section of over two thousand black professionals, approximately 45 percent self-identified as Democrats, 35 percent as Republican, and 20 percent as independent/other. In the mid-1950s, the NAACP's Henry Lee Moon described "the increasing economic stratification within the Negro community with the development of a more stable and substantial middle class with Republican leanings." Similarly, E. Frederic Morrow wrote in 1956 that there was a distinct "cleavage of class" in black communities, and that those from the professional classes "have been pre-dominantly Republican." After a meeting with the National Negro Insurance Association, Val Washington reported high levels of Republican support from the organization's leaders, who supported Eisenhower's civil rights stance and were not moved by "the depression psychology which is being spread by the Democrats."[27]

Support for the Republican Party was particularly strong in black fraternal organizations, most of which drew their membership from middle-class ministers, lawyers, physicians, and businessmen. Atlanta Republican leader John Wesley Dobbs, for example, was also the longstanding Grand Master of Georgia's black Masons. The national president of Phi Beta Sigma, one of the largest black college fraternities, was a devout Republican who actively campaigned on behalf of GOP candidates. In Baltimore in 1951, members of the Knights of Pythias formed the State Allied Republican Club, which convened in local lodges and lobbied for civil rights and state patronage for black Republicans.[28]

The group with the strongest ties to the GOP was the Improved Benevolent and Protective Order of Elks of the World (IBPOEW). Known for their purple fezzes and ubiquitous lodges that spanned the country from the Deep South to the urban North and far West, the IBPOEW, often referred to as the "black Elks," was the country's largest black fraternal organization, having a peak membership of eight hundred thousand by the late 1950s. The black Elks had practically been an extension of the Republican Party since the

1920s, and their national leadership was composed of some of the biggest Republican names of the era, including Black-and-Tans Perry Howard and Henry Lincoln Johnson. From the 1920s through the 1940s, Grand Exalted Ruler J. Finley Wilson, a follower of Robert Church, Jr., rallied members behind the GOP. In the early 1950s, Wilson was replaced by Robert H. Johnson, a veteran of the Philadelphia Republican machine and past chairman of the Negro Division of the Pennsylvania Republican State Committee. As Grand Exalted Ruler, he toured on behalf of the Republican ticket in 1954, and on his watch Republicans continued to dominate IBPOEW leadership. His second in command was a friend from Philadelphia GOP circles, Hobson Reynolds, who succeeded him as Grand Exalted Ruler in 1960.[29]

Republicans interested in appealing to black voters recognized the black Elks as an important base. RNC Chairman Hugh Scott was the keynote speaker at the 1948 Grand Lodge Session, and black entertainer Lionel Hampton used California Elk lodges as concert venues that doubled as GOP voter registration centers in the mid-1940s. Perry Howard claimed at a meeting of the RNC Executive Session in 1950 that the Elk "political machine . . . is about 90 per cent Republican," and inside the White House, E. Frederic Morrow told an IBPOEW official, "I stand ready at all times to be of whatever assistance I possibly can and certainly will continue to work to have all Elkdom embrace the Republican Party."[30]

Like other black Republicans, IBPOEW leadership was committed to promoting racial equality and prodding party leaders to endorse civil rights. During the debate over fair employment laws in the 1940s and early 1950s, the Elks petitioned for state and national legislation, and provided their Baltimore lodges as headquarters for the National Negro Congress's fair employment lobbying campaign. As a delegate to the 1948 Republican National Convention, Hobson Reynolds publicly protested its weak civil rights platform, and Elk representatives frequently appeared before congressional committees on behalf of a federal FEPC and military desegregation. In 1956, Reynolds traveled to Alabama to present an IBPOEW financial contribution to the Montgomery Improvement Association to help sustain their bus boycott. That same year at the Elks' national convention, Grand Exalted Ruler Johnson told members from Louisiana and Alabama, states where the NAACP had been outlawed, that they could meet in Elk lodges so that the NAACP could "carry on its work . . . under the banner of the Elks." The IBPOEW also heavily promoted black higher education. Memphis Black-and-Tan leader George W. Lee served as Grand Commissioner of Education of the

Figure 4. George W. Lee, in IBPOEW regalia, with New York Senator Kenneth Keating
and A. Philip Randolph, circa 1950s. Photograph by Maurice Sorrell. Amistad
Research Center, Tulane University.

national Elks throughout the 1950s, and dramatically intensified their college
scholarship program. Using his fundraising network in middle-class and Republican circles, Lee doled out over four million dollars in Elk scholarships
during his tenure, many of them given to future civil rights leaders.[31]

Throughout the 1950s, black Republicans continued to earn ranking positions within local parties and state governments. In 1952, Roberta Church
of Tennessee became the first black woman elected to a southern party's state
executive committee. By the middle of the decade, Julius Adams secured one
of the most powerful spots in New York Republican politics, serving on the
executive committee of the New York Republican Committee. William O.
Walker headed the Ohio Republican Council and served on the Republican
State Central and Executive Committee. In Pennsylvania, E. Washington
Rhodes served on the state parole board, and in Illinois Joseph D. Bibb headed
the Department of Public Safety, which had jurisdiction over the state police.

Arthur Fletcher, the first black player for professional football's Baltimore Colts, served as a vice chairman of the Kansas State Republican Central Committee, alongside another African American, Prentice Townsend. In 1954, he became vice campaign chairman to progressive Republican gubernatorial candidate Fred Hall. Emphasizing Hall's support for a state fair-employment law, Fletcher spearheaded registration drives that added ten thousand blacks to voting rolls, and convinced African Americans to join his crusade to oust the party's conservative Republican machine. Following Hall's upset victories in both the primary and general elections, in which black voters played a pivotal role, Fletcher was named deputy state highway commissioner, an important position in a decade of extensive interstate highway expansion.[32]

Republicans in the 1950s also experimented with slating African American Congressional candidates in mixed-race, Democratic-leaning districts, hoping to draw black votes away from white incumbents. In 1952, Lawrence O. Payne won the endorsement of the GOP in his campaign against Robert Crosser in Ohio's twenty-first district. Though Payne did significantly better than previous Republicans, Crosser, bolstered by strong ties to unions, easily won the race with biracial working-class support. In 1958, Republicans in Los Angeles nominated Crispus A. Wright to challenge Franklin Roosevelt's oldest son, Congressman James Roosevelt. An active member in the California civil rights movement of the 1940s, Wright actively promoted the *Los Angeles Sentinel*'s "Don't Spend Your Money Where You Can't Work" campaign and prepared briefs in the NAACP's successful case before the U.S. Supreme Court that prohibited restrictive covenants. On election day, Wright lost not only the election, but also the majority of black voters. The name Roosevelt was particularly powerful among the black working class, and Wright, himself one of Los Angeles's wealthiest African Americans, could not shake the perception of the Republican Party as elitist. The *Los Angeles Tribune* summed up Wright's difficulty, and the difficulty of many black Republican candidates in the 1950s, noting that while he was "intelligent . . . well educated . . . personal, respectable, [and] militant . . . Wright is also, and regrettably, a Republican." That even black Republicans with militant civil rights agendas could not garner a majority of black votes against white candidates again pointed to the priority working-class African Americans placed on Democratic economic policies.[33]

This preference among the black working class was also borne out in Chicago. With Windy City residents Archibald Carey, Jr., and Val Washington in positions of national prominence, one of the central targets of black

Republicans in the 1950s was the city's black Democratic Congressman, William Dawson. As a cog in the city's Democratic machine, Dawson had unfettered access to power and organizational resources. In return for his unwavering support, Illinois Democrats provided him with immense patronage power and leadership positions inside the party. Though this ensured that government jobs and benefits flowed to black Chicagoans, it also came a price: his silence on controversial issues that might embarrass Democrats, especially civil rights. By the 1950s, black activists had grown weary of Dawson's refusal to criticize southern Democrats or embrace civil rights; he even joined the majority of Congressional Democrats in voting against a school-integration bill. Even the solidly Democratic *Chicago Defender* criticized his "evasive" civil rights stance, concluding, "Bill Dawson is, by all odds, ultra-conservative."[34]

In 1950, the local and state Republican party endorsed Carey as their congressional candidate. Val Washington's Minorities Division dedicated six weeks exclusively to the campaign, which centered on a platform that contrasted Carey's civil rights militancy to Dawson's accommodationist role within the Democratic Party. According to Carey, Dawson was incapable of challenging his party to reject its southern wing, but Carey already had enough clout within GOP circles to join liberal Republicans in pressuring conservatives and businessmen to back civil rights. Regardless of his respected stature within Chicago's black community, and solid civil rights record, Carey lost handily to Dawson. Throughout the rest of the decade, Washington continued his "buck Dawson" crusade, sponsoring numerous progressive candidates, including Edgar G. Brown of the National Negro Council. As part of his failed congressional campaign, Brown led a hundred-minister delegation to Washington to demand that the Senate investigate the fatal bombing of Florida activist Harry Moore. Like Carey, he lost in a landslide.[35]

In 1958, black Republicans nominated one of the best-known activists in the country, T. R. M. Howard to run against Dawson. Howard had previously headed Mound Bayou, Mississippi's NAACP, and founded one of the most important organizations in the state's civil rights movement, the Regional Council of Negro Leadership. He joined Charles Evers in attempting to register black voters in Philadelphia, Mississippi, and made national headlines with his vocal criticisms of the state following the lynching of Emmett Till. In the field of civil rights, there was no comparison between the aggressive, bombastic Howard and the ever cautious Dawson, who remained characteristically quiet after Till's murder. In 1956, Dawson was greeted with boos and forced to leave the stage, speech unfinished, at a meeting of six-hundred ministers in Chicago after he discouraged them from sending church contributions to help southern black protest movements, arguing that change in the South was best handled by politicians. Howard tackled Dawson's civil rights reticence head on with slogans like "'Uncle Tom' leadership has got to go." However, like Dawson's opponents before him, Howard received less than 30 percent of the vote, even with a campaign appearance by President Eisenhower on his behalf. Of three hundred and fifty precincts, Howard won only five, which were located in the district's wealthiest areas.[36]

Black Republican congressional candidates like Carey, Brown, and Howard epitomized the Republican Party's central problem in connecting with the black working class. While they had stronger civil rights records than their Democratic opponent, they lacked the organizational resources of political machines and labor unions. Most importantly, the economic record of Democrats proved far more vital to securing mass black support. While middle-class African Americans could potentially be swung by an emphasis on civil rights, the failure of black Republicans to systematically address issues of economics and poverty lay at the center of their congressional defeats. A particularly revealing 1957 survey of African Americans nationwide found that a *majority* of those polled selected the Republican Party when asked which party was best for them on the issue of civil rights. When asked "the best party for jobs," however, the same respondents chose Democrats by a margin of almost four to one. There certainly was sympathy towards eradicating southern Jim Crow, but the harsh economic realities that plagued black communities in northern cities provided little incentive for most workers to leave a party they perceived as on the side of unions, workers, and the poor. In the words of a black Democrat from Philadelphia, "It does not matter very much to colored people here what is going on in the South. The colored man votes according to what will affect his pocket-book, and he knows that the Democrats are the party of the poor man." On the other hand, to many black Republicans, the civil rights of black southerners took precedence over the bread-and-butter economic issues of northern workers.[37]

Nevertheless, black Republicans did find electoral success at the state level. In Chicago, each legislative district elected three representatives to the Illinois General Assembly. In the voting booth, one could select three different candidates or cast all three votes for the same candidate. A number of Republicans found success in this ballot-sharing method. In 1957, for example, three Republicans were among the ten African Americans in the Illinois legislature. The most prominent of these legislators was William H. Robinson, who served from 1954 to 1964. A social worker and militant advocate for racial equality, Robinson was a vocal critic of William Dawson's stranglehold over the district. To him, Dawson was the "king of Uncle Toms in this country," whose cautious approach to civil rights and kowtowing to the Democratic machine were a "disgrace." As a Republican, Robinson argued that he truly represented the interests of Chicago's black citizens because he was free to speak out against Democrats without repercussions. His outspoken rhetoric earned him the support of the city's most radical black activists, including communist labor organizer Frank Lumpkin. In the Illinois House, Robinson became one of the leading supporters of open housing legislation and laws that required equal rent for white and black tenants.[38]

Black Republicans also had electoral success in state races elsewhere. In 1950, Charles Stokes became Seattle's first African American state legislator, and represented the city's black voters in Olympia until 1958. Like many black Republican politicians, he had a long record of both GOP and civil rights activism. He had previously served as vice chairman of the Young Republican National Federation, and, as president of the Seattle NAACP, he was the chief lobbyist for Washington's Fair Employment Practice Act of 1949. Likewise, Harry A. Cole became Maryland's first black state senator in 1954. Prior to his victory, Cole had served as an assistant attorney general, where he focused his attention on increasing and protecting the state's black voters. He furthered his civil rights agenda in Annapolis, sponsoring numerous bills to eliminate the state's remaining racial barriers.[39]

As demonstrated by their political candidates, black Republicans in the 1950s were strong advocates and intraparty lobbyists for civil rights. Throughout the decade, Archibald Carey remained active in the Congress of Racial Equality, National Urban League, and Chicago NAACP. During the Montgomery bus boycott, he organized a prayer meeting at the Chicago Coliseum attended by 7,000 people, which raised thousands of dollars for the Montgomery Improvement Association. He was subsequently invited by his friend, Martin Luther King, Jr., to speak at an association rally in Montgomery. At King's request, Carey also chaired a committee that pressured the Chicago-based National City Lines, Inc. to desegregate their buses in Montgomery. In 1957, he joined Adam Clayton Powell in Detroit to protest discrimination in labor unions, and to promote local black candidates for city council.[40]

Similarly, prominent New York Republican Francis E. Rivers was elected to the NAACP Legal Defense Fund board of directors in the 1950s, and by the 1960s had become its president. In addition to Art Fletcher's Republican activism in Kansas, he also joined the Topeka NAACP in raising money for the local case that evolved into *Brown*, a case argued by several black Republican lawyers before the Supreme Court. John H. Calhoun, a GOP organizer from Atlanta, also headed the city NAACP in the 1950s, and initiated lawsuits to desegregate the city parks and golf courses. In 1960, Calhoun, John Wesley Dobbs, and other black Republican leaders joined Martin Luther King, Jr., in direct action protests against segregated downtown businesses. His successor as head of the city NAACP was another Republican, C. Clayton Powell. Similarly, Clayton Yates, a member of the Georgia Republican Party Executive Committee, also served on the advisory committee of the National Urban League. These were far from marginal figures in their communities.[41]

Despite their partisan differences, Roy Wilkins, who became NAACP executive director in 1955, told Archibald Carey, "When all angles are considered we really are not too far apart," and expressed his hope that the GOP would "be wise enough" to follow Carey's advice. Indeed, black Republicans during the 1950s were essential agents of the civil rights movement, serving as leaders in local NAACP branches, as financiers of civil rights campaigns, and as legislators that sponsored state-level civil rights measures. Moreover, they also served as an inner-party voice that continually demanded that the GOP live up to its campaign promises to support racial equality. As one political scientist noted in the early 1950s, "The Negroes who remained with the Republicans demanded more of the party than ever before: more liberal reforms, more jobs for more people, more consideration in the party council, while organizing more resistance to the undemocratic practices of the South." To most black Republicans, the GOP represented a legitimate, practical, means to achieve the same objectives as the NAACP, Martin Luther King, and other activists in eliminating state-sanctioned discrimination.[42]

Early in 1956, the *Christian Science Monitor* speculated on "The Negro Defection," asking, "are the Negroes going to desert the Democrats in this year's elections?" Acting on a potential increase in black support, Attorney General Brownell convinced a skeptical Eisenhower to support a new civil rights law. Brownell worked closely with the NAACP's Clarence Mitchell in writing a moderate bill that strengthened the federal government's ability to protect southern black voters. By the end of May, the Civil Rights Act of 1956 had sailed through the Democratic-controlled House of Representatives by a vote of 279-126 (of that figure, the Republican vote was 168-24). In the Senate, however, the legislation never even made it to the floor, as it was stalled in the Judiciary Committee, chaired by Mississippi's third-term Democratic senator James Eastland. It remained in the committee, and under the threat of a southern Democratic filibuster, until it died when the session ended. And because of the way seniority worked in the Senate, as long as Democrats controlled Congress, Eastland and other southern Democrats would continue to chair the chamber's most powerful committees.[43]

At the 1956 national convention, the GOP touted Eisenhower's civil rights bill, but carefully avoided endorsing *Brown v. Board of Education* in its platform, which instead "accepted" the court's decision and concurred that it should be implemented with "all deliberate speed." The rest of the platform was short on specific pledges, but provided a thorough list of Eisenhower's modest civil rights accomplishments. E. Frederic Morrow made it his personal mission to include a black woman "who would appear on a television screen as a Negro, rather than some fair-skinned person who might be mistaken for white," in a prime-time speaking slot. He selected Dr. Helen Edmonds, a history professor at North Carolina College, who has been described by contemporary scholar Pero Dagbovie as "arguably the most widely known black woman historian before the post-civil rights era." Although North Carolina's Lily-White Republican leadership warned that a television appearance by Edmonds would hurt them back home, RNC chairman Leonard Hall sided with Morrow, and agreed to give Edmonds one of the eight coveted slots to second Eisenhower's nomination. While her boilerplate speech was not as stirring as Carey's four years prior, her appearance as the first black woman to second the nomination of a presidential candidate had the symbolic resonance desired by Morrow and Hall.[44]

Though hosting an unremarkable convention, the Republicans managed to outshine Democrats on civil rights. Thirty-six black delegates attended the Republican convention, compared to twenty-four at the Democratic convention. Adlai Stevenson again received the party's nomination, and he again selected a moderate southerner, Tennessee's Estes Kefauver, as his running mate. Though the Republican civil rights plank was meticulously restrained regarding *Brown*, the Democratic plank avoided even a pledge to follow the court's orders, simply stating that the decision had "consequences of vast importance." Roy Wilkins criticized both platforms, but noted that the GOP's was "a thin shade stronger than the Democratic platform." The NAACP's chief lobbyist, Clarence Mitchell, declared, "the liberals in the Democratic party sold us out."[45]

Vice President Richard Nixon stood out among the two parties' tickets as the most vocal advocate of civil rights during the campaign. Simeon Booker, the Washington bureau chief of *Jet* magazine, later described the vice president as the GOP's "civil-rights workhorse" and "Mr. Civil Rights during the Eisenhower Administration." Nixon gained respect and publicity in black communities through his work as the head of the President's Committee on Government Contracts (PCGC), Eisenhower's alternative to a national FEPC. The committee was created by a 1953 executive order, and was tasked with ensuring fair employment in businesses that held federal contracts. Its first noteworthy success occurred in Washington, D.C., when, as a direct result of private meetings between Nixon and city leaders, the Chesapeake & Potomac Telephone Company desegregated its business offices and hired its first black clerical and switchboard workers. The Capital Transit Company soon followed and employed its first black bus and trolley drivers. Among other limited successes, the committee was responsible for four hundred black workers being hired at a South Carolina power plant, and for the first African Americans hired at an Esso refinery in Louisiana.[46]

Though the PCGC offered imperfect solutions to systemic employment discrimination, many credited Nixon with its piecemeal success. E. Frederic Morrow was "impressed" by "Nixon's keenness of mind, deep perception of a centuries-old problem, and his apparent sincerity of purpose." The NAACP's Henry Lee Moon privately remarked, "If the election were held today and I had to choose between Stevenson and Nixon, I'd vote for Nixon." However, many southern whites criticized the vice president's newfound interest in civil rights. One journalist wrote, "generally speaking, the south does not go along with a lot of his views," and Eisenhower's personal friend, South Carolina Governor James Byrnes, complained bitterly of Nixon's position on the committee. Even press secretary James Hagerty admitted that Nixon was becoming increasingly unpopular in the South because he was "connected in Southerners' minds with the Negro difficulty."[47]

Nixon embraced his role as the administration's "civil rights workhorse" in the 1956 campaign. At a Lincoln Day speech in New York, he linked the GOP directly to *Brown*, proclaiming that "a great Republican Chief Justice, Earl Warren, ordered an end to racial segregation in the nation's schools." On April 22, he appeared before and after *Commencement*, a made-for-television movie about racial discrimination that aired on the NBC network. In his prime time remarks, Nixon called for an end to discrimination in private enterprise, telling viewers that fair employment made "good business, good citizenship and plain good sense." In an October speech, he described his hope that "most of us here will live to see the day when American boys and girls shall sit, side by side, at any school—public or private—with no regard paid to the color of their skin." Just weeks before the election, he campaigned in Harlem, and received national headlines for his attack on the Democratic Party's southern bloc, arguing, "a political party at the national level cannot long endure or merit support when it's half for and half against equality of treatment."[48]

In denouncing the prominence of the Democratic Party's southern wing, Nixon had tapped into increasing disillusionment among black leaders with the party of James Eastland. In addition to the failure of Eisenhower's civil rights bill to survive the Judiciary Committee, the signing of the "Southern Manifesto" in the spring of 1956 fully revealed the commitment of southern Democrats to Jim Crow. Written primarily as a denunciation of *Brown*, the manifesto condemned "the Supreme Court's encroachment on the rights reserved to the States," and symbolized the immense weight southerners still carried inside the Democratic Party's congressional delegation. Signed by nineteen Democratic senators and eighty-two representatives, the document drew the signatures of every southern senator except Estes Kefauver, Albert Gore, Sr., and Lyndon Johnson.[49]

Republicans attempted to exploit black discontent with the Democratic Party's southern wing throughout the 1956 campaign. E. Frederic Morrow wrote in his diary that black cynicism toward Democrats "has been detected . . . and the results have been gratifying to me and to all of us here at the White House." Former RNC Chairman, and staunch supporter of the Eastern Establishment, Representative Hugh Scott of Pennsylvania spoke on behalf of the party at the NAACP's annual convention. Prior to his appearance, he convinced Illinois representative Leo Allen to support Eisenhower's civil rights bill in the House Rules Committee so that he could contrast the Democrats' four-four split with unanimous Republican support. The rift in the Democratic Party served as the central theme of Scott's June 29 NAACP address, where he declared, "The Democratic Party is split hopelessly . . . its Congress is in control of the Southern Do-Naught-Crats." He concluded with an argument that would be repeated again and again by Republicans throughout the fall: "A vote for the Democrats this year in San Francisco, Los Angeles,

Chicago, New York, Philadelphia is a vote for Southern Democrat control of Congress, it's a vote for the Democrat control of the House Rules Committee where Civil Rights bills get their suffocation treatment. A vote for any Democrat in a Federal election is a vote for Eastland."[50]

Former GOP congressional candidate Grant Reynolds, who joined the Liberal Party in 1950, returned to the Republican aisle out of his anger that "Eastland was made chairman of the Judiciary Committee." Touring across the country with boxer Joe Louis, Reynolds declared, "I'm supporting the entire Republican ticket . . . the people who signed the Southern Manifesto were among the leaders of the Democratic Party, and I can't see Negroes in the same party." T. R. M. Howard, who had recently fled from Mississippi to Chicago because of death threats to his family after he condemned Emmett Till's murder, formed Task Force '56, an organization designed to attract black voters to the Republican Party. In speeches across the country, he exclaimed, "the hell and damnation heaped on Negroes in the south today is being heaped by southern Democrats. I cannot see how the Negro is going to be able to vote for Democrats in the north, without at the same time voting for my neighbor, Jim Eastland." In a campaign form letter sent to black voters by the RNC's Minorities Division, Val Washington asked, "*Haven't many of us been cutting our own throats by voting for Democrat Congressmen and Senators?* What has it gotten us? Nothing but headaches, because we have been voting committee chairmanships to race-hating manifesto signers like Eastland of Mississippi."[51]

Black Republicans were more active on the campaign trail in 1956 than they had been in years. The Minorities Division printed ninety thousand copies of "Abe and Ike, In Deed Alike," a booklet that documented Eisenhower's civil rights accomplishments and profiled high-ranking black appointees. Thalia Thomas, the division's ranking woman, conducted a cross-country speaking tour of an estimated hundred thousand miles. Helen Edmonds was given her own tour after a black Republican field agent in Ohio reported favorable responses to her speech at the national convention. By the end of the campaign, she had delivered approximately fifty speeches across the Midwest and the East coast, and was interviewed on numerous television and radio broadcasts. Archibald Carey similarly spoke on the GOP's behalf across the country, served as cochair of the Friends for Ike organization, and wrote a widely distributed campaign pamphlet. On the grassroots level, George W. Lee spent $15,000 to expand the Lincoln League in Memphis; by the end of the election he had amassed nearly seven hundred and fifty ward and precinct workers, distributed eighty-nine thousand pieces of literature, and sponsored almost forty rallies.[52]

Eisenhower's most renowned black supporter was also one of the most surprising: Harlem's Democratic representative, Adam Clayton Powell. Given limited access to President Truman, Powell had been cultivating a relationship with Eisenhower since the inauguration. In February 1954, he told a union rally that Eisenhower did more "to restore the Negro to the status of first class citizenship than any President since Abraham Lincoln." In an October 1954 essay published in *Reader's Digest*, Powell wrote, "In less than two years in the White House President Eisenhower, without political trumpeting, has quietly started a revolution which, I firmly believe, means an era of greater promise for Negro citizens." In an early October 1956 meeting at the White House attended by Eisenhower, Val Washington, and others, Powell announced that he was "prepared to lead an independent movement for the President on a nationwide basis and take an active part in the balance of the campaign." On October 19, he officially launched "Independent Democrats for Eisenhower," and was given a $50,000 budget from the GOP for a national tour. His rhetoric closely mirrored that of black Republicans, praising Eisenhower's "silent revolution" and arguing that Stevenson "has to be either a hypocrite, a liar, a double-talker, or a double-dealer" for accepting the endorsements of both Eleanor Roosevelt and James Eastland.[53]

Although Eisenhower gladly accepted the active role of black supporters on the campaign trail, civil rights remained relatively absent from his rhetoric. One of the major reasons Eisenhower could generally avoid this issue was Adlai Stevenson's silence. Following the president's endorsement of the Civil Rights Act of 1956, the NAACP condemned Stevenson for having "not even given lip service" to the proposed bill. Two days after a white mob drove Autherine Lucy out of the University of Alabama, Stevenson, engaged in a tight February primary race against Kefauver, told a black audience that "gradualism" was the key to successful integration of southern schools. Throughout the fall, he continued to assure the South that he would not rock the boat on civil rights, peppering his speeches with phrases that were becoming increasingly unacceptable to black voters: "We must proceed gradually"; "We cannot by the stroke of a pen reverse customs and traditions that are older than the Republic"; "We will not improve the present condition [of southern blacks] . . . by coercive Federal action." While Stevenson finally endorsed *Brown* before a Harlem audience late in the campaign, it appeared to many as pandering, particularly as he still refused to support the use of federal troops to enforce the decision. Failing to spark much enthusiasm among African Americans, Stevenson secured the endorsement of only one of the nation's ten largest black newspapers.[54]

After the votes were counted on election day, it was evident that not only had Eisenhower won in a landslide (Stevenson won only the Deep South and Missouri), but that he had made gains among black voters. Pollster George Gallup reported in January 1957 that "of all the major groups of the nation's population, the one that shifted most to the Eisenhower-Nixon ticket last November was the Negro voter." He estimated that the national black vote for Eisenhower was approximately 38 percent, an increase of 18 percentage points from 1952. A 1957 report by the NAACP came to a similar conclusion after a study of predominantly black areas in sixty-three cities, estimating that Eisenhower received 36.8 percent of the black vote. Of the cities examined, Eisenhower won the majority of black voters in ten northern cities and thirteen southern ones.[55]

Eisenhower made his most substantial gains among southern blacks, prompting the *New York Times* to declare, "if you look South, the Negro voter has returned to the Republican party." Moreover, while black turnout decreased in the North, the same was not true of the South, where turnout increased in many of the South's largest cities, including Atlanta, Norfolk, Charlotte, Chattanooga, and Tampa. Though many southern blacks remained disenfranchised, those who could vote overwhelmingly supported Eisenhower. Black voters in Jefferson County (Birmingham), Alabama, cast an estimated 75 percent of their ballots for Eisenhower, and upwards of 90 percent of black voters in Macon County (Tuskegee) supported him. In Montgomery, civil rights leaders Martin Luther King, Jr., and Ralph Abernathy joined approximately 59 percent of the city's black voters in casting ballots for the president. King later remarked that "I do not recall a single person telling me he voted for Stevenson." African Americans in Atlanta, who had cast 74 percent of their votes for Stevenson in 1952, gave Eisenhower 86 percent of their votes in 1956. Similarly dramatic increases were reported in New Orleans and in Columbia, Darlington, and Charleston, South Carolina. In North Carolina, Eisenhower received over 60 percent of the vote in predominantly black precincts in Durham, Raleigh, and Greensboro.[56]

Southern black voters also helped secure Eisenhower victories in Florida, Louisiana, Kentucky, Tennessee, and Virginia. A 1957 report by the RNC Research Division concluded that Eisenhower's slim six-thousand-vote plurality in Tennessee "can be accounted for by the increased Republican vote among

Negroes of the city of Memphis alone." Due in large part to George W. Lee's organizing, the Republicans won twenty-three of the city's thirty-eight majority-black precincts, giving Eisenhower 54 percent of the city's African American vote. Likewise, the majority of black voters in Virginia supported a Republican presidential candidate for the first time since the New Deal. While Eisenhower had won just over 25 percent of the black vote in Richmond in 1952, he received almost 75 percent in 1956. His support among black voters in Norfolk soared from 16 to 77 percent.[57]

Though support for Eisenhower among northern blacks was far less impressive than his showings in the South, he made modest inroads in many black districts. He even won the majority of black votes in cities like Baltimore, Atlantic City, New Jersey, and Columbus, Ohio. The vote for Eisenhower increased in Harlem from 20.8 percent in 1952 to 33.7 percent in 1956. In Chicago's black districts, the vote for the president rose from under 30 to 37 percent, and his support in seven majority-black wards in Cleveland rose from 31 to 48 percent. In Boston's majority-black Ward Nine, support for Eisenhower grew from 28.1 to 48.9 percent, and his support in thirty-nine of Gary, Indiana's, majority-black precincts grew from 26 to 41 percent. In only a handful of cities did Eisenhower's black support remain stagnant.[58]

In their post-election analysis, black leaders were careful to point out that support for the GOP was just as much a vote against the Democratic Party as it was an endorsement of Eisenhower. Roy Wilkins attributed Republican victory to "the growing resentment against the pernicious role of southern Democrats in hamstringing all civil rights legislation and especially in slowing down school desegregation." Black Republican P. B. Young argued that in his state of Virginia, "the shift was in large part an expression of protest. Negroes resented the insults, and smears hurled at them by angry state officials, legislators and newspapers, because of the Supreme Court decision." A post-election study conducted by the RNC suggested that black voters in Maryland supported the GOP largely in response to the southern leanings of the state's Democratic leadership. Overall, the report found that Republican gains were "moderate" in cities where local Democrats "give recognition to Negroes," but "the big switch" toward Republicans occurred in areas where "Negroes enjoy no status in the Democratic Party and Democratic leaders oppose civil rights."[59]

Other factors also explain Eisenhower's strong showing. *Louisiana Weekly*, a black newspaper, argued in its endorsement of the president, "Without a question Ike has moved forward on the civil rights question." A 1957 study of black voters by Virginia Union University professors found that in addition to disillusionment with Democrats, African Americans were swayed by "the number of high level governmental appointments by Eisenhower," "the personal prestige of the President," and the successful desegregation of Washington, D.C. Harry A. Cole, Maryland's black Republican state senator, claimed that the shift in his state "was mostly due to the great respect for Eisenhower and to intensive organizing efforts on the precinct level." Economic prosperity also played a part, at the very least calming black fears of a depression under a Republican administration. According to a black Republican congressional candidate from Philadelphia, "if a man is hungry, he's mainly interested in feeding himself and his family, and doesn't have much time to worry about broader things. . . . Now times are good, and he has time to look around." Though this argument did not convince most black workers in northern cities to support the Republican presidential candidate, many within the middle class and in the South believed that the GOP offered a means to achieve civil rights reform outside a deeply divided Democratic Party.[60]

Modest black support for the GOP in 1956 extended beyond Eisenhower. New York Senate candidate Jacob Javits's campaign advertisements urged black voters to "MAKE YOUR VOTE COUNT FOR CIVIL RIGHTS! PUT JAVITS IN THE SENATE. . . . So I can block Eastland . . . and other manifesto signers." Also earning the endorsement of Adam Clayton Powell, Javits won the race and received over 30 percent of Harlem's vote. In Kentucky, black voters were credited by Republicans and the NAACP with providing Thurston Morton a slim majority over the incumbent Democrat, Senator Earle Clements. Maryland's incumbent GOP Senator, John Marshall Butler, won the majority of Baltimore's black precincts. Atlanta's Republican Congressional candidate, Randolph Thrower, received 86 percent of the black vote. Likewise, black voters in Richmond, Virginia, cast the majority of their votes for the Republican Congressional candidate, and black areas of Durham and Charlotte, North Carolina, voted overwhelmingly for Republican gubernatorial candidate Kyle Hayes. Black Republicans still hadn't found a convincing argument that appealed to working-class pocket books, but as the 1956 election demonstrated, they held the upper hand, if tentatively, on civil rights.[61]

On January 20, 1957, Marian Anderson, the renowned black vocalist who had been barred from performing at Washington's segregated Constitution Hall eighteen years earlier, performed in a fully integrated city at President

Eisenhower's inauguration ceremony, and was assigned a front row seat on the presidential inaugural platform. E. Frederic Morrow became the first African American to marshal a division of the inaugural parade, and, later that day, he and his wife became the first African Americans invited to sit in the presidential review stand. As the Democratic Party continued to be weighed down by its powerful southern wing in the 1950s, a wing that party liberals like Adlai Stevenson carefully avoided offending, the Republican Party made significant inroads among black voters, especially in the middle class and in southern cities. The results of the 1956 election indicated that many African Americans were willing to support Republican candidates who promised to advance the cause of civil rights. However, as James Hicks suggested, while many blacks had temporarily "divorced" the Democratic Party and begun a flirtation with a new Republican suitor, "the divorcee . . . isn't going to let him in unless he puts a ring on her finger." The question that remained in the minds of many African Americans who had flirted with Eisenhower and the GOP was how far he and his party would go to win their affection.[62]

CHAPTER 3

Bit by Bit: Civil Rights and the Eisenhower Administration

Though many African Americans supported Dwight Eisenhower in 1956 in hopes that the GOP would surpass the Democratic Party on issues of civil rights, the president proved to be a lukewarm ally. He had had few interactions with African Americans in his life before the presidency. Born in Jim Crow Texas and spending nearly all his adult life in a segregated army, he was insulated from racial discrimination and black protests. He was not a white supremacist by any means, but civil rights was not an issue he spent time thinking, or talking, about unless pressed to do so. More pragmatic than ideological, Eisenhower's self-touted brand of "Modern Republicanism" emphasized moderation and stability over rigid dogma and radical change. As such, he balked at conservative calls to overturn the New Deal, but was also skeptical of idealistic liberals who sought to upend the South's deeply entrenched racial order. By his second term, he found it increasingly difficult to strike a moderate balance on civil rights that would placate both black and white southerners. Together, these two groups had played an important role in his 1956 victories in Texas, Louisiana, and the border South, with African Americans seeing him as a potential alternative to Democrats and whites valuing his military service and down-to-earth persona. Without decisive leadership from the White House, the Republican Party of the 1950s lacked ideological and strategic moorings, sharing the president's hope that they could both retain black gains and expand deeper into the Democratic South.

This balancing act became even harder to maneuver by the late 1950s, as grassroots protests like the Montgomery bus boycott mobilized African Americans across the South and launched a new phase of the civil rights movement. If Eisenhower didn't want to rock the boat on race relations, the undercurrents of black discontent that had risen to the surface would rock it for him. As E. Frederic Morrow noted, "American Blacks were set to love President Eisenhower. But when he failed to come to grips with their hopes and aspirations, the Black community soured and the expressions of protest became physical rather than just verbal." As black dissatisfaction morphed into nonviolent demonstrations, and white backlash against activists intensified, Eisenhower's second term would be marred by his cautious approach that confused and offended both blacks and segregationists. Moderate support for civil rights might have been acceptable, even progressive, in the early 1950s when Eisenhower first entered the political arena, but by the end of the decade African Americans were no longer content with gradual reform. Martin Luther King, Jr., who had cast his ballot for Eisenhower in 1956, reflected the frustrations of many African Americans by the late 1950s, describing the president's remedy for cancerous Jim Crow as "bit by bit with a tweezer because the surgeon's knife was an instrument too radical."[1]

Eisenhower was willing, however, to combat egregious forms of black disenfranchisement. Despite a steady rise in black voter registration in the region since the 1940s, only 25 percent of voting-age African Americans in eleven southern states voted in 1956. In Mississippi, where blacks composed over 40 percent of the state's adult population, they made up less than 4 percent of registered voters. African Americans represented one-third of Alabama's population, but only 8 percent of the state's voters. Approximately 75 percent of Georgia's voting-age African Americans were not registered. Sixteen counties in the Deep South with majority black populations had zero registered black voters, and just 5 percent of African Americans were registered in forty-nine additional black belt counties. These registration numbers were a byproduct of over sixty years of violence and intimidation. For those who risked their lives and attempted to register, local officials disenfranchised them through a legal maze of poll taxes and restrictions, including literacy tests that featured intentionally impossible questions, such as "How many bubbles are there in a cake of soap?"[2]

Central to Eisenhower's focus on eliminating voter discrimination was his belief that if black voters could be protected, they would end Jim Crow themselves at the ballot box. This would allow for state-level repeals of segregation rather than sweeping federal decrees. By targeting the most obviously unconstitutional denial of black citizenship rights, it also let him off the hook when it came to dealing directly with the social and cultural forms of discrimination that permeated the South. In January 1957, Eisenhower reintroduced voter-protection legislation similar to the failed bill from the previous year. Again written by Attorney General Herbert Brownell, the law made it a federal crime to interfere with voters in federal elections, created a new assistant attorney general to handle civil rights violations, and gave federal judges the power to issue injunctions to protect the right to vote and declare in contempt anyone who interfered. By placing this power in the hands of judges, Brownell intended to remove the matter from criminal trials, where he was well aware that southern juries would side with local officials.[3]

While the administration's bill made it through the House without any substantial changes, the Senate, where southern Democrats chaired five of the eight most powerful committees, was a much more hostile environment. Even northern Democrats, including John F. Kennedy (Massachusetts) and Warren Magnuson (Washington), voted to send the 1957 bill to James Eastland's Judiciary Committee, where its most effective sections were diluted. Opposition to the legislation initially focused on Title III, which provided civil and criminal penalties for anyone who violated another's rights, including, but not limited to, voting rights, and gave the president the authority to use troops to enforce civil rights laws. Led by Majority Leader Lyndon B. Johnson, who claimed that it would create "new and drastic procedures to cover a wide variety of vaguely defined so-called civil rights," the Senate rejected the provisions. Despite protests from Jacob Javits, William Knowland, and other Senate Republicans, Eisenhower agreed to a compromise that excluded the controversial section.[4]

The president was less conciliatory on the issue of jury trials. On August 1, the Senate passed a jury trial amendment that placed the power to prosecute a person held in contempt of a federal judge's orders in the hands of southern juries. Twelve conservative Republicans joined thirty-nine Democrats in supporting the amendment, which significantly weakened the federal government's ability to enforce the law, as southern juries were notorious for acquitting those accused of civil rights violations. Even Mississippi's segregationist governor described the new bill as a "fairly harmless proposition." Among those who voted for the amendment were emerging conservative Republican icon Barry Goldwater (Arizona) and liberal Democrats Paul Douglas (Illinois) and Hubert Humphrey (Minnesota). Vice President Richard Nixon, one of the amendment's most vocal critics, described its passage as "a vote against the right to vote." Senate minority leader William Knowland called it "a vote to kill . . . an effective voting rights bill," and was later found crying in his office by the NAACP's Clarence Mitchell. At a cabinet meeting the following day, Eisenhower described the amendment as "one of the most serious political defeats of the past four years," and issued a statement lamenting that millions of black voters "will continue . . . to be disenfranchised."[5]

It remained initially unclear whether Eisenhower would sign or veto the compromised law. The NAACP took a "calculated risk" and endorsed the bill, telling members, "even though it has been weakened by the Senate . . . [it] will constitute a start toward our goal, and a start is better than standing still." They were joined by the Leadership Conference on Civil Rights and union leader Joseph Rauh, who argued that to a starving man "a half-loaf of bread was better than no bread at all." King followed suit, telling Vice President Nixon, who supported a veto, that "while I sympathize with your point of view, I feel that civil rights legislation is urgent now, and the present bill will go a long way to insure it." Other black luminaries, including Ralph Bunche, baseball legend Jackie Robinson, John Sengstacke of the *Chicago Defender*, and Earl Dickerson of the NAACP board of directors, were less willing to compromise, echoing A. Philip Randolph in declaring that a weak bill was "worse than no bill at all."[6]

Leading black Republicans supported a veto. Val Washington argued, "it is better to have no bill at all than to have one with no teeth in it." The Grand Exalted Ruler of the black Elks, Robert H. Johnson, declared that his organization opposed the weakened bill, and Elk official Larry Foster wrote Eisenhower, "your veto of the bill . . . will be welcomed by all those who hate deception and love justice. The bill as it now stands is a farce." Though the impetus for the legislation came from Eisenhower's Justice Department, its compromised form belonged to Lyndon Johnson, who rallied his party behind a tame bill acceptable to all but its most rabid segregationists. Northern Democrats could tell black constituents they passed a civil rights bill, while southern Democrats could return home to highlight their role in rendering the same bill ineffective. Though the NAACP's national leadership and union leaders would have preferred a stronger bill, their strong ties to northern Democrats provided incentive to accept concessions, as a presidential veto would draw attention to the role of high-profile Democrats in scrapping its strongest sections. Many black Republicans, such as Julius Adams of the *New York Amsterdam News*, believed the NAACP had sold out to protect Democrats. E. Frederic Morrow publicly expressed his "shock" that the organization used "the long-ago discarded 'half-a-loaf' theory" to support the legislation, "no matter how emasculating or insulting." Their willingness to compromise provided shelter for Democrats to "run for cover," he noted, and, "it is strange to see the NAACP agreeing with men of the South like Eastland, Lyndon Johnson and Senator Russell of Georgia on the same bill."[7]

Guaranteed by Lyndon Johnson that a bill without a jury trial amendment would never get through the Senate, Eisenhower agreed to support a compromise bill. He feared that his opponents would never stop reminding black voters that a Republican president vetoed the first civil rights legislation in over eighty years, but understood that supporting the bill would be seen by many in his own party as caving in to Johnson and the Democrats. With Eisenhower promising his support, the Senate passed the Civil Rights Act of 1957 on August 29 by a vote of 60–15. All 15 votes against it were cast by southern Democrats.[8]

While the law did not endear Eisenhower to African Americans, it enhanced the vice president's image as the administration's most prominent supporter of civil rights. According to a September edition of the *Reporter* magazine, the bill "turned Vice-President Richard Nixon . . . into an avowed champion in this field." The day after the bill was passed, Martin Luther King, Jr., wrote Nixon to say "how grateful all people of goodwill are to you for your assiduous labor and dauntless courage in seeking to make the Civil Rights Bill a reality. . . . This is certainly an expression of your devotion to the highest mandates of the moral law." NAACP lawyer James Nabrit, Jr., sent the vice president a telegram, asserting, "The Negro people will not forget your great contribution toward the passage of the Civil Rights Bill." Jackie Robinson, who would become a confidant of the vice president by 1960, promised "we will not forget those of you with enough courage to stand by your conviction," and would "never forget the fight you made and what you stand for."[9]

Though supporters of civil rights could be found inside Eisenhower's administration, including Nixon, E. Frederic Morrow, Maxwell Rabb, and Sherman Adams, it also housed conservatives who were far less willing to endorse even moderate advances. At cabinet meetings, secretaries John Foster Dulles, Charles Wilson, and Marion Folsom called Brownell's civil rights bills "impractical," and warned they would "aggravate the situation" in the South. secretary of health, education and welfare (HEW) Oveta Culp Hobby, wife of a former Democratic governor of Texas, fired Jane Morrow Spaulding, a black HEW appointee, after Spaulding publicly targeted southern hospitals that refused to hire black doctors. Behind the scenes, Eisenhower's conservative chief of staff during his second term, Wilton Persons, told Morrow, "I would appreciate it if you never approach me or come to me with anything involving

civil rights," and advised him to "discuss any matters in this area with somebody else." The conversation confirmed Morrow's fears that "the South looks
hopefully" to Persons "to exercise restraining influences on the President in
matters of race."[10]

While his hands-off leadership gave liberal cabinet members like Brownell
room to pursue a civil rights agenda, Eisenhower himself typically avoided
the issue altogether. Simeon Booker of *Jet* stopped attending presidential
press conferences, because Eisenhower refused to recognize black reporters
and said little on issues of race. Journalist Alice Dunnigan similarly recalled
that the president "was not familiar with many questions raised on civil
rights . . . he would become very annoyed whenever such questions were
raised." Morrow wrote in his diary that while Eisenhower may have "noble
instincts about things that are right and just . . . [his] closest personal friends
are Southerners," and he had a difficult time "in formulating an opinion or a
policy" on issues of racial equality. Nor did he care for the direct action protests and tactics of the civil rights movement, once telling Morrow that "progress does not necessarily demand noisy conflict." The president's desire to
place domestic issues like civil rights in the hands of cabinet members left
matters of equality at the mercy of department secretaries. While a cabinet
member like Brownell could actively pursue a progressive agenda, others
could placate the South. Without a clear, strong voice from inside the Oval
Office, administration policy was disjointed and confused, giving only
glimpses of hope to African Americans looking for national leadership.[11]

Morrow observed that "civil rights in the Eisenhower Administration was
handled like a bad dream, or like something that's not very nice, and you
shield yourself from it as long as you possibly can." Many civil rights leaders
echoed this sentiment. Fred Shuttlesworth declared African Americans had
"no friend in Ike," who "saw nothing, felt nothing, heard nothing, and he did
nothing until he had to." Martin Luther King, Jr., claimed that while Eisenhower was "a man of genuine integrity and good will . . . I don't think he feels
like being a crusader for integration." The president instead favored gradual
change, where "you just wait 50 or 100 years and it will work itself out." Roy
Wilkins bemoaned that while Eisenhower "made inroads into the Negro vote,"
his administration "demonstrated their ineptitude in expanding their gains . . .
acting as though they were ashamed to be forthright on the issues."[12]

As the administration's highest profile African American, Morrow implored the president to take a stronger stand against southern violence. Following the murder of fourteen-year-old Emmett Till in August 1955, he

suggested that the administration "issue some kind of statement deploring the breakdown of law and order in Mississippi, and stating that it is un-American and undemocratic and contrary to the American way." To his dismay, he found that "there seems to be complete fright when it is suggested that such action be taken," and warned, "it is things like the refusal of the Republicans to issue any kind of fear-allaying statement on conditions in Mississippi that contributes to the Negro's thinking that the Republican Party deserts him in crisis." Morrow, Val Washington, James Nabrit, J. Ernest Wilkins, and Maxwell Rabb concluded after a strategy meeting that "the Republicans missed the ball when no prominent member of the administration spoke out against the Till matter." Rabb, a white advisor who had the closest ear of the group to the president, claimed to have a difficult time getting anyone "close to the President to go along with this kind of thing on the matter of civil rights." Morrow could only conclude "there seems to be some uncanny fear that to alienate the South on this matter of race will be disastrous." Even Sherman Adams, Morrow's closest ally inside the White House, opposed issuing a statement condemning southern violence, claiming, "Eisenhower is the President of all the country and could not make speeches designed to influence or castigate any segment of the American public."[13]

African Americans from across the country joined Morrow in urging the president to speak out against racial violence. Morrow described daily "sacks of mail" brought to his office "berating the president for his failure to denounce the breakdown of law and order." The editor of the *Pittsburgh Courier*, William Nunn, warned party officials that his paper was "swamped" with letters from readers who "feel that a miscarriage of justice such as this should call for some official statement from the Justice Department." Roy Wilkins told Val Washington that if the administration had simply "made a move and been rebuffed it could have collected some kudos for effort. . . . But it said and did nothing." Realistically, a presidential statement would have had a minimal effect on curbing southern violence, but symbolically to African Americans Eisenhower's silence proved his apathy to their suffering.[14]

The Eisenhower administration's muted response occurred during a decade of sustained terrorism against southern blacks. The Ku Klux Klan grew exponentially in the 1950s, having significantly more members and committing more acts of violence than it had in decades. On Christmas night 1951, activist Harry T. Moore and his wife were killed after a bomb exploded outside his Florida home. In 1955, two of Mississippi's leading civil rights workers, Rev. George W. Lee and Lamar Smith, were murdered for encouraging

Figure 5. President Eisenhower meets with E. Frederic Morrow in the White House,
October 4, 1956. National Park Service photo, 72-1908, Dwight D. Eisenhower
Presidential Library and Museum.

blacks to register to vote. Lee, no relation to George W. Lee of Memphis, was
the first African American since Reconstruction to register to vote in Belzoni,
Mississippi. During the Montgomery bus boycott, Klansmen bombed the
homes and businesses of activists, and murdered a black truck driver who
they believed had a white girlfriend. In 1956, Fred Shuttlesworth was nearly
killed in Birmingham after sixteen sticks of dynamite were set off underneath
his bedroom.[15]

A distraught E. Frederic Morrow wrote in his diary that though "the
bombings and the racial strife in the country continues. . . . There does not
seem to be leadership forthcoming from anywhere." When juxtaposed to the
presidential proclamations against Soviet tyranny in Eastern Europe, he observed, "Hungarians seem to be getting a better break in their efforts to find
freedom" than black citizens of America. Roy Wilkins believed that "the 'soft'
and 'slow' policy of the President" bore "some blame for the tensions and

ugliness now breaking out all over," and Martin Luther King, Jr., feared that Eisenhower's inability "to render positive leadership in this area . . . will serve to push the moderates more and more in the background." Soon after King became head of the newly created Southern Christian Leadership Conference, the organization joined with Roy Wilkins, A. Philip Randolph, and other civil rights leaders in announcing a large-scale demonstration in Washington, D.C. A primary intent of the 1957 "Prayer Pilgrimage," scheduled on the third anniversary of *Brown*, was to condemn Eisenhower's silence on racial violence. Speaking on the steps of the Lincoln Memorial, King denounced the president as "all too silent and apathetic."[16]

Much to the chagrin of black Republicans, on the few occasions when Eisenhower mentioned civil rights, he emphasized gradualism. In a letter to Roy Wilkins, he repeated his standard response when addressing the issue, arguing that "laws on the statute book are not enough . . . patience and forbearance and wisdom are required of all of us if we are to solve effectively the perplexing problems of this trying period of adjustment." Such language was seen as antiquated not only by civil rights leaders, but by black Republicans as well. Throughout his time in the White House, E. Frederic Morrow constantly reminded members of the administration that most blacks "are against any talk of moderation and the use of the term 'gradualism' is fatal when addressing any Negro audience." George W. Lee of Memphis told Young Republicans in Atlanta, "we would have been in a devil of a fix if gradualism had been employed" during Reconstruction, when Republicans used "rapid right now action" to push through the Thirteenth, Fourteenth, and Fifteenth Amendments. Jackie Robinson, who would become the best-known black Republican of the 1960s, asked the president, to "whom you are referring when you say we must be patient," reminding him that African Americans "have patiently waited all these years for the rights supposedly guaranteed us under our Constitution."[17]

After "much sparring behind the scenes" and "several conferences" with Sherman Adams, Morrow convinced the president to speak before the Negro Publishers Association's annual meeting in May 1958. Recognizing Eisenhower's unpopular rhetoric, Morrow prepared a "fact sheet" on the terms and phrases to avoid when speaking to black audiences. During the limousine ride with the president to the event, he again emphasized black discomfort with Eisenhower's standard responses. After receiving loud cheers from a crowd of nearly four hundred leading black newspaper publishers, editors, and journalists, many of whom were sympathetic to the GOP, Eisenhower began his speech by describing a variety of domestic and international issues confronting the nation. As he transitioned to the topic of civil rights, he set aside his prepared remarks to speak extemporaneously, and told the audience that "you people" need to have "patience and forbearance," as "there are no revolutionary cures" to combat discrimination. Upon hearing the president repeat this string of objectionable phrases, Morrow observed, "the audience reacted as if a time bomb had exploded. Their contorted and pained faces expressed their disbelief and disdain. Sitting on the platform next to the President, I could feel life draining from me."[18]

The reaction of black Republicans to the speech was overwhelmingly negative. The chairman of the meeting, William O. Walker, whose Cleveland *Call and Post* had consistently been one of the most loyal Republican newspapers in the country, declined to accompany Eisenhower out of the room, complaining that this was "the kind of advice we have been getting" since the *Brown* decision. The *Iowa Bystander*, another solidly Republican paper, editorialized that the president had pulled "the rug from under law abiding citizens . . . and has encouraged the rabble to push harder against the very thing he is pledged to uphold—law and order." Jackie Robinson, who was in attendance, wrote Eisenhower that he "felt like standing up and saying 'Oh no! Not again,'" and reminded him that "we have been the most patient of all people." The president's words, "unwittingly crush the spirit of freedom in Negroes by constantly urging forbearance and give hope to those . . . who would take from us even those freedoms we now enjoy."[19]

The fall 1957 desegregation crisis at Central High School in Little Rock, Arkansas, further exposed the inadequacies of Eisenhower's gradualist approach to race relations. As his former speechwriter, Emmet John Hughes, later wrote, Eisenhower's "limp direction" in the field of civil rights "served almost as a pathetic and inviting prologue to Little Rock." Prior to the crisis, the president's rhetoric regarding school desegregation suggested to many southern whites that there was little he would do to actively enforce desegregation. In April 1956, he remarked, "civil rights extremists never stop to consider that although you can send in troops, troops can't make anyone operate schools," and as late as July 1957 claimed, "I can't imagine any set of circumstances that would ever induce me to send federal troops . . . to enforce the orders of a federal court." As Little Rock officials prepared to implement the court-ordered desegregation of Central High in September, Governor Orval Faubus ordered the state National Guard to block the nine enrolled black students from entering the school. Seeking a quiet solution, Eisenhower publicly stated, "you cannot change people's hearts merely by laws," and expressed his hope that the people of Little Rock would peacefully comply with the court order. He invited Faubus to join him in Newport, Rhode Island, and convinced the governor to call off the National Guard. Many of Little Rock's white citizens, however, were not prepared to have their children attend an integrated school, and the black students faced a rabid mob as they approached Central High. Police and law enforcement personnel tepidly intervened only after the confrontation descended into violent chaos.[20]

As photographs of defenseless black children accosted by angry crowds circulated throughout the country, African Americans blamed Eisenhower for not denouncing violence and enforcing the court order. Roy Wilkins claimed that the president "has been absolutely and thoroughly disappointing and disillusioning" in his handling of the crisis. Helen Edmonds, who had endorsed Eisenhower at the national convention just one year earlier, reported to Val Washington that even African Americans who "formerly manifested a love for the President, are saying that they are no longer enchanted and that the seeming indecision on the Arkansas situation was the breaking point." The crisis galvanized the nation, and threatened America's self-portrayal as an international beacon of freedom, giving the president little choice but to act. On September 24, weeks after the crisis began, Eisenhower finally addressed the nation in a televised speech. Surrounded by portraits that strategically included both Abraham Lincoln and Robert E. Lee, the president sympathized with white southerners, but claimed that even if the Supreme Court was wrong in *Brown*, "Our personal opinions about the decision have no bearing on the matter of enforcement; the responsibility and authority of the Supreme Court to interpret the Constitution are very clear." He then federalized Arkansas's National Guard and sent a thousand troops from the 101st Airborne Division to supervise the desegregation of Central High. Though some whites harassed the black students throughout the rest of the school year, the continued presence of armed soldiers, the first federal troops dispatched to the South since Reconstruction, were a visible sign of Eisenhower's reluctant action to preserve the credibility of the federal judiciary. Little Rock would hardly become an integration success story, however, as Governor Faubus closed all four of Little Rock's high schools for the 1958–1959 school year.[21]

Little Rock illustrated the Republican electoral quandary. On the one hand, Republicans saw significant gains among African Americans in Eisenhower's reelection effort. On the other hand, with his decisive southern wins in 1952 and 1956, the GOP believed they could form a new and potentially permanent coalition of businessmen, fiscal conservatives, and middle-class suburbanites in the South. Early in 1957, Meade Alcorn, a former state legislator from Connecticut and recently named chairman of the Republican National Committee, created a Southern Division, often called "Operation Dixie," to expand the party in the South. The division's director, I. Lee Potter, a real estate investor and state chairman of the Virginia Republican Party, embodied the attitude of young southern Republicans. Though he could be described as a moderate by southern standards, believing the rabid racism of Democrats damaged southern economic progress, he publicly declared "our party is for segregation" soon after taking charge of Operation Dixie. Revealing Republican priorities, Potter received the third highest budget of any special division of the national committee, behind only Young Republicans and the Women's Division. His initial six-month budget was $20,000, which doubled by 1960.[22]

On the other hand, the RNC Minorities Division played a more limited role in party affairs, inhibiting Val Washington's already difficult endeavors in black communities. Monetarily, the division's budget varied annually. In 1956, it had a six-month campaign budget of $161,500, which contributed to the party's best presidential showing among African Americans since the New Deal. In other years, however, Washington's annual budget dropped below $30,000, and he was given just one assistant and a secretary. This was not nearly enough to compete with Democrats, whose city machines had extensive grassroots networks, and whose union allies had access to millions of black voters. Even more than budgetary complaints, Washington lamented that party leaders "have been unwilling to accept us in the high councils of the party," and rarely sought black advice.[23]

Indeed, black Republicans in the 1950s were often ignored during the party's discussions of racial policy. During the debate over the Civil Rights Act of 1957, Washington wrote the president to encourage a veto. Eisenhower's secretary, Ann Whitman, told Maxwell Rabb that "Val is very worked up about this letter," and noted that he "thinks I have shown [it] to the president, which I haven't." She asked Rabb to help craft a perfunctory response on Eisenhower's behalf. On another occasion, prominent Republican and civil rights activist T. R. M. Howard requested a meeting with Richard Nixon, Sherman Adams, and Herbert Brownell to discuss racial violence in Mississippi. He never made it past Rabb, who advised Nixon's secretary that the vice president "should stay out of this if possible." At the outbreak of the Little

Rock crisis, E. Frederic Morrow complained that, despite joining the president in Rhode Island, he was "powerless," as no one with any influence "asked me my thinking on these matters."[24]

As much as Eisenhower's approach marginalized black voices of protest, its willingness to act when pushed to address patently unconstitutional violations of civil rights also irritated many white southerners. Democrats were especially quick to exploit the federal "invasion" of Little Rock. Senator Eastland called Eisenhower's action "an attempt to destroy the social order of the South," and Senator Richard Russell of Georgia denounced "Hitler-like storm-trooper tactics." Southern newspapers triumphantly declared, "the followers of Eisenhower in Mississippi have departed faster than the Israelites out of Egypt," and claimed the president was under the spell of "that political lick-spittle, Herbert Brownell, Jr., who takes his orders from the NAACP." I. Lee Potter feared for the future success of Operation Dixie, and asked the RNC Executive Committee "if something can be done to pull the last semblance of Federal Intervention out of Little Rock . . . for the president to say now we are through and turn it back over to the states." White Republican leaders from Mississippi were particularly critical of the president. E. O. Spencer resigned in protest as head of Mississippi's Citizens for Eisenhower, and Wirt Yerger, head of the state GOP, accused Eisenhower of "joining hands with the NAACP and the Democratic High Command in a scheme to destroy the Constitution of the United States."[25]

Though the Little Rock crisis marked a temporary setback, the Republican Party continued to grow in the South. Demographic changes were rapidly shifting the urban-rural balance, as "New South" cities like Atlanta and Charlotte grew exponentially in the postwar years and created a new base among the urban and suburban white middle class. Though many of these Republicans were businessmen and professionals, not diehard segregationists, most were not integrationists or deeply concerned with issues of black equality. Unlike the Lily-Whites of past decades, this new generation of white southern Republicans were sometimes willing to allow black participation in the party, though they often stopped short of providing African Americans with meaningful power. Their rise generated inevitable tension with the pro-civil rights stance of Black-and-Tan holdouts. Indeed, while there was significant variation from state to state during the 1950s, many Republican factions could be found throughout the South with competing ideas of what, and whom, the party represented.[26]

In Potter's home state of Virginia, the black president of Norfolk's 7th Division Republican Club, Melvin E. Diggs, argued that "every Dixiecrat and Manifesto signer should be challenged," and called on Republicans to "stand for human rights as against so-called 'states rights' in the tradition of our party." On the other hand, both Virginia's Republican representatives, Joel Broyhill and Richard Poff, joined Democrats in signing the Southern Manifesto and encouraging "massive resistance" against school desegregation. Other white party leaders took more moderate positions, hoping to bring black voters into party ranks. Linwood Holton, a white lawyer from Roanoke who would become governor in the 1960s, rallied many in the GOP to oppose the forces of "massive resistance" led by Senator Harry Byrd's Democratic machine. Holton recognized that, in large part because of Byrd, Virginia was home to a growing network of black Republicans. Helen Edmonds noted after visiting the state in 1956, "The Virginia Negroes are so mad" at the Democratic establishment "that they don't need too much prodding" to support the GOP. Clarence Townes, for example, who became the RNC's highest ranking black official in the mid-1960s, was initially drawn to the party in the 1950s in response to Democratic efforts to close public schools entirely rather than comply with *Brown*. By the end of the decade, he had become an integral member of the Richmond City Republican Committee. The black vice president of the committee, David E. Longley, also served as director of the state's Central Republican League.[27]

Though Atlanta's suburban whites flocked to the GOP in record numbers in the 1950s, African Americans continued to wield influence within the state party, and the widely circulated *Atlanta Daily World* stood out as black America's most reliably Republican newspaper. Black Republicans like John H. Calhoun, L. B. Toomer, and William Shaw attended national conventions as delegates, and John Wesley Dobbs served as vice chairman of the Republican State Central Committee. Outside Atlanta, African Americans continued to control much of the state's patronage. Indeed, the black chairman of the Eighth District's Republican Party, Tom Williams, and the head of the GOP in Pierce County, Isaac J. White, were arraigned in the 1950s on charges of soliciting bribes from people seeking government jobs. Though this did not help the perception of the party among white voters, the arrests indicated the entrenched position blacks continued to hold in the state's Republican establishment. These were influential roles not just for the acquisition of patronage, but also for shaping the party's overall outlook. For example, the integrated

Executive Committee of the Republican State Central Committee of Georgia—led by African Americans Clayton R. Yates and William Shaw— approved a 1957 statement supporting Eisenhower's decision to send troops into Little Rock, a widely unpopular sentiment in the white South that would not have been approved without significant black participation inside the party.[28]

Similarly, George W. Lee, who was referred to by the *Pittsburgh Courier Magazine* in 1959 as "undoubtedly the most effective Negro Republican leader in the U.S.A. at this time," remained firmly in control of the Memphis GOP. His power did not go unchallenged, however, as a "New Guard" faction vied for control. Most New Guards were wealthy businessmen and house-wives who were drawn to conservative economic policies. They also, with a few exceptions, opposed civil rights, prompting Lee to claim that their vision of the GOP had "drawn its strength almost all together from racial prejudice." Lee and fellow Republican Benjamin Hooks organized one of the most suc-cessful registration drives in the country, increasing the number of black vot-ers in the city from eight thousand in 1951 to fifty-seven thousand by 1959, providing him a solid base to maintain influence.[29]

In 1952, Lee discovered from black waiters at a local hotel that New Guards were secretly staging a coup to take control of the local party at the upcoming Shelby County Republican Convention. On the morning of the convention, he gathered six hundred black Republicans at the Beale Street Elk lodge for a free breakfast, packed them aboard chartered buses, and assem-bled at the meeting four hours before it was scheduled to convene. When white Republicans arrived to a packed building that could seat only three hundred, they demanded a larger room. Their request was denied by meeting chairman George Kleper, a white ally of Lee. Though New Guards complained to state leaders, Congressman B. Carroll Reece, one of the most powerful Southern Republicans, sided with his longtime Black-and-Tan colleague. Lee continued to oversee the Memphis GOP and Western Tennessee patronage throughout the decade. At his suggestion, Raymond Lymon of the Lincoln League became the twentieth century's first black deputy marshal in Tennes-see, and Evelyn Stuart, president of the Lincoln League of Republican Women, was named to the Shelby County Primary Board. At the insistence of Con-gressman Reece, Memphis's newest post office was named after Lee in 1956, making it the nation's first postal station to bear the name of an African American. Under Lee's direction in 1960, at the height of the sit-in

Figure 6. Black-and-Tan leaders in Memphis gather in 1960 to work on behalf of
Richard Nixon's presidential campaign. At far right are longtime allies George W. Lee
and Millsaps Fitzhugh. Photograph courtesy of Memphis and Shelby County Room,
Memphis Public Library and Information Center.

movement, the Shelby County Republican Executive Committee unani-
mously approved a strong statement endorsing the objectives and tactics of
civil rights demonstrators.[30]

Unlike those in Georgia and Tennessee, North and South Carolina's Republican organizations had been Lily-White for decades, but by the 1950s
were willing to accept limited black participation. In 1954, North Carolina's
party slated "a militant Negro Republican" from Durham, Alexander Barnes,
to run for the state senate. However, at a GOP fundraising dinner, Barnes was
told to eat at a segregated table. Refusing to be a "special Republican," he
dropped out of the race in protest. Republicans in South Carolina had a better
track record with African Americans. A study of the state's black newspapers
in the 1950s found zero Democratic papers, nine independent papers, and

thirty Republican papers. African Americans led numerous county-level organizations, and white leaders expressed a desire to reach out toward black voters. In 1958, Republican state chairman David Dows affirmed that African Americans had "a right to vote" and were "going to vote, more and more as time goes on, so it behooves the Republican Party to realize this and make every effort that they can to see that their civil rights under the law are amply protected." Elliot Turnage, a party organizer from Darlington, asked Val Washington to secure more patronage for African Americans so the state might "increase the Negro vote for the Republican ticket." However, though they saw potential in black voters, party chiefs proved unwilling to share state-level leadership with African Americans, and Earl M. Middleton, a black businessman from Orangeburg, claimed the party made sure blacks made up no more than 10 percent of the state's organization. By 1960, South Carolina's two most respected black Republicans, Middleton and I. De-Quincey Newman, had switched affiliation to the Democratic Party.[31]

In Alabama, only shades of difference separated white Republicans from their Democratic counterparts on issues of Jim Crow. In 1952, attorney Oscar W. Adams, Jr., and other black Republicans interested in creating a "liberal organization in Alabama" formed the Abraham Lincoln Club in Birmingham. During its first two years, the club contributed financially to the state and national Republican parties, and was assured by Val Washington of the full support of the RNC. Prior to the 1954 state GOP convention in Birmingham, the club sought to ensure their voice was included in party affairs. The state chairman of the Republican Party, Claude O. Vardaman, told Adams, "it probably would be better if we did not attempt to attend the state meeting," because "our presence at the meeting would hurt the Republican Party." Though unwelcome, members of the club attended the convention, where they were herded to the balcony and denied official recognition. Adams submitted a complaint to the national committee, prompting Chairman Leonard Hall to intervene personally. He told Vardaman, "the Republican Party must be a party of all the people if it is to be the dominant party. I cannot see how you can build a strong Republican Party in Alabama and ignore some 516,000 potential voters." The state party continued to resist black membership (Vardaman replied to Hall that "not one single negro showed any interest in participating in our precinct meetings"), but the RNC made direct appeals to the club. Its members were invited to the 1956 national convention and the presidential inauguration ceremonies. Adams was appointed to the party's Speakers' Bureau, and the national committee secured a charter for the black-owned

Citizens Federal Savings and Loan Association at the organization's request.[32]

Upon launching Operation Dixie in 1957, Meade Alcorn sought to "obliterate any semblance of division, segregation, between white Republicans and Negro Republicans" in Alabama. Wanting to ensure "that there would be no effort to exclude anybody," he requested that party leaders include blacks in their meetings, and spoke before an integrated Republican gathering in Birmingham in 1957. Whites, however, continued to dominate the state party through the late 1950s. According to a black citizen of Tuskegee, though he was inclined to vote for the Republican Party, "There is no choice for the Negro locally. Those who 'Like Ike' do not like their neighbors." The white chairman of Tuscaloosa's Republican Executive Committee, for example, urged Eisenhower in 1956 that the party could "carry the majority of the southern states if he will stay mum" on civil rights. Even more outspoken, the Dixiecrat-turned-Republican Thomas Abernethy conducted competitive campaigns for governor in 1954 and 1958, where he asked voters "whether the NAACP or the people are to run Alabama."[33]

White leaders in Mississippi's GOP closely resembled those in Alabama. The state's most prominent Eisenhower supporter, E. O. Spencer, also owned the Walthall Hotel, headquarters of Jackson's White Citizens' Council. Young attorney Wirt Yerger sought to replace Black-and-Tan leaders with white Republicans closely aligned with his conservative views, and mocked the state's highest ranking black party official, S. D. Redmond, as the "supposed chairman of the flimsy pseudo-GOP state executive committee." Though he refused to use the outdated label "Lily-White," there would be no cooperation between Yerger's faction and black Republicans. During the early 1950s, the state passed a law designed to promote Democratic unity by permitting only one organization to use a party name. Yerger took advantage of the legislation by claiming exclusive rights to the name "Mississippi Republican Party." In March 1956, the newly founded Mississippi Republican Party met in the Hinds County courthouse to choose delegates for the national convention in San Francisco. With Spencer's endorsement, Yerger became party chairman, and a slate of all white delegates were elected. Perry Howard, the state's seventy-nine-year-old black national committeeman, launched an aggressive campaign to unseat Yerger's delegation. Because of Howard's long-established ties to the national committee, the Black-and-Tan delegation was given eight of the state's fifteen delegate slots, in a compromise rejected by Yerger as a "dirty deal." Despite Howard's victory, and white disillusionment with

Eisenhower following Little Rock, Yerger's aggressive organization eventually became the state's official Republican Party, as it controlled patronage in Eisenhower's second term and was fully recognized at the 1960 national convention.[34]

As demonstrated by Perry Howard, George W. Lee, and the Abraham Lincoln Club, southern black Republicans vehemently opposed what they saw as a resurgence of Lily-White Republicanism in the 1950s. Though there were whites like B. Carroll Reece who supported civil rights legislation and accepted blacks in leadership positions, there were many more like Wirt Yerger who were ambivalent or openly hostile to the political aspirations of African Americans. A report by Helen Edmonds based on her experiences in North Carolina condemned the " 'Lily White' tendencies" that still plagued the state's party, and George W. Lee castigated white GOP leaders of the Deep South, proclaiming, "You shall not crucify the Republican Party on a cross of race hate. You shall not press down upon its brow a crown of intolerance." Though Edmonds and Lee were more than willing to work with whites who were willing to work with them, it was clear that their vision of the Republican Party was counter to the vision of conservatives like Yerger. On issues of civil rights and black inclusion in party leadership, there was little room for compromise by either side.[35]

The split between African Americans and conservative whites in the South reflected a larger national division between the party's Eastern Establishment and the bourgeoning conservative movement, derided by Eisenhower aide Gabriel Hauge as the "Neanderthal Wing." Though Eisenhower's pragmatic "Modern Republicanism" obscured party divisions, the GOP was fiercely split between a moderate-liberal coalition that sought black votes on the basis of civil rights, and a conservative faction whose vision of states' rights protected Jim Crow. To many conservatives, even Eisenhower, whom black Republicans criticized as too passive, was too liberal. Barry Goldwater denounced Eisenhower's policies as a "dime store New Deal," and Wirt Yerger criticized his "federal civil rights bill" and "big-budget brand of taxing and spending adored by Northern pinstripe Republicans." Goldwater, who had become the leader of the GOP's conservative wing by the end of the decade, drew loud cheers in 1959 before Yerger's Mississippi Republican Party when he vowed "to let the states handle segregation" and called fellow Republican Earl Warren a "socialist" who was unqualified to head the Supreme Court.[36]

On the other end of the spectrum, the party housed some of the nation's most aggressively pro-civil rights politicians. In fact, one study of congressional voting patterns and "racial liberalism" determined that Republicans were "substantially more liberal than Democrats" throughout the 1950s. Jacob Javits and Kenneth Keating (New York), Clifford Case (New Jersey), Margaret Chase Smith (Maine), Hugh Scott (Pennsylvania), and others formed a solid bloc of liberal northeastern Republican senators who continually pressed for aggressive civil rights legislation throughout the late 1950s and 1960s. Border state Republican senators John Sherman Cooper and Thruston Morton (Kentucky), John Glenn Beall and John Butler (Maryland), and W. Chapman Revercomb (West Virginia) had similarly solid voting records on civil rights. In 1959, Javits declared that "the great piece of unfinished business now before Congress is civil rights legislation." Throughout the rest of the year, he joined Keating, Scott, Case, Cooper, and other Republicans in sponsoring legislation that would revitalize the aggressive provisions struck from Title III of the Civil Rights Act of 1957. Their efforts were blocked by Senate Democrats.[37]

The eventual namesake of the party's liberal wing, Nelson A. Rockefeller, emerged on the political scene in his 1958 campaign for New York governor. A strong supporter of civil rights, he took pride in the involvement of his great-grandparents in the Underground Railroad and his grandfather's support of black universities. Fliers touting him as "A Man Who Believes in and Practices Equality" could be found throughout New York City, and campaign letters sent to thousands of black households claimed, "As governor of New York, NELSON A. ROCKEFELLER will continue his fight for Civil Rights and job opportunity for all. Join this 'CRUSADE FOR FREEDOM!'" His campaign won the endorsement of chairman of the National Urban League Lester Granger, renowned journalist (and former publicity director for the Democratic National Committee) Louis E. Martin, and other prominent African Americans. On election day, Rockefeller not only won, but secured a third of New York's African American vote, triple the percentage the Republican Party had received in its failed 1954 gubernatorial bid.[38]

Except for Rockefeller's victory, the 1958 midterm elections were a disaster for the GOP, with the Democratic Party winning its largest margin in Congress since the New Deal. Outside the South, and with the notable exception of Barry Goldwater in Arizona, conservative Republicans fared the worst, as incumbent conservative senators from Ohio, Michigan, Wyoming, and Utah went down in defeat. On the other hand, many of the party's most liberal politicians cruised to easy victories. In addition to Rockefeller's success, Kenneth Keating won the vacated Senate seat of Irving Ives in New York, and Hugh Scott defeated Pennsylvania governor George Leader by 100,000 votes in his race for the Senate. Though the conservative movement was on the rise, the Eastern Establishment remained in firm control of the party.[39]

Along with disillusionment with Eisenhower's gradual approach to civil rights, an economic recession added to a growing weariness of his party, and the GOP lost ground among African Americans, still maintaining more black voters than they had in 1954, but not to the same extent as in 1956. From 1957 to 1958, nonwhite income dropped from 54 to 51 percent of white income, and African Americans made up 25 percent of the country's long-term unemployed. As a public opinion report conducted in 1958 observed: "Detroit's unemployment lines have more political significance to Negro voters today than Little Rock's picket lines." And while Eisenhower spent some federal dollars on public works projects as a means to alleviate unemployment, he was willing to accept higher unemployment if it meant a balanced budget and limited inflation, two of his economic priorities. This response to the recession only reinforced the perception among the black working class that the Republican Party was uninterested in the plight of the poor, and black voters helped secure Democratic victories in states like Ohio and Michigan hit hardest by the recession.[40]

As the 1950s concluded, it was evident that despite President Eisenhower's personal appeal, he had failed to solidify the Republican Party in the same way Franklin Roosevelt had united Democrats behind the New Deal. Where Roosevelt provided African Americans with symbolic gestures and tangible economic benefits, Eisenhower offered them only a moderate alternative to the Democratic Party. In many ways, Eisenhower "left the Republican party— politically and intellectually—where he first found it," as his former speechwriter Emmet John Hughes later wrote. Eisenhower's vague "Modern Republicanism" lacked an ideological core of policies and principles that the party could rally behind. By the end of 1959, Republicans had lost 24 percent of the House offices they had held before Eisenhower's first year as president in 1953, and the number of Republican senators during that same period decreased from twenty-five to fourteen.[41]

It was clear to many black Republicans that though the party accepted their votes, they were not considered an essential component of the party's coalition. Conservative whites throughout the South frequently challenged Black-and-Tans, and the national committee's Operation Dixie made only

token efforts toward black outreach. Helen Edmonds wrote that from her discussions with black Republicans, "one gathers the feeling that they are temporary instruments only for the election." E. Frederic Morrow noted in a 1958
diary entry that in his experience with many local Republican organizations,
the white leadership were "aloof" and "still look upon Negroes as 'boys' and
talk down to them rather than giving them any chance of equality" in party
ranks. Conversely, though the Democratic Party housed the country's most
devoted segregationists, many of whom were given important congressional
committee chairmanships, the party's northern wing far surpassed the GOP
"in making it possible for Negroes to participate in party councils as well as
appointing them to jobs of influence and position in the states and cities in
the North." It was "difficult when one goes into certain states where Republicans have been in power for many years, to discover that the Eisenhower
philosophy does not prevail and that Negroes are not represented in any important degree in the political life and councils of the Republican Party."[42]

On April 14, 1959, Morrow publicly expressed these critiques. Speaking
before the all-white Republican Women's Convention in Washington, D.C.,
he launched a scathing tirade against the lack of inclusion of African Americans in Republican leadership posts, despite sustained support for the GOP
among black southerners and the middle class. Attacking the "basic failure
of the party to recognize Negro-Americans as first-class citizens" at all levels
of party infrastructure, Morrow noted, "Eisenhower's philosophy of
Democracy . . . has not penetrated the local precinct, the county and state
governments and local party machinery." The only way the GOP could ever
"overcome the Democratic party's ballyhoo that it is the poor man's party"
would be for Republicans to openly support black equality and to promote
African Americans to top-level party posts. Following the speech, which was
quickly disseminated nationally by the Associated Press, "all hell broke loose,"
and many white Republicans branded him "a traitor, an ingrate, and many
other uncomplimentary names." One member of the national committee demanded his resignation. On the other hand, Morrow claimed, "the response
from the Black community was tremendous!" Black Republicans joined independents and Democrats in flooding his office with telegrams, letters, and
phone calls of support for saying what had long been on their minds.[43]

Regardless of his criticisms, Morrow never questioned his allegiance to
the Republican Party. Rather, he believed that in the speech "I had carried out
my duty to my party and the Administration." Jackie Robinson summed up
the feelings of many black Republicans toward Morrow's candid remarks,

writing him, "Congratulations on your speech. I sincerely believe you have done the Republican Party a great service." Despite their criticisms of the GOP, many black Republicans in the late 1950s remained loyal to the party they believed could surpass the Democrats in advancing the cause of racial equality. Liberal Republican politicians like Jacob Javits, Hugh Scott, and Nelson Rockefeller helped sustain their hope in the potential of the GOP. As the country entered into the 1960s at the conclusion of Eisenhower's presidency, black Republicans, from Black-and-Tans like George W. Lee in the South, to Val Washington in the nation's capital, to Julius Adams in Harlem, would continue their effort to steer the Republican Party toward racial equality.[44]

CHAPTER 4

Ye Cannot Serve Both God and Mammon: The 1960 Presidential Election

In a 1958 letter to journalist Earl Mazo, Martin Luther King, Jr., confessed that he had been "strongly opposed to Vice-President Nixon before meeting him personally." Now, one year after their first meeting, King's opinion had "changed," and he believed the vice president had "matured" and "grown a great deal" since the 1940s. King even ventured to say, "It is altogether possible that he has no basic racial prejudice." He then criticized Dwight Eisenhower for not speaking out on the "pressing moral issue" of civil rights, adding, "Nixon, I believe, would have done that." King's candid remarks reflected an optimistic view of the vice president held by many middle-class African Americans in the late 1950s. As the nation entered into the 1960 election season, Nixon had carefully crafted a formidable record in the field of civil rights. However, like many in his party, he not only hoped to maintain 1956's level of black support, but also sought to further the GOP's gains in the South. This ultimately proved to be an impossible balancing act. As L. K. Jackson, a black Republican minister from Indiana, articulated to the party in 1960, "ye cannot serve both God and mammon"—African Americans and conservative southerners—"you will have to . . . hold fast to the one and turn loose the other."[1]

King first met Nixon at Ghana's March 1957 independence ceremonies, where the vice president promised an extended meeting after returning home. On June 13, he invited King and his associate in the Southern Christian Leadership Conference, Ralph Abernathy, to the Formal Room of the U.S. Capitol. A positive relationship with the civil rights icon represented enormous potential for Nixon. King always stressed his nonpartisanship, and publicly argued, like many black Republicans and independents, that African

Americans needed a strong presence in both parties. Moreover, he was born and raised in the black Republican stronghold of Atlanta, where the GOP counted his father among its supporters. During the closed-door meeting, which lasted over two hours, King and Abernathy expressed their discontent with Eisenhower's failure to endorse *Brown* and take a stronger public stand on civil rights. They also told the vice president that, despite these shortcomings, they had voted for the Republican ticket in 1956, and suggested that even more African Americans could support the GOP under Nixon's leadership. At a press conference afterward, King remarked that while he remained unsure of Eisenhower's personal feelings on civil rights, Nixon "assured us that he is strongly in favor of the inevitable move toward integration."[2]

The meeting encouraged Nixon to continue prioritizing his work on employment discrimination as chairman of the President's Committee on Government Contracts. Earlier that year, he had announced a shift in PCGC strategy toward "specific results rather than general education." Shortly thereafter, he asked the head of every federal agency that issued contracts to take a "firmer approach" in rejecting bids from businesses with a history of discrimination. He also convinced the administration to increase the PCGC staff, and to establish four regional offices. In 1959, he invited King and A. Philip Randolph to speak at a PCGC-sponsored conference attended by four hundred black ministers. In his keynote address, Nixon called on the activists in attendance to "mobilize the country in the struggle to achieve the unrestricted access to employment." However, because the PCGC could only encourage voluntary compliance, it remained unable to implement its objectives. Neither the president nor Congress proved willing to fight for Nixon's requests for statutory authority and enforcement power. "This is no way to run a committee," he once fumed. His discontent was broadcast to the nation during televised debates with John F. Kennedy in 1960, after the Massachusetts senator criticized the PCGC's failures. Nixon shot back that he had been "handicapped" and denied "adequate powers."[3]

By 1960, it was also obvious that the Civil Rights Act of 1957 inadequately protected voting rights, as 70 percent of black southerners remained disenfranchised. The Eisenhower administration responded by introducing new legislation during his final year in office. Surviving a nine-day filibuster by southern Democrats, the Civil Rights Act of 1960 was passed in the spring by a bipartisan coalition under the guidance of Senate Majority Leader Lyndon Johnson. Among other moderate measures, it allowed for potential black voters to request federal "referees" to oversee registration in areas with patterns

of discrimination, though their contested ballots would not be counted unless they survived a complex maze of court proceedings. The limited legislation came at the inception of a more militant, student-driven phase of the
civil rights movement, which was no longer satisfied with piecemeal reform.
Sparked by a February sit-in by four black college students at a segregated
lunch counter in Greensboro, North Carolina, the year saw the formation of
a new organization, the Student Nonviolent Coordinating Committee
(SNCC), which ushered in an even more militant phase of direct action protests. By January 1961, 50,000 activists had participated, and over 3,500 had
been arrested, in protests across the South.[4]

Entering the election year, many black Republicans and civil rights leaders were confident of the vice president's potential to maintain, or even increase, Eisenhower's showing among African Americans. The *Industrial
Statesman*, a black newsletter published under the direction of Philadelphia
Republican Joseph V. Baker, argued that even the NAACP "would have to
admit, if it were faced with the tabled records, that nothing the Democrats are
likely to muster, in way of a standard bearer, can touch the Nixon testimony
in the area of the Association's major objectives." The RNC's Val Washington
reported after a 1959 meeting between NAACP officials and prominent Republicans, including Roy Wilkins, Clarence Mitchell, Kenneth Keating, and
Thruston Morton, that the black leaders in attendance believed the "GOP was
more willing to take positive action in civil rights field than Democrats," and
expressed "strong support" for Nixon's record. Even more encouraging to Republicans was the relationship that had developed between Nixon and Martin
Luther King, Jr. White Democrat and activist Virginia Durr wrote after a December 1959 dinner party attended by King that she was "horrified" by his
observation that "Negroes more and more are turning to Dick Nixon," and
that he was "strongly tempted" to do the same. King told Durr, "Nixon calls
him over long distance for advice, he invites him to his home, he is making
every effort possible to get him on his side." Though "he has some doubts
about Nixon, still he is the ONLY candidate that does these things."[5]

As implied in King's comments, the Democratic frontrunner, John F.
Kennedy, entered the primaries facing skepticism from African Americans.
Tellingly, in November 1959, when Kennedy attempted to meet with King for
the first time, King simply ignored the request. Two years prior, Senator Kennedy had voted to send the Civil Rights Act of 1957 to James Eastland's Judiciary Committee and supported its jury trial amendment. Moreover, during
a 1957 speech at the University of South Carolina, Kennedy extolled the

legacy of John C. Calhoun, the nineteenth century's zealous proponent of slavery and white supremacy. That same year, after speaking at the University of Georgia's commencement ceremony, he appeared on a local television show alongside arch-segregationists Richard Russell and Herman Talmadge. As the cameras rolled, Kennedy called Russell "a Senator's Senator" and praised Talmadge's "remarkable record." He further drew the ire of African Americans for inviting the segregationist governor of Alabama, John Patterson, and the head of the state's White Citizens' Council, Sam Englehardt, to a private breakfast at his home. By 1959, Patterson had officially backed Kennedy's presidential run.[6]

Many liberals questioned Kennedy's ability to restore the black vote to pre-1956 levels. The NAACP's Roy Wilkins warned that African Americans "feel uneasy over this apparent entente cordiale between Kennedy of Massachusetts and . . . Talmadge, Eastland, et al., of Dixie." As late as August 1960, Eleanor Roosevelt claimed, "Kennedy can't win the Negro vote." Black journalist Carl Rowan reported "observations by politically astute Negroes that 'Kennedy will get a smaller percentage of the Negro vote than any Democrat since 1932.'" Black Republicans were especially eager to highlight Kennedy's mixed record. The *Industrial Statesman* declared that when the 1957 civil rights bill "was almost literally gasping for breath on its rocky journey through the congress," Kennedy "did not raise either a voice or any strong hand to help that legislation pass." The RNC's Minorities Division issued press releases emphasizing that not only had Kennedy missed over thirty important roll call votes on civil rights, but "he voted to send the GOP civil rights bill to a gas chamber death in the Eastland Judiciary Committee."[7]

Campaign manager Robert Kennedy recognized that his brother's engagement with segregationists could cost him black votes, and enlisted the help of Harris Wofford, a white activist and law professor at Notre Dame. On Wofford's advice, Kennedy took a strong civil rights position at the Democratic National Convention, and his supporters pushed through an aggressive platform that far outpaced the moderate 1956 provisions. The civil rights plank promised to to pass and execute measures ensuring equality in the voting booth, in education, and in employment, and to appoint an attorney general who would "vigorously" enforce civil rights laws. Adam Clayton Powell, who had been one of Kennedy's loudest Democratic critics, proclaimed, "This is the best platform either party has written in the history of politics."[8]

On the other hand, since Kennedy did not want to alienate the southerners he had spent years courting, he named Lyndon Johnson as his running mate. As a Texas New Dealer, Johnson was moderate by southern standards, but still had voted against every major civil rights measure until the watered-down bills of 1957 and 1960. Black delegates to the Democratic convention told reporters, "Senator Johnson is perhaps a symbol against sit-ins," and warned, "The problem of the negro vote may become more difficult." Soon after the convention, Johnson fueled black fears by publicly referencing the party's civil rights plank at a southern rally, promising to "oppose that part of the platform when it gets up in congress."[9]

On the Republican side, Nelson Rockefeller threatened Nixon's presumed presidential coronation. Although never publicly announcing his intention to run against the vice president, the New York governor privately courted delegates and had become one of the administration's most outspoken intraparty critics, dissatisfied with its cautious approach to civil rights and other issues. Anonymous Republican strategists expressed fears to reporters that New York's forty-five electoral votes might even be jeopardized if Nixon did not receive Rockefeller's unequivocal endorsement. Seeking a seamless nomination at the national convention, Nixon flew to New York City on July 22 and offered Rockefeller the vice presidential nomination. Rockefeller turned it down, and, instead, the two hammered out a series of compromises in what the press called the "Treaty of Fifth Avenue" (or, the "Munich of the Republican Party," according to Barry Goldwater, who loathed liberal "Rockefeller Republicans"). On civil rights, Rockefeller and Nixon agreed to "assure aggressive action to remove the remaining vestiges of segregation or discrimination in all areas of national life—voting and housing, schools and jobs," and pledged support for "the objectives of the sit-in demonstrators."[10]

Nixon's next step was to ensure that the Platform Committee at the Republican National Convention in Chicago adopted the same positions as those in the "treaty." The initial platform draft, however, had been written to appease Goldwater's conservative wing and featured a halfhearted civil rights plank. A Nixon aide commented that the vice president's staff "collected every political IOU we held in the country," and journalist Theodore White wrote that Nixon "one by one . . . summoned key members" of the committee and "insisted that the civil rights plank be rewritten to please Rockefeller and match the Democrats." The final civil rights plank was the strongest in party history. It connected the GOP directly to *Brown*, noting that it was Republicans who "supported the position of the Negro school children before the Supreme Court," and pledged the party's "vigorous support" of school desegregation. It further promised to pass legislation that would eliminate literacy tests, strengthen the President's

Committee on Government Contracts, and prohibit discrimination in housing built with federal assistance. Nixon not only supported the plank, but bragged to the NAACP's Clarence Mitchell that it "was drafted under my supervision and approved by me before it was sent to the Resolutions Committee." In his floor speech, Goldwater attempted to salvage the conservatives' platform defeat, as well as a failed, last-ditch "Draft Goldwater" movement, by telling followers that if they "want to take this party back . . . let's get to work." Though his remarks would prove to be a prophetic rallying call for the conservative movement, in 1960 it was still the Eastern Establishment, personified by Rockefeller, that appeared in control of the national convention.[11]

In his acceptance speech, Nixon evoked Abraham Lincoln's name six times, promising, "For those millions of Americans who are still denied equality of rights and opportunity, I say there shall be the greatest progress in human rights since the days of Lincoln one hundred years ago." He reiterated the same point toward the end of the speech, pledging to end "the prejudice which one hundred years after Lincoln, to our shame, still embarrasses us abroad and saps our strength at home." The White House's E. Frederic Morrow, who had spent years failing to convince Eisenhower to make similar remarks, wrote in his diary that the speech was "a masterpiece" and the "high point of the campaign and perhaps of his career," and praised Nixon's "conviction, sincerity, determination, fight, and boldness."[12]

The convention itself was a positive experience for black Republicans. Morrow flew to Chicago aboard Air Force One and delivered an impassioned prime-time floor speech. Nixon also invited him to a "secret mid-night caucus of the party greats to pick the vice-presidential candidate," and told the room that Morrow "was invited on the same basis as any of them." One of the first asked to speak, Morrow endorsed Henry Cabot Lodge, Jr., arguing that "not even the NAACP can be against his superb liberal record." A former Massachusetts senator and ambassador to the United Nations, Lodge was a prominent member of the Eastern Establishment and a vocal proponent of civil rights. His ultimate selection as Nixon's running mate stood in direct contrast to Kennedy's choice of Lyndon Johnson. The convention highlight was a cocktail party hosted by T. R. M. Howard, S. B. Fuller, and Golden B. Darby, three of Chicago's most respected black Republicans. According to *Jet* magazine, it was "the first major political convention party given by Negroes," and the trio provided their nearly seven hundred guests with 5,000 hors d'oeuvres, 2,500 glasses of pink champagne, sixty-two pounds of beef, and "untold" amounts of Maine lobster and cocktail shrimp.[13]

Beyond the glitz of cocktail parties, however, the convention revealed troubling trends for black Republicans as they entered a new decade. Despite receiving record support from black voters in 1956, the party failed to capitalize on its success among middle-class and southern African Americans. Even the Republican National Committee, where moderates held key leadership posts, seemed to believe that Eisenhower's gain among African Americans was a satisfactory ceiling, and a major push for even more black voters might alienate their growing number of white supporters in the South. The committee did not backpedal on civil rights, but rather stayed in place, hoping that supporting Eisenhower's mild civil rights bills and backing court orders to desegregate was enough to placate black voters who had supported the GOP in the past election. Cutbacks to the Minorities Division after 1956, and the creation of a well-funded Operation Dixie in 1957, reflected this approach.

Moreover, African Americans held fourteen fewer delegate positions than they had in 1956, and, from 1960 onward, black delegates to Republican conventions would never again outnumber their Democratic counterparts. As Operation Dixie focused its attention on white voters, occasionally even endorsing Jim Crow, it generally ignored Black-and-Tan organizations that had long been a staple of Republican politics in the region. Though black Republicans had been active in cities across the 1950s South, the rise of conservative white factions inside the party was too promising for many in the GOP to ignore. By 1964, these groups would assume control of every southern Republican organization, where they pushed out persistent Black-and-Tan factions. This process began in the summer of 1960, when Wirt Yerger's conservative Mississippi Republican Party delivered the final blow to Perry Howard's Black-and-Tan group, which was not offered a single delegate slot at the convention. Howard's defeat could be chalked up to his failing health, and to Yerger's aggressive hostility toward rival factions, but it also reflected a larger trend in the region. African Americans across the South had been largely excluded from national support since the inception of Operation Dixie in 1957, and the Minorities Division of the national committee had become a one-man operation led by an increasingly isolated Val Washington.[14]

The growing marginalization of African Americans inside GOP ranks was masked early in the campaign by the favorable response from black leaders toward Nixon's record. The vice president became even more confident after securing one of the most coveted endorsements of the campaign, that of baseball star Jackie Robinson. Since his retirement in 1957, Robinson had served as a member of the NAACP's National Board of Directors and a columnist for the *New York Post*. His initial endorsement went to Democrat Hubert Humphrey, whom he campaigned for in the primaries, but his harshest criticisms were directed toward Kennedy. He was particularly concerned about the senator's relationship with Alabama's governor John Patterson, telling Democratic advisor Chester Bowles, "It's difficult for me or my friends to see how [Kennedy] can be a friend of the kind of South that Patterson represents." Hoping to change Robinson's opinion, Bowles arranged a private meeting with Kennedy in early July, where Robinson asked the senator to explain his "very bleak record on civil rights." Kennedy, who, Robinson complained, "couldn't or wouldn't look me straight in the eye," confessed, "I don't know much about the problems of colored people since I come from New England." The meeting ultimately backfired, with Robinson leaving "even less an admirer" of Kennedy.[15]

By contrast, Nixon had an established relationship with Robinson. The two first met at the 1952 Republican National Convention, where Robinson was "charmed" and "dazzled" by Nixon's "evident admiration" for his athletic talent, as the vice president retold in specific detail his favorite plays Robinson made while playing college football. Robinson wrote the vice president on several occasions from 1957 to 1960, once describing his "deep sense of appreciation for your constant efforts to provide a greater measure of justice for Negro Americans." Even while endorsing Humphrey, Robinson wrote in one of his columns, if Kennedy or another "weak and indecisive" Democrat won the party's nomination, "I, for one, would enthusiastically support Nixon." In January 1960, he wrote a Democratic friend to defend his praise of the vice president, confessing, "I feel as strongly in favor of Nixon's principles, ethic and intellectual honesty as you are against."[16]

In March, a Republican operative contacted Nixon's secretary to describe a recent lunch he had had with Robinson. He felt "that with the slightest persuasion" Robinson would endorse Nixon, and stressed "how important Jackie was as far as the Negro vote was concerned." Senator Hugh Scott took the lead in pursuing Robinson, telling him in private correspondence, "If the Congress were Republican, not a single Southern Democrat would head any committee in either the House or the Senate." Nixon himself assured Robinson that he understood "no political party or special interest group can take the American Negro vote for granted," and promised he would offer them more than lip service. In July, Robinson met with Nixon and Scott at the White House, where the vice president emphasized "that he was really very different

from his boss, the President." It was clear to Robinson that Nixon "wanted me
to disassociate him from Eisenhower since he knew that blacks, in the main,
didn't like Ike." Though the disparaging remarks against Eisenhower "had the
feel of a cheap trick," Robinson was pleased with the meeting, as Nixon "certainly said all the right things."[17]

While Robinson described himself as politically independent in 1960, he
was, according to biographer Arnold Rampersad, "a Republican at heart." A
strong supporter of civil rights, Robinson also identified with Republican no-
tions of self-sufficiency and the free market, particularly after becoming a
vice president of Chock full o'Nuts Coffee in the late 1950s. Additionally, he
was an outspoken anti-communist, who had previously praised Nixon for his
"telling refutation of anti-American charges made by the Communists," and
chastised actor Paul Robeson before the House Un-American Activities
Committee for his alleged communist sympathies. Most important, Robinson disliked the Democratic Party's affiliation with corrupt urban machines
and southern segregationists, and believed that "blacks should have a say in
both parties" as the best means to obtain civil rights reform—a stance common among black Republicans and their independent allies.[18]

By the end of the national conventions, Robinson had officially endorsed
Nixon, and launched a massive hundred-city tour. His speaking arrange-
ments were coordinated directly with Nixon's camp, whom he sometimes accompanied on the campaign trail. His speeches emphasized that he was
"black first" and "not beholden to any political party." He didn't want "a job"
or "money" from Republicans—"All I want is civil rights." Though "not an Ike
supporter," he believed Nixon was "better qualified" and "more aggressive" on
issues of race than Kennedy, who "goes the way the wind blows." He further
claimed, "Mr. Nixon has given me a pledge he's going to give civil-rights legislation all the support he can."[19]

For his own campaign, Nixon pledged to visit all fifty states, guaranteeing
that he, not coincidentally, would tour more of the South than any candidate
in party history. His first major speech after the convention was in Greensboro, North Carolina, where just months earlier students had inspired the
sit-in movement. During the August 17 visit, Nixon reaffirmed his "strong
convictions on civil rights" to an integrated (but mostly white) crowd. At a
locally televised news conference, he claimed that he was "proud of the record
of our Administration" on issues of racial equality, expressed support for the
objectives of sit-in demonstrators, and highlighted the party's progressive
civil rights plank. The *Washington Post* praised Nixon's "serious and

Figure 7. Jackie Robinson meets with black Republicans at a Memphis campaign rally for Richard Nixon in 1960. Left to right: Robinson, Sandy Ray, Leonard Carr, and George W. Lee (seated). Photograph by Justin Westerfield, *Memphis Commercial Appeal.* Amistad Research Center, Tulane University.

commendable" remarks, which indicated his refusal to give "any intention to trim on civil rights issues."[20]

Weeks later, Nixon actively courted black voters in a September stop in Memphis. After being greeted by sixty thousand people at the airport, his motorcade proceeded toward the heart of the city's black community. In a tour "sponsored" by George W. Lee, the vice president visited W. C. Handy Park, where he placed flowers on a statue honoring the "Father of the Blues" and greeted a crowd of African Americans. He made a deliberate point to shake hands with each child in a line of black kindergarteners, a moment captured by photographers and reprinted the next day on the front page of the *Washington Star* and other newspapers across the country. Upon reaching downtown, Lee, Benjamin Hooks, and four other black Republicans joined Nixon on stage as he delivered his main address, in which he reiterated his

"deep conviction" on civil rights. Lee described the event as "highly successful," and a black aide employed by the RNC remarked, "It was wonderful!"
But it would also be Nixon's last major campaign stop that featured a significant black presence.[21]

Reminiscing on Nixon's open embrace of civil rights in the summer and early
fall, E. Frederic Morrow bemoaned, "One of the unsolved mysteries of the
1960 campaign is what happened to that Nixon." By October, Nixon's campaign seemed to have shifted toward a strong play for southern conservatives.
He did not run away from his record, but the emphasis of his speeches tilted
to distinctly conservative themes, particularly states' rights. The month following the national convention, while encouraging to African Americans,
was a disaster for Nixon. In Greensboro, he injured his knee, which became
infected and sidelined him in the hospital for two weeks. Even more painful
than his staph infection were impromptu remarks by Eisenhower at a press
conference. When asked for a time when he adopted an idea of Nixon's during
his eight years in office, the president responded, "If you give me a week, I
might think of one." The remarks pushed Nixon, who had a notoriously paranoid personality, to forge his own course in the campaign. Not only would
Eisenhower be underutilized on the campaign trail, but Nixon trusted only
his inner circle of personal advisors. He even eschewed help from the RNC,
which had been a central coordinator of black outreach in past presidential
campaigns. Whereas the Minorities Division played a central role in Eisenhower's 1956 successes among black voters, particularly in working closely
with black newspapers and producing campaign literature, Nixon's campaign
declined its assistance.[22]

Concluding Nixon's disastrous first month of campaigning was his infamously poor showing in the first televised debate with Kennedy on September
26. In the days after the debate, at the same time that his campaign needed
revitalization, Nixon's promise to visit all fifty states brought him to Tennessee
and Arkansas, where, as he wrote in his memoirs, "significantly, the crowds
were bigger than ever." Even during his tumultuous September, the South had
been a bright spot of the campaign. Nixon told an aide after the Greensboro
appearance, "That is the kind of crowd you get in the last months of a campaign. . . . There is something happening down there. We are going to have to
look at those southern states again." As the campaign sought to put September
behind them, the South, which had already been on Nixon's radar, looked particularly promising.[23]

Greensboro and Memphis notwithstanding, Nixon's selection of I. Lee Pot-ter as director of his southern campaign indicated a tin ear when it came to southern black voters. As head of Operation Dixie, Potter was among the few RNC staffers close to the campaign. He had also supported state segregation laws and disregarded counsel from the national committee to work with south-ern African Americans, despite their noteworthy support of the GOP in 1956. As the campaign progressed, Nixon followed Potter's example in emphasizing states' rights in southern speeches. Though Republicans had traditionally sup-ported limited federal power, Nixon was well aware that "states' rights," specif-ically, had been a mainstay of rhetoric against desegregation, especially since *Brown v. Board of Education* and Little Rock. For example, the South's most prominent segregationist organization, the Citizens' Council, officially pledged itself to "the preservation of our States' Rights" in its motto. Likewise, the noto-rious Southern Manifesto never explicitly used racist language, but instead de-fended Jim Crow by focusing on the "rights of the states."[24]

By October and November, Nixon's campaign speeches in the South fol-lowed a predictable formula. While still occasionally alluding to his record on issues of race, he often included it in gratuitous lines that generalized civil rights as a "complex issue" that "will not be solved by demagoguery." After these obligatory references, he proceeded to more impassioned discussions of states' rights, often declaring that Republicans "stand for strengthening the states and our opponents stand for weakening them." In trips to Virginia and North Carolina, he highlighted his belief in not only states' rights, but local control of education, a phrase directly associated in southern politics with federally imposed school desegregation. In Nashville, he declared that "An-drew Jackson would turn over in his grave" at the sight of Kennedy's platform. Quoting the slave-owning, Democratic president, Nixon concurred with Jackson's declaration that "My countrymen will never find me arresting mea-sures which encroach on the rights of the states." The *Louisville Courier-Journal* remarked that, compared to earlier speeches, these comments were "of such remarkably different cast. . . . He is clearly trying to make Southern segregationists believe that he and the Republicans offer them a haven" by "playing footsie with the segregationists."[25]

As part of his fifty-state tour, Nixon also became the first presidential can-didate to campaign in Mississippi since Jackson in 1828. While there, he reit-erated that Democrats had "abandoned" the South, and declared, "what we Republicans stand for is closer to what you stand for." He told President Ei-senhower by telephone that "he was tremendously pleased with the crowds" in Mississippi and Louisiana, and "in the south the thing that appeals most is a statement to the effect that we are not going to weaken states' rights but we are going to strengthen them." In Georgia, he proclaimed, "the best guarantee of freedom is local government." The idea that "freedom" was best guaranteed at the local level went against all that black southerners knew about government, where Jim Crow was preserved and protected most fervently by local officials, from registrars who refused to recognize black voters to sheriffs and juries who turned a blind eye to racial violence. In one of his final campaign appearances, Nixon told a crowd in Columbia, South Carolina, after being introduced by the state's segregationist governor, that the Democratic Party had abandoned southern heroes like Andrew Jackson for northerners who disregarded the "fundamental principle" of "local and State responsibility." As a trained lawyer, Nixon surely knew that strengthening states' rights in the South was directly at odds with the civil rights measures he claimed to support. These measures would have dramatically expanded the federal government's authority over the single state-level issue closest to the hearts of many white southerners: segregated schools and public facilities.[26]

As the vice president wooed white southerners, Kennedy worked on resuscitating his image among African Americans. On sit-ins he declared, "It is in the American tradition to stand up for one's rights—even if the new way to stand up for one's rights is to sit down." He attacked Eisenhower for not issuing an executive order against discrimination in federally funded housing, and promised, if elected, he would do so with "a stroke of the Presidential pen." He also reminded voters that Eisenhower "never indicated what he thought of" *Brown*, and criticized the president's failure to set "a moral atmosphere for the implementation of the Supreme Court decision." He even blamed the president for the "inadequate" nature of the Civil Rights Act of 1957, omitting his own role in watering down the legislation.[27]

Lyndon Johnson provided Kennedy cover to move to the left on civil rights. While Kennedy only made select appearances in a few competitive southern states, Johnson focused exclusively on the region. He reminded audiences that he was "the grandson of a Confederate soldier," mocked Nixon's honorary membership in the NAACP, and emphasized Kennedy's history of racial moderation. An October press release issued by Johnson's campaign declared, "The present Republican administration has certainly racked up a record which is dangerously close to the evils of Reconstruction times," criticizing "the bayonets and paratroopers in Little Rock." It then claimed that Nixon believed "white southerners accused of violating civil rights statutes should be deprived of the ancient Anglo-Saxon right of the jury trial." Johnson also personally convinced reluctant segregationists to endorse Kennedy, including Orval Faubus, Richard Russell, and Herman Talmadge.[28]

Unlike Kennedy and Johnson, who carefully delineated campaign strategies, there was no such coordination between Nixon and his running mate Henry Cabot Lodge. In an October 12 speech in Harlem, Lodge stated, "There should be a Negro in the Cabinet. . . . It is offered as a pledge—and as a pledge that will be redeemed . . . if you elect Richard Nixon President." Unlike many of Johnson's controversial statements, Lodge's promise was widely reported in news outlets across the country, hindering Nixon's efforts to recast himself as an ally of the white South. Nixon headquarters immediately retracted the pledge, claiming that race would not play a factor in political appointments. The following day, hundreds of African Americans greeted Lodge in Winston-Salem, North Carolina, where he amended his comments by reminding them that, as vice president, he could not pledge anything. While Kennedy also attacked Lodge's pledge, calling it "racism in reverse at its worst," press coverage centered on Nixon, and the event bolstered a growing perception that he had become increasingly timid on issues of race.[29]

By the time Lodge made his pledge, the poor planning of Nixon's black outreach was evident. Black Republican insiders saw this early on in the campaign. In August, Val Washington complained to Nixon's staff that "no work is being done among Negroes," and asked for a plan of action. The aide who spoke to Washington dismissed the warning, noting to his superiors, "It's my impression that Val is perpetually inclined to the belief that nothing is being done among his people, but I pass it along for what it's worth." Nixon's campaign believed he had already moved to the left to accommodate Nelson Rockefeller prior to the convention, a move that, combined with his solid civil rights record, warranted black support. This was itself enough, they seemed to believe, to maintain moderate levels of black support on election day.[30]

Black Republicans played a far less active role in the 1960 campaign than they had four years earlier. Given a two-month leave from the White House, E. Frederic Morrow headed Nixon's skeletal crew of seven black aides. Many of the same black Republicans who had played prominent roles in Eisenhower's 1956 campaign returned to assist Nixon, but their roles were largely diminished. For instance, Archibald Carey served as a Nixon field coordinator in Chicago, and Helen Edmonds cochaired North Carolina's Women for Nixon-Lodge. Neither, though, was given the funds to conduct another nationwide tour. Although Edmonds expressed a willingness to devote her time exclusively to campaign appearances, her offer was ignored. She lamented that, unlike Eisenhower's campaign, "There was never a well defined, cohesive Negro unit of speakers and workers on a national level" to promote Nixon in 1960. Jackie Robinson consistently drew large crowds and media attention, but "the task to be done . . . was more than one Negro could carry."[31]

Journalists assigned to follow Nixon, such as Simeon Booker, were surprised "to notice the thoroughness of his campaign managers in ignoring Negro communities," and saw an alarming pattern of "keeping Negro VIPs from platforms of rallies." Reflecting after the election, Grant Reynolds blasted Nixon for treating "areas of concentrated Negro voter strength as if they were afflicted with small pox." Jackie Robinson claimed campaign advisors told him that the vice president would not visit Harlem because he "would lose South Carolina and Georgia." Late in the campaign, the Rev. L. K. Jackson of Gary, Indiana, even found a donor willing to pay one-third the cost ($10,000) of an hour-long national television spot that would allow "some of the best Negro leaders in the Republican Party to go on the air and appeal directly to the Negro." The offer was declined. Days later, Nixon's campaign purchased four hours of national television air time that omitted the topic of civil rights altogether.[32]

Jim Bassett, a Nixon aide and onetime RNC public relations director, recalled that the vice president was "in mortal fear of some kind of demonstration," and deliberately avoided black areas of northern cities. Bassett had been in contact with Archibald Carey, who offered a standing invitation for the vice president to use his influential Quinn Chapel AME Church, the city's oldest black church, to reach out to African Americans. Nixon declined the offer. Bassett also coordinated with an unnamed Chicago field agent (perhaps also Carey), who arranged a meeting between Nixon and the city's leading black ministers and businessmen. Two days before the scheduled meeting, Bassett received a telephone call from Nixon advance man H. R. Haldeman, who said, "The boss says he ain't going to do that nigger thing in Chicago." Bassett protested that the field agent "busted his ass to arrange this," and asked Haldeman if he tried "to talk Nixon out of it." Haldeman simply repeated, "The Boss says he ain't going to do that nigger thing."[33]

Nixon and his closest aides routinely ignored the suggestions of their few black advisors and provided them with almost no funding. E. Frederic Morrow would craft memos and strategies for Nixon's staff, but "often those notes were ignored or the replies innocuous. It was maddening." It was apparent to him that Nixon's young campaign managers "never accepted, or needed advice" on black outreach. Their belief was that Nixon had a strong record on civil rights, and that he had Jackie Robinson, one of the most admired black men in the nation, working the campaign trail with them. Much more beyond this in terms of black outreach would be a diversion of precious time and money. In contrast to 1952 and 1956, Morrow was not invited to travel with the nominee's entourage and did not attend any major strategy meetings during the fall campaign. He could not afford to print campaign literature specifically targeting African Americans or even hire a secretary to answer campaign mail. Though black Republicans "called me day and night for help, financial help, and literature," Morrow had to turn them down because he could offer neither.[34]

Val Washington's Minorities Division in the RNC faced a similar situation. He was given a negligible budget and assigned only five workers. John H. Calhoun, a prominent Republican leader in Atlanta, gave Washington drafts of campaign literature he had written for black communities and asked if the Minorities Division could print copies for national distribution. Washington replied that not only did he not have money to do so, but he was also "going to have a time" even communicating with Nixon's staff for approval. Shunning assistance and advice from the national committee and Minorities Division, both of which had played active roles in Eisenhower's campaigns, Nixon instead coordinated strategy with his personal advisors and independent organizations focused on southern outreach, such as Democrats for Nixon. None of his close advisors had meaningful connections to African Americans. In the previous election, Morrow and the Minorities Division were conduits to black leaders, organizations, and publications, and even if Eisenhower did not often reach out to African Americans, he had well-funded black supporters who did. Nixon, on the other hand, held fast to a belief that the African Americans who supported Eisenhower would also be drawn to him strictly on the merit of his past support for civil rights. Continued harping on this record in speeches and advertisements was gratuitous, and might also push away southerners who liked the GOP's economic policies but were still wary of the party of Lincoln. What they failed to realize, or chose to disregard, was that even by those African Americans who praised Nixon's past stances, his avoidance of that record and of black communities was duly noted. It appeared to many, as the NAACP's Gloster Current observed, that despite Nixon's record, "the Negro vote was not wanted or needed."[35]

Val Washington was not alone among those in the RNC who were frustrated with Nixon's approach to African Americans. By October, chairman Thruston Morton of Kentucky feared that the "amateurs" running Nixon's campaign would "result in murder for us," and tasked A. B. Hermann, the RNC's campaign director, to convince Nixon's ambivalent staff to pay attention to African Americans. Though the committee itself had prioritized Operation Dixie over the Minorities Division, it still recognized the need for, at a minimum, the creation of campaign literature targeting African Americans and the purchase of ads in black newspapers. In a series of memos to Nixon's campaign chairman, Leonard Hall, and campaign manager, Robert Finch, Hermann belabored that "there should be an endless flood" of pro-Nixon material to black newspapers. They responded that there was not enough money to do so. Undeterred, Hermann continued to stress that it was unwise "to not at least provide one piece of literature for distribution among the Negro population," but was again met with apathetic replies. He then sent Hall a sampling of letters from black Republicans requesting materials to circulate in their communities and asked for Hall's plan of action. Without any constructive replies from the Nixon camp, Hermann sent a final message: "This has been a very badly neglected area. I do not know why. I am fearful of it coming home to haunt us."[36]

In contrast, the Kennedy campaign created an organized and well-funded Civil Rights Section (CRS) to handle its black outreach. Frank Reeves, an outspoken Washington, D.C., attorney and advisor to Hubert Humphrey's primary campaign, headed the division. His partner, Harris Wofford, coordinated an extensive voter registration campaign with black churches. In mid-October, the CRS sponsored a two-day civil rights conference in New York, which culminated in a Kennedy rally in Harlem. Kennedy also personally cultivated a positive relationship with black journalists and hired the editor of the *Chicago Defender*, Louis E. Martin, to coordinate with black newspapers. Martin maintained constant communication with editors and publishers, even staunch Republicans, whose newspapers he filled with campaign ads. The end result, Gloster Current observed, was that even "pro-Republican newspapers . . . became filled with pro-Kennedy information." Kennedy's extensive advertising in black publications provided his campaign the ability to craft messages that saturated black communities but left white voters largely unaware of much of his campaign's most dramatic civil rights rhetoric.[37]

Nixon's approach could not have been more different. Though he was notoriously contemptuous of reporters, he was completely inattentive to the black press. In November 1959, Claude Barnett, a Republican and the director of the Associated Negro Press, which distributed articles to almost every major black newspaper, told Nixon's press secretary, "we would be delighted to make use of" pro-Nixon stories that "affect Negroes in one way or another that would not normally be in your regular press releases." Despite this unparalleled offer for free publicity in black newspapers across the nation, there is no indication that Nixon's campaign accepted the offer. Moreover, by the time of his 1960 campaign, Nixon's staff not only balked at advertising in black newspapers but avoided black reporters. Black journalists generally asked questions on race and civil rights, topics Nixon reserved for his carefully worded speeches, not unscripted remarks that could backfire in the South. By mid-October, Simeon Booker, the Washington Bureau Chief of *Jet* assigned to follow Nixon, requested to be transferred to Kennedy's campaign after consistently being evaded by Republican staffers.[38]

Disillusionment and discontent thus reigned in the fall of 1960 among black Republicans. Val Washington swore that he would never "go through another campaign which was as stupidly run as this one." Jackie Robinson later claimed, "Several times during the Nixon campaign, I was on the verge of quitting and denouncing the Vice President." Archibald Carey and Helen Edmonds lamented the failure of the party to capitalize on its potential to make inroads among African Americans, noting that although the vice president "had a much better story" than Kennedy, who actually "went after" black voters, Nixon "did nothing with it." Similarly, George W. Lee argued, "our party had so much to sell, but men on the higher echelon failed to organize a sales campaign." The GOP's lack of support for southern black Republicans since 1957 also left Lee vulnerable, as he faced rigorous, organized competition from Democrats for black voters in Memphis. The state Democratic Party recognized the role African Americans had played in past Republican victories in Tennessee, and paid campaign workers to canvass every majority-black ward in Memphis. Unlike 1956, the city's Democrats offered black voters a well-funded and organized alternative to Lee's Lincoln League, which found few allies inside Nixon's camp.[39]

One of the few places in the country where Nixon continued to maintain high levels of black support was Atlanta. Black Republicans in the southern capital of black business were not dependent on outside funding, but drew their strength from the city's concentration of middle and upper-class African Americans. Additionally, white Republicans in the state not only accepted black support but shared power with African Americans inside party ranks.

In fact, Georgia's nine black delegates made up 40 percent of the party's total number of African American convention delegates. The state's Democratic delegation, by contrast, did not have a single black representative. Prior to the fall campaign, at a meeting of the nonpartisan Atlanta Negro Voters League, whose membership included some of the most respected African Americans in the city, John H. Calhoun asked every ward leader if he supported Nixon or Kennedy. "And to a man," he soon found, "they said Nixon." Calhoun, who also served as vice chairman of the state Republican Party, convinced the preachers who were present to sign a petition supporting Nixon, and later commented that Republicans "had all of the leadership practically tied up." By November, the Atlanta Baptist Ministers' Union, which included Martin Luther King, Sr., had also officially endorsed Nixon, as had the perennially Republican *Atlanta Daily World*.[40]

Atlanta also became the site of the 1960 election's defining event. On

Figure 8. John H. Calhoun in his Atlanta office in 1977. Copyright *Atlanta Journal-Constitution*, courtesy of Georgia State University.

October 19, Martin Luther King, Jr., was arrested after joining seventy-five black protestors in a demonstration at a segregated lunch counter. His arrest violated parole from a previous minor traffic violation, and Judge Oscar Mitchell sentenced him to four months of hard labor in a rural prison. John Calhoun, who had participated with King at the demonstration, immediately recognized the need for the vice president to respond, and urged campaign advisors "to make some kind of statement, because Kennedy didn't know King, but Nixon did." After it became apparent that he would not receive a return phone call, Calhoun warned Val Washington, "This is gon' have some terrific repercussions, and you oughta get ahold of Nixon to get him to say something." Washington suggested that Calhoun might reach the vice president through the Democrats for Nixon organization. According to Calhoun, he eventually spoke with the leaders of the group, who relayed his warnings to the vice president. When they called Calhoun back, they claimed Nixon said, "He would lose some black votes, but he'd gain white votes, so he was gonna sit it out, and he wouldn't say anything."[41]

Calhoun was not alone among black Republicans in pleading with Nixon to intervene on King's behalf. George W. Lee implored Robert Finch and other ranking campaign officials to assist King, arguing, "It was the Democrats who arrested Mr. King, and put him in jail. . . . He is a martyr, a hero to Negroes." E. Frederic Morrow "begged the Nixon managers" to have the campaign "make a statement deploring the situations under which King was jailed. They demurred. They thought it bad strategy." He then met up with the campaign in Illinois to personally give press secretary Herbert Klein a draft statement that expressed Nixon's support of King. Klein "put the draft in his pocket to 'think about it.'" Another staffer told Morrow, "You're always thinking up things to get us into difficulty, so forget it." Jackie Robinson, who was traveling with Nixon, told staffer William Safire that the vice president "has to call Martin right now." Safire brought Robinson to Robert Finch, who arranged a meeting with Nixon. After a ten-minute discussion, Robinson left the room with "tears of frustration in his eyes," telling Safire that the vice president "thinks calling Martin would be 'grandstanding.'" Robinson then exclaimed, "Nixon doesn't deserve to win." In the end, the only public statement issued by Nixon's campaign came from press secretary Klein, who told reporters that the vice president had no comment on the matter.[42]

Though Kennedy also turned down advice to publicly condemn the arrest, his brother-in-law, Sargent Shriver, told him that black voters "want to know whether you care. If you telephone Mrs. King, they will know that you understand and will help. You will reach their hearts." Kennedy took the advice, called King's pregnant wife, and consoled her when she started crying. On hearing about the phone call to Coretta Scott King, Robert Kennedy telephoned Harris Wofford and Louis Martin, shouting, "Close down your Civil Rights Section. You've shot your bolt. You've probably lost the election." According to the traditional narrative of the story, that same night, Robert was so irate that he called the judge who had sentenced King and demanded his release. Judge Mitchell complied and freed King the following day.[43]

Both Kennedy brothers knew the potential risks involved in their phone calls. Three southern governors warned Robert that if there were any connections made between Kennedy and "Khrushchev, Castro, or Martin Luther King, we're going to throw our votes to Nixon." However, unbeknownst to campaign outsiders, Georgia's governor Ernest Vandiver was personally involved in King's release. In August, the Kennedys privately promised the segregationist governor that if he endorsed their campaign, they would not send federal troops into Georgia to enforce school desegregation. Once the King crisis broke out, they reminded Vandiver of their promise. The governor, through channels within the state's Democratic establishment, received word from Judge Mitchell that he was willing to release King if Kennedy privately requested it. Vandiver would later suggest that Democratic officials tempted Mitchell to cooperate by referencing positions on the federal bench that might open up after Kennedy became president. While the back-channel story of King's release is not as flattering as the sanitized accounts later detailed by pro-Kennedy writers, it still reveals a willingness on the part of the Kennedy campaign to take a political risk in being associated with the polarizing Martin Luther King.[44]

Unlike the fallout that followed Lodge's Harlem speech, the Kennedy phone calls did not sustain prolonged attention from the national media. The *New York Times* story on Kennedy's role in the events was given two inches of copy on page 22, and a *U.S. News and World Report* article on King's release did not mention Kennedy's telephone call to Coretta Scott King. Conversely, the story received extensive coverage in black newspapers. When contacting journalists about Kennedy's role in the events, Louis Martin of the CRS deliberately left white reporters off his call list, telling the story exclusively to African Americans. The front page of major black papers across the country featured dramatic headlines, such as "King Freed After Senator Kennedy Intervened." The Memphis *Tri-State Defender* remarked, "This was the action of a man with deep convictions," and black columnist Ted Poston noted that while Kennedy acted in "full awareness that his words and deeds would inflame the Southern racists . . . Nixon remained passive and silent."[45]

While never formally endorsing the Democratic nominee, King expressed gratitude for the "genuine concern" Kennedy showed after his arrest. In a radio interview three days before the election, he praised Kennedy's "forthright position" on civil rights and claimed there had been "too much disagreement and double-talk" from Nixon. King later described the vice president as a "moral coward," because "he had been supposedly close to me . . . yet, when this moment came, it was like he had never heard of me." Martin Luther King, Sr., went a step farther, rescinding his endorsement of Nixon, who did not say "a mumbling word" in defense of his son, and declared, "I've got a suitcase of votes, and I'm going to take them to Mr. Kennedy and dump them in his lap."[46]

Word of Kennedy's role in the King affair circulated throughout African American communities across the country via black newspapers and campaign fliers. With less than two weeks until election day, Kennedy's Civil Rights Section and union allies distributed a pamphlet entitled " 'No Comment' Nixon Versus a Candidate with a Heart, Senator Kennedy: The Case of Martin Luther King." It featured a plea from King's closest associate, Ralph Abernathy, imploring African Americans "to take off our Nixon buttons . . . since Mr. Nixon has been silent through all this, I am going to return his silence when I go into the voting booth." Two million copies were printed and distributed via churches throughout the country on the Sunday prior to the election. Sargent Shriver even personally handed out pamphlets as he stood by the front doors of a black church in Chicago.[47]

Many middle-class black leaders could echo Mississippi activist Charles Evers, who claimed that until October, "I was backing the Republican, Richard Nixon. So were most Negroes," because he had "spoken out against racism for years." However, "overnight" following King's release, Evers, along with his brother Medgar, took off his Nixon button and publicly endorsed Kennedy. On election day, Kennedy won just under 70 percent of the nation's black vote, including 40 percent of the *black Republican* vote. In the closest election of the twentieth century, mobilized black voters propelled him to victory in tight races in pivotal states. Had African Americans voted for Nixon at the same levels as they supported Eisenhower in 1956, he would have won the election. Kennedy won Illinois by a mere nine thousand votes and Michigan by just sixty-seven thousand. In each state, he received an estimated two hundred and fifty thousand black votes. In South Carolina, where Eisenhower had made significant gains among African Americans in 1956, Kennedy received forty thousand black votes, contributing to his slim ten thousand vote victory in the state. Similarly, 90 percent of Louisiana's black voters helped bring the state back into the Democratic column. The same was true of African Americans in North Carolina and Texas, whose support helped secure narrow Democratic wins.[48]

Despite Nixon's gamble for white southerners, he still lost most of the region. Many white southerners felt the same way as Senator Richard Russell, who observed that while he was "not enamored of Kennedy . . . I am frank to say that I cannot see any reason to prefer Nixon." Johnson's presence on the ticket, contrasted to Henry Cabot Lodge, no doubt contributed to easing southern fears of Kennedy. Moreover, despite Nixon's emphasis on states' rights in October and November, white southerners, according to the *New York Times*, and confirmed by poll data, felt "they had little choice between the two parties." Many had not forgotten Nixon's civil rights record as vice president and his compromises with Nelson Rockefeller at the convention. As suggested by one Kennedy aide, Nixon's courtship of conservative white southerners was a "curse in disguise," because the strategy pushed him to mute his advocacy of civil rights to court a demographic he still ultimately lost. He ended up alienating both African Americans and white southerners.[49]

Economics also played a role in solidifying black support for Kennedy, particularly in northern cities. While the 1950s saw an unprecedented boom in the national economy, black poverty rates dropped by only 3 percent, compared to 27 percent for whites. From 1950 to 1960, the number of black-owned businesses declined by one-third, and by the time Eisenhower left office, nonwhite household income remained only 53 percent of average white income. Though Nixon claimed that mass unemployment had been wiped out, black unemployment in the nation's largest cities ranged between 20 and 40 percent. For all the emphasis black civil rights leaders placed on eliminating Jim Crow in the South, black voters in the North continued to face their own harsh economic realities, left unaddressed by eight years of Republican rule. Tellingly, of black Democrats interviewed in 1961, over 60 percent claimed the main reason they supported the party was because it was "good for the working man" and "conditions are good under Democrats." Only a third claimed their support stemmed primarily from the party's civil rights positions.[50]

It should not be overlooked, however, that Nixon won almost half of the black middle class, and received 46 percent of the total black vote in the eleven former Confederate states, according to the *Washington Post*. His record, and party, still carried some weight. No Republican presidential candidate since 1960 has even come close to receiving his 32 percent of the national black vote. Moreover, while Nixon obtained only a fourth of the black vote in cities with total populations over 500,000, he received 40 percent of the black vote in mid-sized cities. He also won the majority of black votes in Alabama and Georgia. In Atlanta, where John Calhoun and John W. Dobbs ran the most extensive black Republican campaign in the country, Nixon attained a decisive 58 percent of the city's black vote. So entrenched was the GOP within Atlanta's black leadership that even after Martin Luther King, Jr., was released from prison, the city's leading black ministers, with the lone exception of King, Sr., issued a statement "firmly re-endorsing" Nixon. Many southern African Americans still associated the Democratic Party with Jim Crow, and, as Atlanta exemplified, they were willing to support the GOP when the party actively courted and mobilized their communities at the grassroots level.[51]

Black Republicans used the defeat as an opportunity to reproach their party in hopes of shaping its future direction. To L. K. Jackson, the fundamental decision faced by the GOP was whether it would reject the "reactionary, lily-white wing." They could not "be true to the principles upon which the party was founded, and the causes for which Lincoln died; and at the same time for political expediency, form coalitions with the Dixiecrats, do the biddings of the Ku Klux Klan, the White Citizens' Council and carry out the mandates of Jefferson Davis and Robert E. Lee." In April 1961, Ed Sexton, chairman of the Young Republicans Minorities Committee, organized a three-day symposium in Chicago attended by seventy-five of the country's leading black Republicans to express their discontent with the party's approach to their communities. William H. Robinson, a militant state legislator from Chicago, delivered the keynote address, where he condemned the strategy that "wrote the Negro off" and formed an "unholy alliance" with southern conservatives. He then targeted institutional impediments against African Americans inside the party, which, despite sustained support for the GOP by middle-class and southern blacks throughout the 1950s, kept them out of meaningful national positions. "Negroes wanted to be on the policy-making level, and especially when the policy is determined relative to minorities," he proclaimed. Instead, "minorities had not been given equal opportunities within the Party," a failure that "manifests a 'Sergeant-at-Arms' policy" that often relegated them to token positions.[52]

Rather than deserting the party, many black Republicans, who had personally invested their political careers and reputations inside the GOP, sought
to reform it from within. As discontented as he may have been with Nixon,
Jackie Robinson told reporters soon after the election, "I'm just about ready
to become a Republican." To him, the party's loss highlighted that "what we
need now more than anything else is a real two-party system." Robinson told
A.B. Hermann, "there are a great number of aggressive Negroes" willing to
work with the GOP, "and I believe we could do a good job if we were given
help." George W. Lee remained equally committed to the two-party system,
calling it "the only bargaining point that the Negro has." L. K. Jackson declared after the election that he was offered "everything but Lake Michigan" to
join the Democratic Party, but "remained loyal, true, faithful and patriotic to
the Republican Party." Not only did he stick with the GOP as "a protest against
what the Democrats are now doing against us throughout the South," but also
because he believed in the "principles upon which the party was founded"—
principles that included racial equality, which he had to defend against conservative incursions.[53]

Just days before Kennedy's inauguration, a contingent of prominent Democrats greeted E. Frederic Morrow at his Washington, D.C., home, and offered him a well-paying job in the new administration if he switched parties.
Rather than being flattered by the opportunity, Morrow recalled, "I was livid!"
He admitted to his Democratic visitors that "the Republican Party has many
flaws. . . . Its record on civil rights leaves much to be desired." However, rather
than this being a reason for Morrow to leave the party, it was because of these
flaws that the GOP "needs some Blacks with guts, courage, and toughness to
stay in it and fight like hell for reforms and changes." As black Republicans
entered the 1960s, the fight for the soul of the Grand Old Party would only
grow more bitter and more imperative. As with the sit-ins that spread across
the nation in 1960, black Republicans demanded to sit at the tables of power
and influence in their party. That their voices were often ignored, and their
ranks continually denied entry into the "Whites Only" positions of elite party
leadership, only underscored the need that they fight for inclusion and respect. Their continued presence inside the GOP did not signify a naive loyalty, or acquiescence to conservatives, but represented their willingness to
embrace the challenge of steering the party toward black voters and civil
rights.[54]

CHAPTER 5

Somebody Had to Stay and Fight:
Black Republicans and the Rise of the Right

"During my life I have had few nightmares which happened to me while I was awake," Jackie Robinson wrote in a 1967 column. One of them, according to the baseball legend, was the rise of Barry Goldwater and a conservative movement that "disgraced and vilified every decent thing which had ever been Republican." Indeed, not only did the 1964 presidential nomination of Goldwater mark the nadir of the GOP's relationship with black voters, it also fractured the party's relationship with black Republicans. Though discontented with the direction of the national party in the wake of Nixon's 1960 presidential campaign, black Republicans like Robinson still maintained the value of the "two-party system" to African American political power, and pointed to moderate and liberal Republicans, such as Nelson Rockefeller, as practical alternatives to Democrats. As allies of the Eastern Establishment, they maintained a discernible presence in states with liberal Republican governors like New York, Pennsylvania, and Ohio, and continued to fight for black equality as leaders of NAACP branches, politicians, and intraparty critics. But in the face of Goldwater's successful grassroots organizing, their power in the party would face a significant challenge.[1]

Staunch conservative Patrick Buchanan wrote that "by the day of Kennedy's inaugural" in 1961, "conservatives were shouldering aside Eisenhower Republicans to engage the Eastern Establishment in a war for the soul of the party." In this war, conservatives had no desire to ally with black Republicans, who collaborated with liberals and supported sweeping civil rights legislation, and whose presence in southern parties might discourage white Democrats from considering the GOP. From 1961 to 1964, F. Clifton White and other conservative activists worked tirelessly behind the scenes on the grassroots level reorganizing state parties and procuring Goldwater delegates in preparation for the 1964 national convention. They also assumed control of the boards of directors of auxiliary organizations, such as the Federation of Republican Women and Young Republicans. The plan, White asserted, "amounted to nothing less than a long-term guerrilla operation" to ensure that conservatives dominated the party apparatus from the precinct to national level.[2]

The conservative movement's first major coup came in June 1961 with the installation of William Miller as chairman of the Republican National Committee. A conservative congressman from Buffalo, New York, Miller turned the RNC into a stronghold of the right over the next three years. This change in direction was apparent as early as November, when the GOP held a two-day workshop in Atlanta to discuss southern strategies. Though it was organized by the segregationist head of Mississippi's party, Wirt Yerger, moderates and fifty black Republicans attended to voice their perspective. "Sooner or later there are going to be 2,000,000 Negro voters in Georgia," the state's GOP chairman cautioned his party, and he hoped "a majority of them will vote Republican." To their consternation, however, the keynote speaker was Goldwater, who promised that he "would bend every muscle to see that the South has a voice on everything that affects the South" and reiterated his opposition to measures that would "enforce integration of the schools." At a separate press conference while in Atlanta, he proclaimed, "We're not going to get the Negro vote as a bloc in 1964 and 1968, so we ought to go hunting where the ducks are." Despite his speaking in a state where a majority of African Americans and a minority of whites had voted Republican the previous year, Goldwater's "ducks" were conservative white southerners.[3]

These comments typified Goldwater's southern strategy. In his 1960 bestseller, *The Conscience of a Conservative*, the Arizona senator argued that while personally opposing segregation, he was "not prepared, however, to impose that judgment of mine on the people of Mississippi or South Carolina." He also wrote that black children did "not have a civil right" to attend integrated schools, and called *Brown v. Board of Education* unconstitutional. In the three years leading up to his presidential bid, Goldwater frequently stressed his belief that "we have no right to tell the Southern states what they must do about school integration and segregation," and questioned if the country could "survive against the pressures" of African Americans who seek civil rights laws that "would destroy our Constitution." On CBS's *Face the Nation* television program, he expressed opposition to any federal intervention that

mandated integration, adding, "I think the South is doing a good job in this."
Though Goldwater may not have been a white supremacist—having supported voluntary desegregation in his home town of Phoenix—by 1964, he
had become, in the words of Ralph McGill of the *Atlanta Constitution*, the
"unexpected hero of the Klans, Klaverns, and councils" as the country's most
prominent opponent of federal intervention in the field of civil rights.[1]

Bolstered by Goldwater's popularity in the South, conservatives redoubled their efforts to make the GOP a viable alternative for weary Democrats,
including segregationists. South Carolina Young Republicans and the state
party of Mississippi passed resolutions in opposition to civil rights. Louisiana's Republican Platform Committee endorsed a constitutional amendment
to reverse "all encroachments by the federal government in the field of so-
called 'civil rights' in the past several years" and pledged to preserve the
"Southern tradition of the separation of the races." In Tennessee, a stronghold
of black Republicans since the 1920s thanks to George W. Lee, conservatives
formed the all-white Shelby County Republican Association, which met in
the city's segregated Peabody Hotel, in order to circumvent Lee's Lincoln
League for control of the Memphis GOP. Though Lee had the endorsement of
one hundred and fifty black ministers in his 1962 reelection campaign to the
state's Republican Executive Committee, his tenure came to an abrupt end
when conservatives, buoyed by Democratic converts, rallied behind the Republican Association. Unlike a decade prior, when conservatives first attempted to replace Lee, this time there were significantly more white
conservatives and a dwindling number of black Republicans, and Lee fin-
ished in third place in the GOP primary. One of his opponents was a member
of the anti-civil rights John Birch Society.[5]

The Republican National Committee actively promoted conservative
southerners who opposed civil rights. Their campaigns received an influx of
cash from Chairman Miller, who by 1964 had directed half a million dollars
toward Operation Dixie. For perspective, the total expenditures of the entire
national committee in 1963 were only $1.7 million. Miller's first significant
victory came in 1961, when John Tower won a special election to fill the vacated seat of Lyndon Johnson in Texas. Winning on a states' rights platform,
he would serve as one of the Senate's most reliable opponents of civil rights
legislation for the next two decades. In 1962, the GOP slated staunch segregationists across the South, in one of its most concerted efforts in the region
since Reconstruction. South Carolina's candidate for the U.S. Senate, William
Workman, Jr., mocked "sociologists and psychologists who preach the

doctrine of equal capacity of whites and Negroes" and justified discriminating against African Americans on the basis of their "intellectual inertia" and "moral laxity." Likewise, James Martin, Alabama's Republican nominee for the Senate, pledged to "forestall collusion between the government and the NAACP to integrate schools, unions, and neighborhoods." Though Workman and Martin lost in the general election, they dramatically improved their party's percentage of the vote. Republican congressional candidates were even more successful, as the GOP picked up new seats in Florida, North Carolina, Texas, and Tennessee, and earned at least 45 percent of the vote in an additional eight congressional races. This midterm success solidified conservatives' belief that the South could be won by the Republican right, and not through building a coalition of African Americans and moderates.[6]

The rise of conservatives within the GOP was aided by missteps of the Eastern Establishment, who approached politics in the 1960s with an outmoded strategy that centered on party elites and made little effort to mobilize grassroots excitement. Conservatives, on the other hand, had a network of publications, organizations, and local activists that reached out to voters on the local level. Though moderate and liberal Republicans continued to wield influence in Congress and within their respective states, they would be unprepared for the intense organizational strength of Goldwater forces by the time of the 1964 primary season. The establishment recognized far too late that they could not contain Goldwater supporters as they had the conservative, but pragmatic, Robert Taft wing of the 1940s. Where Taft was willing to compromise within the party, Goldwater's followers maintained a strict allegiance to ideological purity, leaving little room for negotiation with moderates and liberals. As Wirt Yerger wrote in his memoirs, "New Republicans in the South detested the liberal-leaning Republicanism of the North." Nelson Rockefeller was as much his political enemy as the Democratic Party. Outraged by eight years of Modern Republicanism under President Eisenhower, the man responsible for protecting New Deal programs like Social Security, nominating liberal Earl Warren to the Supreme Court, and deploying troops in Little Rock to enforce desegregation, the Republican right launched an uncompromising movement to wrest control of a party that had long minimized their influence on the national level.[7]

Most important, they outflanked the establishment by assuming control of the local Republican organizations that selected delegates to the national convention. Black representation in southern delegations had been a feature of the party since Reconstruction. Conservatives knew all too well that it was

African Americans in Georgia, Tennessee, Mississippi, and elsewhere that had provided a typically solid bloc in favor of Eastern Establishment presidential candidates since the 1940s. If the party was going to nominate Goldwater, or any staunch conservative for that matter, black delegates in the South would have to be removed. Most moderate Republicans, whose bases lay in places like New York, Ohio, and Michigan, while urging the party to reach out to black Republicans in the South, did little in terms of exhausting internal party mechanisms to ensure a continued black presence. Black Republicans themselves, without support from the national committee, found it difficult to continue urging black voters to join local parties whose civil rights stances were identical to those of segregationist Democrats. By 1962 many precincts had already selected conservative delegates, inspired by a grassroots "draft Goldwater" movement, which meant that Goldwater was on his way to becoming the party's nominee well before the first primary ballots were ever cast in 1964. By the time the overconfident establishment began prepping for the election, they were too late.

Though far fewer in number than conservatives, black Republicans had their own vision of the party's future and sought to implement reforms in the RNC by reinvigorating the Minorities Division. While its director, Val Washington, had lacked money and institutional support since 1957, his reputation as a behind-the-scenes negotiator, rather than outspoken activist, drew the ire of those seeking a more aggressive presence inside the GOP after the 1960 debacle with black voters. Helen Edmonds argued that most black Republicans "don't think a damn thing of Val Washington's ability as an organizer," and complained that he failed to exploit the talents of younger, more militant black Republicans because "he does not know them. He does not travel in that group." Similarly, George W. Lee concluded that Washington "has no genius for organization nor imagination; no capacity for showmanship," and recommended a complete overhaul of the division. With few allies, Washington resigned in the fall of 1961 and was replaced by Grant Reynolds and Louis Lautier. Reynolds had gained national prominence in the 1940s through his efforts to eliminate military segregation and remained active in New York civil rights circles in the 1950s. Lautier was the former Washington Bureau chief of the National Negro Press Association, but died in 1962 shortly after his appointment. His successor, Clay Claiborne, had previously worked in public relations for the national committee and had served as the national press secretary for the black Elks.[8]

While Reynolds was far more outspoken and aggressive than

Washington, he was just as powerless when it came to implementing an agenda. The Minorities Division received one-third the budget of Operation Dixie, barely enough to cover the salary and personal expenses of Reynolds and Claiborne. In spite of financial constraints, Reynolds wrote several reports detailing an alternate agenda for expanding the party's base. He called for the RNC to counterbalance Operation Dixie with an "Operation Big City" (a name occasionally used in the early 1960s to describe the Minorities Division), noting that diverse urban areas represented Nixon's largest margin of defeat in 1960. He also encouraged the national committee to draft a new party platform, where "every effort must be made to broaden and strengthen the civil rights plank." As for the South, he suggested that Operation Dixie hire black field organizers and an operative with extensive connections to black newspapers. Arguing that Republican strength could best be established in the South if the party won the rapidly expanding black electorate, which would continue to grow if the GOP pressed for protection of voting rights, Reynolds urged Operation Dixie to partner with the Voter Education Project in registering black voters. This would not only undercut President Kennedy, who provided federal funding to the project, but could supply Republicans with an untapped source of first-time voters who would be drawn to a party that offered a viable alternative to segregationist Democrats.[9]

The Eastern Establishment also championed Reynolds's approach, believing the South could be won through a strategy that preserved their heritage as the party of Lincoln by reaching out to African Americans and moderates in the expanding white middle class. The moderate Republican magazine, *Advance*, accused Goldwater of "hitching the party wagon to the falling star of segregation," and called for the GOP "to orient its Southern campaign toward responsible Southern progress, rather than toward Southern prejudices and reaction." Former RNC chairman Thruston Morton knew from experience that the approach could work, as he himself had been elected by a coalition of African Americans and moderate whites in Kentucky. Reminding his party that, more and more, "the negro in the South is going to vote," he stressed that if the GOP could win 40 percent of the black vote, their candidates "can win anywhere." To him, it was vital that the party focus on moderate southern states like Kentucky, Florida, and North Carolina, which could provide a "sound foundation for Republicanism not based on racism." Similarly, Jacob Javits's 1964 book—written to critique Goldwater's "disconnect . . . from the traditions of the Republican Party"—urged the GOP to win converts "by appealing to the new commercial and economic order of the South" and "on the civil rights issue." Even Operation Dixie's original founder, Meade Alcorn of Connecticut, who had encouraged at least the appearance of black outreach, claimed that his program had been "perverted . . . into a lily white Republican organization," as he lamented its refusal "to mold a modern, forward-looking, progressive Republican organization."[10]

In light of strong black support for the GOP in the South during the 1950s, black Republicans were particularly concerned with Democratic advances in the region. As a member of the Fulton County Republican Executive Committee, Atlanta's C. Clayton Powell called for the creation of minority branches across the South patterned after the Democratic regional offices formed by their national committee's leading black advisor, Louis Martin. Grant Reynolds asked Republicans to follow the Democratic Party's example in providing "hospitality rooms and good speakers" to all major black conventions, and recommended that the RNC create measures to ensure black representation within its leadership. While the Democratic National Committee had three black members, a black Republican had not served as a national committeeperson since the death of Perry Howard in 1961. To remedy this lack of black representation, which lent credence to claims that the GOP was rapidly becoming lily-white, Reynolds joined George W. Lee in calling for the emergency appointment of a black vice chairman, or five black members at large, until party rules could be amended to ensure adequate African American representation. Like Reynolds's other suggestions, these too were ignored by Chairman Miller.[11]

Miller's and Reynolds's polarized visions of the party led to inevitable tension inside the national committee. A champion of the "draft Goldwater" movement, Miller sought to build a new, conservative base in the South, while Reynolds believed the party's livelihood remained with the Eastern Establishment. Reynolds was livid in the spring of 1963 when Miller, who served on the House Judiciary Committee, refused to support a Republican civil rights bill, and by 1964 Reynolds had become so exasperated that he described the Minorities Division to reporters as a "front" and "simply window dressing." This was not a hyperbolic description. Chairman Miller explicitly prohibited Reynolds from issuing statements that touted Republican-sponsored civil rights legislation or the party's positive record on issues of race. He also rejected the division's requests to create a black newsletter comparable to Operation Dixie's monthly publication, which had a circulation of fifty thousand. Similarly, while I. Lee Potter of Operation Dixie traveled two hundred and fifty thousand miles and delivered over one

hundred speeches in 1963 alone, the national committee tabled Clay Claiborne's planned speaking tour because of "budgetary problems." In December 1962, the committee took away Reynolds's secretary, forcing him to
devote considerable time to reading and responding to mail, a task he described as "costly and exasperating beyond the point of tolerance." He complained to Nelson Rockefeller's aides that "he is not really accepted or wanted"
by the committee and "could be more effective out in the field organizing the
contacts which he has made." So futile was the work of the Minorities Division that a 1963 survey of twenty-five leading southern black Republicans
found only one individual who even knew the division existed. All twenty-
five, on the other hand, received a weekly mailing from the Democratic National Committee's black division.[12]

Despite being ignored by the national committee, many black Republicans
still did not see the Democratic Party as a worthwhile alternative. Though
President Kennedy exceeded Eisenhower in high-ranking black appointments, he and Attorney General Robert Kennedy adamantly opposed new
civil rights legislation during the administration's first two years. Democrats
dominated both houses of Congress, and the president feared that a failed
civil rights bill would expose divisions inside the party and jeopardize needed
southern support for other legislation. He would not even fulfill his campaign
promise to sign an executive order banning discrimination in federal housing
until after the 1962 election. Most egregiously, he named staunch segregationists to newly created federal judiciary posts to placate southern supporters. When the Justice Department opted to prosecute cases involving
discrimination against black voters, many of the very same judges blocking
the administration were the president's own appointees. One judge would infamously describe black plaintiffs in a 1964 voting rights case as "a bunch of
niggers . . . acting like a bunch of chimpanzees." Without decisive action from
the White House during Kennedy's first two and a half years in office, civil
rights demonstrations further intensified, and racist backlash became more
violent, as beatings, bombings, and terror plagued the South.[13]

   Black Republicans frequently highlighted Kennedy's trepidation, which
they used as evidence to support their argument that African Americans
should join the GOP to prevent Democrats from taking their vote for granted.
Grant Reynolds denounced Kennedy as the "phoniest" president in history,
because he "has given much lip service to civil liberties, but not one legislative
proposal has had any backing by the President." George Fowler of New York

called the president a "fraud" and "an insult to Negroes," and George W. Lee proclaimed, "There isn't anything new" in Kennedy's New Frontier, as "nothing has been done thus far on the Civil Rights front." In his nationally syndicated column, Jackie Robinson described Kennedy as "a clever tokenist," who intended to "pull the wool over the eyes of the Negro."[14]

At the same time, black Republicans continued to see the GOP's Eastern Establishment as a viable option. In 1961, representatives John Lindsay of New York, Charles Mathias of Maryland, and other Republicans backed legislation that banned discrimination in unions, employment, and places of public accommodation. Though Kennedy had supported these measures as a candidate, his press secretary dismissively said in response to the proposals, "The President has made it clear that he does not think it necessary at this time to enact civil rights legislation." In 1962, Republicans reintroduced strong legislation, again without significant Democratic support, which human rights lawyer Joseph Rauh called "the most complete answer to segregation and discrimination yet offered in Congress." In the spring of 1963, after the president signaled a willingness to consider a civil rights bill, Mathias and other Republicans proposed an even stronger civil rights legislative package that included a plan of rapid school desegregation, greater protection of voting rights, and the establishment of a permanent Fair Employment Practices Commission. Not a single liberal Democrat cosponsored the measures, as they awaited Kennedy's plan. Meg Greenfield of the *Washington Post* summed up the surprise of many political insiders in the early 1960s, noting that "the principal force truly committed to taking *immediate* action against the kinds of crude racial oppression still officially in place seemed to be, of all things, a bunch of Republicans."[15]

A number of Republican governors also embraced civil rights in the early 1960s. William Scranton gave Pennsylvania's Human Relations Commission subpoena and injunction power to actively combat racial discrimination, and James Rhodes supported legislation that prohibited discrimination in the sale or rental of housing in Ohio. George Romney of Michigan supported measures that banned segregation in housing, public accommodations, employment, and education, and even led an NAACP march against segregated housing in suburban Detroit. Similarly, Nelson Rockefeller helped pass laws in New York that barred discrimination in employment, housing, bank loans, insurance policies, and places of public accommodation. He also served as one of the most important financial benefactors of the civil rights movement, often channeling funds directly to Martin Luther King, Jr., who occasionally traveled aboard Rockefeller's private jet. Specific contributions included

financing the rebuilding of Mount Olive Baptist Church after it was torched
by white supremacists in Albany, Georgia, and providing $100,000 in bail to
secure the release of King, Ralph Abernathy, and hundreds of activists arrested during the Birmingham movement of 1963.[16]

Like black Republicans, moderates in the party criticized Goldwater's
southern strategy. Governor Scranton urged the GOP to reject Democrats-
turned-Republican who used "the phrase 'states rights' only as a cloak to deny
Negroes," and "whose only reason for joining us is one hope of leaving his
Negro neighbors outside." Kentucky's John Sherman Cooper suggested that if
Republicans embraced "the expedient argument of States' rights with respect
to constitutional and human rights . . . such a position will destroy the Republican Party, and worse, it will do a great wrong" to African Americans.
Jacob Javits warned that it would be "a very serious threat to the country if the
Republican Party should go lily white," and Kenneth Keating called conservative opposition to civil rights "wrong politically and morally." Even Richard
Nixon called the RNC's conservative leadership "just stupid" in its lack of attention to black voters, and feared, "if Goldwater wins his fight, our party
would eventually become the first major all-white political party."[17]

Many African Americans responded positively to moderate and liberal
Republicans in the voting booth. Senator Cooper received a majority of Kentucky's black votes in 1960, and two years later his colleague, Thruston Morton, obtained 46 percent. In 1961, 69 percent of Louisville's black voters led a
coalition that successfully elected the city's first Republican mayor in almost
thirty years. Mayor William Cowger would go on to sign the first law in a
southern city that banned segregation in places of public accommodation.
The following year, Senator Jacob Javits received 42 percent of the black vote
in heavily Democratic New York. Indeed, substantial black support propelled
Governors Rockefeller, Romney, Scranton, and Rhodes into office, as well as
other moderate Republicans in municipal and state elections in Baltimore, St.
Louis, Kansas City, and Oklahoma in 1962 and 1963.[18]

Black Republicans still wielded power inside local parties and in state
governments with moderate Republican leadership in the early to mid-1960s.
In 1961, the Republican Party of Washington, D.C., had three black vice
chairmen, and one-third of its committee members were African American.
Governor Rhodes appointed William O. Walker, publisher of Cleveland's *Call
and Post*, as Director of Industrial Relations, making him Ohio's first black
cabinet member. George Fowler, a close ally of Nelson Rockefeller, served
over five years as the chairman of the powerful New York State Commission

for Human Rights. Similarly, Governor Scranton appointed Republican Theodore O. Spaulding as Pennsylvania's first black appellate court judge, and
named a prominent social worker, William P. Young, as Pennsylvania's secretary of labor and industry, a position with jurisdiction over the state's media-
tion services, fair employment, vocational education, and workmen's
compensation. Shortly after his appointment, Young also became the chairman of the Republican Committee of Allegheny County, which included the
state's second largest city, Pittsburgh.[19]

Black Republicans also continued to run for meaningful political offices.
In 1960, the GOP fielded Charles Stokes as Washington's first black candidate
for lieutenant governor, and Republicans in Massachusetts nominated Edward W. Brooke as secretary of state, the Bay State's first black nominee for a
statewide office. In 1962, William D. Graham became Connecticut's first African American to run for a statewide post after securing the GOP nomination for state treasurer. Indeed, black journalist Chuck Stone observed that
when it came to the nomination of African Americans to statewide races in
the early 1960s, it was Republicans who "had taken the first giant step." Conversely, Democrats, who preferred to slate black candidates in heavily black
districts, "were dragged along by the scruff of the neck," often running their
first black statewide candidates in response to the GOP.[20]

On the local level, four black Republicans in Indianapolis served on the
county superior court, and Rufus Kuykendall represented African Americans
on the city council. In 1961, black Republicans in Louisville won several positions on the Board of Aldermen, and Amelia Tucker defeated a black Democratic opponent for a seat in the Kentucky General Assembly, making her
the first black woman to serve in the legislature of a southern state. The following year, in a victory hailed by African Americans of both parties, Edward
Brooke became one of the most powerful black men in the country after winning his race for attorney general of Massachusetts.[21]

As they had since the 1940s, black Republican politicians prioritized civil
rights in their agenda. Prior to his tenure as a public official, Brooke had
served as vice president and legislative chairman of the Boston NAACP,
where he lobbied the state legislature for antidiscrimination laws. In one of
his first acts as attorney general, he became the only state official to submit a
brief in support of a proposed fair housing law, and assisted in the drafting of
legislation designed to eradicate discrimination in unions and businesses.
Amelia Tucker sponsored a public accommodations act in Kentucky's General Assembly, and Rufus Kuykendall introduced a fair housing ordinance in

Indianapolis. David Albritton, a black Republican state legislator from Dayton, Ohio, partnered with Democrat Carl Stokes in sponsoring a 1963 bill that banned discrimination in the sale and rental of housing. They eventually secured passage of the legislation with the assistance of Russell M. Jones, a Republican and president of the Columbus NAACP, who led a statewide lobbying campaign on its behalf.[22]

In addition to sponsoring legislation as elected officials, black Republicans remained active in state and local NAACP branches and civil rights campaigns. Throughout the 1960s, the NAACP Legal Defense and Education Fund, which served as the legal backbone of the civil rights movement, had at least two black Republicans on its board, Francis Rivers and William Coleman, Jr. Both would serve terms as president of the organization. Herman Smith, a member of the Los Angeles Republican Advisory Committee and 1962 GOP congressional candidate, chaired the Watts NAACP branch, where he led a massive legal campaign on behalf of the four thousand African Americans arrested in the aftermath of the 1965 Watts uprising. David Longley, who served as vice president of Richmond, Virginia's, GOP in the 1950s, became the state NAACP's treasurer and led protests of segregated businesses in Richmond in the 1960s. The most prominent black aide inside George Romney's administration, Charles M. Tucker, headed the Oakland County NAACP, and was vice president of Michigan's state NAACP. Charles Lunderman of Louisville's Republican Executive Committee had previously served as president of the city's NAACP and participated in a number of desegregation lawsuits. Reverend L. K. Jackson, called "the Daddy of the militant civil rights movement" by Martin Luther King, Sr., not only hosted political rallies at his church as one of Gary, Indiana's, most prominent Republicans, but also led crusades to integrate the city's public facilities and combat employment discrimination.[23]

Black Republican activism included denouncing the influence of civil rights opponents within their party. L. K. Jackson criticized RNC Chairman William Miller for ignoring "the groans, lamentations and prayers of the Negro for freedom, justice and equality." In his newspaper columns and public appearances, Jackie Robinson condemned Republicans who sought to win the South "by catering to the Dixiecrats and to the rightist policies of people like Barry Goldwater." In a speech at Yale University, George W. Lee censured Goldwater followers who "temporize and compromise upon the barriers of freedom for the negro," and seek to "drive negroes in the South from membership." Edward Brooke lamented that members of the GOP were "fighting for wrong" on the "absolutely clear-cut ethical issue" of civil rights. "At best," he claimed, Operation Dixie and courtship of conservative Southerners "were repudiations of the Lincoln tradition. At worst, they were appeals to naked racism."[24]

Perhaps because her name appeared on lists of North Carolina's most active Republicans, Helen Edmonds received mailings from William F. Buckley's *National Review*, one of the right's most influential publications. One advertisement touted the periodical as "the only Northern magazine that consistently upholds Southern liberties," and featured a defense of segregation headlined, "Why the South Must Prevail." Outraged, Edmonds wrote Buckley that she would never be "interested in your periodical . . . which seeks to support a point of view which deprives me as a human being of my God-given liberties and freedoms." She resented the implication that "the South" only referred to conservative whites, noting that millions of African Americans like herself were "bred and born" southerners. She concluded, "I cannot wish your magazine success," because of its efforts to set "one class of citizens apart from another."[25]

Edmonds received a reply from Maureen Buckley, William's sister, that typified the dismissive attitude of many conservatives toward black Republicans. Buckley argued that it was futile for the *National Review* to respond to Edmonds's charges, because her "emotionalism . . . reminded us of the practical impossibility of discussing the segregation issue rationally." The RNC similarly disregarded the concerns of African Americans, including Reynolds and Claiborne of its own Minorities Division, who were not even invited to strategy meetings. When George W. Lee warned Chairman Miller that avowed segregationists had removed him and other African Americans from southern Republican organizations, Miller disingenuously responded that the effort of Operation Dixie "satisfies me that our Party is doing everything possible to enlist support from all voters." Miller, whose committee amply funded the campaigns of outspoken segregationists, complained to black journalist Simeon Booker of the "badly mistaken . . . view among Negroes that the Democratic Party offers them more than does the Party of Abraham Lincoln," arguing that the GOP would only become "all-white" if "Negro leaders should themselves drum every last Negro into the Democratic Party."[26]

Miller's national committee itself, however, had drummed countless black Republicans out of GOP ranks. Not a single African American received an invitation to the RNC's 1963 annual meeting, prompting the moderate Republican editors of *Advance* magazine to claim that the gathering had been "deliberately contrived to give an impression of indifference to the Negro drive." The only African Americans present at the Denver summit were the waiters at a closed-door luncheon, where southern state chairmen had "boisterous conversation about 'niggers' and 'nigger-lovers,'" according to journalist Robert Novak. One northern state chairman noted his shock "that nobody criticized them for doing it and only a few of us were uncomfortable." When one official expressed concern that the party increasingly appealed to white supremacists, another retorted, "You have to remember that this isn't South Africa. The whites outnumber the Negroes 9 to 1." Held during the peak of the violent backlash against civil rights demonstrators in Birmingham, the conference did not address civil rights except for a brief statement criticizing President Kennedy for stoking racial violence.[27]

In reality, the president remained characteristically quiet as the civil rights movement in Birmingham dominated headlines in the spring of 1963. But as images of police dogs biting black protestors, and officers blasting black children with high-pressure water hoses, gripped the nation, Kennedy's cautious approach was no longer a viable strategy. On June 12, he appeared on national television to announce his support for sweeping civil rights legislation that, most notably, banned segregation in places of public accommodation, such as hotels, restaurants, and theaters. That same evening, a member of the Ku Klux Klan shot and killed Mississippi's most prominent civil rights icon, Medgar Evers. In August, more than a hundred thousand men and women, black and white, participated in the March on Washington, where they heard one of the twentieth century's most revered speeches. But, as much as Martin Luther King, Jr.'s "I Have a Dream" speech inspired activists, it also hardened the resolve of his opponents. On Sunday, September 15, Klansmen detonated explosives outside Birmingham's Sixteenth Street Baptist Church, killing four girls, ages eleven to fourteen. One month later, a nation beleaguered by years of internal strife and violence watched helplessly as television broadcasts delivered the news that President Kennedy had been assassinated during a visit to Texas. With the eyes of history upon him, Kennedy's successor, Lyndon Johnson, now freed from the limitations of southern politics, placed the passage of the civil rights bill at the forefront of his agenda.[28]

Eastern Establishment Republicans stressed the importance of unified GOP support for the bill. Richard Nixon cautioned that "it would be disastrous to the party in the long run" if conservatives voted against it, and Dwight Eisenhower emphasized the party's historic "obligation to be vigorous in the furtherance of civil rights." In the House of Representatives, John Lindsay and

William McCulloch guided the legislation through the Judiciary Committee, and Minority Leader Charles Halleck of Indiana, who had previously opposed similar bills, ensured that 80 percent of Republican congressmen supported the measure. Minority Leader Everett Dirksen led the charge in the Senate as twenty-seven of thirty-three Republicans backed the legislation. In the final tally, Republican senators far outpaced their Democratic counterparts in percentage support of the bill, and made up an essential bloc that broke a southern filibuster. Civil rights leaders openly acknowledged the GOP's crucial role. The NAACP's chief lobbyist, Clarence Mitchell, said of Republicans, "It is no exaggeration to say that this bill would not have become law without them," and Roy Wilkins claimed they "once more echoed Abraham Lincoln." Charles Evers later wrote, "It's a damn myth that all the real civil rights work was done by Democrats."[29]

To black Republicans, the bipartisan bill validated their argument that African Americans should embrace two-party politics as a means to pressure both sides to support civil rights. However, tragically for the GOP's image given the central role Republicans played in the bill's passage, the party's presidential frontrunner was among the six Republican senators who voted against the most significant civil rights measure of the century. Taking the advice of his legal advisors, William Rehnquist and Robert Bork, Barry Goldwater echoed segregationists in calling the bill unconstitutional, a "usurpation" of federal power against states and private business owners, and a "threat to the very essence of our basic system." While he stressed he remained morally opposed to segregation, he argued, "I don't feel an unconstitutional law that strikes at the freedoms of everyone will solve the problems of a few." On July 2, less than two weeks before Goldwater's nomination at the Republican National Convention, President Johnson signed the Civil Rights Act of 1964, officially casting his administration firmly against the segregationist South.[30]

Entering into the primary season, not only did Goldwater have an organizational advantage, but the most popular Eastern Establishment candidate, Henry Cabot Lodge, Jr., declined to run. Goldwater's opponents eventually coalesced behind Nelson Rockefeller, the namesake of the party's liberal wing. Though Rockefeller's highly publicized divorce and controversial remarriage had been the fodder of tabloids in 1963, he had some of the party's strongest ties to both industry and labor, and promised to expand the party's reach based on his past support of social programs in housing, education, and welfare. Like other establishment figures, he did not join conservatives in

unilaterally opposing "big government." Rather, even though some of his programs could be hard to distinguish from those of Democrats, Rockefeller emphasized the ideal of "good government," one not corrupted by machine
politics or bogged down by bureaucratic inefficiency. And while he relished
his role as the one "pushing the party forward," Rockefeller still had GOP
bona fides, particularly his connections to Wall Street and hard-line anticom-
munist foreign policy. The middle-class leadership of the civil rights movement also held Rockefeller in high esteem. *Jet* magazine devoted a 1962
edition to a glowing overview of his civil rights record, and Charles Evers
claimed Rockefeller "was the kind of powerful white man that I'd always been
looking for." Roy Wilkins noted that the governor was a lone "exception"
among national politicians, one the NAACP could rely on as an unwavering
"friend."[31]

Rockefeller's campaign made direct appeals to African Americans, and
campaign literature featured photographs of him with Martin Luther King.
Jackie Robinson resigned as vice president of Chock full o'Nuts Coffee to
work for Rockefeller's campaign as a deputy director. In public appearances,
he warned Republicans that Goldwater "will set back the course of the country," and that Rockefeller could "make the Democrats live up to some of their
promises" on civil rights. After winning West Virginia and Oregon, Rockefeller set his sights on the delegate-rich state of California, where he described
Goldwater's ideology as "an extremism outside the main currents of American political life." Black Republicans held well-attended rallies, raised money
in Elk lodges, and formed Independent-Citizens for Rockefeller to recruit
African Americans. By election day, Rockefeller's campaign manager estimated that fifty thousand blacks had registered with the Republican Party.
Goldwater, however, had a mobilized and well connected base in the massive
suburbs of southern California, and Rockefeller narrowly lost the pivotal
state by less than sixty thousand votes, out of a total of two million cast.
Though Goldwater won only three counties, Los Angeles, Orange, and San
Diego, his victory ensured that California, one of the largest and most diverse
states in the Union, would send an all-white delegation to the national
convention.[32]

An infamously fickle candidate, Rockefeller dropped out of the race after
the loss. But, although Goldwater's victory put him well ahead in the delegate
count, it did not indicate widespread support for the conservative icon among
the party's rank and file. When an April 1964 Gallup poll asked Republicans
whom they would most like to see nominated as president, only 15 percent

named Goldwater; 52 percent named Rockefeller, Lodge, Romney, or Scranton, all liberals on civil rights with support among African Americans. Outraged by Goldwater's opposition to the Civil Rights Act, Governor Scranton stepped into the race and launched a "stop-Goldwater" bid with Rockefeller's endorsement just five weeks before the national convention. Though too late to win any primaries, he hoped that his campaign could sway delegates who agreed with him that Goldwater's extremism represented "a weird parody of Republicanism."[33]

Conservatives, however, had a three-year head start packing state delegations with Goldwater supporters. Eliminating Black-and-Tan remnants from southern delegations was essential to this strategy. South Carolina's state party, which had been open to black inclusion in the 1950s, issued a report in the early 1960s boasting that "not a single Negro showed any interest" in the party, which "was welcomed by new Party leaders as victory in the South at any level could never be achieved by a Negro dominated party." Georgia's Republican Party continued to welcome black participation through the early 1960s, and an African American served as vice chairman of the state party. One white official bragged that the GOP was one of only two "integrated public organization[s] in the state." At the 1963 state party convention, the Fulton County Republican Committee proposed a platform endorsing black equality. Not only was the statement rejected, but the delegation from Atlanta was not prepared for the onslaught of conservatives who had only recently become interested in the mechanics of party gatherings. Whereas previous state conventions had averaged fewer than four hundred participants, conservatives, including many former Democrats, filled the convention with more than fifteen hundred delegates. By the final day, they had removed every single black leader from power, including John H. Calhoun, the man who delivered Atlanta's black vote to Nixon in 1960. For the first time in forty years, Georgia's delegation to the Republican National Convention was entirely white. One of the party's new officials proclaimed, "The Negro has been read out of the Republican Party of Georgia here today," and members celebrated with an all-white banquet.[34]

That same year, conservatives in Memphis successfully removed George W. Lee's white ally, Millsaps Fitzhugh, as chairman of the city's Republican Party. Refusing to concede without a fight, Lee swore that it would be a "vice . . . to sit by lifeless when an evil thing walks the earth," and attended the March 1964 Shelby County Republican Convention. Still maintaining a base among the city's black middle class, Lee's Lincoln League had sixty-five

precinct clubs as late as 1963. When the county convention began, he arose
from the audience, denounced the party's conservative leadership, and led
one hundred and eighty black Republicans outside the convention hall to
conduct their own "rump convention." The group elected an alternate Republican committee, and chose Lee and Benjamin Hooks as delegates to the national convention.[35]

Two months later, Lee took two busloads of African Americans to the
state convention in Nashville to protest Shelby County's first all-white delegation in decades. In a closed-door session, reporters outside could hear him
shouting that African Americans in Memphis had "stood first for the Republican Party for 50 years.... If you abandon the Negro to the Democratic
Party, it will be a travesty." He also documented a number of "irregularities,"
alleging that his opponents violated state party rules by sending white delegates to the state convention from black precincts that did not even hold elections. In one precinct that allegedly held an election, conservatives moved its
polling place to a segregated hotel located outside precinct boundaries. The
following day of the state convention, Goldwater supporters flooded Nashville's War Memorial Auditorium, initially barring African Americans from
even stepping onto the convention floor. Lee's old Black-and-Tan friends
from eastern Tennessee intervened, granted him permission to attend, and
implored their colleagues to not abandon the state party's tradition of inter-
racial cooperation. Their appeal to seat Lee's delegation was ultimately rejected by the executive committee.[36]

Undeterred, Lee believed he was "fighting for a cause that is bigger than
this state," and began work on a final appeal at the Republican National Convention. He felt that a floor fight over the Tennessee delegation at the convention would "dramatize our fight for freedom," and "expose the efforts of
turncoat Democrats . . . who are moving heaven and hell to take over the Republican Party in this area and follow the Goldwater line." Finding evidence
that members of the Shelby County delegation had affiliations with racist organizations like the White Citizens' Council and the John Birch Society, he
reached out to high-profile party leaders to describe his efforts "to keep the
Republican Party from wrapping itself in a blanket of ultra-conservatism."
More than just infighting between local rivals, he claimed his "contest represents the Negro's fight all over the nation to save the Republican Party."[37]

The Eastern Establishment rallied behind Lee's cause. William Scranton
personally paid a prominent white lawyer from Knoxville to present Lee's
appeal to the national convention, and Henry Cabot Lodge claimed the

Memphis Republican had been "railroaded" by conservatives "because he's a Negro." On the first day of the national convention in San Francisco, the Rules Committee voted down a proposal by Scranton supporters that would have rejected delegations elected through procedures that had the "purpose or effect" of racial discrimination. Lee's allies then took the matter before the Credentials Committee, where all three major television networks dispatched cameramen to the nearly four-hour hearing. Taking the stand, Lee affirmed, "I am Republican born and I am Republican bred, and I shall stay Republican until I am dead and gone," and emphasized his desire to represent southern blacks who believed in the party's "great record . . . in the matter of civil rights." His opponents from the Shelby County Republican Association argued that if the committee seated Lee, "we would be handing the Democrats a powerful weapon that could cost us" the election, and warned "any agreement or accommodation with Mr. Lee can result in no benefit to the Republican Party . . . and most assuredly will result in the active disapproval of those Republicans who have worked so long and so hard to reform the Republican Party in Shelby County." In this case, "reform" signified the removal of African Americans and their white allies.[38]

Split along Goldwater-Scranton lines, the Credentials Committee ruled against Lee, with the result that at the same time as Tennessee Democrats elected black delegates for the first time in their party's history, the state's Republican Party would send its first all-white delegation to the national convention since the turn of the century. "To add insult to injury," the *Pittsburgh Courier* commented, the new caucus of southern Republicans named their hotel headquarters "Fort Sumter," after the Confederate assault that launched the Civil War, and Jack Craddock, who would later become chairman of the Republican Party of Memphis, proudly called his organization "a white Republican party." Later reminiscing on his efforts against Lee in San Francisco, Craddock remarked, "We loved it because it was all on TV. They seated our delegates. Lee sort of went fishing after that. . . . That's when the party came around."[39]

After Lee's defeat, Scranton's supporters turned their attention to the party's platform, and introduced amendments that called for additional civil rights legislation and condemned "extremist groups," including a bastion of Goldwater support, the John Birch Society. Refusing to compromise with liberals on the platform as Richard Nixon had done in 1960, Goldwater appeared at the Platform Committee's final hearing to personally advocate an unamended platform, which noticeably did not endorse the recently passed

Civil Rights Act. Rather, it only pledged to "enforce" the law, as already required of the next president by his oath of office. When it came time for the committee's only black member, George A. Parker of Washington, D.C., to speak, he turned to Goldwater and bemoaned his vote with segregationists against the Civil Rights Act, in a move that "forsook all your colleagues." Parker then asked the senator how he could "in good faith" enforce the bill as president while openly doubting its constitutionality. Offended, Goldwater lashed out at Parker for "questioning my integrity," but an unfazed Parker responded, "I request your frankness in answering my question." Goldwater reiterated his belief in the bill's unconstitutionality, and emphasized that discrimination would never be "solved by law." A black reporter described Goldwater's demeanor as "chilling and aloof," and black Republicans William Nunn and John Clay observed that he "visibly showed his deep disturbance over the fact that Parker had the nerve to question his position on civil rights."[40]

Scranton's civil rights and anti-extremism amendments had little chance of passage. Determined to write an unyieldingly conservative platform, Goldwater's supporters successfully changed procedural rules so that subcommittees would no longer create their own planks, which together would form the larger platform. Instead, the Platform Committee's executive committee, stacked with Goldwater supporters, now held the final say on each issue. The final platform did not endorse the Civil Rights Act or any additional legislation to protect African Americans. It did, however, express opposition to discrimination against white citizens through "Federally sponsored 'inverse discrimination' whether by the shifting of jobs or the abandonment of neighborhood schools for reasons of race." Pleased with the final draft, Goldwater praised the unamended platform as an expression of the party's new "conservative majority."[41]

Finally in control of the party's most powerful committees, and inspired by the GOP's first staunchly conservative presidential nominee in decades, Goldwater delegates sought to humiliate their establishment enemies at the convention in San Francisco's Cow Palace. Dwight Eisenhower was "bitterly ashamed" of the behavior of Goldwater supporters, who he alleged "molested" his niece with insults. Conservatives intentionally delayed proceedings so that Nelson Rockefeller could not deliver his convention address until midnight, or 3:00 a.m. on the East Coast. When the New York governor finally stepped on stage, a steady stream of boos interrupted him for a solid three minutes. Black delegates faced similar disrespectful treatment from members of their own party. Jackie Robinson wrote that African Americans "distinguished in their communities, identified with the cause of Republicanism . . . had no real standing in the convention, no clout. They were unimportant and ignored." The vice chairman of the D.C. Republican Committee, Elaine Jenkins, similarly recalled, "There was *no* inclusion of black Republicans as a group at the convention. White staffers treated the few of us present as truly non-existent or invisible." On one occasion, Goldwater's "Junior Sergeant at Arms" blocked four black men from entering the convention floor, including Edward Brooke, one of the most powerful public officials in Massachusetts. It was not until a Nixon associate, John Ehrlichman, intervened on their behalf that they were granted entry.[42]

African Americans in attendance even faced verbal and physical abuse. George W. Lee had to be escorted from Scranton headquarters to an undisclosed motel after receiving death threats during his contest against Memphis conservatives. When Clarence Townes, the only African American in Virginia's delegation, cast his vote for Rockefeller, he "was forced to flee from the convention hall in company with television newscasters to escape angry conservatives." A group of men in the Cow Palace public gallery similarly chased off radio journalist Belva Davis and her news director from the proceedings, shouting, "What the hell are you niggers doing in here?" and "Get out of here, boy! You too nigger bitch." As Davis and her colleague hurriedly packed their equipment, the hecklers pelted them with "wadded up convention programs, mustard-soaked hotdogs, [and] half-eaten Snickers bars." In one of the most shocking events of the convention, William P. Young, Pennsylvania secretary of labor and industry, noticed smoke coming from his clothes after a heated exchange with a group of Goldwater delegates. After burning his hand to extinguish the flames, he discovered four holes burned into his suit jacket from a lit cigar placed in his pocket by an unknown assailant. The event was witnessed live by television cameras and reporters on scene. Shortly thereafter, one southern entrepreneur began selling "Goldwater Cigars," which included a card that read, "These cigars can be used in many ways. . . . Some Republican People at the San Francisco Convention Slipped a Lighted Cigar Into a Negro Delegate's Pocket! They Say He Seemed to Get the Idea That He Wasn't Wanted. And He Left the Room in a Hurry!"[43]

The events at Cow Palace confirmed many black Republicans' worst fears about their party. Edward Brooke described the convention as "an exercise in manipulation by a zealous organization which operated with a militancy, a lack of toleration, at times a ruthlessness totally alien to Republican

Figure 9. Clarence Townes, a delegate from Virginia at the 1964 Republican National Conventions, holds a sign featuring Nelson A. Rockefeller. 306-RC-2-4-12, National Archives and Records Administration.

Figure 10. Jackie Robinson is interviewed at the 1964 Republican National Convention in San Francisco. 306-RC-2-2-13, National Archives and Records Administration.

practices." In a convention hall filled with Confederate flags waved by southern delegations, one African American remarked, "It's clear to me . . . that
this taking over of our party is based on resentment of civil rights advances."
Other black delegates compared the spectacle to "downtown Birmingham"
and described the crowd as "an ocean of hatred and bigotry." Sandy Ray of
New York lamented that his party had become home to "extremists, racists,
crackpots, and rightists. What we experienced at the convention television
onlookers could not believe." Jackie Robinson declared, "As I watched this
steamroller operation in San Francisco, I had a better understanding of how
it must have felt to be a Jew in Hitler's Germany."[44]

Scranton's last-ditch campaign failed, and Goldwater easily secured the
GOP nomination. Although a July poll of registered Republicans found that
60 percent favored Scranton, conventions are not democratic proceedings,
and Goldwater had a firm grasp over delegates. Southern delegations, who
under Black-and-Tans had previously supported the victorious Eastern Establishment candidates Wendell Willkie, Thomas Dewey, and Dwight Eisenhower, cast over 97 percent of their votes for Goldwater under their newfound
all-white leadership. By refusing to slate African Americans as delegates even
from diverse states like California, and replacing black leaders in Georgia and
Tennessee with conservative whites, Goldwater's forces had reduced black
representation at the national convention to its lowest numbers in over fifty
years. Especially disconcerting to moderates was that 7 percent of the convention's thirteen hundred convention delegates were members of the anti-
civil rights John Birch Society, while only 1 percent, or fourteen individuals,
were African American. Conversely, the 1964 Democratic convention featured a record sixty-five black delegates.[45]

In his acceptance speech, Goldwater rejected another opportunity to rec-
oncile with moderates and liberals. Although civil rights had been the nation's most pressing domestic issue for the past four years, the nominee did
not make a single reference to the movement. He identified communism and
an ever-expanding federal government as the primary threats to American
"liberty," but conspicuously left Jim Crow off the list. He used the words "free"
and "freedom" twenty-six times, though none referred to the ongoing struggle for black equality that raged in the South. The same summer as Goldwater
delivered his convention speech, four civil rights activists had been murdered, eighty had been beaten, and sixty-seven black churches, homes, and
businesses had been burned or bombed, in Mississippi alone. Goldwater was
silent on this wave of violence in the South in his convention speech, and yet

railed against violence in the "streets" of northern cities. He also expressed his disdain for moderate Republicans, who had so often dismissed him as an extremist, and famously proclaimed, "Extremism in the defense of liberty is no vice! And . . . moderation in the pursuit of justice is no virtue!" For his running mate, Goldwater named RNC chairman William Miller, the man responsible for crippling the Minorities Division and emboldening racial conservatives through Operation Dixie.[46]

Despite efforts to alienate African Americans at the convention, they refused to withdraw quietly without a fight. According to *Jet*, black Republicans "poured out in numbers" to attend an anti-Goldwater rally led by Jackie Robinson and the Congress of Racial Equality. The rally, whose participants also included Nelson Rockefeller, Henry Cabot Lodge, George Romney, Jacob Javits, and Kenneth Keating, culminated in a forty-thousand-person march from Market Street to Cow Palace. On July 15, African Americans assembled at the Fairmont Hotel to discuss protest strategies. Temporarily naming themselves the Negro Republican Organization (NRO), the group issued a statement read by William Young to the press. "We have no confidence" in Goldwater's "ability to enforce" the civil rights bill, they announced, and pledged to "defeat that minority segment" of the GOP, "which appears determined to establish a lily-white Republican party." They further vowed "to return to our home communities . . . to work for the building of a strong Republican party that truly reflects the established ideals and traditions of support for civil rights." At the convention, the NRO distributed copies of their statement, alongside other anti-Goldwater literature that described how his supporters openly discriminated against "Negroes, Jews, and Catholics" in their selection of delegates.[47]

Jackie Robinson called for a coordinated NRO walkout from the convention floor, but George Parker cautioned that because of their small numbers, "It would look as if they were just going out to lunch." They ultimately agreed to stage a "walk around" instead of a walkout, hoping that television cameras would broadcast their protest. The demonstration occurred as the convention began counting verbal votes for the presidential nominee. Marching the perimeter of the convention floor, NRO members carried signs that read "We Protest the GOP Civil Rights Plank" and "We Are Not Walking Out But In & Around." However, a counter-protest soon eclipsed the demonstration, and journalists found it difficult to see the marchers amid "a tunnel of Goldwater banners, signs, pennants, streamers, and flying hats." As the confrontation between the black marchers and Goldwater delegates intensified, George

Fleming, an alternate delegate from New Jersey, stormed out of the hall in tears. When asked by reporters what happened, he said, "They called me a nigger," and claimed that other black delegates "had been shoved, pushed, spat on, and cursed with a liberal sprinkling of racial epithets."[48]

Though marginalized at the national convention, black Republicans' protests demonstrated their continued fight for the future of their party. The strategic importance of the "two-party system" still held a central place in their rationale. Grant Reynolds even blamed African Americans for Goldwater's nomination, suggesting that had only a fraction of black Democrats in California temporarily switched parties to vote in the GOP primary for Nelson Rockefeller, they "could have changed the entire political complexion of the nation. . . . We've got to do something about all of us being in one party." Jackie Robinson, whose newspaper columns often centered on his revulsion toward the Republican right, argued at a 1964 fundraising dinner for New York Republicans that he equally abhorred "the attitude of the Democrats who believe they have the Negro in their pocket." The rest of his remarks then turned to the need for African Americans to use the two-party system to pressure both parties into taking stronger stands on behalf of black voters. Even in the midst of George W. Lee's unsuccessful campaign for black representation inside Tennessee's GOP, he continued to stress that "it would be fatal for the Negro . . . to abandon the Republican Party and go over whole soul to the Democrats." In so doing, blacks would lose their "bargaining power."[49]

To the black delegates who formed the NRO, leaving the party was not an option. The hostile national convention provided motivation to continue their fight against an uncompromising conservative movement. As Sandy Ray declared after the convention, "If we sit quietly and allow this band of racists to take over the party, we not only signal the end of the party of freedom, we also help to bring about the total destruction of America through racism." When asked in 1968 if he had ever considered leaving the GOP, George W. Lee somberly replied, "during my Goldwater fight in San Francisco . . . I was a lone individual down there," but he never thought of ever leaving the GOP, because "somebody had to stay there in the Republican Party and fight, and fight, and fight with the hope that the Republican Party wouldn't be made a party of ultra-conservatism and further than that, a party for the white man." This would be the fight of black Republicans for years to come.[50]

CHAPTER 6

Fighting the Enemy Within:
Black Republicans in the Wake of Goldwater

"We are going to work like hell . . . for those people who have given substantial support to our efforts to achieve first-class citizenship. And we are going to work within the framework of the Republican Party," William P. Young declared on behalf of black delegates after Barry Goldwater's nomination. Soon after the 1964 national convention, Young, Grant Reynolds, Clarence Townes, Jr., and other delegates who had formed the impromptu Negro Republican Organization called for black Republicans across the country to attend an August conference in Philadelphia "to create a new atmosphere within . . . the Republican Party that will make it unmistakably clear that the Negro is needed, wanted and welcome." The fifty who attended named themselves the National Negro Republican Assembly (NNRA). While denouncing Goldwater, they still believed two-party politics were "vital" to black progress, and promised to work for "Republican candidates whose concepts are compatible with ours."[1]

By 1965, after Goldwater lost the general election to Lyndon Johnson in one of the most crushing defeats in presidential history, liberal, moderate, and conservative Republicans competed for control of a disoriented party. Like other factions inside the GOP, African Americans sought to exploit this state of instability and soul searching, and partnered with members of the Eastern Establishment seeking to reestablish civil rights as a central tenet of the party. Though the damage done by Goldwater was severe, the mid-1960s were a time of continued viability for a moderate strain of Republicanism that reached out to black voters on civil rights. The party's decisively conservative, and predominantly white, future was far from guaranteed, as moderate and liberal Republicans continued to corral significant black support in the voting booth, and as black Republicans continued to fight for their civil rights agenda as elected politicians, advisors, and activists.

At its Philadelphia convention, the NNRA elected John H. Clay, an active member of Philadelphia's GOP, as executive director and George G. Fleming, a New Jersey life insurance executive, as president. In his passionate keynote address, Fleming voiced the indignation of black Republicans across the country toward the Goldwater wing, proclaiming, "We are here to let it be known throughout this land that we have looked upon the face of the enemy within . . . and we have understood his danger to the party of Abraham Lincoln." Emphasizing the importance of the two-party system to black progress, he continued, "We are here to raise an army led by Negroes . . . to defeat those who have infiltrated the party and are seeking to drive the Negro out." He feared that if black Republicans deserted the GOP, "progress toward human dignity cannot be maintained or advanced," because it would allow one party "to put the Negro vote in its pocket."[2]

Similarly, during the fall campaign, Clay and Grant Reynolds sent form letters on organization letterhead imploring fellow black Republicans "to resist any effort to drive them out of the Republican Party" and to join the NNRA, which sought "to salvage their Republican Heritage." In September, the organization held a southern conference in Richmond, Virginia, and worked with the city's Crusade for Voters in registering record numbers of African Americans. Prior to the election, the NNRA issued a press release, covered by newspapers across the country, listing its endorsement of forty-one Republican senators, congressmen, and governors who openly embraced civil rights. Given the vast unpopularity of Goldwater, the NNRA remained small, but within four months of the August convention it had grown to two hundred fifty members, with chapters in more than twenty-five states.[3]

Many black Republicans outside the NNRA also refused to support Goldwater. A September poll of thirty-five black Republicans in five major cities found only three who would even consider voting for their party's nominee. Chester Gillespie of Ohio's Republican State Central Committee publicly stated that no "Negro with any self-respect can vote for Goldwater," who should be "disowned and excommunicated by our party." Edward W. Brooke, running for reelection as attorney general of Massachusetts, and James Flournoy, the black vice president of the California Republican Assembly, both refused to campaign for Goldwater. Jesse Carter, a member of West Virginia's State Executive Committee, similarly declined to endorse the party's nominee, and G. E. Ferguson, who served in Charleston's local party, claimed

Goldwater "will destroy the image of the Republican Party." Harold C. Burton, the veteran black delegate from New York, told reporters, "I'd rather be lynched than vote for this guy."[4]

Even the traditionally nonpartisan civil rights establishment publicly opposed the Republican nominee. Martin Luther King, Jr., Roy Wilkins, John Lewis, James Farmer, A. Philip Randolph, and Whitney Young, Jr., called for a moratorium on demonstrations until after the election, so that the full attention of the movement could be focused on voter registration to ensure Goldwater's defeat. At the National Urban League annual conference, a gathering that had favorably treated Republican candidates in the past, Young alleged that Goldwater "has no consideration of sympathy for the plight of Negroes," and that his victory would be "a mistake from which the Nation may never recover." For the first time in its fifty-five-year history, the NAACP explicitly rejected a presidential nominee. They were careful, however, to emphasize that their opposition to Goldwater did not apply to his entire party, and they simultaneously endorsed a number of Republican allies, such as John Lindsay, William McCulloch, and Hugh Scott. Even one of the most adamantly nonpartisan black leaders, Martin Luther King, Jr., told crowds, "I'm not going to tell you who to vote for . . . but I will tell you who I'm not going to vote for." To him, Goldwater was "the most dangerous man in America," whose campaign "gave aid and comfort to the most vicious racists" and showed "dangerous signs of Hitlerism."[5]

While black Republicans' rhetoric centered on their opposition to Goldwater, some actively supported President Johnson. The Central Ward Young Republicans of Newark, New Jersey, and the United Republican Club of Harlem, both predominantly black and Puerto Rican organizations, worked for their party on the state level, but publicly endorsed Johnson. Crispus Wright, a former congressional candidate in California who served as a vice chairman of the Richard Nixon for Governor Committee in 1962, created a national organization named "Republicans for Johnson." He believed that by supporting the president, black Republicans could "repudiate once and for all the ultraconservative wing of the party." The group attracted some of the biggest black Republican names of the era, with Jackie Robinson becoming its national chairman, and Hobson Reynolds, the Grand Exalted Ruler of the black Elks, serving as head of its eastern division. In his nationwide speaking tour and syndicated columns, Robinson stressed his continued support of liberal Republicans, while repeating that Goldwater was a "bigot" and "advocate of white supremacy."[6]

Some distinguished black Republicans completely abandoned the party after the national convention. Archibald Carey, Jr., the most prominent black Republican of the 1950s, endorsed Nelson Rockefeller and William Scranton in the primaries, and considered backing the Republican slate of local candidates in Illinois after Goldwater's nomination. But, after "agonizing deliberation," he decided to officially join the Democratic Party, because the "image" of the Republican Party had so badly deteriorated. He subsequently traveled across the country on a tour sponsored by the Democratic National Committee. Veteran NAACP lawyer James Nabrit, another prominent Chicago resident who had been "a Republican all my life," also switched parties and vowed to work for the entire slate of Illinois Democrats. In the South, Benjamin Hooks of Memphis "left the Republican Party for good" after George W. Lee was denied a seat at the national convention. Hooks would spend the next decade as a major figure in Tennessee's Democratic Party, and succeeded Roy Wilkins as head of the NAACP in 1977.[7]

Shortly after the national convention, a Goldwater ally, Dean Burch, replaced William Miller as chairman of the Republican National Committee. In one of his first acts, Burch shut down the Minorities Division and fired Grant Reynolds, who had become increasingly active in the anti-Goldwater NNRA. Clay Claiborne, however, agreed to stay on board as Burch's "special assistant." Early in the fall campaign, Claiborne created a short brochure that attacked Johnson's civil rights record in Congress. However, fearing that such a publication might alienate Goldwater's segregationist supporters, who *wanted* to link the president to civil rights, the national committee refused to print the document. Claiborne then printed over fifty thousand copies of a brochure entitled "What About Civil Rights and Barry Goldwater," which emphasized the Arizona senator's personal objections to racism. Again concerned with its reception in the South, the RNC halted distribution before he could disperse even half the copies.[8]

Rather than abandoning Goldwater, Claiborne changed his tactics to accommodate campaign strategy. In one of the more underhanded events of the 1964 election, he circulated 1.4 million simulated telegrams from a fictitious "Committee for Negroes in Government," which urged African Americans to write in Martin Luther King, Jr.'s name for president. King denounced the leaflets as a blatant attempt to take black votes away from Johnson, and journalists quickly traced them to a New Jersey printing company linked to Claiborne. The NNRA publicly demanded his termination from the national committee, and apologized to King "on behalf of those within the Republican

Party who will refuse to surrender . . . to racist elements." Claiborne remained on the RNC's staff, but spent the next two years in court fighting an indictment for violating New Jersey election statutes.[9]

While many black Republicans endorsed Johnson or abstained from backing either candidate, a small number joined Claiborne in supporting Goldwater. Most were marginal figures in both Republican circles and their communities. The most prominent was George Schuyler, a leftist-turned-conservative associate editor of the *Pittsburgh Courier*, who openly backed Goldwater in his columns, which also criticized the objectives and strategies of the civil rights movement. A member of the John Birch Society, Schuyler ran on the Conservative Party ticket against Congressman Adam Clayton Powell in 1964. Alvin Smith, the publisher of an obscure Ohio newspaper, also endorsed Goldwater's presidential bid. Unlike Schuyler, Smith maintained he "whole-heartedly" supported civil rights, but believed President Johnson was a hypocrite who "uses the Negro for selfish political gain." Goldwater also received positive coverage from the black-owned *Arizona Tribune*, published by a personal friend and neighbor, Edward Banks, who felt the senator had been unfairly labeled a racist. However, as the campaign progressed, Banks became increasingly "bothered" by Goldwater's positions, and ultimately refused to write an official editorial endorsement for his longtime friend.[10]

At the outset of the fall campaign, Goldwater announced, "I don't even intend to talk about civil rights," and issues of race were indeed ignored in most of his campaign rhetoric. This was not true, however, of his base. A Republican worker in Arkansas's Goldwater headquarters attached pictures to car windshields of President Johnson meeting with African Americans, and Republicans in Alabama, Louisiana, and Texas printed literature distributed in black neighborhoods that claimed they could be arrested for voting if they had unresolved traffic violations or a past criminal record. Goldwater also received the endorsement of the head of Georgia's Ku Klux Klan. An Alabama Klan leader told a three-hundred-person rally, "I like Barry Goldwater. I believe what he believes in. I think the same way he thinks." The Grand Dragon of South Carolina's Klan sat on stage behind Goldwater during a campaign speech in Spartanburg. Though Goldwater ultimately rejected Klan endorsements, his running mate, William Miller, refused to do the same, claiming he would "accept the support of any American citizen who believes in our posture." National Committee Chairman Burch similarly told viewers of NBC's *Today* show, "we're not in the business of discouraging votes," when asked about Klan endorsements. In additional to dismantling the Minorities Division, Burch also allowed portraits of Abraham Lincoln and Dwight Eisenhower to be removed from RNC headquarters, lest the GOP be associated with its two most prominent figures linked to civil rights.[11]

Many white Republicans, including George Romney, Kenneth Keating, and John Lindsay, joined African Americans in refusing to endorse Goldwater. On election day, half the Republicans in New England voted for Johnson, who became the first Democrat to ever win the state of Vermont. Indeed, Goldwater's only victories came in his home state of Arizona and five states in the Deep South where many African Americans still could not vote. He became the first Republican presidential candidate to receive the majority of the southern white vote, including 87 percent in Mississippi. On the other hand, well over 90 percent of black voters in the metropolitan areas of Arkansas, Florida, Tennessee, Virginia, and North Carolina helped secure Johnson's victory in the peripheral South. Across much of the South, Goldwater acquired less than 1 percent of the black vote, including in Tennessee and Georgia, bastions of black Republicanism less than eight years earlier. Nationally, he received a dismal 6 percent of the black vote. Johnson won over 60 percent of the entire nation's vote in the largest margin of victory in American history.[12]

Though it was a banner year for Democrats, moderate and liberal Republican candidates fared better than the national ticket. Every single Republican congressman who voted for the Civil Rights Act of 1964 was reelected, and almost half who opposed it were defeated. While 65 percent of voters in Pennsylvania voted for Johnson, Republican Senator Hugh Scott was handily reelected. In Massachusetts, Edward W. Brooke won his race for attorney general by the largest plurality of any Republican in the history of the state. Other liberals, however, did not survive the Democratic landslide. Senator Kenneth Keating lost his seat in New York to Robert Kennedy, and Robert Taft, Jr., who was far more liberal than his father on almost every issue, narrowly lost his senatorial race in Ohio. Illinois gubernatorial candidate Charles Percy publicly blamed his defeat on Republicans who used the party "as a means to promote hate and bigotry."[13]

Although individual Republicans may have received support from African Americans in 1964, the nomination of one of the most prominent opponents of the Civil Rights Act left a lasting impression on African Americans. When a 1962 National Election Studies poll asked white and black respondents which party was more likely "to see to it that Negroes get fair treatment in jobs and housing," 55.9 percent said there was no difference between the parties, 22.7 percent said Democrats, and 21.3 percent said Republicans. When asked the same question in 1964, 33 percent said no difference, 60 percent said Democrats, and only 7 percent said Republicans, despite significant GOP support for the Civil Rights Act in Congress. The year of Goldwater's nomination, 94 percent of new black voters in Baltimore, a border city with a previously strong black Republican base, registered as Democrats. Similar Democratic registration patterns were seen across the South, where the number of registered black voters grew exponentially in the mid-1960s. While large numbers of southern blacks in the 1950s and early 1960s still identified as Republican, particularly when compared to their northern counterparts, after 1964 there was virtually no geographic difference in black Democratic registration between North and South.[14]

At the same time that conservative opposition to civil rights became synonymous with the GOP in the minds of black voters, so too did Lyndon Johnson's Great Society, which included civil rights and a sweeping War on Poverty, become the defining expression of the Democratic Party. While southern racists were still represented in the Democratic caucus, President Johnson set his party on the side of traditionally marginalized voters, especially African Americans and the poor. Moreover, while middle-class African Americans who could vote in the South in the 1940s and 1950s had found a welcome home in the Republican Party of Memphis, Atlanta, and other southern cities, many of the new southern GOP organizations of the 1960s often worked explicitly to keep blacks out. The Democratic Party, which already included African Americans in its northern coalition, and whose president was the politician most closely associated with civil rights, was a natural fit for newly registered black voters in the South. As more African Americans entered into the ranks of southern Democratic parties after the passage of the Voting Rights Act of 1965, many conservative whites saw the GOP as a better alternative, intensifying the ideological outlook and lily-white nature of southern Republican organizations.

Moderate Republicans of both races saw Goldwater's loss as a rejection of conservatism, and called for the party to reclaim its civil rights legacy. Soon after the election, Massachusetts Attorney General Edward Brooke declared that moderate whites and blacks must "take back the State GOP organizations in the South," and the NNRA redoubled its mission "to prevent control of the Republican party by racist elements among the Goldwater supporters." The Ripon Society, a predominantly white organization headquartered in

Harvard Square, issued well publicized position papers that insisted the party address "the shortage of capable Negro Republicans" in leadership. Ripon even adopted many of the NNRA's positions in a 1965 report, *Republicans and the Negro Revolution*, which offered a seven-point program to improve the GOP's relationship with black voters, and proposed a southern strategy that centered on the rapidly expanding black electorate. Another group, Republicans for Progress, whose leaders included Grant Reynolds and Henry Cabot Lodge, Jr., similarly called for Republicans to focus on newly registered African Americans and place civil rights at the forefront of their southern strategy. Also under the leadership of Reynolds, the Council of Republican Organizations (CRO) served as an umbrella organization that represented the NNRA, Ripon, and other Republican groups opposed to Goldwater's brand of conservatism. In 1966, the CRO partnered with the Leadership Conference on Civil Rights in sharing memos to help their lobbying of Republicans on issues of civil rights.[15]

Still reeling from Goldwater's defeat, and under intense pressure from moderates and liberals, the Republican National Committee replaced Chairman Burch in January 1965 with Ray Bliss, a former state chairman of Ohio's GOP who had had success in urban areas. As a pragmatic moderate, Bliss sought a big-tent party that included both conservatives and liberals, with the RNC serving as a mediator between factions. This approach included reconciliation with black Republicans, and he met with a delegation of NNRA leaders early in his tenure. In February 1966, he created the Negro Advisory Committee, whose twelve members included NNRA leaders George Fowler and James Flournoy. Two months later, Bliss reactivated the Minorities Division and named Clarence Townes, Jr., as its director. An insurance company executive, Townes had joined the Republican Party of Virginia in the 1950s to protest Democratic resistance to school desegregation, and had worked with the Crusade for Voters, Student Nonviolent Coordinating Committee (SNCC), and NAACP in registering black voters in Richmond. In 1965, he served as special assistant to the head of Virginia's GOP, the highest position attained by an African American in either of the state's parties since Reconstruction. That fall, Republicans fielded Townes as a candidate for the Virginia House of Delegates, and gave him a $30,000 budget. Despite support from party bosses and 300 campaign volunteers, Townes lost the general election to a conservative write-in candidate.[16]

While Townes was among the few remaining African Americans with allies inside a southern Republican organization, and had cofounded the

Figure 11: Vince Callahan (center, left) and Clarence Townes (center, right) canvass black voters in Virginia circa mid-1960s. Clarence L. Townes Jr. Papers, M293, Special Collections and Archives, James Branch Cabell Library, Virginia Commonwealth University.

NNRA, his nomination drew the ire of Grant Reynolds, who claimed Bliss ignored other black leaders, including himself, because they were "too aggressive and outspoken." Alternately, Reynolds believed that Townes was too cautious and measured in his critiques of the party. These claims were not without merit. Townes supported civil rights and personally sided with liberals, but his personality did not lend itself to public displays of outrage. A behind-the-scenes tactician, Townes was even willing to curry favor with conservatives to maintain influence. For example, he sent an unprompted letter to Barry Goldwater soon after the 1964 campaign, in which he claimed, "I had no difficulty in working wholeheartedly and enthusiastically for your election." In reality, Townes supported Scranton at the national convention, held a leadership post in the staunchly anti-Goldwater NNRA, and publicly stated from the 1970s through the 2000s that he did not vote for Goldwater. In interviews after leaving the national committee, he claimed he "tried to straddle" the divisions inside the national committee, and had to "show a degree of loyalty" in hopes that he would "be able to remain here and hopefully make this system work" for African Americans.[17]

Under pressure from Townes, who served as NNRA treasurer and imagined a future partnership between the organization and the national committee, the NNRA removed Grant Reynolds from his position as National Director of Political Activities in December 1965. However, as the former director of the Minorities Division, Reynolds remained a prominent member of the NNRA, and still spoke on its behalf to the national press, where he intensified his critiques of Townes and Chairman Bliss as weak moderates whose big-tent philosophy emboldened conservatives. To him, Goldwater's conservative wing simply could not be tolerated by any organization seeking black support, noting that "on every issue vital to [black] progress . . . and in some instances their very existence, there are *Conservatives* in vociferous opposition."[18]

Tensions flared at the 1966 NNRA annual meeting. Sponsored by the Wolverine State Republican Organization (WSRO), a group of black Republicans from Michigan with ties to George Romney, the May convention was held at Detroit's Sheraton-Cadillac Hotel. In the days leading up to the event, Townes invited WSRO members to his suite, where he claimed that Reynolds's abrasive and self-serving rhetoric hampered the NNRA's potential to develop a mutually beneficial relationship with the RNC. It initially appeared that his whisper campaign had paid off. George Washington, Governor Romney's highest-ranking black appointee, privately cautioned the governor to avoid Reynolds, and a number of WSRO members suddenly claimed at the last minute that they could not attend convention proceedings.[19]

Townes's allies launched a "Robinson for President" drive, hoping that Jackie Robinson would replace Reynolds as the organization's public face. However, as rumors circulated that orders had come down from Chairman Bliss for Townes to "stop Reynolds at all cost," even Robinson became skeptical of the movement, and removed his name from consideration. Townes's efforts backfired, and members elected Reynolds as their new president, with Robinson becoming chairman of the executive board. Despite the early concerns from his black advisors, Governor Romney met privately with Reynolds and Robinson, and delivered the convention's keynote address. In Robinson's closing remarks, he asserted that unlike Townes, who was notably absent from the ceremony, the NNRA did not blindly march behind the principle of "our party right and wrong." Instead, it demanded that "our party must be right," and vowed its members would "stand up, speak up and act vigorously as Negro Republicans." In one of their first acts as heads of the NNRA, Robinson and Reynolds sent a letter to Chairman Bliss expressing their disapproval of Townes's efforts "to interfere in our right to independently select and elect our own slate of leadership." Though they still "want very much to work with you for the triumph of the Republican Party and the perpetuation of the two-party system," they refused "to do it wearing the collar of an outside force."[20]

Only a year removed from Goldwater's defeat, 1965 offered black Republicans promising candidates in off-year municipal elections. The NNRA joined James Farmer, Wyatt Tee Walker, and Sammy Davis, Jr., in endorsing John Lindsay's bid for mayor of New York City. Touting his congressional record as a staunch advocate of civil rights, Lindsay received approximately 40 percent of the black vote on election day. Similarly, African Americans helped elect another moderate Republican mayor in Louisville, as well as the city's first African American prosecutor of the police court. And with his election as Philadelphia's District Attorney, Arlen Spector, a former Democrat and up-and-coming star in the GOP, became the city's first successful Republican in a major race in over a decade. Openly campaigning in black neighborhoods, Spector received 40 percent of the vote in middle-class black precincts and 20 to 30 percent in poorer black precincts.[21]

In the 1966 midterms, the NNRA issued press releases covered by national newspapers listing their endorsements of eighty-two moderate Republican candidates, hoping their publicized support would "encourage more Republican civil rights initiative." Under the direction of Grant Reynolds and Jackie Robinson, who both had close ties to the Republican Party of New York, the NNRA also became a virtual auxiliary of Nelson Rockefeller's campaign organization. In 1966, they held a fifty-dollar per plate Rockefeller fundraising dinner that drew four hundred and fifty black Republicans from across the country. The following year, Reynolds privately assured the governor that NNRA members were "committed to the principles of Rockefeller Republicanism," and promised to use the organization "as an effective instrument . . . in the coming presidential campaign." Rockefeller responded by claiming, "I can think of nothing more significant and important than what the National Negro Republican Assembly is now doing," and provided funds for its annual meeting in Albany.[22]

Though its membership had grown to almost three thousand by 1967, the NNRA's only meaningful actions were political endorsements, which were usually well covered by the national press. It occasionally proposed grassroots registration and recruitment efforts, but these rarely panned out. Reynolds privately compared the NNRA to a "paper tiger" that had a loud enough roar to be heard by reporters, but was otherwise unable to provoke substantive action. Despite the organization's relationship with Rockefeller, one of the wealthiest men in America, the NNRA had a limited budget, and Reynolds occasionally paid overdue telephone and postage debts with his own money. Not surprisingly, given Reynolds's public criticisms of the national committee, Ray Bliss cut off any meaningful communication with the NNRA after 1966, wanting "no part of splinter groups." Privately, even Nelson Rockefeller's inner circle questioned Reynolds's tactics, believing that moderates like Bliss could provide support to the NNRA's effort to recruit African Americans. One aide remarked, "Why in the world would anybody be so stupid as to kick [Bliss] around publicly," and feared that Reynolds was "isolating himself and destroying his own usefulness." Though their endorsements and press releases continued to make national headlines through 1968, the NNRA had neither a sufficient membership base nor the resources to organize effective grassroots campaigns.[23]

The RNC proceeded without the NNRA in developing its own program of black outreach. In three years, the paid staff of Townes's Minorities Division was increased from five to twelve, and included Junius Griffin, who resigned as a public relations aide with Martin Luther King's SCLC to join the division; Theodore Brown, a former research director for A. Philip Randolph; and Samuel C. Jackson, an NAACP leader from Kansas and original member of President Johnson's Equal Employment Opportunity Commission. The division's budget provided funds for Townes to travel across the country and to print materials that touted the Republican civil rights record. Both were logical functions of a political division of the national committee, but had been routinely denied to Grant Reynolds and Clay Claiborne in the early 1960s. Townes also convinced the RNC to write specific press releases to black newspapers, and his staff frequently consulted governors, congressmen, and senators, so at the very least they could "get Black opinion involved into Republican decision-making." In 1967 and 1968, the division had canvassed more than thirty states, and set up "ghetto outreach centers" in Kansas City, Minneapolis, and other cities. These centers investigated discrimination complaints, sponsored Little League teams, tutored school children, and provided job placement, budgeting, and meal planning services. Volunteers were in-structed to assist anyone "on a 'no strings attached' basis," with the objective of providing tangible services to those in need, while softening the GOP's image on the grassroots level.[24]

By the end of the year, Republicans in Michigan, California, New York, and Washington, D.C., had created similar programs. The most popular, the New Illinois Committee (NIC), actually predated Townes's endeavors. After blaming his 1964 gubernatorial defeat on pitifully low black support, Charles Percy, a Chicago millionaire and political maverick, began his 1966 campaign for the U.S. Senate by founding the NIC. Its services included adult education classes, legal counsel, and day care assistance. Its most popular program, "Call for Action," was a telephone help line that mediated services with bu-reaucracies on behalf of citizens with problems that ranged from absentee landlords to trash removal and rat control. By 1968, the chair of Michigan's state party, Elly Peterson, followed Townes's and Percy's examples and estab-lished the Detroit Action Center, which provided similar services to constit-uents. When massive riots broke out in July, the Action Center sent four truckloads of food into devastated areas within twelve hours of the initial uprising, and convinced surrounding Republican county chairmen to con-vert their headquarters into food distribution centers, which donated eighty tons of food by the end of the summer, in addition to medical supplies, cloth-ing, and other necessities.[25]

Though Republican community centers may have improved the image of local GOP organizations, and contributed to increased black support for Re-publicans like Percy, who won his 1966 Senate race, they were insufficient to eliminate intense skepticism of the national party among black voters. Townes admitted that even with unprecedented support, "The Minorities Division . . . has only been equipped to fight a guerilla war in a political campaign where organized, well trained troops are necessary to engage in every skirmish." The damage done by Goldwater, and the continued persistence of anti-civil rights conservatives inside party ranks, could not be erased by his division and community centers alone. At the end of his tenure in the early 1970s, Townes told an interviewer, "I'm not going to sit here and try to lie to you that this [had] some ringing impact." Nevertheless, he remained positive, noting, "like all other things that Black people are doing, we're trying to open up those cracks in those doors. And we're . . . making a little bit of progress."[26]

By November 1966, Townes could point to modest success among black voters in the midterm elections. Republican candidates received a national average of 19 percent of the black vote on election day, more than triple the percentage received by Goldwater two years earlier. Republicans identified as "moderate" by political analysts William Brink and Louis Harris received an average of 38 percent of the black vote, including George Romney, Nelson Rockefeller, and Clifford Case. John Sherman Cooper won 55 percent of Kentucky's black vote, and John Volpe, Massachusetts's liberal Republican candidate for governor, received over 60 percent of the vote in Boston's black communities; 94 percent of African Americans in Maryland cast ballots for Spiro Agnew, a civil rights moderate who ran against a conservative Democrat, in his gubernatorial victory. Howard Baker, an ally of George W. Lee, became Tennessee's first Republican U.S. Senator in over fifty years. Unafraid to reach out to African Americans and support civil rights, Howard received 35 percent of the state's black vote.[27]

Black Republicans were particularly interested in Winthrop Rockefeller's campaign for governor of Arkansas. Nelson Rockefeller's brother Winthrop opened a cattle ranch at Petit Jean Mountain after a scandalous divorce in 1953. Though he opposed the Civil Rights Act of 1964, he still outshone his Democratic opponent, a notorious race-baiter who refused to even shake hands with African Americans. Long before his gubernatorial bid, Rockefeller hired an African American as the foreman of his ranch, served on the executive board of the National Urban League, and blamed segregation for the state's economic woes. During the election, he actively recruited African Americans through registration drives that received grassroots support from state branches of the NAACP, SNCC, and Voter Education Project. Irene Samuel, a respected civil rights worker who led efforts to reopen Little Rock's integrated public schools in 1959, organized African Americans across the state on his behalf. On election day, Rockefeller *lost* the majority of white votes, but obtained over 90 percent of the black vote according to some estimates, enough to secure his victory as the first Republican governor of Arkansas since Reconstruction. This was exactly the coalition of moderate whites and African Americans that black Republicans had long urged their party to build in the South. This same coalition secured Rockefeller's narrow reelection in 1968.[28]

Another groundbreaking moment of 1966 was the nomination of five black Republican congressional candidates in majority-white districts in California, Minnesota, New Jersey, and Ohio. Though none won election, black journalist Chuck Stone noted that while Democrats only nominated African Americans in majority-black urban areas, the GOP took "the leadership in breakthroughs for black candidates in elective offices" in predominantly white or multiracial districts. This was nowhere more apparent than in Massachusetts, where Republicans selected Attorney General Edward Brooke as their nominee for the U.S. Senate. Not only was Brooke's nomination unprecedented, but his election day victory represented one of the most significant milestones in American history. Though he did not shy away from his racial heritage, Brooke departed from the campaign strategy of black Democratic congressmen, who ran as distinctly black candidates in majority-black districts. Recognizing that whites made up the largest percentage of his constituents, Brooke frequently described his vision of America as "an integrated society of magnificent pluralism," and promised to represent all peoples of his state. He defeated former Democratic governor Endicott Peabody in a landslide, receiving over 60 percent of the total vote and 90 percent of black ballots. The victory made Brooke the first African American ever elected to the U.S. Senate by popular vote. He instantly became a GOP star, with his image featured on the November 18 cover of *Time* magazine.[29]

Journalists and historians have occasionally credited Brooke's light skin and blue eyes for his success as a black politician. A May 1966 poll, however, found that 80 percent of Massachusetts residents identified Brooke as black, and it is not a far stretch to believe that even more were aware of his racial identity by the end of a highly publicized fall campaign. He also did not shy from civil rights, promising "a broadly based, massive assault against all remaining forms of discrimination." Jackie Robinson declared, "There never was any doubt in my mind about Ed Brooke's devotion to his race," and called his victory "the most resounding reply which could have been given" to Republicans who wrote off the black vote. The NAACP saw his election as not only a win for the GOP, but one for African Americans that "heralds the dawn at a new day." Black journalist Carl Rowan wrote that black Democrats were "secretly pulling and praying for Brooke's victory . . . [and] regard Brooke as one of their own."[30]

Brooke "understood that as the only African American senator, I was viewed by millions of black Americans, in every state, as 'their' senator." During his twelve years in the Senate, Brooke became a power broker on issues of civil rights, housing, and employment. He served as the ranking Republican on the Banking, Housing, and Urban Affairs Committee, and the party's ranking member on the Urban Affairs Subcommittee. He consistently voted with liberals on social issues relating to women's rights, health care, education, and anti-discrimination. After his first three years in Washington,

Figure 12. Edward W. Brooke at 1968 Republican National Convention in Miami. LC-U9-19514-9A, U.S. News and World Report Collection, Library of Congress.

the NAACP, who awarded him their highest honor, the Spingarn Medal, in 1967, praised Brooke's "consistent and strong support of civil rights legislation and goals." Their chief lobbyist, Clarence Mitchell, claimed Brooke "is more informed and knowledgeable on civil rights than any other first term senator I have met."[31]

Similar in many ways to the Urban League's Whitney Young, Brooke rarely marched in demonstrations, but instead pressed for civil rights legislation behind the scenes through alliances with powerful white politicians. As the keynote speaker at the 1963 National Urban League annual conference, he warned that while "the ballot and the picket line and the demonstration are all weapons of persuasion," civil rights activists should not "abandon the traditional approaches" used by African Americans in the past, which emphasized "cooperation and coordination" with white allies. Indeed, Brooke became a lynchpin in the Senate's bloc of moderate Republicans who partnered with Democrats to enact much of the liberal agenda of the 1960s. Though his style differed from the more bombastic approach of many members of the Congressional Black Caucus, founded in 1969 by black Democrats in the House of Representatives, they saw themselves as allies. Brooke was the keynote speaker at the caucus's 1973 annual banquet, and Harlem Congressman Charles Rangel referred to him as the "Senate Black Caucus." Shirley Chisholm defended Brooke in 1975 after a member of NBC's Today show claimed the senator had "never met another black person in his life." In a letter to the network's chairman, Chisholm said the claim "libels his character and his record in Congress. I know the Senator and I know that he has worked long and hard to improve the education and employment opportunities of blacks, and indeed, all underprivileged people."[32]

In his first year in the Senate, Brooke was the only black elected official named to the President's National Advisory Commission on Civil Disorders, also known as the Kerner Commission after its chair, Illinois governor Otto Kerner. By the summer of 1967, riots had spread to seventy-five cities, as economic and racial inequalities plagued urban America. President Johnson tasked the commission with finding solutions to urban racial violence. Though Brooke condemned riots as "the mortal enemies" of civil rights, he placed the blame largely on poverty and poor housing. He was joined on the commission by fellow liberal Republicans John Lindsay and William McCulloch; their views on the root causes of the violence corresponded with the commission's final report, which offered one of the most striking government-sanctioned assessments of American race relations ever published. Its introduction warned, "Our nation is moving toward two societies, one black, one white—separate and unequal," and blamed rioting on structural racism. To solve its underlying causes, they proposed the extension of anti-poverty programs, the hiring of more black police officers, the passage of fair housing legislation, and the construction of new government housing aimed to end de facto segregation.[33]

These recommendations largely fell on deaf ears, as politicians of both parties believed that anything but strong condemnations of urban violence amounted to political suicide. President Johnson did not invite its members to the White House upon the report's release, and Robert Kennedy declared that anyone affiliated with rioting "must know that swift justice will be done and effective punishment meted out for their deeds." Gearing up for a presidential run centered on law and order, Richard Nixon blasted the report for blaming "the riots on everyone but the rioters," and called for courts to double the conviction rate of accused criminals. Everett Dirksen hinted at a communist conspiracy, alleging there was "a touch of Red" behind the disorder. Brooke, however, remained steadfast, and continued to emphasize that violence was "the product of years of deprivation—in jobs, housing, [and] the good things in life."[34]

Brooke had long supported fair housing legislation, one of the commission's most pressing recommendations, believing that "as long as white people could refuse to sell or rent property" to African Americans, there could be no lasting way to "break education and employment barriers and show that the ghetto was not an immutable institution in America." In early 1968, Brooke and Democrat Walter Mondale cosponsored legislation that banned discrimination in the sale or rental of housing. He then worked with Dirksen to pass a compromise bill that included anti-riot provisions and banned discrimination in an estimated 80 percent of the nation's housing. As the GOP's leading advocate of the bill, Brooke personally persuaded a number of Republicans, including arch-conservative Jack Miller of Iowa, to reverse their previous opposition to fair housing and vote to end a filibuster of the bill. As the legislation moved to the House, Brooke worked closely with Republican congressman John Anderson of Illinois in guiding it through a hostile Rules Committee. Three days after the assassination of Martin Luther King, Jr., Brooke appeared on CBS's *Face the Nation*, and warned that failure to pass the legislation would further stoke racial tensions in the wake of uprisings in response to King's murder. Within a week, the House passed the bill, and President Johnson signed the Civil Rights Act of 1968 into law.[35]

Though Brooke was the only elected black Republican on the national stage, others wielded influence at the state and local levels during the mid- to late 1960s. In 1966, nine black Republicans were elected to state legislatures, and Robert C. Henry became the nation's first African American mayor of a sizeable city (Springfield, Ohio, which at the time had a population of over eighty thousand). Like Brooke, Henry represented a majority-white elector- ate and emphasized that he "happens to be a Negro rather than a Negro Mayor." He was not isolated from the black community, though, serving as the vice president of the city's Urban League and on the board of the NAACP. Chicago's Paul P. Boswell, a dermatologist and Whitney Young, Jr.'s brother- in-law, survived the Democratic landslide of 1964 in his election to the Illi- nois legislature. During his two years in office, Boswell sponsored open housing legislation and led a massive protest against segregated medical soci- eties. Throughout the 1960s, voters in Cleveland's majority-black eighteenth ward repeatedly elected Republican John Kellogg to the city council. A pros- perous lawyer and Republican delegate to several national conventions, Kel- logg successfully pushed through a zoning ordinance that combated overcrowding, and procured services for his neighborhood that ranged from free house paint to community gardens.[36]

In 1966, Kentucky's only black legislator, Republican Jesse Warders of Louisville, cosponsored a civil rights bill that prohibited discrimination in places of public accommodation and employment. Jackie Robinson and Mar- tin Luther King, Jr., championed the legislation, leading a ten-thousand- person "March on Frankfort" to lobby for its passage. The law ultimately was passed with bipartisan support, and was described by King as "the strongest and most comprehensive civil rights bill passed by a southern state." Warders also led the effort to repeal Kentucky's "dead letter" laws, offensive legislation such as slave codes and segregated education that was no longer enforced but had never been repealed. Another Kentucky Republican, Louise Reynolds of Louisville's Board of Aldermen, introduced a 1967 open housing measure that was, to her dismay, rejected by the majority of white Republicans on the board. In the November municipal elections, black voters played a significant role in replacing eleven of the twelve Republican aldermen with Democrats. Reynolds was the sole member of the GOP reelected to the board, where she secured passage of an enforceable open housing ordinance.[37]

Black Republicans also continued to receive high-ranking appointments in state and local governments and parties. Only three African Americans served in state cabinet posts in 1967, all three appointed by Republican governors. By 1968, the number of meaningful black appointees under Republican governors and mayors totaled over one hundred. Nelson Rockefeller appointed Jackie Robinson to a paid position on the governor's Executive Chamber as his Special Assistant for Community Affairs in 1966. For the next two years, Robinson represented the governor before legislative committees and constituent groups, and coordinated the efforts of other black appointees in advising Rockefeller on matters of concern to black communities. Other African Americans on Rockefeller's staff included the acclaimed *Pittsburgh Courier* journalist and editor, Evelyn Cunningham, and veteran civil rights activist Wyatt Tee Walker. In 1965, the NNRA's president, George Fleming, became treasurer of the New Jersey Republican Executive Committee, and his NNRA colleague Joseph Bell became vice chairman of Michigan's Republican State Central Committee. Black advisors with the Democratic National Committee privately lamented in 1965 that "all but two" of Louisville's "approximately 14 Negro lawyers are on the GOP payroll, at least six of which are above the $10,000 level." Louisville's black legislator, Jesse Warders, resigned from the Kentucky General Assembly at the end of 1966 after the city's Republican mayor appointed him Director of Sanitation, making him the first black director of a major southern city's municipal agency.[38]

While African Americans showed a willingness to support individual Republicans in the 1966 midterm elections, polls taken throughout the decade showed a dramatic drop from the 1950s in the number of self-identified black Republicans. The decline began during Nixon's 1960 presidential campaign, and fell to record lows with Goldwater's nomination. Whereas 28 percent of southern blacks had considered themselves Republicans in the spring of 1960, only 17 percent did by December. Throughout the early 1960s, percentages varied from poll to poll, but on average about 14 percent of blacks in the North and only slightly more in the South self-identified as Republican. By 1964, the national average of black Republicans had dropped to just 7 percent, and less than 4 percent in the South. By 1968, the numbers had fallen even further, with approximately 2 percent of African Americans nationwide willing to describe themselves as members of the Republican Party.[39]

The rise of Goldwater's conservative wing, and the purge of black leadership from southern Republican organizations in the early 1960s, corresponded with this decline. At the same time, though some southern Democrats remained among the most virulent racists on the political scene, their influence had waned by the mid- to late 1960s. President Johnson became the symbol of federal civil rights legislation, and named the nation's first African Americans to the presidential cabinet and the U.S. Supreme Court. In 1965, following the assault on peaceful civil rights activists in Selma, Alabama, he sided unequivocally with demonstrators, bringing tears to the eyes of Martin Luther King by proclaiming "we shall overcome" before a joint session of Congress. Even Edward Brooke admitted on national television in 1968 that "no President in the history of this country has done more for civil rights than has Lyndon Baines Johnson."[40]

At the same time that Johnson was identifying his administration with the aspirations of African Americans, black Republicans found it difficult to shake the image of the GOP as the new home to old racists. In 1964, South Carolina Senator Strom Thurmond, the former Dixiecrat presidential nominee whose filibuster against the Civil Rights Act of 1957 was the longest in U.S. history, declared on television, "The Democratic Party has forsaken the people to become the party of minority groups," and announced he would leave the party of Johnson to join the "Goldwater Republican Party." The following year, another South Carolina Democrat, Congressman Albert Watson, ran as a Republican in his successful reelection bid. As a staunch segregationist, Watson in his campaign highlighted his opposition to the pending Voting Rights Act, and his supporters warned of illiterate "Negro mobs" dominating southern elections if the bill passed. Mississippi's GOP called segregation "absolutely essential" to the state's social order, and its state chairman, Wirt Yerger, refused to give in to pressure from national Republicans to reach out to African Americans. In 1965, House Minority Leader Gerald Ford of Michigan drew national headlines for canceling an appearance at a Mississippi GOP luncheon after civil rights activist Charles Evers informed him that black Republicans would be denied entry to the event. Incredulous at Ford's rebuke, Yerger informed him that Barry Goldwater and other high-profile Republicans had spoken at all-white events in the state in the past without incident, and called black Republicans interested in participating "radicals" and "Negro agitators" who should be denied access to the party. On the floor of the House of Representatives, Alabama's Republican congressman William Dickinson described civil rights marchers, who included nuns, ministers, young children, and even registered Republicans, as "beatniks, prostitutes, and communists" who participated in "sex orgies of the rawest sort."[41]

Unsavory Republican racism and opposition to civil rights extended beyond the South. In January 1966, newspapers across the country covered a controversial faction of the New Jersey Young Republicans who called themselves the "Rat Finks." The group had become popular in conservative circles for writing satirical songs with lyrics that mocked Jews, called for the lynching of GOP moderates, and bemoaned lost tax dollars that had "Gone to niggers." On another occasion documented by the press, the head of Washington, D.C.'s Republican Party blamed riots on "well-dressed, responsible Negroes running wild like in the Congo." A Michigan Republican who had grown tired of George Romney's proclivity to join civil rights marches recommend he instead demonstrate for "the white people that are stabbed, clubbed, knifed, etc., at the hands of colored people." In California, conservatives gathered enough petitions to bring a repeal of the 1963 Rumford Open Housing Act to a statewide ballot in 1964. While more than Republicans voted for the proposition, which passed by a vote of almost two to one, the state chairman of Goldwater's campaign became one of the anti-housing drive's most vocal proponents. Regardless of the continued presence of the Eastern Establishment after 1964, racial conservatives persisted as a central faction of the party in the minds of many voters. Tellingly, an October 1966 Harris poll found that almost 70 percent of Americans nationwide selected the GOP when asked which party they thought would "slow the civil rights pace."[42]

One of California's own, Ronald Reagan, a former Hollywood actor and president of the Screen Actors Guild, emerged on the political stage in 1964 as one of Goldwater's most charismatic supporters. By the time he announced his 1966 bid for governor, Reagan had become a conservative icon. Like Goldwater, Reagan claimed to abhor racism on a personal level, but opposed the Civil Rights Act of 1964 and Voting Rights Act of 1965 on constitutional grounds as federal intrusions into states' rights. In California, civil rights emerged as a major campaign issue after a federal court reinstated open housing in the state. The repeal of open housing and the restoration of "law and order" in cities (where, according to Reagan, "every day the jungle draws a little closer") played a central role in his campaign. "If an individual wants to discriminate against Negroes . . . in selling or renting his house," Reagan declared, "it is his right to do so." James Flournoy, a member of the Republican State Central Committee and National Negro Republican Assembly leader, warned Reagan that every time he called for the repeal of the Rumford Act, "you are automatically slapping one million Negroes in the face," but, as a Goldwater conservative, Reagan's base existed in nearly all-white suburbia, the communities that feared open housing the most.[43]

During the spring primaries, Reagan appeared in a debate with two Republican opponents sponsored by Flournoy's California NNRA chapter.

Though one aide admitted, "We knew Ron wasn't going to get anywhere with Negroes," he recognized, "it would look bad if he stayed away." From the outset, Reagan's moderate opponents attacked his support for Goldwater and opposition to civil rights legislation. Increasingly agitated by the tone of the debate, Reagan lost his temper in the question-and-answer session after an audience member joined the chorus of attacks on his civil rights record. According to news reports, Reagan "shouted in a voice cracking with emotion" that he resented "the implication that there is any bigotry in my nature . . . I will not stand silent and let anyone imply that—in this or any other group." He then balled up his notes, hurled them into the audience, and audibly mumbled "sons of bitches" as he stormed off stage. He made it all the way to his home before aides convinced him to return to a post-debate cocktail party, lest it appear "that you don't like blacks or that you're afraid to face them." The debate performance confirmed the negative opinion of Reagan among many of the hundred NNRA members in attendance, and the national NNRA listed Reagan as one of the Republican candidates whose election they adamantly opposed.[44]

Given the prominence of conservatives like Goldwater, Reagan, and Strom Thurmond inside the GOP, black Republicans had a steep hill to climb in recruiting new followers. Moreover, with the determined effort of every president since Harry Truman to include African Americans in all levels of the federal government, by the mid-1960s the public sector had become the largest employer of the black middle class. Republican rhetoric of eliminating the size of government thus automatically fell on deaf ears to a constituency that had shown a willingness to join the GOP's moderate ranks in the 1940s and 1950s. Additionally, in an economy African Americans believed to be undergirded by structural racism, most could not identify with Republican rhetoric of "free enterprise" and "property rights," which they saw as the instruments used to maintain the discriminatory status quo. To the majority of working-class African Americans, Democrats represented their economic interests in their support of welfare, public housing, workers' rights, and labor unions. Many African Americans saw themselves as members of a coalition that included organized labor and Great Society Democrats, committed not just to civil rights, but, perhaps even more important, to economic equality.[45]

Why then did a distinct minority of African Americans remain loyal to the GOP? For one thing, the elite and professional classes that filled the ranks of black Republicans had no personal interest in Democratic economic issues. Edward Brooke, who described himself as "a liberal in civil rights and a conservative in fiscal matters," grew up attending operas at Carnegie Hall as the son of a prominent Washington, D.C., attorney. *Time* labeled Brooke a "NASP," the Negro version of the stereotypical White Anglo-Saxon Protestant that dominated New England's sociopolitical elite. From this privileged position, his father taught him to admire "the Republican virtues of duty and self-help," and to oppose Democratic welfare policies that fostered "a chain of dependence." George W. Lee, who worked as an insurance-company executive in addition to his political activism in Memphis, described his ideal party as one of "fiscal responsibility and Civil Rights," and argued that the average black Democrat "turned away from his quest for Civil Rights in the quest for bread and butter." In speeches across the country on behalf of the Minorities Division, Junius Griffin criticized "heavy reliance on government programs," and emphasized "the individual's responsibility toward the betterment of his community." L. K. Jackson frequently denounced "brainwashed" African Americans who sold out for "relief, welfare and hand-out programs," which were "the biggest political racket that has ever been turned loose in America."[46]

Edward Brooke's notion of an "Open Society," a term he used to contrast his beliefs to the Democrat's Great Society, represented the civil rights ideology of many black Republicans. His ideal government was one that "extends to *all* Americans the freedom and opportunity to have equal justice under the law, to obtain quality education, to enjoy decent housing and good health, and to gain equal access to the economic benefits available in a free enterprise system." This vision paralleled many of the major objectives of the early civil rights movement, and underpinned Brooke's support for voting rights, protections against employment discrimination, and the use of busing as a means to desegregate public education. It also justified his support of liberal Democratic programs, such as Head Start and improved public housing, which he believed provided a safety net that gave single mothers and other marginalized workers the institutional support needed before they could find gainful employment. One of his signature measures in the Senate, the "Brooke Amendment," placed a ceiling on the amount charged in public housing so that tenants would not have to pay more than one-fourth of their income on rent. While this was in line with much of the Great Society legislation of the decade, Brooke believed this cap would encourage work and decrease welfare rolls. Equal access, not redistribution of wealth through welfare programs, would best ensure African American progress. In Brooke's Open Society, equality of opportunity was protected by anti-discrimination legislation, and impoverished individuals were assisted in areas that had traditionally limited black social mobility, such as housing and education. Ultimately, however, it would be the individual who was responsible for succeeding through his own initiative.[47]

To other black Republicans, working within the GOP was as much a pragmatic decision as an ideological one. Even those without formal positions could benefit from a relationship with powerful Republicans like Nelson Rockefeller. Sandy Ray, a former Republican legislator from Ohio who served as Jackie Robinson's spiritual mentor as pastor of New York City's Cornerstone Baptist Church, closely allied himself with the state's establishment in the 1960s and 1970s. Not only did New York's Republican elites, including Governor Rockefeller and John Lindsay, frequent his church, but Ray's endorsement of the party ensured that his pet community projects received adequate government resources and support. Similarly, musician Lionel Hampton, whose entertainment was a staple at Republican campaign events from the 1950s through the 1980s, used his GOP contacts to spearhead the construction of multimillion-dollar public housing complexes in New York City, such as the Lionel Hampton Houses. Even Percy Sutton, a prominent Harlem Democrat, saw the value of black Republicanism, noting that Jackie Robinson and others "got things done" because association with Governor Rockefeller "gave you access and opportunity and contacts."[48]

Black Republicans also continued to see the Eastern Establishment as a positive political force that should be rewarded in the voting booth. A self-professed "Rockefeller Republican" by the mid-1960s, Jackie Robinson supported New York's GOP establishment, which had "consistently fought and spoken out for justice and honor in the treatment of minorities groups in our society." Edward Brooke claimed his loyalty to the party stemmed both from his disdain for the "corrupt" Democratic machine of Massachusetts and from his admiration of Henry Cabot Lodge, Jr., and other "moderates who were among its national leaders." A Republican until his death in 1977, L. K. Jackson wrote in his unpublished memoirs that he proudly stood alongside any Republican who "follows the philosophy and concepts of . . . Earl Warren, Nelson A. Rockefeller, Jacob Javits, Henry Cabot Lodge, Clifford Case, Hugh Scott," and other establishment figures.[49]

Through the late 1960s, moderate and liberal Republicans had a solid record that black Republicans could point to when justifying their partisan affiliation. As with the Civil Rights Act of 1964, a greater percentage of

Republicans than of Democrats supported the Voting Rights Act of 1965. In Michigan, George Romney sponsored an open housing law and led a ten-thousand person march through Detroit in solidarity with civil rights demonstrators in Selma. Governors Daniel Evans, Raymond Shafer, and Spiro Agnew vocally backed open housing, fair employment, and other civil rights measures in Washington, Pennsylvania, and Maryland. Nelson Rockefeller, who "did more for the Negro than any governor in the country" according to civil rights leader Charles Evers, continued to play a key role in strengthening New York's open housing laws, job training programs, and other issues important to African Americans. During the peak of American involvement in Vietnam, a war that disproportionately affected black communities, Agnew's Maryland and Winthrop Rockefeller's Arkansas had the nation's largest percentages of African Americans appointed to local draft boards. Rockefeller also named the first African American head of a state agency in Arkansas, and famously held hands with black leaders outside the state capitol, singing "We Shall Overcome" in a memorial service after Martin Luther King's death.[50]

The common thread uniting almost all black Republicans, regardless of their personal ideology, was the notion that civil rights could best be obtained in a strong, two-party system where African Americans pressured both parties from within. Members of the New York chapter of the National Negro Republican Assembly published a five-hundred-word declaration in 1967 that emphasized to black voters "blind allegiance and apparent chronic affinity to the Democratic Party that seeks only to exploit their inequitable position is unwise, and self-defeating." Jackie Robinson argued that the NNRA's main objective was to foster the "two-party system so that Americans—and especially minorities—may have the bargaining power necessary to gain for them the best of everything in our society." In his tours across the country with the Minorities Division, Clarence Townes called for African Americans to "infiltrate this great party of Lincoln," because "there's no moral person in this world who'll give you a damn thing unless he needs . . . some of your votes." Edward Brooke's 1966 book, subtitled *Crisis in Our Two-Party System*, emphasized the benefits of two-party politics, and called for moderates to remain vigilant in making the party competitive among minority groups. Even George W. Lee, who had been publicly evicted from power in Memphis by conservatives in 1964, contended until his death in 1976 that it would be "suicidal" for a voter to "abandon completely a party and lose his bargaining power because of the temporary ascendency of objectionable personalities."[51]

Black Republicans in major cities with powerful Democratic machines were particularly drawn to the idea of the two-party system. Black journalist Evelyn Cunningham became a Republican and joined Nelson Rockefeller's administration when she realized that "in Harlem the Democrats owned everything and did nothing." Similarly, Cora Walker's motivation for running for a state senate seat in Harlem as a Republican was that African Americans were being "neglected" by Democratic bosses. "It is only the threat of loss of political power" to entrenched machines, she argued, "that brings good government, which is responsive to the wishes of the citizens." While working for the SCLC, Junius Griffin organized King's civil rights marches in Chicago during the summer of 1966. His experiences with Mayor Richard Daley, whose machine thrived on the "exploitation of the Negro voter," led him to join the RNC's Minorities Division to assist Charles Percy and other liberal Republicans in Illinois. L. K. Jackson of nearby Gary frequently emphasized that while the Democratic establishment of the city made appeals to African Americans during election season, they also condoned "police brutality as bad as they do in Birmingham, Alabama, and work as hard to perpetuate segregation in Gary as they do in South Carolina."[52]

In 1966, twenty-five-year-old activist David Reed switched his party affiliation to Republican after becoming frustrated with the lack of reform in Daley's Chicago. He befriended Charles Percy, and organized the New Breed Committee in the Ghetto, whose members were described by *Jet* magazine as "young militant Negroes." They believed veteran Democratic congressman William Dawson was a "Super Tom" who capitulated to white party bosses, encouraged political corruption, and did not sponsor any meaningful legislation for the betterment of his district. When the New Breed slated a candidate to challenge Dawson in the Democratic primaries, he was shot in the shoulder by an unknown assailant while on the campaign trail. Reed then launched his own congressional bid as a Republican to challenge Dawson in the general election. In campaign speeches, he retold stories of Democratic bureaucrats who routinely denied licenses to black businessmen who criticized Daley, and claimed that precinct captains threatened single mothers with eviction from public housing if they did not vote Democratic. He even reached out to the city's most notorious gang, the Blackstone Rangers, who had personally experienced machine-sanctioned police brutality and racial profiling. Reed argued if voters would elect him to Congress, along with liberal white Republican candidates, they could break Daley's stranglehold over the city. He received financial support from the state party, and prominent white

Republicans campaigned on his behalf, including Richard Nixon, who had long blamed his 1960 loss in Illinois on machine-sanctioned election fraud. On election day, New Breed poll watchers alleged to have witnessed overt ballot stuffing, but their complaints were ignored by election officials. Nevertheless, Reed obtained over 25 percent of the vote in the heavily gerrymandered, machine-dominated district, and was among the first five staffers hired by Richard Ogilvie, the newly elected Republican president of the Cook County Board.[53]

Black Republicans were not alone in their belief that African Americans should actively participate in both parties. Civil rights leaders continued to emphasize the need for bipartisanship within black communities. The NAACP wrote in 1965, "it is not politically healthy for any group to be tied completely to any single party," and feared black voters were susceptible to being "taken for granted by one party and discounted by others." Andrew Young proclaimed at the SCLC's 1965 annual convention that, even though Goldwater forces "ran us out of the Republican Party," African Americans "must still find every opportunity to encourage the development of a two-party South." Mississippi activist James Bevel urged African Americans to participate in both parties and force them compete for their votes, "otherwise we can have no real political power as a group." Ralph Abernathy went so far as to claim that the GOP's success among conservatives was the fault of African Americans for failing to divide their ballots judiciously between the two parties. In 1967 and 1968, civil rights activists James Meredith, who integrated the University of Mississippi and initiated the 1966 March Against Fear, and James Farmer, the former national director of the Congress of Racial Equality, ran as Republican congressional candidates in their challenges to New York City's entrenched Democratic Party.[54]

The congressional races of Reed, Meredith, and Farmer, led many commentators to question the Democratic Party's ability to maintain 1964 levels of black support. John Conyers, a black Democratic congressman from Michigan, warned his party in 1967, "It's no secret . . . that the Republican party has been attracting a large number of disaffected Negroes." Political scientist Everett Carll Ladd, Jr., observed that outside powerful urban Democratic machines, the black vote "is highly fluid" and "appears to be potentially less stable than that of virtually any other demographic group." The *New York Post* similarly claimed, "it is no longer safe to assume that Negroes will automatically vote Democratic." Simeon Booker, one of the country's foremost experts on black politics as the Washington, D.C., bureau chief of *Ebony*, even predicted in a 1967 article that "with an appealing national ticket in 1968, Republicans could well make their greatest showing among Negroes since Reconstruction."[55]

While these predictions never panned out, they reveal a moment of potential viability for the GOP among black voters after 1964. Far from being outside the mainstream of black political thought, moderate and liberal Republicans and the two-party system were embraced by black voters across the country in their support of Winthrop Rockefeller, John Lindsay, John Sherman Cooper, George Romney, and other Republicans willing to actively pursue their vote. One poll found that nearly half of African Americans would consider voting for a Republican if given the right candidate. While Goldwater may have solidified black identification with the Democratic Party on the national level, the black vote remained fluid on the state and local levels, when given the choice between conservative Democrats or apathetic Democratic machines and Republicans who made sincere efforts to demonstrate their genuine concern for issues affecting black communities.[56]

CHAPTER 7

A Piece of the Action: Black Capitalism and the Nixon Administration

"Only the ignorant or the frightened could misunderstand Black Power," declared Nathan Wright in 1969. To him, black Americans "are, in fact, a community set apart," and Black Power meant that wherever "Blacks predominate, whites must not dominate any more." This definition of black nationalism and power sought black control of the schools, businesses, utilities, and other entities inside majority-black communities. A veteran activist since the 1940s, Wright was a seminal figure in the nascent Black Power movement of the mid-1960s. He was the chief organizer of the first, and second, national Black Power conferences, and the founding chairman of the Department of African and Afro-American Studies at the State University of New York at Albany. He was also a lifelong Republican, believing the GOP represented the principles necessary to achieving his goal of black self-sufficiency—"local control, the encouragement of personal dignity, independence . . . and that the sky is the only limit for ambition."[1]

Black Power first reached a national audience in the summer of 1966, after James Meredith launched a one-man March Against Fear in protest of continued discrimination in the Deep South. A white assailant shot him on the second day. Seeking to once again galvanize the nation, civil rights leaders arranged to complete Meredith's trek from Memphis, Tennessee, to Jackson, Mississippi. They represented a cross section of the movement, with Martin Luther King, Jr., leading the respectable Southern Christian Leadership Conference (SCLC), Stokely Carmichael heading an increasingly frustrated Student Nonviolent Coordinating Committee (SNCC), and Floyd McKissick guiding the Congress of Racial Equality (CORE) toward black nationalism.

By the end of the march, chants of "Black Power" rang out from young, disillusioned marchers in SNCC and CORE.[2]

By 1968, Black Power marked a new phase in the civil rights movement. Although it has often been described as a more radicalized version of the movement, Black Power included many diverse, but often overlapping, perspectives emphasizing racial identity and self-determination, from the austere moral code of the Nation of Islam to the Marxism of the Black Panther Party. Another strain was a conservative interpretation of black nationalism that spurred a new generation of Republicans drawn to the party's self-help and pro-business ideology. To Nathan Wright and black nationalist supporters of self-help, integration should no longer be a priority, but needed to be replaced by economic plans centered on "helping people help themselves." Central to this ideology was the notion that one could pull himself out of poverty by his own "bootstraps" and initiative, and that black communities could be uplifted through entrepreneurship. Bootstrap black nationalists lamented that African Americans controlled less than one-half of 1 percent of the nation's total business assets, and they forged an alliance with those in the GOP, particularly Richard Nixon, who were willing to embrace black capitalism.[3]

Support for bootstrap black capitalism and economic independence had deep roots in African American political thought. In the early twentieth century, Booker T. Washington emphasized self-help and entrepreneurship, and Marcus Garvey's Universal Negro Improvement Association called for African Americans to rally behind black-owned businesses. Since the 1930s, black entrepreneurs, many of whom remained loyal to the Republican Party, continued to emphasize economic self-determination through free enterprise. Prominent Republican and civil rights activist T. R. M. Howard, who held board positions with the black-owned Tri-State Bank and the Universal Life Insurance Company, urged African Americans to follow the dogma of always "talking about Negro business, singing Negro business, preaching Negro business." Memphis Republican leader George W. Lee, who cofounded the National Negro Insurance Association, championed "Dollar Power" as the key to black self-determination, believing African Americans "have to be behind the counter" as owners of the businesses that serve their communities. In the North, "Don't Buy Where You Can't Work" campaigns were a staple of black protests. Philadelphia's Leon Sullivan, for example, perfected the use of selective patronage drives in the 1950s and 1960s as a method to

encourage black solidarity against purchasing goods and services from businesses with a history of employment discrimination. By the mid-1960s, his
emphasis remained on economics, though he moved away from mass protest
and political action toward self-help and job training as the keys to black
autonomy.[4]

By the late 1960s, black Republicans turned their attention to economic
policies they believed promoted self-sufficiency. Senator Edward Brooke
lauded the principle of "a hand-up, not a hand-out," and sponsored a 1968
amendment to the Small Business Act that relaxed government regulations in
high-risk urban areas in order to help black businesses secure loans. Speaking
at the 1967 annual convention of the SCLC, Clarence Townes chastised mainstream civil rights leaders for their reluctance to embrace "Black Power," arguing, "Black folks will win acceptance from the larger society only by
developing their own bases of power," not simply integrating into the nation's
white infrastructure. By the 1968 election, Townes argued that "never before
has the negro community been more insistent upon self determination," and
directed the Minorities Division to give "special attention" to cultivating and
organizing disillusioned black youth.[5]

Welfare was anathema to most black Republicans. But, while many Goldwater conservatives argued that welfare was not the responsibility of the federal government and was a waste of public money on an undeserving poor,
black Republicans focused almost exclusively on its perceived effect on its
recipients. Clarence Townes lambasted the Democratic Party's "steady diet of
this frustrating, humiliating, degrading, deteriorating welfarism," which they
used like opium "to control their masses." Edward Brooke believed welfare
created "a chain of dependence and lack of self-respect," and "sometimes if
you have too many crutches, you will never learn to walk." William Coleman,
Jr., a civil rights lawyer and member of President Gerald Ford's cabinet, similarly held that "well-intentioned but ill-conceived" Democratic policies led to
dependence on federal programs, "deterring minorities from competing in
the economic mainstream."[6]

Nevertheless, black Republicans were not opposed to government actions
that they believed rewarded work and ensured equal opportunities, such as a
hike in the minimum wage and substantial federal investment in education.
Coleman held that the federal government had the responsibility to invest in
education, skills training, housing, and jobs programs, all of which he associated with promoting self-help. Central to his vision of civil rights was his belief that it was the government's responsibility to protect equal opportunities

for all. This not only meant that Coleman supported federal protections against discrimination, and believed in the value of personal responsibility and hard work, but that it was the government's obligation to actively work to ensure jobs through affirmative action. Similarly, Arthur Fletcher of Richard Nixon's cabinet defended affirmative action programs that favored black workers, on the basis that such policies helped break historical barriers that prevented African Americans from fully entering into the work force. Employment, including that which was made possible by federal anti-discrimination laws and racial quotas, provided African Americans "dignity," potential for "personal advancement," and the "ability to make choices" that were essential to full participation in a capitalistic society. Many black Republicans were among the nation's most fervent defenders of both public and private affirmative action policies in the 1960s and 1970s, and supported the use of racial quotas and set-asides in the allotment of federal jobs and contracts as a means to secure black employment and to empower black businesses.[7]

Black Republicans on the local level also shifted their emphasis to economic self-help by the late 1960s. In 1967, a hundred black professionals in California, led by Republican Norman Hodges, formed the Green Power Foundation, which ran job training programs, a trucking company, and two factories in Watts that made baseball bats, wood paneling, and electronic equipment. Republican real estate broker Al Hicks partnered with San Francisco's Chamber of Commerce to create a job training program for black youth and the chamber's first equal employment office. Black Republicans in Houston worked with Congressman George H. W. Bush in starting a local minority bank deposit initiative and a youth summer job program. That same year, Michigan's Republican black outreach division, the Metropolitan Action Center, hosted the first Black Power seminar endorsed by either of the city's political parties, which touted its job training and day care programs. In 1969, the Wolverine State Republican Organization, formed by black supporters of George Romney in the mid-1960s, rededicated itself to the principle of "Black self-determination in predominantly Black districts."[8]

In New York, disheartened that whites from outside Harlem controlled nearly all of the borough's property, Cora T. Walker, a two-time Republican candidate for state senate and delegate to the 1972 Republican National Convention, spearheaded a community-owned supermarket. More than 2,500 local residents purchased inexpensive stocks, raising over $200,000 for the Harlem River Cooperative Supermarket, opened in 1967. The 10,000-

square-foot store featured high-quality merchandise, air-conditioning, automatic doors, and fluorescent lighting, and its forty-three previously "underemployed" workers were given competitive wages. Within a year, it had over three thousand shareholders, who received annual dividends. The cooperative remained open until 1976, when it was forced to shut down after Walker refused to meet the demands of local Democrats to unionize its employees. Harlem would remain without a black-owned supermarket for the next thirty years.[9]

Nowhere were black Republican efforts at economic self-determination more successful than under Washington State's Arthur Fletcher. A key figure in the Kansas GOP during the 1950s, Fletcher settled in Pasco, Washington, in the 1960s, where he won election to the city council and served on the governor's Urban Affairs Advisory Council. In 1965, he founded the East Pasco Self-Help Cooperation Association, which he described as a "model self-help program." The association raised money among black residents, who bought stocks that paid for the construction of community-owned businesses built by workers from the community. Within three years, the neighborhood had built a shopping center, gas station, grocery store, barber shop, dry cleaners, credit union, and police station. The success of East Pasco secured Fletcher the 1968 Republican nomination for lieutenant governor, which he obtained by winning every single county in the state primary. On the campaign trail, he emphasized his record of "teaching people what they can do for themselves," and promised to initiate self-help projects across the state. As a rising star in the party, Fletcher appeared before the Platform Committee at the Republican National Convention, and served as an advisor for Richard Nixon's presidential campaign.[10]

At the national level, the Congress of Racial Equality, under the leadership of Floyd McKissick, became the biggest civil rights organization to openly embrace self-help as its guiding philosophy. A veteran activist, McKissick participated in the 1947 Freedom Ride, and his North Carolina law firm litigated almost five thousand civil rights cases. He became national director of CORE in 1966 and, in joining Stokely Carmichael to promote Black Power during the March Against Fear, was one of the most prominent early supporters of the movement. Under his leadership, CORE dropped the terms "multiracial" and "nonviolent" from its constitution, expelled whites from leadership, and moved its national office from Manhattan to Harlem. He reached out to the Nation of Islam, which historically supported self-segregation and black business, and shifted CORE's goals away from integration and toward economic self-determination through the establishment of black-owned businesses, cooperatives, and credit unions. "Black Capitalism is so long overdue and of such importance," McKissick declared, "that it takes precedence over job training programs and general education."[11]

Though he was a political independent at the time, McKissick's attitude concerning welfare and free enterprise closely aligned him with Republicans. He urged African Americans to turn toward themselves for uplift, and to reject "handouts," which "do violence to a man, strip him of dignity, and breed in him a hatred of the system." He left CORE in 1968 to focus exclusively on promoting black capitalism through his Harlem-based consulting firm, Floyd B. McKissick Enterprises. Among its business ventures were a black-owned restaurant, shopping center, and Afro-centric drama production company. Its publishing house acquired the rights to one of the decade's most popular books among young nationalists, Robert F. Williams's *Negroes with Guns*. The firm's promotional literature urged militants to accept capitalism as a "fact of life," and argued, "If Black people are to survive in a capitalist society, they must control and productively use capital." The struggle in black communities was not for social integration, but "for Economic Power and Self-determination. . . . These bring respect to those who gain them." According to McKissick, "there are two concepts of black power." While those on the Left wanted "to tear down, burn down, [and] destroy" American society, his version sought "to get involved in economics, in politics . . . in the whole fabric of life." The civil rights movement had "kicked down a door," but the era of direct action protest had passed. Now was the time for African Americans to focus on participating "on every level of the capitalist structure."[12]

McKissick's successor at CORE, Roy Innis, further entwined the organization with self-help. A native of the Virgin Islands and former chairman of Harlem's CORE, Innis rejected integration and urged African Americans to take control of their own businesses and schools. Under his leadership in the late 1960s, CORE created model economic self-help programs in Cleveland and Baltimore, and worked with Nelson Rockefeller to establish a community-owned hospital in Harlem. According to Innis, "the total thrust of CORE's endeavors to build a viable and positive black minority is directed toward self-help bootstrap efforts," as local branches redirected their emphasis away from integration and civil disobedience toward programs centered on self-determination. The St. Louis branch held seminars on business management attended by white corporate representatives, and its chairman claimed CORE's new motto was "build, baby, build," as it focused on "constructive programs to rebuild the ghetto."[13]

Another influential supporter of bootstrap self-help was Nathan Wright, Jr. Like McKissick, Wright participated in the 1947 Freedom Ride and had close ties to the Nation of Islam, officiating at the wedding of the organization's future leader, Louis Farrakhan. In the late 1960s, he left his position as a minister in the Episcopal Church to chair the newly formed Department of African and Afro-American Studies at the State University of New York at Albany. Philosophically opposed to "the degrading welfare system," Wright argued that "all men should have some kind of responsibility . . . before they receive any money. Earning for self spells dignity." He rejected integration as an "insult on its face," because it implied a black man's worth was dependent upon the presence of whites, and insisted that African Americans take control of their own education and businesses. He also urged black voters to reject the Democratic Party—"the plantation," as he called it—and to "take over the Republican organization and force the Republican Party to give full support to your efforts." If African Americans explained their demands in the "language" of white Republicanism—"subsidies in the place of welfare, self-determination, local control, the encouragement of personal dignity, independence and self-sufficiency"—Wright believed they would find natural allies among "conservative business-oriented Republicans."[14]

Wright chaired the planning committee of the nation's first major Black Power conference. His vice chairman was Maulana Karenga, the creator of Kwanzaa. Held in Newark, New Jersey, the forum highlighted the myriad perspectives within the emerging Black Power movement, from pro-business Republicans to Marxists. Bootstrap self-help was among the ideas presented, with Wright urging African Americans to stop carping on "the deficiencies of the white community," and to work toward "the empowerment of black people" by helping them "take care of their own needs." Numerous workshops focused on black business, and the convention approved a concluding statement demanding that African Americans get a "fair share" of American capitalism. Wright also organized the 1968 national Black Power conference in Philadelphia, which was sponsored by a white-owned corporation, Clairol, where Wright's brother held an executive position. Invitations to the conference featured Clairol's logo and included a message from its president, who urged prospective participants to "forget . . . all this foolish talk of revolution" and to ally themselves with "the American businessman."[15]

Though bootstrap nationalists played a public role in the Black Power movement, organizing national conferences, establishing business enterprises, and taking over CORE's leadership, theirs was a small voice in the cacophony of late 1960s Black Power debates. Indeed, many individuals affiliated with the movement saw the ideas of Wright, McKissick, and Innis as antithetical to the needs of black communities. Ernie Allen of *Soulbook* mocked their self-help ideology as "cullud nationalism" that fostered "illusions about 'Whitey's so-called free enterprize chiefly in order to bolster their own economic position in racist U.S. 'society.'" The Black Panthers' Eldridge Cleaver expressed his desire "to drag this decadent system of capitalism over the cliff," and criticized the "regime of puppets" inside CORE who "coopted" Black Power. To the Black Panther Party and other Leftists, black capitalism offered little more than "a few crumbs for the small Black bourgeoisie and acceptance of a system of continued racial oppression for 30 million Black people."[16]

To supporters of what Huey Newton called "Revolutionary nationalism," capitalism was an inherently racist system that perpetuated black poverty. Although the Panthers and others emphasized self-sufficiency and self-determination, their version was of a different sort—a complete overhaul of American society, politics, and economics—from the bootstrap, individualistic, and middle-class approach of Wright and CORE. Revolutionary nationalism looked past the black middle class to emphasize structural racism's effects on the black underclass. Many of their programs, from free breakfasts to liberation schools, highlighted the failures of American capitalism to meet the needs of African Americans. The Black Panthers' Ten Point Program demanded self-determination, but through the redistribution of U.S. wealth that was built on the backs of slaves. Similar Black Power organizations, such as Baltimore's Mother Rescuers from Poverty, saw the expansion of welfare and government programs for the poor as essential to securing self-determination for single mothers and low-wage workers. In the words of one welfare activist, "How can we better ourselves with nothing?"[17]

The mainstream civil rights establishment, which itself was transitioning from an emphasis on integration to economic empowerment, was also not enamored with black capitalism. The National Black Economic Development Conference of 1969 devoted an entire panel to "The Myth and Irrationality of Black Capitalism." Martin Luther King called for a hundred-billion-dollar plan that would redistribute U.S. wealth to urban renewal projects patterned after the postwar Marshall Plan in Europe, and denounced the individualism and greed that capitalism encouraged. A. Philip Randolph, Whitney Young, and Bayard Rustin proposed a "Freedom Budget" that would invest massive amounts of federal dollars in programs that guaranteed universal health care, decent housing for all, and full employment through public works projects.

Rustin feared that an emphasis on black capitalism would "let both the federal government and the white community off the hook" on addressing issues of socioeconomic inequality, and that the government's focus should be on black workers. Roy Wilkins of the NAACP and Ralph Abernathy of the SCLC claimed that black capitalism was inadequate to solve the drastic economic hardships black neighborhoods faced, and would help only a handful of already well-connected professionals. "What we need is rich communities," noted Abernathy, not "rich individuals."[18]

At the start of the 1968 Republican primaries, most seasoned black Republicans still identified with the Eastern Establishment. When George Romney's presidential bid folded after he claimed to have been "brainwashed" into supporting the Vietnam War, Nelson Rockefeller tepidly entered the primaries as the liberal standard bearer. Black Republicans, 85 percent according to one poll, rallied behind his candidacy. Jackie Robinson hosted an event with the governor attended by seventy of the nation's leading black publishers, and Edward Brooke helped establish the national Rockefeller for President organization. Musicians Louis Armstrong and Lionel Hampton headed a pro-Rockefeller committee of entertainers, and civil rights leaders James Farmer and Ralph Abernathy publicly embraced the governor. Regardless of black enthusiasm, Rockefeller's presidential bid was marred for months by his coy denial of even being a candidate, and by the time he became serious about the race it was too late. Even so, any establishment contender would have had a difficult time securing the nomination. In the past, their coalition included urban states and Black-and-Tan southern delegations, but, in the wake of the Goldwater campaign, by 1968 southern delegates had become mostly white and conservative, depriving the party's liberals of a traditional ally. And while the ten most populous states represented 56 percent of the nation's voters in 1968, they represented only 43 percent of Republican delegates, due to party rules that favored rural states.[19]

Meanwhile, Richard Nixon headed a juggernaut campaign that painted the former vice president as a unifying force between moderates and conservatives. Since 1964, Nixon had maintained ties to the establishment and supported all the major federal civil rights laws of the decade. Careful to differentiate himself from Goldwater, Nixon asserted, "If there is one thing that classifies me it is that I'm a non-extremist," claiming, "on the race issue I'm a liberal." At the same time, he also campaigned for Republican candidates, including segregationists, in all eleven ex-Confederate states in 1965 and 1966. Nixon recognized that not only had southern whites become an important bloc of GOP delegates, but that the establishment's influence within the national party had given way to the suburban voters of the rapidly growing Sunbelt that stretched across the South from Florida to California. White suburbanites, be they from Atlanta, Georgia, or Orange County, California, were the party's new base.[20]

Though Nixon supported the Civil Rights Act of 1968 during the primaries, he devoted far more attention to the racially charged issue of law and order, repeatedly emphasizing his belief that "the most fundamental civil right is the right to be safe from violence." In addition to condemning white anti-war protestors, the Black Panther Party, and other Leftists, he also denounced Martin Luther King, Jr.'s plans for the Poor People's March on Washington. The intent of Nixon's carefully worded appeals for a restoration of law and order was not lost on white voters tired of demonstrations and unrest. Encouraged by his disapproval of mass protests and his emphasis on law and order, many conservatives were willing to overlook his more liberal positions. "You know he *has* to say what he does, for the Northern press," remarked one Atlanta Republican when asked about Nixon's civil rights record.[21]

Ronald Reagan's late entry into the race, and his subsequent victory in the California primary, pushed Nixon farther toward the South. Nixon staffers feared Reagan would steal votes in the region, warning in memos that the California governor's campaign relied on "the emotional distress of those who fear or resent the Negro, and who expect Reagan somehow to keep him 'in his place.'" Whereas Nixon ran to the left before the 1960 national convention to placate Nelson Rockefeller, he ran to the right in 1968 to outflank Reagan in the South. He held private meetings with southern leaders to assure them he would select an acceptable vice presidential candidate, appoint conservative judges, and slow the pace of school integration. His remarks were leaked to the press, along with his claim that he only supported the new open housing law "to get it out of the way" before the election. His most influential southern supporter, Strom Thurmond, lobbied southern delegates to ensure they did not cast renegade votes for Reagan or defect to former Alabama governor George Wallace, a Democrat who ran as an independent in the fall election.[22]

Though most black delegates at the Republican National Convention backed Rockefeller, and criticized Nixon's law-and-order rhetoric, the proceedings were not tarnished by open hostility toward African Americans as they had been four years earlier. Southern delegations remained mostly white, but George W. Lee and Senator Howard Baker reintegrated Tennessee's by fighting to ensure that Sarah Moore Greene, state NAACP president, served as a delegate. In total, the number of black delegates was almost doubled from 1964. Senator Edward Brooke delivered a prime-time address and was a coveted commentator in televised press coverage. Clarence Townes and the Minorities Division successfully placed African Americans on important convention committees and hosted an event attended by three hundred people.[23]

On the other hand, the convention placed minimal emphasis on civil rights. The platform did not include a specific civil rights plank, but simply offered a generic sentence pledging to support existing legislation. Nixon's vice-presidential selection, Governor Spiro Agnew, who had been overwhelmingly supported by Maryland's black voters as a civil rights advocate in 1966, exemplified the GOP's law and order wing by 1968. Condemning even peaceful civil disobedience, Agnew authorized the mass arrests of hundreds of protestors, blamed riots on "the misguided compassion of public opinion," and supported a policy that would have allowed state law enforcement officers to shoot unarmed looters. With Agnew, Nixon signaled that he not only would oppose radical black militants, but would resist the public protests that had been a staple of the civil rights movement for a decade.[24]

Black delegates initially responded negatively to the Nixon-Agnew ticket. William O. Walker accused Nixon of "selling out" to Strom Thurmond, and Edward Brooke claimed that law and order rhetoric was "a code word for, basically, racism." One black delegate told the *New York Times*, "there is no way in hell I can justify Nixon and Agnew to Negroes," and another remarked, "They're telling us flatly that they want the white backlash and that they don't give a damn about us." Ohio's Chester Gillespie lamented that Agnew's "image is worse than Nixon's," and feared the nomination indicated that the party "reckons it can do without the Negro." Regardless, most delegates, displeased as they may have been with Nixon, reluctantly endorsed him in the general election, emphasizing the need for black participation in the two-party system. As New York's Deighton Edwards put it, "I'll work for Nixon because we must fight this thing from within the party."[25]

Unlike the events of 1964, when the national committee fired Grant Reynolds and shut down the Minorities Division, Clarence Townes' division in 1968 expanded to twenty-nine staffers and over forty black field workers. Townes alone traveled twenty-five thousand miles, established black Republican clubs on college campuses, organized rallies, and coordinated a speaking tour featuring Edward Brooke. He devoted special attention to the black press, which had been a mainstay of black Republicanism prior to 1964, paying full advertising rates without haggling over prices and maintaining constant communication with publishers in order to get "preferential treatment" during news cycles. By election day, the *Atlanta Daily World*, *Denver Blade*, Cleveland *Call and Post*, *Iowa Bystander*, and other black newspapers returned to their roots and endorsed Nixon. Townes also established a "celebrity committee" composed of high-profile black entertainers and athletes, most notably basketball star Wilt Chamberlain. As Jackie Robinson had done in 1960, Chamberlain traveled with Nixon on the campaign trail, even accompanying him to Martin Luther King's funeral. Like many black Republicans, Chamberlain emphasized that black voters needed to pragmatically support both parties. "It is just common sense," he argued, "that the black American must stay in a position to talk to and influence any man who has [a chance] to become the next President."[26]

While Nixon was far more acceptable to black Republicans than Barry Goldwater had been, some still endorsed the Democratic candidate, Hubert Humphrey. Asa Spaulding, a prominent Republican businessman from North Carolina, was a founding member of the National Citizens for Humphrey Committee. Most notable was Jackie Robinson, who claimed that Nixon "prostituted himself" to segregationists, and that his nomination signified "the GOP didn't give a damn about my vote or the votes—or welfare—of my people." Though Robinson vowed to remain a Republican for the sake of the two-party system, he resigned from Nelson Rockefeller's staff to campaign for Humphrey. As he was the chairman of the board of the National Negro Republican Assembly, Robinson's defection initiated the organization's collapse, and by the 1970s NNRA president, Grant Reynolds, had moved to the Bahamas.[27]

The black Republicans who endorsed Humphrey, along with other black leaders, believed Nixon's speeches used thinly veiled code language just vague enough to allow the campaign to deny any racial undertones. When Nixon spoke of "law and order" and "crime in the streets," they heard a crackdown on demonstrations and black neighborhoods. His support of "states' rights" and opposition to "federal interference" meant an end to federal intervention in civil rights. "Neighborhood schools" signaled a slowdown of integration, and denunciations of "giveaway programs" and "welfare cheats" played on stereotypes of black laziness. This rhetoric increasingly paralleled that of savvy southern Republicans, who couched their opposition to civil rights in a

palatable language of property rights and individual freedom. Despite carefully selected terminology, it became clear by the end of the campaign that
Nixon deliberately intended for racist listeners to hear anti-black messages.
After recording a television advertisement on crime, Nixon told aides, "this
hits it right on the nose . . . it's all about law and order and the damn Negro-
Puerto Rican groups out there." His right-hand man, John Ehrlichman, later
confessed, "there were subliminal racial messages in a lot of Nixon's campaigning," and admitted the president's intent to "go after the racists."[28]

It is important to note, however, that Nixon openly endorsed civil rights
legislation and did not pursue a strategy centered on the segregationists of the
Deep South, whose Electoral College votes ultimately went to George Wallace. He instead focused his attention on the rapidly converging and expanding middle class of the metropolitan Sunbelt (and northern) suburbs, many
of whose residents accepted civil rights and gradual reform but had grown
tired of demonstrations and feared black militants. Many suburbanites touted
a nominally color-blind notion of an individual meritocracy, where self-
initiative supplanted government intervention in economic advancement. If
African Americans lagged behind whites economically, this thinking went, it
was because of their own laziness, dependency on welfare, or cultural deficiencies, not the result of discrimination or structural impediments.[29]

Even in reaching out to Sunbelt suburbia, Nixon did not fully embrace
their colorblind ideology in his economic policies. In December 1967, he
foreshadowed the affirmative action initiatives of his administration by suggesting that the country owed African Americans a "dividend" in economic
prosperity, claiming, "the people in the ghetto have got to have more than an
equal chance." He subsequently told an audience in Virginia that civil rights
laws were part of a "necessary revolution," but the country's focus should now
turn to "a period of helping people walk through those doors" of opportunity.
On policies that helped African Americans enter the work force, such as
government-funded training programs and affirmative action policies that
gave preferential treatment to minorities, Nixon told a reporter, "I would be
considered almost radical." Affirmative action was compatible with Republican ideology, according to Nixon, because it fostered self-help by giving a
"little extra start" to "those who haven't had their chance, who've had it denied for a hundred years."[30]

The thrust of Nixon's economic plan centered on "black capitalism,"
whereby the government provided black businesses with tax breaks, guaranteed loans, and contract set-asides. He claimed not only that the program

would assist entrepreneurs, but that the success of black businesses would trickle down in the form of jobs and revenue inside their communities. Initially, some of his conservative advisors warned him not to endorse a program that appeared to redirect government resources away from white businesses toward black endeavors, lest he be accused of "reverse discrimination." Even while fearing he might lose some white votes, admitting, "I don't think this is a good political move," Nixon told aides, "we'll do it, because it's the right thing to do." Moreover, he was the only presidential candidate in 1968 to use the controversial "Black Power" phrase, predicting that his programs would spur "black pride, black jobs, black opportunity, and yes, black power." He told a Boston audience in February that "the answer to the militants is not to say 'never,' " but to work with them and "forge new alliances." The following month, he told supporters in Milwaukee to not be afraid of Black Power, because it promoted "the power that people should have over their own destinies." His carefully worded definitions fit securely within the self-reliance, free market ideology of the Republican Party, and his black capitalism plan won the endorsement of the *Wall Street Journal*. Indeed, it faced little resistance from most conservatives, including the *National Review*, who championed the idea that "respect and access to jobs must be earned by the Negroes themselves."[31]

Nixon introduced his program to a national audience with two addresses broadcast by the CBS and NBC radio networks on April 25 and May 2. The two speeches were later used in radio advertisements and reprinted in campaign literature circulated in black communities. He criticized the Great Society programs of "payments to the poor, but not for anything except keeping out of sight: payments that perpetuate poverty, and that kept the endless dismal cycle of dependency spinning from generation to generation." Assuring white listeners that "much of the black militant talk these days is actually in terms far closer to the doctrines of free enterprise than to those of the welfarist 30's," he urged them to "listen to the militants," hearing not just their "threats" but their usage of "the terms of 'pride,' 'ownership,' 'private enterprise,' 'capital,' 'self-assurance,' [and] 'self-respect.'" According to Nixon, the fundamental aspiration of African Americans was "to be included in—not as supplicants, but as owners, as entrepreneurs—to have a share of the wealth and a piece of the action." Rather than fearing Black Power, Americans needed to understand "the black man's pride is the white man's hope" for a peaceful society.[32]

While occasionally mentioning black capitalism in campaign speeches,

Nixon rarely reached out to majority-black audiences in person, but, unlike his 1960 campaign, he encouraged black staffers and the Minorities Division to target African Americans on his behalf. His only campaign stop in a black neighborhood was at Philadelphia's Progress Plaza shopping center, where he promoted the virtues of self-determination. At his side was the project's founder, Leon Sullivan, a "quiet" Nixon supporter who had become one of the nation's most prominent advocates of self-help by 1968, and whose Opportunities Industrialization Center was designed to help move African Americans from "welfare to work, from tax dependent to tax payer." In October, an estimated one thousand African Americans attended a Nixon rally in New York that included Hobson Reynolds of the black Elks, Lionel Hampton, and a dance troupe of black "Nixonettes."[33]

The Minorities Division similarly ensured that local black leaders were included on stage with Nixon in campaign stops in Knoxville, Atlanta, and other southern cities. Many of the stops featured the Nixonettes, and provided chartered buses for black attendees. The division also flooded black communities with literature using Black Power "catch themes attributed to Nixon," such as "a piece of the action." Just days prior to the election, subscribers to *Jet* saw a two-page, glossy advertisement purchased by Nixon's campaign that featured a well-dressed black college student named Homer Pitts. It informed readers that Pitts would soon graduate, but asked, "Then what?" Its answer: "a vote for Richard Nixon for President is a vote for a man who wants Homer to have the chance to own his own business," concluding, "black capitalism is black power. . . . It's the key to the black man's fight for equality—for a piece of the action."[34]

Nixon also met privately with Floyd McKissick and Roy Innis at his New York apartment, where he promised to support CORE's Community Self Determination Act. The bill was the centerpiece of CORE's legislative campaign, proposing "a new institutional structure" in black communities, "based not on governmental paternalism, but on local self-help." It called for government loans and tax incentives that assisted in the creation of a Community Development Corporation and Community Development Bank to be owned by members of a neighborhood who purchased five-dollar stocks. The corporation would manage subsidiary businesses and social programs, with profits staying exclusively inside each community. Innis was invited to discuss the bill at the Republican National Convention, and numerous Republicans cosponsored it in Congress. Nixon dispatched three staffers to help guide the act through Congress, and instructed his law firm to assist in drafting its most legally technical sections.[35]

Though the bill did not pass through the Democratic-controlled Congress, and neither Innis nor McKissick officially endorsed a presidential candidate, Nixon earned their respect. On NBC's *Meet the Press*, Innis lauded Nixon's acknowledgement that "black nationalism is relevant, black power is the relevant philosophy in this country," adding, "I praise him when he endorses CORE's plan." McKissick told reporters, "Nixon may fool a lot of people and do one Hell of a job as president," and expressed his certainty that "Nixon is a first rate American and there's no doubt about that." The editor of *The Liberator*, a popular magazine among nationalists, told readers that while conservatives were the "natural ally" of the Black Power movement, economic self-determination was a precursor to political power and equality. "As Roy Innis of CORE has attested," the publication declared, "only Richard Nixon is . . . hospitable to Black Power."[36]

While Nixon doubled Goldwater in terms of black votes on election day, his program of black capitalism was not enough to sway the vast majority of African Americans to ignore his racially coded rhetoric. He secured victories in the Midwest and across the Sunbelt in California, Arizona, New Mexico, Florida, and the Carolinas, but did not win in the Deep South, writing off Alabama, Mississippi, Georgia, and Louisiana to arch-segregationist George Wallace. He did particularly well among the white middle class, in the nation's first election where suburban voters outnumbered rural and urban voters, and made inroads among traditionally Democratic constituencies—Catholics, ethnic whites, and blue-collar workers—who were drawn to his conservative populism and emphasis on law and order, family, and patriotism. Nationally, he drew only 10 to 15 percent of the black vote, but received upward of 25 to 30 percent in a few silk-stocking precincts. Black Republicans were quick to point out that, despite minimal black support on the national stage, crucial middle-class black precincts in Ohio, Tennessee, Kentucky, and New Jersey provided over 20 percent of their votes for Nixon, helping to secure narrow victories in those states.[37]

Black Republicans played a prominent role in Nixon's inaugural ceremonies. Business leader Berkeley Burrell served as the first black chair of an inaugural concession committee, and made a concerted effort to secure over one million dollars in profit for black businesses contracted to provide photography, transportation, food, and other services. The inauguration featured

1,500 black VIPs, and a Republican civil rights activist from Kentucky, Bishop C. Ewbank Tucker of the African Methodist Episcopal Church, delivered the invocation. Senator Brooke hosted one of the largest receptions of the day, with guests ranging from high-ranking Nixon cabinet members to Nathan Wright, who arrived in "flowing, colorful African-style robes". The inaugural concert featured the talents of Dinah Shore, Lionel Hampton, and Duke Ellington. In one of the liveliest musical performances of the evening, James Brown slid onto the stage and black Republicans in the audience sang along as he delivered his signature lyrics: "Say It Loud, I'm Black and I'm Proud!"[38]

As president, Nixon approached civil rights with a series of what advisor John Ehrlichman described as liberal "zigs" and conservative "zags." Far more personally devoted to foreign policy, Nixon lacked a guiding ideology on most domestic issues, basing many of his decisions on opportunistic political calculations that defy "conservative" and "liberal" categorization; indeed, Nixon obliquely described himself as a "progressive conservative". On issues of civil rights, his "zig-zag" strategy was complemented by a policy of "benign neglect." The term entered the public lexicon after a memo written by advisor Daniel Patrick Moynihan was leaked to the press, in which he suggested, "the time may have come when the issue of race could benefit from a period of 'benign neglect' . . . a period in which Negro progress continues and racial rhetoric fades." Because "benign neglect" downplayed the administration's civil rights accomplishments, and the "zig-zag" strategy deliberately muddied the administration's policy, Nixon's elusive civil rights record remains contested. For example, the same Nixon who oversaw an 800-percent increase in the civil rights enforcement budget also made racist remarks in private, publicly embraced Strom Thurmond and other segregationists, and condoned the FBI's repression of militant black organizations.[39]

The "zig-zag" strategy was particularly loathsome to Secretary of Housing and Urban Development (HUD) George Romney, who had long advocated housing integration. With Nixon's approval, Romney oversaw the construction of more housing units for low-income families in three years than under all previous administrations combined. He also attempted to integrate middle-class white neighborhoods through the construction of low-income housing. This strategy spurred intense backlash from his former constituents when he targeted a suburb of Detroit that was 99 percent white. Nixon intervened and demanded Romney no longer "force" integration on white neighborhoods by constructing "cheap houses." Later, when the city of Blackjack,

Missouri, contested the construction of a HUD-sponsored housing project, Attorney General John Mitchell refused to step in, further undermining Romney's ability to pursue his agenda. A disgruntled Romney resigned from the president's cabinet after the 1972 election.[40]

The "zig-zag" approach also impacted the administration's handling of school desegregation. Secretary of Health, Education and Welfare Robert Finch outraged conservatives by revoking the tax-exempt status of segregated private schools, which served as lily-white alternatives to public education. However, when it came to public school districts that remained segregated, more than fifteen years after *Brown v. Board of Education*, HEW shifted its focus away from withholding funds from noncompliant districts to challenging them in court. School desegregation still progressed, although with a low profile, and already unpopular courts, rather than the administration, took the blame from conservatives. The strategy infuriated liberals and civil rights leaders, who wanted not only presidential action, but moral leadership and resounding rhetorical support for integration. However, though it was not touted by the president, the proportion of segregated schools in the South dropped from 68 percent in 1969 to just 8 percent by 1974, integrating more students than the combined efforts of all previous administrations since *Brown*.[41]

Also disconcerting to liberals was Nixon's appointment of conservative Supreme Court justices. In one of his first major acts as president, he replaced the iconic liberal Republican, Chief Justice Earl Warren, with a more conservative Warren Burger. To replace Democrat Abe Fortas, he nominated Clement Haynsworth of South Carolina, who had previously opposed school desegregation. Edward Brooke joined the NAACP in denouncing the nomination, and his lobbying efforts played a significant role in unifying Senate opposition. A nearly unprecedented 40 percent of Republicans joined Democrats in rejecting the nominee. To the delight of southerners, Nixon doubled down and nominated G. Harrold Carswell, who once ran on a white-supremacy platform in a race for the Georgia state legislature. Brooke and the NAACP again led the opposition, and, again, enough Republicans joined Democrats in denying the appointment. The president ultimately moved outside the South, and successfully appointed a more moderate judge from Minnesota, Harry Blackmun. When tasked with filling another Supreme Court vacancy in 1971, Nixon turned to Barry Goldwater's former advisor, William Rehnquist, who had once argued that the legal backbone of segregation, *Plessy v. Ferguson*, "was right and should be reaffirmed."[42]

On the other hand, Nixon also fulfilled his pledge to black capitalists early in his tenure, signing an executive order on March 5, 1969, that created the Office of Minority Business Enterprise (OMBE). Dozens of black entrepreneurs and activists attended the signing ceremony, where the president promised them full "involvement in business," which "has always been a major route toward participation in the mainstream of American life." The OMBE had jurisdiction over more than one hundred programs designed to "encourage pride, dignity, and a sense of independence" by providing guaranteed loans, credit, insurance, and assistance to minority-owned businesses. Unlike his handling of most civil rights policies, Nixon personally embraced the OMBE, privately telling Secretary of Commerce Maurice Stans, "this is something long overdue and I want you to give it a high priority." By 1970, the OMBE oversaw the distribution of over $315 million to minority-owned businesses, an amount that continued to grow for the next four years. The program had an immediate short-term impact. Over half of the one hundred largest black businesses in 1975 had been founded since 1968, and the total number of black-owned companies had grown by over thirty thousand.[43]

Coordinating their efforts with the OMBE, other government agencies joined the black-capitalism campaign. In 1970, Nixon issued an executive order authorizing the Small Business Administration (SBA) to become the prime contractor for government agencies that lacked sufficient contracts with black businesses. Contracts under this set-aside program ranged from black janitorial companies hired to clean federal buildings to a multimillion-dollar deal awarded to a black-owned food company that provided the military with canned goods and meat. From 1969 to 1971, federal purchases of minority services and products skyrocketed by over one thousand percent, and by 1973 the federal government had contracted over $200 million with minority businesses, compared to less than $9 million when Nixon first took office. The president also lifted bank-chartering and regulatory safeguards that had previously stunted the formation of black-owned banks. From 1969 to the mid-1970s, the number of black-owned banks, and the amount of federal deposits in black-owned banks, more than doubled. In just three years, the total assets of black banks rose from $400 million to more than $1 billion.[44]

While the OMBE was popular with bootstrap nationalists like Floyd McKissick, most mainstream civi rights leaders were ambivalent. As one activist told Nixon, "You're talking to and about the Negro elite," not "to the black man in the street." In addition to panning Nixon's "zig-zag" strategy and Supreme Court nominees, they lambasted him for failing to name a single

African American to his cabinet. The reality of the administration's black appointees, however, was more complex. Nixon offered Whitney Young, Jr., the top position at HUD, but the Urban League chief declined, fearing that a close affiliation with the administration would taint his legacy. Nixon also offered Edward Brooke his choice of secretary of HUD or HEW, as well as the ambassadorship to the United Nations, but Brooke declined, wanting to build his legacy in the Senate. Many journalists close to Brooke claimed that the president later offered him the position of U.S. attorney general and a spot on the Supreme Court.[45]

In high-ranking subcabinet and executive level appointments, however, Nixon named 37 percent more African Americans than Lyndon Johnson and, in total, tripled the number of African Americans appointed by Johnson. The number of black women appointed by Nixon more than doubled that of his two predecessors, and included the first woman and first African American to serve as deputy solicitor general, Jewel Lafontant-Mankarious. This record was achieved despite Nixon's being rejected by nearly three out of four African Americans who were offered high-level posts in his first eighteen months. Among those who accepted a position was the Republican-turned-Democrat activist from Memphis, Benjamin Hooks, who became the first black chair of the powerful Federal Communications Commission.[46]

Nixon's first major black appointment was Robert J. Brown, who served the White House as special assistant to the president. A wealthy public relations man with humble origins from High Point, North Carolina, Brown personified the self-made, bootstrap ideal of black capitalism. He had also been active in the civil rights movement, working with McKissick in North Carolina's CORE, and serving as a lifetime member of the NAACP, a board member of the SCLC, and the director of the North Carolina Voter Education Project. A registered Democrat in 1968, Brown worked for Robert Kennedy's presidential campaign, but was convinced by Clarence Townes to break ranks and join the Nixon camp during the general election. In his first year with the administration, Brown wrote a memo that encouraged federal agencies to "set goals" regarding contracts with black-owned businesses. The directive received the authoritative signature of the president and reinforced the administration's prioritization of black capitalism within the federal bureaucracy.[47]

Brown was the administration's most passionate supporter of historically black colleges and universities (HBCUs). His suggestions to John Ehrlichman and other key advisors to see to it that "the Administration do whatever it can to assist black colleges" were eventually endorsed by Nixon himself. By 1970, the president saw HBCUs as vehicles of self-help, and told white aides that an alliance with black colleges was now "one of his priorities." Brown arranged a series of meetings between almost a dozen HBCU presidents and Nixon, who subsequently instructed H. R. Haldeman to redirect $100 million to black colleges. Though conservatives in the administration complained that black colleges already received disproportionate federal funding, grants to HBCUs grew dramatically on Nixon's watch. Between 1969 and 1971, federal funding to black colleges increased from $108 to $167 million, and by 1973 had increased to $400 million. Brown served as a central conduit of the funding, negotiating budgetary earmarks for scholarships, salaries, and various campus improvements. Between 1969 and 1977 enrollment at HBCUs grew by 50 percent. Brown also spearheaded the creation of a program that actively recruited top students at black colleges to join the federal government, significantly raising the number of minority applicants to the General Services Administration.[48]

Like Brown, other black appointees worked behind closed doors on behalf of African Americans, often with little media fanfare. Assistant secretary for equal opportunity Samuel J. Simmons, a black Republican from Detroit who had previously worked with the U.S. Civil Rights Commission, oversaw a large-scale education and public relations campaign that taught African Americans their rights under the new open housing law. He also compiled the first National Registry of Minority Contractors and Subcontractors, a six-volume directory created to maximize the government's ability to purchase black firms' goods and services. Similarly, the assistant postmaster general, Ronald Lee, deposited $70 million of Post Office funds in black-owned banks. As the third highest ranking official in HUD, Assistant Secretary Samuel C. Jackson, a former NAACP lawyer and the first black vice chairman of the Kansas state GOP, oversaw the allocation of over one billion dollars a year. His major emphasis was a "more equitable distribution of fiscal resources" to infrastructure development in black communities. As the administrator of a massive water and sewage program, for instance, Jackson directed hundreds of millions of dollars to repairing dilapidated systems in poor, predominantly black towns, such as Grambling, Louisiana, and Robbins, Illinois. In Kansas City, he ensured that the architectural and construction work for a multimillion dollar housing project and community park were contracted to black-owned businesses.[49]

Nixon's best-known black appointee was the former national director of

Figure 13. President Nixon discusses his black capitalism initiatives in the Oval Office in March 1969 with, from left to right: Robert J. Brown, John A. Hannah, and the Reverend Leon Sullivan. White House Press Office, 0596, National Archives and Records Administration.

CORE, James Farmer, who accepted a position as assistant secretary of HEW. Though Farmer was tasked with handling the types of traditional civil rights issues that Nixon generally shied away from, particularly school desegregation, he managed to exert some influence—for instance, ensuring that 50 percent of HEW's management interns came from underrepresented minority groups. On one occasion, the governor of Mississippi threatened to veto Head Start grants to his state, and the secretary of HEW, Robert Finch, opted not to intervene to save the program. Distraught, Farmer called Nixon's office directly, and was granted a private meeting with the president. In the Oval Office, Farmer pled his case, and by the end of the day Nixon had instructed Finch to override the governor's veto. Though Farmer frequently referenced this success story, and maintained he had "a good deal of leverage" during his short time in Washington, he resigned in 1970. He publicly cited "the slowness of the bureaucracy" when announcing his departure, but privately he was the insider responsible for leaking Moynihan's "benign neglect" memo to the press to demonstrate the administration's hesitancy on civil rights.[50]

"The father of affirmative action," Arthur Fletcher, was also among Nixon's black appointees. As assistant secretary of labor, he revived President Johnson's abandoned Philadelphia Plan, which targeted widespread discrimination in the construction industry. With jurisdiction over the Office of Federal Contract Compliance, headed by another black Republican, John Wilks, Fletcher made the restoration of the Philadelphia Plan his primary objective. Philadelphia had a particularly vicious pattern of discrimination, with African Americans representing 30 percent of the population but just one percent of the jobs in a construction industry that received over $600 million annually in federal contracts. With Secretary of Labor George Shultz's support, Fletcher demanded specific "goals or standards for percentages of minority employees" in the construction trades. In order to work on federal projects, Philadelphia's iron trade unions, for example, had to hire between 5 and 9 percent black employees by 1970, and 25 percent by 1975. Fletcher argued that contract compliance had too long been met with vague, noncommittal promises, and that his plan "destroys tokenism, by making specific numeral requirements on the contractor as the price of his doing federal business." To him, affirmative action represented an institutional response to economic disparities between blacks and whites that was more substantial than a welfare check. In lobbying their plan to the administration, Shultz and Fletcher claimed it fit within the Republican "spirit of self-reliance," arguing it would demonstrate Nixon's commitment to "helping people help themselves."[51]

In June 1969, Fletcher formally announced the administration's backing of his revised Philadelphia Plan. Weeks later, the comptroller general declared the policy unconstitutional, arguing that racial quotas violated the Civil Rights Act of 1964, which banned the use of race as a factor in employment. To the surprise of many, Nixon backed Fletcher, eagerly embracing a plan that complemented his self-help initiatives, drove a wedge between two key Democratic constituencies (labor and African Americans), and highlighted Democratic hypocrisy on the issue of union discrimination. With its status in legal limbo, Fletcher rewrote the plan to cover not only the building industry in select cities but all trade unions and businesses with federal contracts nationwide. In March 1970, a federal court sided with the administration, overruled the comptroller general, and gave the green light to what one historian has called "the most radical civil rights employment measure in American history." Though the Philadelphia Plan later fell out of favor with Nixon and was diluted by conservatives inside the administration, who replaced it with weaker "home town" plans, it marked the start of an era of institutionalized affirmative action in the federal government.[52]

The Philadelphia Plan put black Republicans out in front of mainstream black leaders on the issue of union discrimination. Many civil rights leaders had a deep-seated relationship with labor and did not want to alienate their

Figure 14. President Nixon with Arthur Fletcher in the White House, December 2, 1971. White House Press Office, 7901-13, National Archives and Records Administration.

longtime allies. Bayard Rustin, for example, did not oppose affirmative action, but stood with labor leaders in opposing the Philadelphia Plan because he could not "conceive of an effective and progressive coalition which does not include the labor movement." Even while union leaders, including George Meany of the AFL-CIO, balked at racial quotas, Rustin did not want to divide the New Deal coalition. On the other hand, black Republicans had long been ambivalent toward unions and certainly were not afraid to offend powerful labor leaders who opposed affirmative action. Edward Brooke's 1966 "Open Society" policy statement, for example, devoted an entire section to discrimination in trade unions, and highlighted President Johnson's fear of alienating labor by targeting discrimination in its ranks.[53]

Black appointees inside the Nixon administration may not have supported the president's conservative "zags" and gestures toward white southerners, but their pragmatic decision to join his administration provided them access to the power necessary to try to enact their agendas. To most black Republicans, the issue immediately facing black communities was no longer integration, but economic self-sufficiency. Art Fletcher told reporters he was fine with the administration's decision to not "spread itself thin over the whole range of civil rights activities," which allowed it "to concentrate on economic opportunities." Robert Brown shot back to his critics, "We kicked down the doors for the kids calling us Uncle Toms," as he vowed "to keep pressing" from inside the White House. James Farmer agreed with many in the civil rights establishment that "there's good reason to criticize the administration," but noted, "without some of us on the inside . . . all the picket lines in the world won't help." Indeed, Edward Brooke, Robert Brown, Arthur Fletcher, Samuel C. Jackson, Samuel Simmons, and other black Republicans routinely made *Ebony*'s list of the "100 Most Influential Black Americans" in the early 1970s. They successfully secured funding and support for black businesses, colleges, and communities. Their shift away from mainstream civil rights leadership, however, represented a stark break from the black Republicanism of the 1950s and early to mid-1960s as they moved self-reliance to the forefront of their agenda.[54]

Black Republicans since the 1930s had frequently failed to identify with the economic needs of the black working class. The Republican vision of black capitalism, while promising trickle down prosperity, was no different, serving the needs of only a segment of the black middle class. While in previous decades black Republicans had actively engaged in the struggle to integrate public accommodations, protect voting rights, and ensure fair housing, by the late 1960s they had moved on to economic issues, and on these issues they were more unambiguously conservative, touting individual opportunity as the key to black advancement. "I won the right to go to the hotel, and I won the right to go to school, and I won the right to buy a house," asserted Art Fletcher, "now I need the money." Black capitalism was not wholly rejected within the Black Power movement, and its adherents, particularly Nathan Wright, Floyd McKissick, and Roy Innis, held leadership positions in the movement's major conferences and managed to assume control of one of the nation's foremost civil rights organizations, CORE. And while their voice may have been marginal inside black communities who rejected their distinctly middle-class solutions, their relationship with the Nixon administration succeeded in redirecting hundreds of millions of dollars of federal funding to their endeavors. However misguided other black leaders thought black Republicans may have been in their belief that black business was capable of transforming black neighborhoods or achieving parity with white corporations, those close to the Nixon administration succeeded in implementing policies on the national stage that aligned with their ideas. When it came to obtaining actual policies that reflected their agenda, bootstrap black nationalists were perhaps the most successful of any strain of the Black Power movement.[55]

CHAPTER 8

Not a Silent Minority:

Black Republicans in the 1970s

"Not since Democratic President Franklin D. Roosevelt," *Ebony* magazine observed in 1973, "has the inauguration of a Republican President resulted in such a massive black turnout." During the four-day celebration of Richard Nixon's reelection, thousands of black guests attended a star-studded reception at the African Museum of Art and a banquet hosted by the Capitol City Republican Club in honor of retiring presidential aide Robert Brown. At another venue, black Republicans escorted First Lady Pat Nixon through the nation's first inaugural exhibition celebrating minority contributions to art, music, and food. Black Republicans also met with the incoming chairman of the Republican National Committee, George H. W. Bush, who promised to "vigorously seek more black input into the party."[1]

The inauguration marked an active yet frustrating decade for black Republicans. Entrepreneurs and bootstrap nationalists enjoyed massive federal support for black colleges, businesses, and self-help ventures, while others who had allied with the Eastern Establishment found themselves outside Nixon's circle. The president eagerly spent money on an array of black enterprises, and enacted bureaucratic reforms like contract set-asides, but shied away from identification with the civil rights movement or its leaders. By the 1970s, local and state Republican parties, even those in the Deep South, accepted token integration, a major step for some, but staunchly opposed black Republican efforts to integrate party leadership. With the GOP inside the White House for the first time in almost a decade, black Republican organizations of various ideologies sought to influence the direction of the party. Just as the civil rights movement had become fractured and decentralized by the late 1960s, so had black Republicanism become divided along philosophical and strategic lines, as a myriad of leaders and organizations competed for the limited attention their party and president were willing to give African Americans.

By 1968, the RNC Minorities Division, which was accused by party stalwart Grant Reynolds of accommodating conservatives just two years prior, had become a vocal intraparty critic. Its director, Clarence Townes, campaigned for Nixon, but denounced Spiro Agnew's nomination as "a step backward" and refused to have his picture taken with the vice presidential candidate when their paths crossed. Once in office, Nixon declined to offer Townes a position in the administration, and did not ask for his division's input in policy debates. Townes subsequently accused Republicans of underfunding black outreach, and calculated that the party spent an average of "$1 million to reach 250,000 white voters and $25,000 to reach a million black voters." It appeared Republicans were less concerned about meaningful black outreach than about the appearance of black outreach as a cover against allegations of racism. He further complained that black "well-being is being sacrificed to political gain" by the president, who "has placed the name of the Republican party in greater darkness than it was in under Goldwater."[2]

In November 1970, the national committee closed the Minorities Division, and Townes assumed a position as director of a black think tank, joining the ranks of other GOP outcasts who had cast their lot with the waning Eastern Establishment. That same year, the RNC also quietly shut down its Action Now initiative. Established in 1969, the program was patterned after Detroit's Metropolitan Action Center, whose founder, Elly Peterson, became a vice chairperson of the national committee. Peterson attempted to establish centers across the country that would work on the grassroots level to solve "urban ghetto problems." The success of the program hinged on local GOP commitment, which varied from mild support to, more often, ambivalence. Republicans in Connecticut, for example, set up centers that worked with citizens to combat pollution and crime, but other states' operatives were not particularly eager to devote money and time away from white constituents. "After all," one Republican leader from Florida told Peterson, "we don't really want to get involved with Negroes."[3]

Outside the official party apparatus, the Nixon years saw a rise in the number of black Republican organizations. In 1968, one hundred black Republicans in California partnered with a group of young black nationalists to form the Third World Republicans, an organization that promoted the president's policies of black capitalism to black nationalists. Seventy-five disenchanted black Democrats, including the chairman of the New York City Commission on Human Rights, publicly switched parties in 1968, and formed the Liberal Independent Republican Club of Harlem to "bring the two-party system back . . . because it can give the voters a real choice of programs, policies and leadership." They were joined in the 1970s by the New York State Conference of Black Republicans, who dedicated themselves to creating a "NEW Republican Party" by advocating increased numbers of black Republicans as candidates for elective office and other policy-making positions. John Kellogg of Cleveland, Ohio's, city council founded the Black Elected Republican Officials organization to connect the local black Republican politicians with Nixon administration and RNC officials. Their 1970 annual meeting featured appearances by Attorney General John Mitchell and other high-ranking White House representatives, but also concluded by passing a unanimous statement condemning Nixon's Supreme Court nominees and demanding a greater role for African Americans in the national committee.[4]

The country's largest black Republican organization, the National Council of Concerned Afro-American Republicans (NCCAAR), reached ten thousand members less than six months after its founding in 1968, and thirty thousand members by 1972. Ideologically oriented toward the Eastern Establishment, NCCAAR assumed the role of the defunct National Negro Republican Assembly, whose leaders, Jackie Robinson and Grant Reynolds, were among NCCAAR's original members, as a perennial critic of the GOP's lack of diversity within party leadership. Its founder, Thurman L. Dodson, had previously headed the National Council of the Fair Employment Practices Act and worked for over two decades alongside Thurgood Marshall as chief counsel for the Washington, D.C., NAACP. According to NCCAAR bylaws, its purpose was not to serve white Republicans by working to bring African Americans into the party, but "to see to it that our race gets a square deal" in the GOP. It advocated reforms to ensure that African Americans would have "a more meaningful role in the policies, personnel and the promotion of Negro candidates in local, state, and national contests." Their first battle centered on Florida's all-white delegation at the 1968 national convention in Miami. Speaking before the Platform and Rules Committees, NCCAAR representatives called for implementation of new procedures that would require a state delegation to reflect the approximate racial composition of the state, and to create positions in the RNC reserved for minorities. The two committees rejected the proposals.[5]

Throughout Nixon's presidency, NCCAAR, which changed its name to the National Council of Afro-American Republicans (NCAAR) in the early 1970s, continued to speak out against the direction of the party. "Very little of the Republican organization dollar has been spent" on black outreach, complained Dodson's successor, Curtis Perkins, who accused the party of "writing the Black vote off without doing anything about bringing Blacks into the Party." Emphasizing their belief in the two-party system, NCAAR vowed to exercise their right "to fight within the Party for our people and to maintain the right to offer constructive criticism." Their bimonthly newsletter, *The Afro-American Voter*, sided squarely with the Eastern Establishment, and lamented that "the ugly spectre" of the far right "still casts its shadow" over the party. To remedy the state of the GOP, they urged the average black voter to "Become a Forward Thinking Republican Who Demands Full Participation in the Republican Party" by removing "bigoted White Republican leadership."[6]

Though NCAAR was the nation's largest organization representing black Republicans, its unpopular demands alienated it from party leaders, who preferred to work with the National Black Silent Majority Committee (NBSMC). Clay Claiborne, the former RNC aide indicted for violating New Jersey election law in 1964, officially launched the NBSMC in the summer of 1970 to represent "black Americans who work every day . . . have never been to jail . . . [and] have never participated in a riot." According to its publications, NBSMC membership reached over six thousand by 1971. However, once it began to receive national media attention, many of its supposed supporters disavowed their membership. The publisher of a black newspaper in Minneapolis claimed to have tentatively agreed to join, but upon seeing its conservative stands on a range of social issues, she openly disassociated herself from the group. Others, such as Jesse Warders of Louisville, were listed as members on official NBSMC publications, though they never officially agreed to join.[7]

While the organization's real membership included Old Guard Republican leaders C.A. Scott and Hobson Reynolds, there is little evidence outside of its own statements to suggest that the NBSMC had widespread black Republican support. The decade's most active and prominent black Republicans, Edward Brooke, Floyd McKissick, Curtis Perkins, Samuel Jackson, and others, had little to do with the NBSMC, preferring instead to focus on their efforts to reform the GOP infrastructure. Because of the NBSMC's conservative outlook, however, it was one of the only independent black Republican organizations of the early 1970s to consistently draw support from white party elites. Claiborne's office was conveniently located across the street from RNC headquarters, which occasionally wrote NBSMC press releases. The Republican Congressional Campaign Committee (RCCC) paid for Claiborne's national tour of seventy-eight cities. Strom Thurmond and conservative newspaper columnists openly praised the group, and President Nixon wrote a public letter commending Claiborne's "excellent efforts." The RCCC and NBSMC partnered again during Nixon's reelection campaign to create a pamphlet, "Partners in Progress," featuring cartoons of Nixon's accomplishments and photographs of 235 black appointees in the Nixon administration. The publication was featured on an ABC national television news program, and became one of the most ubiquitous pieces of campaign literature produced by the GOP in 1972, with an initial print run of over 1.5 million.[8]

The NBSMC claimed to represent hardworking, nonconfrontational African Americans, and its publications rarely deviated from the official White House line on a range of social issues, from anti-war protests to drugs. Ignoring the lack of black representation within the GOP, the NBSMC saved its attacks for left-wing "shaggy agitators hiding guns in storefronts, selling newspapers and wearing black berets." Claiborne's response to those who complained about racism was simple: "there are black people living better in this country than anywhere else on earth." Rather than challenging racial inequalities in America, his organization stood for "patriotism," "constitutional government," and "law and order." The NBSMC also pledged to "cooperate with police," who they believed had been unfairly targeted "with a barrage of false charges of corruption, racism, and brutality." Though the NBSMC did not represent even a majority of black Republicans, and was far smaller than NCAAR, it was willing to toe the official GOP line—a trait that earned it substantial support from party leadership.[9]

Most of Nixon's staunchest black supporters, however, were attracted to his black-capitalism endeavors, not his positions on social issues. The National Business League (NBL), founded by Booker T. Washington in 1900 to promote black entrepreneurship, essentially became a Republican auxiliary by the 1970s under the leadership of Berkeley Burrell. A black dry-cleaning tycoon and staunch Republican, Burrell championed black capitalism and self-help as the salvation of black neighborhoods. "Get up early and work hard," he preached, "that's what the Republican party is all about." The NBL experienced the largest growth in its long history during Nixon's tenure in office. Believing "you can push this administration into doing more than you can with an administration who already has you in his pocket," Burrell deepened his ties to the GOP, becoming vice president of Nixon's Advisory Council for Minority Enterprise, where he sought to "sit at a table of power and talk

A CALL TO BLACK CONSCIENCE

PATRIOTISM OR MILITANCY?

By Clay J. Claiborne
BSMC National Director

This is a call to the conscience of an overwhelming number of black people in this nation — to the Black Silent Majority.

It is a call to millions of hard-working, responsible men, women, and students who are sick and tired of the agitation, shouting, burning and subversion carried out in their name by self-styled militant groups who want to destroy this country.

We, the legions of black factory workers, beauticians, ministers, teachers, farmers, businessmen, postmen, firemen, transit workers, laborers, plumbers, and lawyers love this nation.

We have never chosen to be represented by Black Panthers, Weathermen, communists and other radical activists. They don't speak for us, and they never could.

No, black militants, America isn't a perfect nation. But look around you at the rest of the world. There are more black people living better in this country than anywhere else on the planet. Maybe that's why misguided Americans who flee to Cuba, Hanoi, Algeria, Peking and even Sweden usually come back to the United States.

And maybe that's also why the independent black nations in Africa and the West Indies are so anxious to send their most promising students to

CLAY CLAIBORNE

school in this country, and why an American education, often from a black college, is so highly prized everywhere in the world.

Americans, working together every day, are ridding the nation of slums, discrimination, poverty, unemployment, and the "welfare-liberalism" stranglehold. All around us things are getting better, and in the light of so much real progress, the militants' call for bloody revolution in America sounds like a dangerous absurdity.

Nothing can be gained for blacks by overthrow of the present political structure, especially if our working democracy is to be replaced with a vague system cooked up in the minds of drug-sodden agitators who are egged on by certain foreign elements anxious to destroy America by dividing her.

This call to conscience urges the majority of silent black citizens to speak out and repudiate violence and militants, so that groups like the Black Panthers can't turn the understandable despair of disadvantaged people into senseless bloodshed.

The time has come to end our long silence. Wake up and speak out, BLACK SILENT MAJORITY!

OUR COVER
Racial Harmony, California Style

Highlight of recent BSMC national executive board meeting was presentation of plaques to citizens who exemplified patriotism during the year. Shown is Rep. Bob Wilson (R-Cal.), chairman National Republican Congressional Committee — a staunch BSMC supporter — and Mrs. Addie Wallace of San Francisco, BSMC deputy national director.

YOU Must Help Silent Blacks!

Panthers Use Commie Dollars For Bail

Communist elements are spending huge sums of money to exploit America's racial difficulties and stir blacks into a frenzy of hatred and violent upheaval. The Black Panther Party, under the guise of "feeding the peoples' children", has raised additional dollars to further its subversive ends.

The following article, reprinted from the Oakland, Cal. "Tribune" (The Panther movement originated in Oakland) shines the light of TRUTH on the sinister forces at work against the United States. You can become directly involved in the battle to keep these forces from succeeding among black Americans by supporting the National Black Silent Majority Committee.

Oakland Tribune
A RESPONSIBLE METROPOLITAN NEWSPAPER

Tues., Nov. 24, 1970

A Congressional investigator says subpoenaed bank records show that a $20,000 donation to the Black Panther Party's program for hungry children was used to raise bail for Panther defense minister Huey P. Newton.

Investigator Neil Wetterman testified last week before the House Internal Security Committee that no tax forms for employees have been filed by the Black Panther Party, although checks drawn to "cash" amounting to almost $12,000 a month during August and September may have been for salaries.

Wetterman said the $20,000 donation, listed as a gift from an anonymous donor to the Black Panther breakfast program for children, came through a New York bank, dated last July 23 and sent to the Panther national headquarters in Berkeley.

The investigator said a Panther official withdrew that amount from the Panther account on Aug. 5, then purchased a cashier's check made out to Alameda County Clerk

Jack G. Blue as part of the $50,000 bail posted for Newton.

Wetterman, according to the Associated Press, informed the House committee a radiogram sent from Peking by the executor of the estate of the late Anna L. Strong, said about $17,000 was being donated to the Black Panthers.

In June and August, he said, checks for about $20,000 were sent from Nassau through the Royal Bank of Canada, and that he believed this money may have come from the estate of Miss Strong, an American Communist and expatriate who lived for many years in China and died in Peking.

From Aug. 10 to Sept. 10, through an account handling Black Panther newspaper finances, Wetterman said 72 money orders from 30 cities had been deposited totaling more than $48,700.

Rep. Richardson Preyer, D-N.C., presiding at the committee hearing, said it appeared from Wetterman's testimony that the program for hungry children was used as a vehicle to get bail money for jailed Black Panthers.

NATIONAL COUNCIL OF SCHOLARS SEEKS BLACK MEMBERS

The National Council of Scholars, a non-partisan academic group, is anxious to enlist black professionals from any field of learning according to its president, Dr. David N. Rowe of Yale University.

Dedicated to "improving the climate of relations between the academic community and the government and the society," the council's membership includes Catholics, Protestants, Jews, men, women, Democrats and Republicans, but few blacks, Dr. Rowe said in a letter addressed to BSMC Director Clay J. Claiborne.

Age is no qualification for membership, and the council welcomes students preparing for the scholarly career. Persons interested should contact:

Dr. David N. Rowe
Department of Political Science
Yale University
New Haven, Connecticut 06502

THE BLACK SILENT MAJORITY COMMITTEE OF THE U.S.A.

The *Newsletter* is published Monthly by the National Black Silent Majority Committee, Executive offices: 33 D Street, S.E., Washington, D.C. (corner of First, two blocks from U.S. Capitol. Mailing address, P.O. Box 7610, Washington, D.C. 20044. Tel. (202) 546-0600.

Figure 15. Clay Claiborne's National Black Silent Majority *Newsletter*, January 1971. Box 219, Rogers C. B. Morton Papers, Special Collections Library, University of Kentucky.

to whites millionaire to millionaire." He secured millions of federal dollars to promote NBL-sponsored training seminars and to fund new chapters across the country. By 1975, the NBL had expanded to one hundred and thirteen chapters (up from just thirty in 1962), with a membership of over ten thousand.[10]

Like Burrell, Floyd McKissick cast his political future with the GOP in hopes that it would institutionalize his brand of economic Black Power by supporting his proposal for the creation of a new black-controlled town, Soul City, North Carolina. For the location of his grand experiment in urban planning, he chose Warren County, one of the poorest, and blackest, counties in the state. Soul City, according to McKissick, would serve as the metropolitan hub of the northeastern Piedmont, providing jobs and political opportunities to black residents, and abundant workers for industrial entrepreneurs. Though white residents were welcome, the town would offer African Americans a path to self-determination as business owners, skilled workers, police officers, and civil servants. Even its streets reflected McKissick's ideals of black capitalism and racial pride, with names that included Opportunity Boulevard and Harriet Tubman Lane.[11]

McKissick sought to pacify white Republicans by arguing that Soul City offered a path for African Americans to obtain "meaningful economic and political power without challenge to those already in control of existing cities." Though it was the type of government-funded project typically dismissed by conservatives, McKissick touted Soul City in the terms of free enterprise, and reminded investors that North Carolina was a right-to-work state unencumbered by unions. Promotional brochures emphasized, "Black people are fighting for respect and dignity, not a handout," and that "additional millions poured into unplanned poverty programs and welfare will not solve the dilemma posed by our ghettos." McKissick won the favor of GOP leaders, including President Nixon, North Carolina Governor Jim Holshouser, and RNC Chairman George H. W. Bush, by suggesting that Soul City could initiate a groundswell of black support for the GOP over the next twenty years. The director of the Office of Minority Business Enterprise pledged his support, instructing McKissick to "let me know of your needs and I will form the various groups to assist you." Others felt the administration had little choice but to support the project. "If we say 'no' to McKissick," Leonard Garment privately noted, "we will stand accused not only of reneging on specific commitments to him, but of reneging on the President's commitment to the whole minority enterprise concept." With Nixon's approval, Garment disseminated the message through all relevant federal agencies that Soul City had Nixon's "green light."[12]

McKissick Enterprises bore much of the early costs of the project, securing over one million dollars in private loans and acquiring a plantation formerly owned by a segregationist state legislator. For the administration's part, George Romney pledged a $14 million guaranteed loan from HUD, and other agencies provided additional millions in grants to fund a healthcare facility, water/ sewage treatment plant, and other infrastructure-building projects. Governor Holshouser provided millions of dollars in state funds as investment capital and to pave roads. Ranking black Republicans took an active role in the project. Robert Brown believed that Soul City would free African Americans in his home state from the "bondage" of welfare, and served as the administration's liaison with McKissick. Assistant Secretary of HUD Sam Jackson personally secured grants for the project, and Edward Brooke fought against Senate opposition to Soul City led by North Carolina's Democratic Senator, Sam Ervin. The administration's support of McKissick's project marked the first time that the federal government provided funding for the development of a new town not affiliated with another urban area, and Soul City became the largest federally funded project underwritten by an African American.[13]

Even some white conservatives within the administration believed that Soul City and black capitalism could lead to newfound support of the GOP within black communities. In 1969, Harry Dent, special counsel to the president and chief architect of Nixon's southern strategy, urged the national committee to enlist black fieldworkers in the South, stressing, "I really do not believe any national money could be better spent." Following a positive midterm election for Republicans in 1970, Nixon publicly urged the party to have an "open door" to African Americans, and encouraged members of his Domestic Council to "pay attention" to black voters. Dent devoted significant attention in the early 1970s to developing what he described as "the changing southern strategy," one that encouraged the GOP to "really intensify its efforts to enlist Negro leaders" within state parties. He hosted southern conferences with Arthur Fletcher and Robert Brown, leading to a more amiable relationship between disgruntled black Republicans and the White House. As one African American from Mississippi remarked, "Dent caught real hell sometimes, but handled it beautifully.... I thought he would be a real Southern cracker, but I left impressed with him."[14]

Black Republicans at the 1972 Republican National Convention in Miami were wined and dined as never before at a late-night party aboard a yacht, where Sammy Davis, Jr., jazz great Lionel Hampton, and football star Jim Brown mingled with an estimated thousand attendants. Though there were

only 56 black delegates of a total 1,348, this represented a 115 percent increase from 1968, one of the largest expansions of black representation in the
party's history. Fifteen states that had zero black delegates in 1968 had at least
one in 1972. Every southern and border state had at least one black delegate,
and African Americans comprised at least 10 percent of the delegates from
Maryland, Delaware, Arkansas, Louisiana, Virginia, and Michigan. Aris T.
Allen of Maryland became the first African American chairman of a state
delegation. Black delegates played an unprecedented role in three of the four
standing convention committees. Seven served on the Credentials Committee, three on the Rules Committee, and two on the Platform Committee. Joan
Crawford, the first black vice chair of Missouri's Republican Party, chaired the
Community and National Development Subcommittee, and Annie Zachary
of Arkansas chaired the Human Concerns Subcommittee.[15]

"The highlight of the whole convention," Harry Dent remarked, "was the
'around the hips' hug Sammy Davis, Jr., gave President Nixon." One year earlier, Robert Brown had first informed Nixon staffers that although the "Rat
Pack" crooner was a Democrat, he was "extremely anti-Kennedy" and had "a
very positive attitude toward the domestic programs the Administration is
offering." Campaigning for John F. Kennedy in 1960, Davis was booed on
stage by segregationists at the Democratic National Convention, and was removed from the list of performers scheduled at Kennedy's inauguration (in
large part, the rumor went, because of his interracial marriage). By 1972,
Davis had been appointed to Nixon's National Advisory Council on Economic Opportunity, represented the White House at Mahalia Jackson's funeral, and privately dined with the president. He rarely provided lengthy
defenses of why he supported Nixon, often quipping one-liners to reporters
that implied a pragmatic alliance with the party in power. "It's better to be
standin' in the Oval Office than bangin' at the gates," he professed.[16]

Davis sat with Nixon's daughter at the 1972 Republican convention, and
performed at a televised Young Voters for Nixon rally, where the president
made a "surprise" appearance. As the partisan crowd cheered, Nixon stepped
to the microphone and quoted a reporter from the previous night who had
asked Davis if he sold out his race for the opportunity to eat lunch at the
White House. Nixon declared before the fawning crowd, "Well let me give
you the answer. . . . You aren't going to buy Sammy Davis, Jr., by inviting him
to the White House. You buy him by doing something for America." At that
moment, Davis rushed from behind to give the president a hug that was
caught on camera and became one of the iconic images of 1972.[17]

"The whole nation saw Sammy Davis, Jr., like a hungry orphan, clutching President Nixon to his bosom at the Republican convention," wrote black columnist Carl Rowan, but what "the nation did not see" were delegates fighting behind the scenes "to get our party to straighten up." An array of black Republicans appeared before the Platform Committee to advocate additional Republican support for black businesses, colleges, and other endeavors that promoted self-sufficiency. Sam Jackson urged the committee to pursue policies that would increase black representation within state delegations and the national committee. Numerous delegates complained to John Mitchell and Robert Finch that while there was a greater African American presence on committees than ever before, the convention was still mired by "non-participation of black people" in the higher echelons of party machinery. Although many states had token delegates, African Americans on the grassroots level were "either ignored or left out" by organizations that had "not spent one dime on black folks." Moreover, while the party was willing to host an extravagant yacht party for black delegates, there were few venues that provided time and space for them to meet as a group. Even the one policy summit organized by black delegates was interrupted by a suspiciously well-timed, unannounced, appearance by the president's daughter, which ground discussion to a halt.[18]

The National Council of Afro-American Republicans remained the most vocal critic of the lack of diversity within the party. Two days before the convention, NCAAR representatives told the press they were "angry and saddened" by the relatively small number of black delegates, and called for changes to the GOP's "downright archaic" rules. Their proposed reforms would have required the national committee to create permanent spots for a black vice chairman and ten black national committee members. To NCAAR, "the right to belong and function in either of the parties is a right of citizenship," and they pledged to "pursue this aim relentlessly." Democrats, they noted, had already made similar adjustments to their party's rules in 1968, under the leadership of 1972 presidential nominee, George McGovern, which resulted in a dramatic increase in black participation at their convention.[19]

Conservatives acquiesced to token integration inside the party in what social critic Norman Mailer called the "Jeannette Weiss Principle," whose namesake was an alternate delegate from Michigan who led the 1972 convention in the Pledge of Allegiance. To Mailer, Weiss represented the GOP's penchant of giving African Americans visually prominent, but ultimately meaningless, roles. In other ways, the party fiercely opposed comprehensive inclusion of black Republicans. Nixon aide Patrick Buchanan urged the Rules Committee at the 1972 convention to reject NCAAR proposals to "McGovernize the Republican Party" by forcing states to include African Americans and other "fashionable minorities." If the party succumbed to "fetishism" of African Americans by guaranteeing them leadership positions, they would "forfeit the Nixon majority" among southerners and white ethnics. Following Buchanan's advice, the Rules Committee, which had been dominated by rural and conservative states since 1964, voted 70 to 27 against a black delegate's proposal to add ten at-large posts reserved for African Americans inside the 312-member national committee. The committee similarly rejected a proposal to require state parties to broaden black participation in leadership. On the other hand, in a move designed to limit the influence of the Eastern Establishment, the committee amended rules to further decrease the delegates allotted to minority-rich, populous states like California, New York, and Pennsylvania, prompting many black delegates to accuse the committee of attempting to "dilute black power in the Republican Party." The only concession to African Americans was a promise to create a new black division whose director would be named to the RNC's Executive Committee, which had not had a black member in over a decade.[20]

In line with the Jeannette Weiss Principle, Nixon's fall campaign focused more on symbolic displays of black outreach than on meaningful grassroots mobilization, and relied heavily on black celebrities. In addition to Sammy Davis, Jr., other Nixon supporters included musicians James Brown, Johnny Mathis, and Billy Eckstein, and athletes Jim Brown, Gale Sayers, Don Newcombe, and Joe Frazier. When discussing their endorsement, most cited the president's support of black capitalism and the influence of his black appointees. Jim Brown, whose organization, the Black Economic Union, received OMBE funds to assist its mission of financing black businesses, praised Nixon for "moving in the areas in which blacks should be concerned . . . self-determination in the business world." Speaking at the headquarters of the Committee for the Re-Election of the President (CRP), James Brown praised the administration's "Blacks in high places . . . taking care of business."[21]

Disillusioned black Democrats also played a prominent role in the campaign. Johnny Ford, the mayor of Tuskegee, Alabama, claimed to have been "virtually ignored" by fellow Democrats, and worked closely with CRP's press section to publicize his endorsement of Nixon. Civil rights leader and mayor of Fayette, Mississippi, Charles Evers privately assured White House aides that while he would not endorse either presidential candidate, he "will be constantly telling of the Administration's accomplishments." True to his word, Evers spent much of 1972 telling African Americans that while Democrats "do a lot of hollering and screaming on minority rights," it was Nixon who "has put more blacks in top positions of government than any other President" and who "cracked down" on discriminatory unions. The president of the Boston NAACP, Jack E. Robinson, switched his voter registration from Democrat to Republican because it was time for "black leadership to put aside 'petty partisanship.'" Though he admitted Nixon had a "serious problem" on civil rights issues, he applauded the president's commitment to black businesses and colleges. Similarly, Milwaukee alderman Orville Pitts expressed his disappointment with Nixon's gestures to the South, but emphasized that African Americans needed to diversify their politics because "Democrats take us for granted. They've been carrying us in their hip pocket." He subsequently attended the Republican convention, and campaigned for Nixon across the country at CRP's expense.[22]

The Black Vote Division (BVD) of CRP, headed by former Peace Corps executive Paul Jones, handled most of the behind-the-scenes work promoting Nixon's high-profile black supporters. The division's "surrogates" included the nation's most vocal proponents of black capitalism, including Sam Jackson, Berkeley Burrell, Robert Brown, and Floyd McKissick, who was christened by the *New York Times* as "chairman emeritus of President Nixon's campaign organization." The BVD kicked off its campaign with a $100-per-plate dinner attended by 2,500 guests, including Malcolm X's widow, Betty Shabazz. Two of Nixon's most influential white officials, Harry Dent and John Mitchell, made brief appearances and recapped the president's support for black capitalism and black colleges. Lionel Hampton provided entertainment, introducing his new song, "We Need Nixon." McKissick delivered the keynote address, declaring that African Americans had too long "been sucking the sugar tit," which "ain't milk—it is a substitute for milk, and it is a pacifier, and it is something that makes you think you have got something when you ain't got it." Black voters, he argued, "have been in the Democratic Party a long, long time," and "we continue sucking the sugar tits not ever tasting milk." It was time to abandon Democrats, and join the Republican Party, which offered genuine "cream"—support for black business ownership.[23]

While Nixon's national campaign centered on hot-button social issues, the BVD focused heavily on wedding the black capitalism movement to the GOP. By 1972, millions of government dollars poured into black businesses, titles such as *Black Capitalism and the Urban Negro* and *Building Black*

Business lined bookstore shelves, and *Jet*, *Ebony*, and *Black Enterprise* magazines glamorized nouveau riche entrepreneurs. Even one of the decade's most
popular television shows, *The Jeffersons*, featured a self-made black businessman, and Republican, George Jefferson. The central message of the BVD, in
the words of McKissick, was that "Black Americans who believe in jobs rather
than welfare; who want a piece of the action, not a part of the dole" should
vote for Nixon. "I talk money and jobs," another black campaign worker declared, "That's all I talk." The division also published a multiedition newsletter, *The Black Advance*, which highlighted Nixon's financial support of black
businesses, banks, and colleges. Stanley Scott, former associate public relations director of the NAACP and son of newspaper magnate C. A. Scott,
worked with black newspapers on the BVD's behalf, recognizing that many
publishers favored black capitalism initiatives. Indeed, by election day, Nixon
received the endorsement of 30 percent of the nation's black newspapers that
endorsed a presidential candidate.[24]

Black Republicans also paid close attention to 1972's largest black confer-
ences. The administration's John Wilks served as an official delegate to the
National Black Political Convention in Gary, Indiana, as did Art Fletcher,
who headed the Washington state delegation. Assistant Secretary of HUD
Sam Jackson chaired the convention's Platform Committee, and Assistant
Secretary of HEW Edward Sylvester chaired the Rules Committee. Robert
Brown, Paul Jones, and members of the National Council of Afro-American
Republicans canvassed the floor promoting two-party competition. Though
the tone of the convention was decisively leftist, the imprint of Republicans
was seen in the passage of resolutions expressing support for "self-reliance"
and "Black owned and operated stores." Brown similarly ensured the "Administration's presence" at the NAACP annual meeting by sponsoring exhibition
booths, and by encouraging an active presence of black Republicans in public
sessions.[25]

Black Republicans were particularly interested in Jesse Jackson's Black
Expo, which paralleled Nixon's initiatives by promoting black-owned businesses. Though Jackson was a Democrat, he was also a disciple of Martin
Luther King, and saw value in bipartisanship, believing Democrats "take us
for granted." It also did not hurt that his Operation PUSH received federal
funding by the time of the fall campaign. In a coup for black Republicans,
Jackson did not endorse either presidential candidate, and left many Democrats aghast by defending African Americans whose support for Nixon had
been criticized by other civil rights leaders. He privately told Republicans that

he could not endorse Nixon and still "maintain credibility in the Black community," but he would not criticize the president during the campaign. He also vehemently opposed Chicago's Democratic machine, endorsed Illinois Republican candidates, and questioned the Left's insistence that law and order rhetoric was inherently racist. Leading up to his Expo, Jackson met with Paul Jones and other black Republicans to plan a "Republican Day" at the event. The day would become a staple of Jackson's expos through the end of the decade.[26]

To many African Americans, however, Nixon's support of black businesses and colleges was poor compensation for his overt appeals to racial conservatives, and black Republicans were ostracized far more than they had been in past elections. Leading black publications labeled them "Uncle Toms" and "house niggers." Protestors greeted James Brown concerts with signs that read "James Brown, Nixon's Clown." Brown sold less than three thousand tickets in a thirteen thousand-seat arena at a concert in Baltimore, where demonstrators passed out leaflets deriding the self-described "Soul Brother Number One" as a "sold brother." Six shots were fired into the office of Charles Hurst at Malcolm X College shortly after his endorsement of the president, and surrogates of the Black Vote Division requested bodyguards after being met with "extreme hostility" and "threats of bodily harm" during public appearances.[27]

One of the most damning criticisms came from Georgia civil rights leader Julian Bond, who called black Republicans "political prostitutes." The comment resonated not only because of Bond's harsh word choice, but because many of Nixon's black supporters were unashamed to admit that their close relationship with the administration ensured that their pet programs received ample government funding. In his speech at the groundbreaking ceremony of Soul City in July 1972, Robert Brown argued that Nixon offered "hard cold, dollars" to black supporters like McKissick. Charles Evers bragged that because of his willingness to support the administration, Fayette, Mississippi, located in the nation's ninth poorest county, received millions of federal dollars to construct public housing, a community center, and the Medgar Evers Medical Center. Tuskegee mayor Johnny Ford later claimed, "my support of Nixon's reelection had nothing to do with Nixon," as he believed that with his endorsement he "could turn around now and go back to all of those guys and get millions and millions of dollars." Turn around he did, as on Ford's watch Tuskegee received approximately fifty million dollars for infrastructural improvements in water and sewage systems, roads, and public housing.[28]

This rationale sounded to many like a quid pro quo. Indeed, the deputy director of CRP, Fred Malek, advised staffers to not only "utilize" African Americans who received federal grants, but also urged "close coordination between the White House and the Campaign team" in the "effective allocation of new grants" to recipients "who will be supportive of the reelection efforts." Many African Americans seeking government funding recognized the eagerness of the administration to dole out money to Nixon supporters. Civil rights leader James Farmer told Paul Jones that he was willing "to work in support of the President" behind the scenes, and, in the same meeting, requested $200,000 to fund his proposed think tank. Jones suggested to Malek that this funding "should be moved on," but that he or Robert Brown needed to oversee its distribution "in order to inforce [sic] Farmer's involvement" in promoting Nixon. On the other hand, others were denied contracts for refusing to endorse the president. The head of the Watts Labor Community Action Committee, for example, lost a $1.5-million contract after he declined to support Nixon. Allegedly, he was told by a group of Republicans "to get in line and I would get my money." Within a year after the election, the Senate Watergate Committee reported the White House's goal in the allotment of grants to black businessmen and activists was to "make sure the right people were being considered and getting grants."[29]

Though Nixon's proclivity to distribute millions of dollars to black allies was motivation among his supporters, the longstanding black Republican idea of influence through participation in the two-party system also resonated. Nathan Wright argued that African Americans "need to learn how to make at least temporary alliances" with Republicans out of "self-interest" in order to maintain a presence in the full spectrum of American politics. Mary Parrish, a Nixon staffer who had previously worked for Shirley Chisholm's presidential-primary campaign, believed that Chisholm's loss symbolized the Democratic tendency to court blacks "with wild promises they always fail to deliver." As one "dedicated to black advancement," Parrish in her campaign speeches urged African Americans "to work within the Republican Party" as a means to pressure both parties to pay greater attention to black issues.[30]

Another prominent Nixon supporter, President Charles Hurst of Chicago's Malcolm X College, certainly benefited from a relationship with Nixon— namely, private meetings with the president and over five million dollars in federal grants to his college—but there is no indication that his endorsement altered the school's "100 percent black" philosophy. After becoming president in 1969, Hurst shifted the racial makeup of the faculty from 80 percent white to 50 percent black within a year, and purchased the majority of school text-books and supplies from black businesses. Focused on recruiting militant youth, his students included Black Panther Fred Hampton, who "helped run interference" for Hurst. After law enforcement officers murdered Hampton, Hurst pledged to educate "a young black army" to continue the Black Pan-thers' fight against racial injustice. Like many black Republicans, he argued that his support for the GOP lay not necessarily in the virtues of Republican-ism, though he lauded Nixon's support of black colleges, but in the failures of the Democratic Party. He frequently lamented that African Americans "have been monolithic in their politics," and must "fight their way into" Republican ranks. A presence in both parties would challenge racial conservatives in the GOP, and send a message to Democrats to "make good some of those phony promises they've made in the past."[31]

As sincere as black Republicans may have been in their support of two-party politics, it was not an argument that swayed the majority of African Americans. On election day, 13 percent of black voters cast ballots for Nixon, only a slight improvement from 1968. White advisors in CRP disparaged Paul Jones's "lack of political experience," but although his division was given an ample budget to print literature and host events, it received minimal funds to disperse among local black Republican organizers. "The Black Vote Division is not effective," Curtis Perkins observed, because it "cannot disburse money where its needed"— to grassroots activists. If there was a strategic blunder, Perkins suggested, it was CRP's overuse of "entertainers" who were "thrust out in front" of black audiences. Moreover, Nixon staffers often rebuked Jones when he attempted to move beyond the narrow parameters of publishing newsletters or scheduling events. "'Paul Jones and Co.' have no business . . . to meet with anyone on matters of substantive policy," remarked a high-ranking campaign advisor, who chastised Jones for "confusing" his role in the campaign structure. When Jones asked for CRP resources to reach out to the leaders of the National Black Political Convention who were critical of Dem-ocrats, deputy director Fred Malek curtly replied, "there is no way we can fund this." In another memo, Jones requested funds for a secretary because his "work load demands are increasingly heavy." On Malek's copy of the memo, this claim was circled with "Bullshit" penciled in the margins. At the height of the campaign, Jones vented, "It is tough . . . fighting a battle inside and outside," against both Democrats and ambivalent Republicans.[32]

However, even had they launched a sweeping grassroots operation, the fundamental problem confronting black Republicans was their candidate,

Richard Nixon, whose personal campaign focused on making further inroads among conservatives and dismantling the Democratic Party's appeal to white ethnics and workers. While he had been willing to reach out to black militants in 1968, he devoted minimal effort in 1972 to tout his support of black capitalism and black colleges, leaving black outreach exclusively in the hands of black surrogates. Following a strategy laid out in Richard Scammon and Ben Wattenberg's *The Real Majority*, Nixon saw the majority of voters as "unyoung, unpoor, and unblack." The new social issues unleashed by the 1960s, drugs, demonstrations, and a counterculture that challenged traditional values, united a wide range of white voters in indignation, from businessmen to blue-collar workers and southerners to northern suburbanites. Reach out to this "Silent Majority," Nixon believed, and leave the Democrats with the outliers: student protestors, intellectuals, the poor, and civil rights activists. This strategy was solidified in May after Alabama Governor George Wallace dropped out of the race following an assassination attempt, as Nixon saw an opportunity to further his standing in the South. He especially distanced himself from the Philadelphia Plan, and targeted blue-collar workers and southerners who feared they would be denied a job "because they don't fit into some numerical quota." So salient had the issue of quotas become by the end of the campaign that even McGovern joined Nixon in publicly opposing them.[33]

Black opinion on one of the most controversial social issues emphasized by Nixon—busing—was more complex. In 1971, the Supreme Court upheld the constitutionality of busing as a means to achieve racial integration in public schools. Polls found that as many as 85 percent of whites nationwide, from Birmingham to Boston, opposed the practice. Seeing an avenue to solidify white support, Nixon condemned the court's decision, and declared, "what we need now is not just speaking out against more busing, we need action to stop it." The NAACP and most of the civil rights establishment largely supported busing as a means to integrate schools, but black opinion was far from monolithic. Polls routinely found that approximately half of African Americans opposed busing. Black Republicans were similarly divided. Those affiliated with the Eastern Establishment, such as Edward Brooke, openly advocated the policy, while conservatives, such as Clay Claiborne's National Black Silent Majority Committee, sided with the administration. Bootstrap nationalists, already skeptical of integration, also opposed busing. Floyd McKissick, Nathan Wright, and Roy Innis called for equal funding of black and white schools, and rejected integration as a positive solution, fearing busing would destroy historically black schools.[34]

Nixon's landslide victory, achieved without meaningful support from black voters, confirmed McKissick's belief that until African Americans competed in the two-party system, they would forever be "used as pawns." He responded by launching the National Committee for a Two-Party System (NCTPS) in August 1972, which received startup money through a fundraising dinner attended by an eclectic array of guests that ranged from Richard Nixon's brother to Sidney Poitier's wife. Dedicated to educating African Americans about the benefits two-party competition would offer their communities, McKissick's press releases and introductory brochures admitted that members of the NCTPS were "not happy about everything" the "white party" had done, but told black voters, "we can't change it without getting in and fighting to change it." The NCTPS established chapters throughout the country, from Chicago, New York City, and Pittsburgh to Tuskegee and Mobile, Alabama. Charles Evers established a chapter in Fayette, Mississippi, and urged African Americans to "adapt to the ideology" of the GOP in order to receive "more consistent funding in our communities for projects beneficial to our people."[35]

Members of the NCTPS's board of directors included some of Nixon's most prominent supporters, such as Sammy Davis, Jr., Robert Brown, Johnny Ford, and Charles Hurst. With many of its members drawn from McKissick's circle of black nationalists, the organization heavily promoted black capitalism. At a speech at Shaw University in Raleigh promoting the NCTPS, Kwame McDonald condemned those of his fellow students who mocked black Republicans but supported "the oppressor class" by shopping at white-owned stores rather than helping to build nearby Soul City. Like McKissick, the NCTPS also deplored welfare "dependency." A 1973 press release criticized those who relied on "handouts or doles," and suggested that black equality would never be fully achieved "without the acceptance of responsibility." At an NCTPS event in Alabama, McKissick warned African Americans "not to get hung up on . . . collectivism," and that it was time they actively promoted a black presence in an economy where "whites have been making all the profits."[36]

In March 1973, McKissick met with the new chairman of the Republican National Committee, George H. W. Bush, to coordinate black outreach. Besides early correspondence with McKissick, however, there is little evidence that points to coordinated efforts between the RNC and the NCTPS. Preferring instead to lend his support to black Republicans directly under his supervision, Bush allocated three hundred thousand dollars to the newly

Figure 16. Floyd McKissick outside his house in Soul City, North Carolina. A former plantation home, the "Green Duke House" would later be used by Soul City as a day care center. Photo by Peter W. Silver. Folder 33, Floyd B. McKissick Papers, #04930, Southern Historical Collection, The Wilson Library, University of North Carolina at Chapel Hill.

formed National Council of Black Republicans (NCBR), whose chairman was guaranteed a spot on the party's Executive Committee in rules adopted at the 1972 national convention. Though the NCBR appeared to be a breakthrough for black Republicans, its members were denied the autonomy to select their leadership, and they angrily protested Bush's decision to name Henry Lucas, a San Francisco dentist with close ties to Ronald Reagan, as the NCBR's first chairman. "It is deeply disturbing that we cannot effectively elect our own leaders," fumed one black Republican, "we are still captives of the white power structure."[37]

After years of infighting between Lucas and the more militant ranks of NCBR members, Sam Jackson and Floyd McKissick led a successful "knock-down, drag-out battle" at the organization's 1976 conference. They replaced Lucas with James Cummings, an Indianapolis businessman and staunch supporter of black capitalism. Under his guidance, the NCBR launched chapters in thirty-two states and boasted a membership of ten thousand by the end of the decade. However, Cummings had minimal influence inside the national committee and never received the support necessary to secure black Republican participation at all levels of party infrastructure. Much of his attention, he complained in memos, was devoted to fighting an internal battle against the party's "paternalistic approach," and the strategy of tasking a handful of African Americans "to attract and recruit to the party masses of Blacks throughout the nation."[38]

Other black Republican organizations in the mid- to late 1970s also focused on fighting for the inclusion of African Americans within party leadership. The Black Council for Republican Politics, formerly the National Council of Afro-American Republicans, continued to demand that the GOP name a black vice chairman and at least ten African Americans to the national committee, and filed an unsuccessful class-action lawsuit in 1976 against the RNC for racial discrimination in leadership posts. Sam Jackson similarly established the Council of 100 to exert pressure on the party's lily-white hierarchy. Members included Floyd McKissick, Charles Hurst, and Evelyn Cunningham, whose prominence drew national media attention to their mission to "make the two-party system work for black people." Because of the council's high-profile membership, party leaders were compelled, at a minimum, to meet with its representatives. Though the GOP rarely acquiesced to their demands, the council scored a political victory from an unlikely source, Strom Thurmond, who reversed his previous opposition to black capitalism after a meeting with the group. He subsequently sponsored a multimillion-dollar contract between the Armed Forces and a black-owned food service company.[39]

With the Voting Rights Act protecting black voters in the South and a rise in northern black political mobilization, the 1970s saw a marked increase in the number of black elected officials. While there were fewer than five hundred black elected officials in 1965, there were almost fifteen hundred in 1970. By 1980, there were more than four thousand. Many of these officials hailed from the South, carried to victory by waves of newly registered voters. The decade also saw the emergence of black mayors at the helm of major cities, such as Carl Stokes in Cleveland, Maynard Jackson in Atlanta, and Lionel Wilson in Oakland. Though most of these were Democrats, black Republicans still found some success. Indeed, while Stokes made national headlines in 1967 when he became the first black mayor of a major city in the country, it was a Republican, Robert C. Henry, who served as Ohio's first black mayor of an integrated city in 1966. Similarly, Michigan's first black mayor was not Coleman Young in Detroit in 1973, but Republican Robert Blackwell in Highland Park in 1967. During Coleman's first year in office, Michigan had five black Republican mayors, including Edward Bivens, Jr., of Inkster and Lyman Parks of Grand Rapids, the state's second largest city. Parks was one of three black Republican mayors of moderate-size, majority white cities in the 1970s, and was joined by Noel Taylor of Roanoke, Virginia, and Kenneth Blackwell of Cincinnati, Ohio.[40]

Black Republicans also found electoral success as state legislators, judges, county commissioners, school board members, and other officials during the 1970s. A black Republican served as chairman of Stamford, Connecticut's, Board of Finance, and another as city controller of Harrisburg, Pennsylvania. In 1972, Edward Brooke handily won reelection to the Senate, where he remained a powerful voice of the Eastern Establishment. In 1971, eight black Republicans served in state legislatures, and in 1973 three served in Illinois alone. Black-and-Tan holdout John Calhoun served on Atlanta's city council from 1974 to 1978. In 1977, black Republican state legislator Aris T. Allen of Annapolis, Maryland, became chairman of the state's Republican Party. Dr. Ethel Allen, a self-described "ghetto practitioner" who treated drug addicts and other marginal residents of Philadelphia, became the city's first black woman elected at large to the city council in the early 1970s. She was also a Republican who had actively campaigned for GOP candidates since the 1950s. By 1979 she had secured one of Pennsylvania's most powerful positions, secretary of state, and was included in *Esquire*'s list of the twelve most powerful women in politics.[41]

Most of these politicians promoted civil rights and other liberal social issues. Edward Brooke continued his fight as one of the Senate's leading advocates of housing, education, affirmative action, and voting rights. "While many other so-called friends deserted the ranks," proclaimed a 1979 NAACP resolution, "Brooke led the sometimes solitary fight against efforts to cut back civil rights progress." According to Pennsylvania's largest black newspaper, Ethel Allen's "voice was constantly heard in defense of women's rights, the disadvantaged and minorities," as she "displayed heartfelt concerns about the environment, housing, gang warfare and drug problems." Robert Blackwell of Highland Park secured over $42 million in federal grants in one of HUD's most extensive "model city" urban renewal projects, and by the end of Lyman Parks's tenure in Grand Rapids, the number of black firefighters and police officers had more than doubled.[42]

On issues of women's rights, African Americans affiliated with the Eastern Establishment, like Evelyn Cunningham, the longtime assistant to Nelson Rockefeller, and Edward W. Brooke, were fierce supporters of the Equal Rights Amendment, and called for increased government funding of abortion services to poor women. Curtis Perkins of the National Council of Afro-American Republicans frequently urged the party to expand its platform on issues of "child care" and "women's rights." Black Republican support of women's rights was not out of step with that of many whites in their party. Numerous Republican governors, including Spiro Agnew and Ronald Reagan, signed laws that dramatically expanded access to abortion, and Republicans from President Ford to future Senate Majority Leader Mitch McConnell backed the Equal Rights Amendment despite fierce conservative backlash. Many black Republican women who supported the Equal Rights Amendment and abortion rights, however, were not afraid to also target white feminists for their lack of attention to the issues confronted by black women. Carole Ann Taylor urged the women's liberation movement to "consider housing, day care, and welfare" as essential causes on a par with abortion rights, and Ethel Allen lamented that white feminists were "more concerned with burning bras" than with attracting average black women through confronting the structural issues that forced black mothers to raise children in "the worst living conditions in the country." Though many black Republicans supported women's rights, issues of socioeconomic racial inequality remained at the top of their agenda. Indeed, black nationalists like Floyd McKissick tended to ignore issues of women's rights altogether in their singular focus on black economic development and promotion of two-party competition.[43]

Given the right circumstances, white Republicans could also win black support in the Nixon years, especially in the South when a racial moderate ran against a more conservative Democrat. In 1968, significant numbers of black voters cast ballots for Arkansas governor Winthrop Rockefeller and Senator Henry Bellmon of Oklahoma. Two Republican candidates for county commissioner in Greensboro, North Carolina, won nearly 70 percent of the black vote. The following year, Virginia's Republican gubernatorial candidate, Linwood Holton, ran as a racial liberal against a moderate Democrat and won half of the state's black vote. Other moderate southern governors, such as Mississippi's Gil Carmichael, Tennessee's Winfield Dunn, and North Carolina's Jim Holshouser, also received meaningful black support. In 1970, 40 percent of black voters in Atlanta cast ballots for the GOP gubernatorial candidate, and a majority of black voters in Birmingham helped secure a victory in 1971 for the city's first Republican mayor.[44]

However, these candidates were the exception, not the norm, as the GOP continued to drift rightward in the 1970s. As one political scientist noted, even when "black leaders see the two-party option as leverage to precipitate socioeconomic change," their only option was a Republican Party "waxing strong on resurgent conservatism." Moreover, compared to Democrats, the GOP only tepidly reached out to black communities. The Republicans, according to the National Council of Black Republicans, "never bother to appear before black or ethnic groups. The Democrats always have someone." Moreover, while Republicans balked at any meaningful procedures to ensure black representation on the national and state level, Democrats installed policies that guaranteed equitable black representation. While Republicans had fifty-six black delegates at the 1972 convention, their highest number in years, the Democratic Party featured four hundred and fifty-two black delegates.[45]

Black Republicans themselves bore some blame for the inability of their party to connect with African Americans, as many shifted their emphasis from civil rights to self-help, business-oriented solutions by the late 1960s. While the black middle class grew rapidly during the 1960s, its expansion came to a standstill in the 1970s, growing just 1 percent from 1970 to 1980. Since less than one third-of African Americans were in the middle class, black Republicans' anti-welfare rhetoric and harsh descriptions of its recipients alienated large numbers of black voters. Berkeley Burrell claimed, "civil rights people are going to have to understand" that even if "we redistributed the wealth tomorrow," the rich would quickly end up back on top because they valued hard work and ingenuity. The poor, on the other hand, would revert back to poverty, having spent their money "foolishly or blew it on a horse race." Likewise, most black Republicans saw no hypocrisy in denouncing welfare but encouraging the acceptance of government dollars for their own projects and businesses. The National Committee for a Two-Party System warned that African Americans who accept "handouts" would never earn the respect "of those who pass out doles." Yet, it had no qualms about encouraging black businessmen "to support their advancement" by pursuing the "full utilization of all federal agencies." When Nixon attempted to dismantle the Office of Economic Opportunity, the chief vehicle for Lyndon Johnson's War on Poverty, the NCTPS publicly backed the administration but simultaneously encouraged black entrepreneurs to tap "the many pockets of funds available in the various agencies in Washington."[46]

The distraction of the Watergate scandal early in Nixon's second term

severely hampered the efforts of his black supporters to develop their relationship with the incumbent. Stanley Scott replaced Robert Brown as special
assistant to the president in 1973, but had little influence within an administration unresponsive to most domestic policy issues in the wake of publicized
illegal activities and coverups. Scott found it difficult to obtain staff assistants,
let alone to enact a proactive agenda. The Watergate disruption particularly
hurt black Republicans in the realm of presidential appointments. Throughout 1972 and 1973, many high-level vacancies in HUD and other federal
agencies remained unfilled, and Scott complained of "the unusually long
delay in fulfilling federal employment promises" to prominent black supporters. "We are being given the run-around," remarked another black Republican, who feared conservatives were "closing ranks."[47]

After Nixon's resignation, black Republicans greeted his moderate successor,
Gerald Ford, optimistically. Ford was never comfortable with overt appeals to
racial conservatives, and maintained an amiable relationship with civil rights
leaders, becoming the first president since Harry Truman to speak before the
NAACP. He named the Eastern Establishment's figurehead, Nelson Rockefeller, as vice president, and supported a five-year extension of the Voting Rights
Act. He also appointed William Coleman, president of the NAACP Legal Defense and Education Fund, as secretary of transportation, making Coleman
only the second African American, and first black Republican, to hold a
cabinet-level post. As transportation secretary, Coleman ensured that black
architects were hired to design Atlanta's subway system and that a substantial
portion of a multibillion-dollar northeastern rail upgrade was contracted to
black-owned businesses. He further implemented an affirmative action program that essentially desegregated air-traffic controllers.[48]
    On the other hand, Ford opposed busing to integrate schools and gener-
ally continued Nixon's policy of benign neglect. In contrast to Nixon's use of
high-profile black supporters in 1972, African Americans were virtually ignored in Ford's 1976 campaign. As a fiscal conservative, he was far more reluctant than Nixon to dole out millions of dollars to black businesses and
colleges, particularly after the Senate Watergate Committee surfaced accusa-
tions of corruption and mismanagement within the OMBE and Small Business Administration. Distancing himself from Nixon's scandals, Ford sat back
as loans to black-owned businesses steadily fell. With the accession of Jimmy
Carter to the presidency in 1976 and Ronald Reagan in 1980, federal funding
to black businesses and colleges was slashed even further.[49]

However, even had Nixon remained in office, it was clear that his black-capitalism programs would not elicit meaningful structural change. While the number of black-owned businesses grew substantially on his watch, they still represented less than 2 percent of the gross income of all U.S. businesses. Indeed, the hundred largest black companies combined would have ranked 284th on *Fortune 500*'s list of American corporations. Even worse, the racial gap in capital ownership between 1969 and 1977 remained virtually unchanged. The 1970s saw the expanding corporatization of the American economy, and the vast majority of businesses supported by black capitalism initiatives were in low-growth industries that provided minimal employment opportunities, such as barbershops and fast-food restaurants. Additionally, white corporations with affirmative action plans proved more alluring career paths to young, educated African Americans than more precarious small business startups. There was also a mid-1970s recession, during which black businesses failed at a rate of over 13 percent, far higher than the national average. In 1975 alone, almost 20 percent of companies affiliated with the National Association of Black Manufactures closed their doors. Many businesses that survived struggled to stay afloat in communities plagued by inflation and unemployment.[50]

The mid-1970s also saw the collapse of Nixon's tentative coalition of Republicans and black nationalists. To a new generation of conservative politicians, and in the chaotic post-Watergate struggle for the GOP, identification with nationalists like Floyd McKissick or affirmative action proponents like Arthur Fletcher was a liability to their efforts to court disaffected white Democrats. Many of the decade's up-and-coming Republicans were themselves former Democrats, such as Trent Lott and Jesse Helms. As a student at Ole Miss, Lott had led opposition to the integration of his fraternity and later worked for one of the state's most ardent segregationist Democrats. Elected to Congress in the 1970s as a Republican, he sponsored a bill to posthumously restore the citizenship of the president of the Confederacy, Jefferson Davis, and proclaimed, "the fundamental principles that Jefferson Davis believed in are very important today to people all across the country, and they apply to the Republican Party." North Carolina's Jesse Helms had been a fixture in state media as a newspaper columnist and television host since the 1950s, where he defended segregation and railed against civil rights activists. Elected to the Senate in 1972, Helms consistently voted against busing, affirmative action, and extensions to the Voting Rights Act, and filibustered the creation of the Martin Luther King, Jr., Holiday.[51]

Following his election in 1972, Helms received a friendly telegram from McKissick expressing a hope that although "no two men think alike, there are many common things that we should work together on." Helms brusquely responded that "at the appropriate time" he would launch a thorough examination into Soul City's expenditures, fully rejecting the pragmatic coalition with black nationalists that Nixon, McKissick, and Governor Holshouser had seen in the party's future. Helms's opportunity came in 1975, when the *Raleigh News and Observer* printed an investigative report on Soul City, leveling allegations of financial malfeasance against McKissick. Helms demanded a full inquiry into the project by the General Accounting Office (GAO), and introduced an appropriations amendment that banned government assistance to McKissick. Calling Soul City "the greatest single waste of public money that anyone in North Carolina can remember," Helms's public outcry prompted HUD Secretary Carla Hills, a Ford appointee who lacked George Romney's willingness to buck conservatives, to freeze Soul City's promised funding. After months of investigation, the GAO found that one-fourth of the project's transactions did not strictly follow the conditions or procedures laid out in their grants, contracts, or loans, but that none violated federal law or warranted further scrutiny. The damage, however, had already been done. In addition to halting the project's progress for almost a year as the GAO investigated Soul City's books, the scandal convinced an already apathetic President Ford to drop administration support.[52]

Though Soul City did not come close to becoming the hub of Black Power McKissick envisioned, it was not a total failure. Over the next two decades, its residents included McKissick, who lived there until his death in 1991, and North Carolina's first black Congressperson since the 1800s, Eva Clayton, who had previously directed the Soul City Foundation. The town had one of Warren County's few recreational facilities, a multimillion-dollar water system that serviced surrounding counties, and a health clinic visited by an average of fifty people per day through the 1990s. However, even had McKissick received continued government support, it seems unlikely that Soul City would have fulfilled his utopian vision. Though he promised abundant workers for corporations, the town's Afrocentric focus scared potential white supporters. One industry consultant also noted the skepticism manufacturers held about majority-black areas, since African Americans had traditionally strong ties to labor. Thus, when automobile and other factories moved south, they were centered in white communities, whose residents were less inclined toward union mobilization. Moreover, in the stagnant economy of the 1970s, few investors were willing to stake massive amounts of capital in an endeavor with as many inherent risks and skeptics as those of Soul City.[53]

By the election of Jimmy Carter in 1976, the hopes that black Republicans had placed in the party seemed to have evaporated. Ever the pragmatist, even Floyd McKissick abandoned the GOP, becoming chairman of the Warren County Democratic Party in 1979. With the return of the Democratic Party to the White House in 1976, Simeon Booker of *Ebony* reflected on the legacy of black Republicans since 1968. "Neglected, forgotten, and unsung," the acclaimed journalist wrote, black Republicans were "sparkplugs for civil rights during the previous GOP administrations." Though they "will be quickly forgotten as the hordes of ambitious Democrats surge into capital town," he continued, "let's give credit to the blacks who struggled against the odds to bring some hope and relief to their people."[54]

Nationally, the Nixon and Ford administrations provided opportunities for black appointees to enact their middle-class agenda of black capitalism and to fund various self-help ventures. They were accompanied by a plethora of black Republican organizations that pressured the GOP, as the party in power, to focus on black businesses, black communities, and black representation within party ranks. And even though, as Booker's comments indicated, the Democratic Party remained the party of most African Americans, especially upon its return to the White House in 1976, black Republicans still left a mark on the decade. From the black capitalism movement to Soul City, to the local successes of politicians like Robert Blackwell and Ethel Allen, black Republicans remained a distinct voice in the political debates of the time. While their emphasis had shifted from a civil rights agenda of the 1960s to an economic message centered on middle class solutions by the 1970s, their goal remained the same. As Floyd McKissick and other black Republicans declared upon launching the National Committee for a Two-Party System in 1972, "The objective is making the American society live up to its moral and political commitments to Black people and other minorities." This had been the objective of black Republicans for more than three decades.[55]

Black Republicans in the Shadow of Reagan

Black delegates at the 1964 Republican National Convention assembled in San Francisco's Fairmont Hotel in opposition to the nomination of Barry Goldwater as their party's presidential nominee. One result of this gathering of civil rights proponents was the formation of the National Negro Republican Assembly, which dedicated itself to opposing the party's rightward turn. Sixteen years later, and a month after Goldwater's protégé, Ronald Reagan, won the 1980 presidential election, a new generation of black Republicans again assembled at the Fairmont, but embraced the conservative ideology their predecessors had united against. Organized by Henry Lucas and Hoover Institution Fellow Thomas Sowell, and funded by a white think tank, the "Black Alternatives Conference" marked a new era of black Republicanism, as attendees railed against minimum wage, rent control, government regulation, and affirmative action. Though they joined bootstrap black nationalists in emphasizing self-help, they rejected Floyd McKissick's brand of black capitalism, advocating instead for "colorblind" policies that paid no special consideration to black entrepreneurs.[1]

Black conservatism was not a new phenomenon in the 1980s, and examples could be found during the civil rights era. Iconoclasts like George Schuyler preached extreme individualism, assailed the liberalism of the civil rights movement, and contributed to right-wing publications. However, their voices were marginal among mainstream black Republicans of the era, many of whom associated conservatism with segregationist Democrats. Schuyler even allied with New York's Conservative Party in the 1960s, not with Nelson Rockefeller's Republican Party, while the decade's most prominent black Republicans, Grant Reynolds, Jackie Robinson, and Edward Brooke, among others, were "Rockefeller Republicans" and fierce advocates of civil rights legislation. Even when black Republicans of the late 1960s and 1970s shifted their focus to distinctly middle-class economic policies, such as affirmative action or the promotion of black businesses, their focus remained on advancing black individuals in society. Moreover, black Republicans from the 1940s through the 1970s had deep ties to the civil rights establishment and major black institutions, holding leadership positions within local, state, and national branches of the NAACP, CORE, SCLC, and black Elks.[2]

To many black Republicans prior to 1980, the use of two-party politics as a means to advance black America was fundamental to their partisanship, not necessarily ideological identification with the party's increasingly conservative leadership. A study of black delegates at the 1976 Republican National Convention found that 84 percent had been "active in the Civil Rights movement," 92 percent favored affirmative action, and 91 percent described themselves as "moderate," "liberal," or "Left Liberal to Radical." As late as 1980, researchers found few ideological differences between black delegates at the Republican or Democratic conventions.[3]

Unlike mainstream black Republicans who served as delegates to national conventions, many of the emerging ideologues at the 1980 Fairmont Conference lacked a substantive prior relationship with the GOP establishment or a base within the black community. Indeed, by the end of the decade, through heavy promotion by the Reagan administration and conservative think tanks, several of the previously obscure participants in the conference, such as Clarence Thomas, Clarence Pendleton, Glenn Loury, and Walter Williams, had become some of the most prominent black Republicans in the country, fulfilling the GOP's need, according to Newt Gingrich in 1983, "to invent new black leaders." This new generation had few prior affiliations with mainstream black organizations, and as John Wilks, a black Republican who served in the Nixon administration, asserted, "they merely say they're conservative, say they're opposed to affirmative action and are immediately picked up by a right-wing sponsor, such as the Hoover Institution [and other] groups not known for their sensitivity to black issues."[4]

It is also important to note the stark number of prominent civil rights leaders who underwent conservative transformations during the Reagan years. Though these are typically ignored by historians or dismissed as idiosyncratic anomalies, the number of black luminaries of the 1960s who supported Reagan in the 1980s points to a pattern of disillusionment with liberalism among battle-worn activists. Black Panther Eldridge Cleaver, who converted to Christianity and befriended evangelist Billy Graham, openly endorsed Reagan and ran as a Republican congressional candidate in Oakland, California. James Bevel, who planned the 1963 Children's Crusade in Birmingham and rallied demonstrators in Selma after Bloody Sunday, also endorsed Reagan and partnered with right-wing organizations. In 1992, Bevel served as the running mate to the fringe presidential campaign of Lyndon LaRouche. Similarly, James Meredith, who integrated the University of Mississippi, claimed he no longer supported the Civil Rights Act of 1964, and declared that his new enemy was no longer the "white supremacist" but the "white liberal." In the early 1990s, he joined the staff of North Carolina Senator Jesse Helms and endorsed the Louisiana gubernatorial bid of Ku Klux Klan leader David Duke in the Republican primaries.[5]

Other civil rights leaders who backed Reagan underwent milder political metamorphoses and supported his candidacy for pragmatic reasons. Stokely Carmichael's mentor, Charles V. Hamilton, argued that because African Americans were still a "relatively powerless minority" they needed to ally with conservatives for access to power. Hamilton attended the Fairmont Conference with another seminal figure of the early Black Power movement, Chuck Stone, who also urged African Americans to rid themselves of the "single-political-party syndrome," and to work with the GOP as a means to leverage both parties. Charles Evers, who concluded his decades-long flirtation with Republicans by officially joining their ranks in the 1980s, supported Reagan as a means to stick it to Democrats who "took us for granted." His cozy relationship with HUD officials secured hundreds of thousands of dollars for Fayette, Mississippi, at a time of substantial cuts to the beleaguered department. Ralph Abernathy and his SCLC associate Hosea Williams also emphasized the need for two-party politics, and not only endorsed Reagan but joined Republicans in attacking welfare dependency. However, early in Reagan's presidency, they found that, despite their support, the administration had little desire to openly identify with civil rights leaders, and both abandoned the GOP in 1984.[6]

Reagan kicked off his 1980 campaign in Neshoba County, Mississippi, the same place where three civil rights workers were infamously murdered in 1964. Declining to acknowledge the tragedy, he reassured the ten thousand whites in attendance, "I believe in state's rights. . . . I believe we've distorted the balance of our government today by giving powers that were never intended in the Constitution to the federal establishment." While Reagan was mostly concerned with federal interference in the economy, he had previously joined segregationists in opposing the Civil Rights Act of 1964 and the

Voting Rights Act of 1965 on the grounds that they violated states' rights. A speech touting states' rights at the location of one of the most horrific events of the civil rights movement in his first speech after receiving the presidential nomination was a profoundly symbolic gesture not lost to Mississippians of either race. In his two election campaigns, Reagan ran on a platform of states' rights, low taxes for the middle and upper classes, cuts in funding for social-welfare programs, and an increase in military expenditures. He won an unprecedented majority of whites across the Deep South, from "colorblind" suburbanites to the Imperial Wizard of the Ku Klux Klan, and lost 90 percent of black voters, including over 40 percent of those registered Republican.[7]

As president, Reagan's few contacts with African Americans came from his small circle of handpicked black conservatives. Of the more than four hundred appointments made during his first year in office, only nineteen were black. Two of these, the chairman of the Equal Employment Opportunity Commission, Clarence Thomas, and the chairman of the U.S. Civil Rights Commission, Clarence Pendleton, reversed three decades of defining employment discrimination as a statistical lack of black representation in a workplace. They instead only pursued cases where individuals had been victimized by specific acts of overt bigotry, although even these cases were backlogged because of staff reductions. Thomas and Pendleton had no patience for civil rights leaders, who, according to Thomas, "bitch, bitch, bitch, moan and moan and whine," and believed the "new racists" were those who supported affirmative action. The administration's highest ranking African American, HUD Secretary Samuel Pierce, acquired the nickname "Silent Sam" for his aloof inaction as his department was systematically dismantled. Pierce was so marginal within the administration during his eight years in Washington that Reagan failed to even recognize him at a White House event, greeting him as "Mr. Mayor."[8]

Reagan also went after the existing remnants of Richard Nixon's black capitalism program, calling for the elimination of contract set-asides and a reduction of federal funding for minority-owned businesses to less than half of what it had been in the 1970s. His assistant attorney general for civil rights, William Bradford Reynolds, focused on eliminating "reverse discrimination" against whites. While Nixon and other Republicans of the 1960s addressed historical patterns of discrimination through race-conscious programs like affirmative action and black capitalism, Reynolds and Reagan supported nominally "colorblind" policies and strongly opposed any program that explicitly aided African Americans. Reynolds also reversed Nixon's directive to deny tax-exempt status to private schools that openly discriminated against black students, and restored federal tax exemptions to Bob Jones University, which expelled students for interracial dating, and Goldsboro Christian Schools, which banned black students outright.[9]

Reagan seldom mentioned African Americans or civil rights in his public comments, but often spoke of a black woman tried for welfare fraud, whom he called "the Chicago welfare queen," and an ambiguous "strapping young buck" who bought T-bone steaks with food stamps. To him, these alleged abuses justified massive cuts to the government programs that enabled the lazy in Chicago and other urban centers at the expense of the hardworking middle class. Though Reagan never explicitly mentioned race in his critiques of government programs for the poor, many heard racial undertones that harkened back to Nixon's code words.[10] As Lee Atwater, a Reagan staffer and future chairman of the Republican National Committee, remarked in a rambling 1981 interview:

> All you have to do to keep the South for Reagan is to run in place on the issues he's campaigned on since 1964. . . . You start out in 1954 by saying "Nigger, nigger, nigger." By 1968 you can't say "nigger"—that hurts you. Backfires. So you say stuff like forced busing, states' rights, and all that stuff. You're getting so abstract now [by the 1980s] you're talking about cutting taxes, and all these things you're talking about are totally economic things and a by-product of them is blacks get hurt worse than whites . . . because obviously sitting around saying, "we want to cut this" is . . . a hell of a lot more abstract than "Nigger, nigger."[11]

Indeed, the programs Reagan cut the deepest, such as welfare and subsidized housing, were programs disproportionately used by African Americans. At the same time, federal programs used by households with incomes of more than $40,000, who also happened to be disproportionately white, remained virtually untouched. Moreover, Reagan's tax plan actually raised taxes on the bottom 50 percent of Americans, and by the end of the decade the earnings of the bottom tenth of workers declined by almost 20 percent. By 1990, African Americans within the poorest fifth of the nation's households were the poorest they had been in relation to whites since the 1950s.[12]

Many black Republicans who had been active during the civil rights era were adamant in their rejection of Reagan, whom Arthur Fletcher called "the

worst president for civil rights in this century." J. Clay Smith, Jr., a lifelong
Republican who served on the Equal Employment Opportunity Commission
in 1977–1982, criticized Reagan's appointment of black conservative new-
comers over longstanding black Republicans, and called his policies "antithetical to the core of Black aspirations." Gerald Ford's secretary of transportation,
William Coleman, Jr., publicly remarked in 1984 that the administration's
civil rights policies "have been just about 100 percent wrong, and despicable."
Three years later, he testified before the Senate against the Supreme Court
nomination of conservative legal scholar Robert Bork. As chairman of the
NAACP Legal Defense and Education Fund, Coleman also argued against
Reagan's Justice Department before the Supreme Court, who concurred with
him that the administration's decision to grant tax-exempt status to discriminatory private schools was in violation of existing civil rights law.[13]

The Republican Party since the 1980s has largely resided in Reagan's shadow.
With minimal efforts to reach out to mainstream black voters, Republican
presidential nominees from Reagan in 1980 to Mitt Romney in 2012 consistently received around ten percent of the black vote. George H.W. Bush
prominently used images of a black rapist, Willie Horton, in his 1988 presidential run, prompting even his closest black ally, Colin Powell, to condemn
the advertising campaign as a "racist . . . cold political calculation." Indeed,
Powell lamented that there existed a "dark vein of intolerance in some parts
of the party," and that part of the GOP's overall election strategy since 1980
was that "if the racial card could be played to appeal to certain constituencies,
play it." Running against a black opponent in 1990, Jesse Helms's reelection
campaign produced a television commercial featuring a white pair of hands
crumpling up a rejection letter as a narrator somberly announced, "You
needed that job, and you were the best qualified. But it had to go to a minority
because of racial quotas."[14]

      From a policy perspective, President Bush vetoed the Civil Rights Act of
1990, a law that strengthened anti-discrimination measures in employment,
and the party's mid-1990s "Contract with America" shifted federal benefits
away from the poor to the "hardworking" middle and upper classes. The
GOP's emphasis remained on deregulation, tax cuts for top earners, and other
economic policies opposed by most African Americans, including those
whose views aligned with conservatives on religion, abortion, and other social issues. Economics remained, as it had since the 1930s, the most difficult
hurdle for Republicans to overcome among black voters. While social issues

influenced how many whites voted, even those whose economic interests did not seem to align with the GOP, economic policy geared towards the working class and impoverished families remained one of the most salient features of black electoral politics.[15]

There were, however, individual Republicans who reached out to black voters and displayed empathy for their communities. New York congressman and George H. W. Bush's secretary of HUD, Jack Kemp, placed economic empowerment of African Americans at the forefront of his agenda throughout the 1980s and 1990s. A self-described "bleeding-heart conservative," Kemp championed cultural diversity and racial justice. His proposed anti-poverty program included tenant management of public housing, a reduction of the payroll tax (a tax increased by Reagan), action against predatory lending, and "urban enterprise zones" that offered tax incentives for businesses to move to inner cities. Kemp was widely praised by both civil rights leaders and black Democrats for his genuine concern for minority communities, but was a solitary figure within a party that believed its electoral future remained with white voters. In 2005, RNC Chairman Ken Mehlman admitted to the NAACP that the GOP had been "wrong" on issues of race for decades, and apologized on behalf of the party, whose strategies included "looking the other way or trying to benefit from racial polarization." A decade later, Senator Rand Paul of Kentucky, a libertarian willing to buck the conservative establishment, became one of the only high-profile Republicans who engaged with black audiences and addressed issues of concern to black voters. He spoke at Howard University and before the National Urban League, quoted Malcolm X, criticized the militarization of police in black neighborhoods, and opened a "GOP engagement office" in a black area of Louisville. He also partnered with Barack Obama's attorney general, Eric Holder, and black Democratic Senator Cory Booker in working to overhaul federal drug sentencing policy and to expand voting rights to ex-felons.[16]

When presented with an attractive Republican candidate who reached out to their communities, black voters continued to show a willingness to cross party lines. At the same time as the vast majority of African Americans voted against Reagan in 1980, for example, approximately 40 percent cast ballots for Senators Don Nickles of Oklahoma and Mack Mattingly of Georgia. Arlen Spector won a third of Pennsylvania's black voters in his senatorial race. In 1985, New Jersey governor Thomas Kean received the endorsement of Coretta Scott King and the vote of 60 percent of African Americans. Ohio governor George Voinovich won 40 percent of the black vote in the 1990s, and governors Christine Todd Whitman of New Jersey and Pete Wilson of California received over 25 percent. Governor Mike Huckabee earned nearly half Arkansas's black vote in 1998.[17]

As the GOP furthered its rightward trajectory by the end of Reagan's two terms, the black Republicans advanced through party ranks were far more conservative than their predecessors. As a U.S. Supreme Court Justice, Clarence Thomas consistently opposed affirmative action and civil rights legislation, including the Voting Rights Act of 1965. In 1990, Gary Franks of Connecticut became the first black Republican congressman since Oscar DePriest in 1935, and focused his attention on cutting the capital gains tax and adding a balanced-budget amendment to the Constitution. By the mid-1990s, he was joined in the House by Oklahoma's J. C. Watts. On its surface, Watts's signature legislation, the American Community Renewal Act, promised to restore the black capitalism ethos of the Nixon years. However, as a staunch proponent of "colorblind" policies, he made no provisions specifically to black entrepreneurs, and his bill almost exclusively benefited white developers who sought tax breaks by expanding into the inner city.[18]

After Barack Obama's 2008 election, the GOP saw a marked rise in viable, high-profile black candidates. In 2010, two black Republicans were elected from majority-white districts in the South. Running as proud members of the Tea Party movement, Allen West of Florida and Tim Scott of South Carolina consistently sided with the most conservative elements of their party, emphasizing deregulation, low taxes, and a strong military. Four years later, Scott became the first African American of either party elected to the Senate from South Carolina since Reconstruction. He was joined in Congress by black Republicans William Hurd of Texas and Mia Love of Utah, the state's first African American congressperson and the nation's first Haitian American congressperson.[19]

The same social issues that have motivated evangelical whites since the 1980s also seem to have a particular salience among contemporary black Republicans. The conservative religious beliefs held by Clarence Thomas, a devout Catholic, Mia Love, a Catholic-turned-Mormon, and J. C. Watts, a Baptist pastor, are central to their political ideology. Whereas many African Americans may have shared similar conservative views on abortion, gay marriage, and other hot-button social issues, most are motivated even more by Christian messages of social justice and community uplift. Black Republicans, on the other hand, tend to join their white counterparts in placing conservative social issues at the fore of their agenda. Clarence Thomas's 2015 dissent in the Supreme Court's gay-marriage decision, for example, quoted the Catholic catechism nearly word for word in its description of human nature. Black Republicans, from Congressmen J. C. Watts and Allen West, to Alveda King (Martin Luther King, Jr.'s niece), to 2016 presidential candidate Ben Carson have consistently placed abortion (a sin and the "number one killer of black people") as the most pressing issue confronting African Americans. Watts and Tim Scott have both cited their involvement in the Fellowship of Christian Athletes, an evangelical organization active on college campuses, as instrumental to their political development, and, once in office, cultivated strong ties with the Family Research Council and other evangelical think tanks.[20]

Although they toed the official GOP line and philosophically embraced conservatism, black Republicans in the post-Reagan years still faced an uphill battle for full acceptance inside the party. In the 1980s and 1990s, the New York-based Freedom Republicans called for the RNC to have more diversity within its executive committee by amending rules to give proportional representation to states, creating more seats for minority-rich, populous states. In 1992, they filed a lawsuit demanding that the Federal Election Commission stop giving millions of dollars to fund the Republican National Convention because it had virtually no black representation in its leadership. Though the Freedom Republicans won their case in U.S. District Court, the decision was overruled two years later after an arduous appeals process by the RNC. Small, rural states continued to have disproportionate representation on the national committee, and as late as 2008 only one African American, a committeewoman from the U.S. Virgin Islands, served on the 165-member committee.[21]

In a rare moment of reflective candor, Clarence Thomas suggested that black conservatives had "to become a caricature of sorts, providing side shows of anti-black quips and attacks" in order to gain acceptance from party leaders, and claimed that black conservatives risked instant excommunication from GOP leadership if they did not remain "adamant and constant" in their opposition to affirmative action and welfare. J.C. Watts frequently criticized the GOP's apathy toward black outreach, and urged Republicans to drop their racially divisive rhetoric on affirmative action, to add single mothers in discussions of family values, and to include more black faces in photo-ops. Assuming leadership in 2009 shortly after the presidential election of Obama, the RNC's first black chairman, Michael Steele, similarly focused his efforts on public relations, promising the party a "hip-hop makeover." On the few occasions when he challenged official GOP policy, such as opposing stringent voter-identification laws or advocating a return to Nixon-era black capitalism initiatives, he was met with indifference or outright hostility. By 2012, Steele had become so isolated within the party that he was not even invited to the Republican convention.[22]

While they were largely excluded from party leadership, there remained a faction of black Republican holdouts from the civil rights era who held to their faith in two-party competition. William Coleman served as the nation's foremost legal defender of affirmative action in the 1980s and 1990s. He remained adamant that his efforts were "those of a committed member of the Republican Party," as he implored the GOP to remember its legacy as the party of Abraham Lincoln and Earl Warren, and "strive not only for greater economic freedom and freedom from unwarranted Government intrusion in our lives but also for true equality of opportunity for black Americans." Former head of the RNC's Minorities Division, Clarence Townes, "was not enthusiastic . . . at all" about the conservative direction his party took in the 1980s, but actively promoted moderates in the Republican Party of Richmond, Virginia, and preached the values of two-party competition through the 2010s. Arthur Fletcher, who became the executive director of the United Negro College Fund after leaving the Nixon administration, continued to ask black audiences, "Why do we have to wait for an invitation to consider the importance of making our influence felt in both major parties?" As chairman of George H. W. Bush's Commission on Civil Rights, Fletcher often locked heads with the administration, and launched a bid for the Republican presidential nomination in 1995 on a platform that promised to "keep affirmative action alive." Though it was a quixotic effort in a party with few black primary voters and a deeply conservative base, it was consistent with Fletcher's fifty-year quest to insert a distinctly black voice into the GOP.[23]

At Fletcher's funeral in 2005, his son eulogized that his father "felt that if he was inside the Republican Party, he could fight for civil rights laws. . . . He didn't have to buy the party line, hook line and sinker, but he was the only voice on the inside." Similarly, Edward Brooke argued shortly before his death in 2015, "I've always believed since I've been in the party that in order to change the party it had to be within and not from without." Fletcher and Brooke both entered GOP ranks in the 1950s at a time when its conservative turn was far from guaranteed. Though they ultimately failed, as did all so-called "Rockefeller Republicans," to wrest control of the party's future, their inability to do so does not mean they did not experience success along the way. The split between the Eastern Establishment and conservatives provided black Republicans an avenue to fight for the future direction of their party. Throughout the 1950s and 1960s, black Republicans like Brooke, Jackie Robinson, Grant Reynolds, and members of the National Negro Republican Assembly joined forces with Nelson Rockefeller, George Romney, Hugh Scott, and other moderates in a fight for a big-tent party capable of competing for the votes of big cities, industrial states, and minorities. Even the Nixon administration of the late 1960s and 1970s provided opportunities for black Republicans and black nationalists to purse an agenda that demonstrably benefited black businesses and colleges, and institutionalized affirmative action within the federal government.[24]

Prior to his death in August 1976, Tennessee's George W. Lee saved his final battle to prevent Reagan from stealing the Republican presidential nomination from Gerald Ford in the spring primaries. "I am afraid of Ronald Reagan," he wrote to members of black Elk lodges, "he represents the extreme ideas of conservatism." But rather than deserting a party that "has not done very much in advancing the cause of black people," Lee implored African Americans to infiltrate the Republican Party and challenge it from the inside. Though the GOP embodied ascendant conservatism, Lee still clung to his belief in "true Republicanism," which stood on "the principles of a free society, a sound fiscal policy and civil rights." It was up to "Real Republicans" to restore the party's lost heritage and ward off the conservatism that "feeds on our community and national frustrations—and undermines our community's purpose of freedom."[25]

This had been the undertaking of black Republicans throughout the civil rights era—from Robert Church and the Republican American Committee's condemnation of the "vicious alliance" between conservative Republicans and Southern Democrats in 1944, to the National Negro Republican Assembly's fight against Barry Goldwater in 1964. George Fleming summed up this militancy at the NNRA's inaugural conference after Goldwater's nomination, declaring that black Republicans "are here to raise an army led by Negroes whose unique contribution through the history of this party and this nation has been to provide a catalyst for the conscience of America." Black Republicans were indeed the conscience of the Grand Old Party during the civil rights era. As members of local, state, and national Republican organizations, as elected politicians, and as activists, they were catalysts for reform in their cities and states. They were also fierce defenders of the party's Eastern Establishment. As Fleming also declared in his 1964 NNRA address, "We are here to support our friends in the Republican Party and, within the framework of the party, we are here to defeat those who have infiltrated the party and are seeking to drive the Negro out."[26]

With a legacy dating back to the first southern Black-and-Tan Republican parties, black Republicans during the civil rights era refused to acquiesce to the party's rising conservative tide. Their failure to permanently reshape the GOP is not just their own, it is the story of moderate Republicanism in postwar America. As today's Republican Party grapples with its future in post-Obama America, with continued racial tension, widening economic disparities, and a shrinking demographic of white voters, it perhaps should heed the advice of its first president, Abraham Lincoln, whose legacy black Republicans in the mid-twentieth century fought to have the party live up to: "The dogmas of the quiet past, are inadequate to the stormy present. . . . As our case is new, so we must think anew, and act anew. . . . The way is plain, peaceful, generous, just—a way which, if followed, the world will forever applaud, and God must forever bless."[27]

ARCHIVAL SOURCES AND ABBREVIATIONS

Manuscript Collections

Buffalo State College, Monroe Fordham Regional History Center (New York)
    Raphael DuBard Papers

Duke University, Rare Book, Manuscript, and Special Collections Library (Durham, North Carolina)
    Asa and Elna Spaulding Papers
    Helen Edmonds Papers

Dwight D. Eisenhower Presidential Library (Abilene, Kansas)
    Bryce Harlow Records (Pre-Acc)
    Columbia University Oral History Project
    Dwight D. Eisenhower Papers as President—Ann Whitman File
    Dwight D. Eisenhower Post-Presidential Papers
    Dwight D. Eisenhower Records as President—White House Central Files
    E. Frederic Morrow Papers
    E. Frederic Morrow Records
    Frederic Fox Records
    James Mitchell Papers
    Leonard Hall, Chairman Republican National Committee Papers
    Maxwell Rabb Papers
    William Rogers Papers

Gerald R. Ford Presidential Library (Ann Arbor, Michigan)
    Gerald R. Ford Vice Presidential Papers
    Melvin R. Laird Papers
    Robert T. Hartmann Papers
    Stanley S. Scott Papers

Indiana University, Lilly Library (Bloomington, Indiana)
   Charles Halleck Mss.

Indiana University Northwest, Calumet Regional Archives (Gary, Indiana)
   City of Gary Collection, Collection No. 10
   Reverend L.K. Jackson Papers, Collection No. 71

Library of Congress, Manuscript Division (Washington, D.C.)
   Edward W. Brooke Papers
   Jackie Robinson Papers
   Leadership Conference on Civil Rights Records
   Roy Wilkins Papers

Lyndon Baines Johnson Presidential Library (Austin, Texas)
   Office Files of Bill Moyers
   Records of the Democratic National Committee
   White House Central Files

Memphis/Shelby County Public Library (Memphis, Tennessee)
   George W. Lee Collection
   Roberta Church Collection

Microfilm
   Papers of the National Association for the Advancement of Colored
      People (NAACP)
      Supplement to Part 1, 1956–1960
      Supplement to Part 1, 1961–1965
      Part 18: Special Subjects, 1940–1955, Series C
   Papers of the Republican Party
      Part I: Meetings of the Republican Committee, 1911–1980
      Part II: Reports and Memoranda of the Research Division of the Re-
         publican National Committee, 1938–1980

Richard Nixon Presidential Library and Birthplace Foundation (Yorba Linda,
California)
   Campaign 1960 Collection
   Campaign 1968 Collection
   Committee for the Re-Election of the President Collection

          Frederic Malek Papers
          Jeb Stuart Magruder Papers
   Nixon Presidential Returned Materials Collection
      White House Special Files
          Contested Materials
   Pre-Presidential Papers of Richard M. Nixon
   White House Central Files
      Staff Member and Office Files
          Bradley H. Patterson Files
          Leonard Garment Files
          Robert H. Finch Files

Rockefeller Archive Center (Sleepy Hollow, New York)
   Graham Molitor Papers
   Rockefeller Family Archives
      Nelson A. Rockefeller, Personal Papers
         George Hinman Files

University of California, Los Angeles, Department of Special Collections, Charles E. Young Research Library
   Ralph J. Bunche Papers (Collection 2051)

University of Kentucky, Special Collections Library (Lexington, Kentucky)
   John Sherman Cooper Collection
   Rogers C. B. Morton Papers
   Thruston Ballard Morton Collection

University of Michigan, Bentley Historical Library (Ann Arbor, Michigan)
   George Romney Papers
   Republican Party (Michigan State Central Committee)

University of North Carolina at Chapel Hill
   Southern Historical Collection
         Floyd McKissick Papers # 4930

University of Texas at Austin, Center for American History
   Stephen Shadegg/Barry Goldwater Collection, 1949–1965

University of Utah, J. Willard Marriott Library (Salt Lake City, Utah)
    Fawn McKay Brodie Papers (Ms. 360)

Virginia Commonwealth University, Special Collections and Archives, James
Branch Cabell Library (Richmond, Virginia)
    Clarence L. Townes Jr. Papers

Abbreviations

CUOHP	Columbia University Oral History Project
DDERP	Dwight D. Eisenhower Records as President
DDEPP	Dwight D. Eisenhower Papers as President
DDEPPP	Dwight D. Eisenhower Post-Presidential Papers
LCCRR	Leadership Conference on Civil Rights Records
LD	*Louisville Defender*
MSRC	Moorland Spingarn Research Center, Howard University
NPC	*New Pittsburgh Courier*
NYT	*New York Times*
PPPRN	Pre-Presidential Papers of Richard Nixon
PPS	Pre-Presidential Series
NARPP	Nelson A. Rockefeller Personal Papers
RDNC	Records of the Democratic National Committee
WHCF	White House Central Files

NOTES

Introduction

1. Republican Party of Shelby County to Roberta Church, January 21, 1986, Folder 2, Roberta Church Collection.

2. David Wesson, "Black Republicans in Chicago," M.A. thesis (University of Maine, 1973), 57–58.

3. James Lane, *"City of the Century": A History of Gary, Indiana* (Bloomington: Indiana University Press, 1978), 276; Cynthia Griggs Fleming, *Yes We Did? From King's Dream to Obama's Promise* (Lexington: University Press of Kentucky, 2009), 117; "Resolutions Adopted by the Sixty-Ninth Annual Convention of the NAACP at Portland, Oregon," *The Crisis,* April 1979; "Transition," *The Crisis,* December 1982; "Honoring Arthur A. Fletcher," *Congressional Record—Senate,* vol. 151, pt. 12, July 21, 2005, 17036.

4. Richard Walter Thomas, *Life for Us Is What We Make It: Building Black Community in Detroit, 1915–1945* (Bloomington: Indiana University Press, 1992), 263. See also Nancy Weiss, *Farewell to the Party of Lincoln: Black Politics in the Age of FDR* (Princeton, N.J.: Princeton University Press, 1983); Patricia Sullivan, *Days of Hope: Race and Democracy in the New Deal Era* (Chapel Hill: University of North Carolina Press, 1996); Roger Biles, *The South and the New Deal* (Lexington: University Press of Kentucky, 2006).

5. Simon Topping, *Lincoln's Lost Legacy: The Republican Party and the African American Vote, 1928–1958* (Gainesville: University Press of Florida, 2008); Paul Frymer, *Uneasy Alliances: Race and Party Competition in America* (Princeton, N.J.: Princeton University Press, 2010); David Lublin, *The Republican South: Democratization and Partisan Change* (Princeton, N.J.: Princeton University Press, 2004); Devin Fergus, *Liberalism, Black Power, and the Making of American Politics, 1965–1980* (Athens: University of Georgia Press, 2009).

6. Lewis L. Gould, *Grand Old Party: A History of the Republicans* (New York: Random House, 2003); Lisa McGirr, *Suburban Warriors: The Origins of the New American Right* (Princeton, N.J.: Princeton University Press, 2001); Dan T. Carter, *From George Wallace to Newt Gingrich: Race in the Conservative Counterrevolution, 1963–1994* (Baton Rouge: Louisiana State University Press, 1996); Matthew D. Lassiter, *The Silent Majority: Suburban Politics in the Sunbelt South* (Princeton, N.J.: Princeton University Press, 2006); Mary C. Brennan, *Turning Right in the Sixties: The Conservative Capture of the GOP* (Chapel Hill: University of North Carolina Press, 1995).

7. For example, Thomas and Mary Edsall's *Chain Reaction: The Impact of Race, Rights, and Taxes on American Politics* (New York: Norton, 1991) briefly mentions black Republican opposition to Barry Goldwater at the 1964 Republican National Convention, but describes them in

the passive terms of victimhood. Allen Lichtman's *White Protestant Nation: The Rise of the American Conservative Movement* (New York: Atlantic Monthly Press, 2008) devotes a paragraph to the anti-civil rights activism of George Schuyler—who wrote from the far-right fringes of black political thought in the 1960s and enjoyed almost no community support—but only mentions Grant Reynolds, who as head of the National Negro Republican Assembly was far more representative of mainstream black Republicans, in a single sentence. Similarly, Rick Perlstein, *Nixonland: The Rise of a President and the Fracturing of America* (New York: Scribner, 2008), references only one black Republican, Edward W. Brooke. Even then, his emphasis is not on the first African American popularly elected to the U.S. Senate, but on the "confused backlashers" who voted for Brooke "because he had an (R) by his name."

8. A notable exception is Elizabeth Gritter, *River of Hope: Black Politics and the Memphis Freedom Movement, 1865–1954* (Lexington: University Press of Kentucky, 2014).

9. Earl Black and Merle Black, *The Rise of Southern Republicans* (Cambridge, Mass.: Belknap Press of Harvard University Press, 2002), 57.

10. Kevin Kruse, *White Flight: Atlanta and the Making of Modern Conservatism* (Princeton, N.J.: Princeton University Press, 2005), 232; Taylor Branch, *Parting the Waters: America in the King Years, 1954–63* (New York: Simon and Schuster, 1988), 349; Biles, 121.

11. Arnold Rampersad, *Jackie Robinson: A Biography* (New York: Knopf, 1997); David Beito and Linda Royster Beito, *Black Maverick: T. R. M. Howard's Fight for Civil Rights and Economic Power* (Urbana: University of Illinois Press, 2009); Dennis Dickerson, *African American Preachers and Politics: The Careys of Chicago* (Jackson: University Press of Mississippi, 2011); David Tucker, *Lieutenant Lee of Beale Street* (Nashville: Vanderbilt University Press, 1971); John Henry Cutler, *Ed Brooke: Biography of a Senator* (Indianapolis: Bobbs-Merrill, 1972); Darius Jamal Young, "The Gentleman from Memphis: Robert R. Church Jr. and the Politics of the Early Civil Rights Movement," PhD dissertation (University of Memphis, 2011), 197.

12. Angela Dillard, *Guess Who's Coming to Dinner Now? Multicultural Conservatism in America* (New York: New York University Press, 2001); Peter Eisenstadt, ed., *Black Conservatism: Essays in Intellectual and Political History* (New York: Garland, 1999); Gayle T. Tate and Lewis A. Randolph, eds., *Dimensions of Black Conservatism* (New York: Palgrave, 2002); Michael Ondaatje, *Black Conservative Intellectuals in Modern America* (Philadelphia: University of Pennsylvania Press, 2009).

13. For example, Christopher Alan Bracey, *Saviors or Sellouts: The Promise and Peril of Black Conservatism, from Booker T. Washington to Condoleezza Rice* (Boston: Beacon, 2008) labels Edward Brooke, a self-described liberal with a progressive voting record, as a "black conservative." Even Leah Wright Rigueur, whose groundbreaking scholarship was among the first to extensively analyze black Republican activism during the civil rights era, labels their ideology "conservative," albeit with a nuanced definition, despite frequent examples in her own work of black Republican leaders who self-identified as "liberal" and saw the conservative movement as antithetical to their ideology. Leah Wright Rigueur, *The Loneliness of the Black Republican: Pragmatic Politics and the Pursuit of Power* (Princeton, N.J.: Princeton University Press, 2015).

14. Nicol Rae, *The Decline and Fall of the Liberal Republicans: From 1952 to the Present* (New York: Oxford University Press, 1989), 7; Geoffrey Kabaservice, *Rule and Ruin: The Downfall of Moderation and the Destruction of the Republican Party, from Eisenhower to the Tea Party* (New York: Oxford University Press, 2012); Timothy Thurber, *Republicans and Race: The GOP's Frayed Relationship with African Americans, 1945–1974* (Lawrence: University Press of Kansas, 2013);

Michael Bowen, *The Roots of Modern Conservatism: Dewey, Taft, and the Battle for the Soul of the Republican Party* (Chapel Hill: University of North Carolina Press, 2011).

15. Donald Critchlow, *The Conservative Ascendancy: How the GOP Right Made Political History* (Cambridge, Mass.: Harvard University Press, 2007), 4-5.

16. William T. Coleman, Jr., with Donald Bliss, *Counsel for the Situation: Shaping the Law to Realize America's Promise* (Washington, D.C.: Brookings Institution Press, 2010), 2, 166, 360-63.

17. George W. Lee, interview by Clayton Braddock, November 1968, MSRC.

Chapter 1. Farewell to the Party of Lincoln?
Black Republicans in the New Deal Era

1. Richard B. Sherman, *The Republican Party and Black America from McKinley to Hoover, 1896-1933* (Charlottesville: University Press of Virginia, 1973), front matter.

2. Eric Foner, *Freedom's Lawmakers: A Directory of Black Office Holders During Reconstruction* (New York: Oxford University Press, 1993), xi; Thomas Holt, *Black over White: Negro Political Leadership in South Carolina During Reconstruction* (Urbana: University of Illinois Press, 1977), 1.

3. LeeAnna Keith, *The Colfax Massacre: The Untold Story of Black Power, White Terror, and the Death of Reconstruction* (New York: Oxford University Press, 2008), xi-xiii; Edward Ayers, *The Promise of the New South: Life After Reconstruction*, 15th anniversary ed. (New York: Oxford University Press, 2007), 6.

4. Tasha Philpot, *Race, Republicans, and the Return of the Party of Lincoln* (Ann Arbor: University of Michigan Press, 2007), 39; Donald Lisio, *Hoover, Blacks, and Lily-Whites: A Study of Southern Strategies* (Chapel Hill: University of North Carolina Press, 1985), 37; Jonathan Martin Kolkey, *The New Right, 1960-1968, with Epilogue, 1969-1980* (Washington, D.C.: University Press of America, 1983), 178-79.

5. Karen Ferguson, *Black Politics in New Deal Atlanta* (Chapel Hill: University of North Carolina Press, 2002), 85; J. Erroll Miller, "The Negro in Present Day Politics with Special Reference to Philadelphia," *Journal of Negro History* 33, 3 (July 1948): 335; Richard Bardolph, *The Negro Vanguard* (New York: Vintage, 1961), 200.

6. C. A. Bacote, "The Negro Voter in Georgia Politics, Today," *Journal of Negro Education*, 26, 3 (Summer 1957): 316-17; Gerald Horne, *Black Liberation/Red Scare: Ben Davis and the Communist Party* (Newark: University of Delaware Press, 1994), 21-23; Catherine Rymph, *Republican Women: Feminism and Conservatism from Suffrage Through the Rise of the New Right* (Chapel Hill: University of North Carolina Press, 2006), 26; Patricia Sullivan, *Lift Every Voice: The NAACP and the Making of the Civil Rights Movement* (New York: New Press, 2009), 77.

7. "Jones, Scipio Africanus," in Henry Louis Gates, Jr., and Evelyn Brooks Higginbotham, eds., *African American Lives* (New York: Oxford University Press, 2004), 479; Peter Lau, *Democracy Rising: South Carolina and the Fight for Black Equality Since 1865* (Lexington: University Press of Kentucky, 2006), 27; "Negro Gets $5,000 Office," *NYT*, November 5, 1922; Michael O'Neil, *Some Outstanding Colored People: Interesting Facts in the Lives of Representative Negroes* (Baltimore: Franciscan Sisters, 1943), 56-57.

8. Glenda Elizabeth Gilmore, "False Friends and Avowed Enemies: Southern African Americans and Party Allegiances in the 1920s," in Jane Dailey, Glenda Elizabeth Gilmore, and Bryant Simon, eds., *Jumpin' Jim Crow: Southern Politics from Civil War to Civil Rights* (Princeton, N.J.: Princeton University Press, 2000), 222; Jere Nash and Andy Taggart, *Mississippi Politics: The*

Struggle for Power, 1976–2006 (Jackson: University Press of Mississippi, 2006), 36; V. O. Key, Jr., with Alexander Heard, *Southern Politics in State and Nation: A New Edition* (Knoxville: University of Tennessee Press, 1984), 286; Hanes Walton, Jr., *Black Political Parties: An Historical and Political Analysis* (New York: Free Press, 1972), 68–69.

9. Neil McMillen, "Perry W. Howard, Boss of Black-and-Tan Republicanism in Mississippi, 1924–1960," *Journal of Southern History* 48, 2 (May 1982): 208–14; David Ginzl, "Lily-Whites Versus Black-and-Tans: Mississippi Republicans During the Hoover Administration," *Journal of Mississippi History* 42, 3 (September 1980): 200; Lisio, 70.

10. Elizabeth Gritter, *River of Hope: Black Politics and the Memphis Freedom Movement, 1865–1954* (Lexington: University Press of Kentucky, 2014), 55; Darius Jamal Young, "The Gentleman from Memphis: Robert R. Church, Jr., and the Politics of the Early Civil Rights Movement," Ph.D. dissertation (University of Memphis, 2011), 33–35.

11. Annette Church and Roberta Church, *The Robert R. Churches of Memphis: A Father and Son Who Achieved in Spite of Race* (Ann Arbor, Mich.: Edwards Brothers, 1974), 74, 112, 129, 173; Young, 127, 202.

12. Gritter, 46–48; Young, 7.

13. Gritter, 60–62; Church and Church, 110.

14. David Tucker, *Lieutenant Lee of Beale Street* (Nashville, Tenn.: Vanderbilt University Press, 1971), 81–83, 172; G. Wayne Dowdy, *Crusades for Freedom: Memphis and the Political Transformation of the American South* (Jackson: University Press of Mississippi, 2010), 9; George W. Lee, interview by Clayton Braddock, November 1968. MSRC.

15. Quintard Taylor, *The Forging of a Black Community: Seattle's Central District from 1870 Through the Civil Rights Era* (Seattle: University of Washington Press, 1994), 77, 102; Charles Pete T. Banner-Haley, *To Do Good and to Do Well: Middle-Class Blacks and the Depression, Philadelphia, 1929–1941* (New York: Garland, 1993), 56; Andrew Kaye, "Roscoe Conkling Simmons and the Significance of African American Oratory," *History Journal* 45, 1 (March 2002): 88; Andrew Kaye, "Colonel Roscoe Conkling Simmons and the Mechanics of Black Leadership," *Journal of American Studies* 37, 1 (April 2003): 92.

16. Simon Topping, *Lincoln's Lost Legacy: The Republican Party and the African American Vote, 1928–1958* (Gainesville: University Press of Florida, 2008), 9.

17. Allan Lichtman, *Prejudice and the Old Politics: The Presidential Election of 1928* (Chapel Hill: University of North Carolina Press, 1979), 152, 156; Hanes Walton, Jr., and Robert C. Smith, *American Politics and the African American Quest for Universal Freedom*, 2nd ed. (New York: Longman, 2003), 142; Lisio, xvi, 93; Young, 185.

18. Roy Wilkins, interview by Lawrence Hogan, December 2, 1976, Accession #76-69, Claude Barnett and the Associated Negro Press Collection, Indiana University Center for the Study of History and Memory; "Why I Am for Hoover," *Chicago Defender*, November 3, 1928; Rymph, 35; Lisio, 111.

19. "G.O.P. South," *Time*, February 18, 1929; George Brown Tindall, *The Emergence of the New South, 1913–1945* (Baton Rouge: Louisiana State University Press, 1967), 251.

20. Lisio, 91; Horne, 22; Wayne Greenhaw, *Elephants in the Cottonfields: Ronald Reagan and the New Republican South* (New York: Macmillan, 1982), 47.

21. Kenneth W. Goings, *"The NAACP Comes of Age": The Defeat of Judge John J. Parker* (Bloomington: Indiana University Press, 1990), xii, 24, 62–66.

22. Editorial, *Pittsburgh Courier*, May 10, 1930; Nancy Weiss, *Farewell to the Party of Lincoln: Black Politics in the Age of FDR* (Princeton, N.J.: Princeton University Press, 1983), 20, 24.

23. Michael K. Brown, *Race, Money, and the American Welfare State* (Ithaca, N.Y.: Cornell University Press, 1999), 77–78; Terry H. Anderson, *The Pursuit of Fairness: A History of Affirmative Action* (New York: Oxford University Press, 2004), 13. See also Nancy Weiss, *Farewell to the Party of Lincoln: Black Politics in the Age of FDR* (Princeton, N.J.: Princeton University Press, 1983); Harvard Sitkoff, *A New Deal for Blacks: The Emergence of Civil Rights as a National Issue: The Depression Decade*, 30th anniversary ed. (New York: Oxford University Press, 2009); Ira Katznelson, *When Affirmative Action Was White: An Untold History of Racial Inequality in Twentieth-Century America* (New York: Norton, 2005).

24. Marcus Boulware, "Roscoe Conkling Simmons: The Golden Voiced Politico," *Negro History Bulletin* 29, 6 (March 1966), 131; Dennis Nordin, *The New Deal's Black Congressman: A Life of Arthur Wergs Mitchell* (Columbia: University of Missouri Press, 1997), 57; Key with Heard, 290.

25. Christopher Robert Reed, *The Depression Comes to the South Side: Protest and Politics in the Black Metropolis, 1930–1933* (Bloomington: Indiana University Press, 2011), 37–41; Nordin, 11; Olen Cole, Jr., *The African American Experience in the Civilian Conservation Corps* (Gainesville: University Press of Florida, 1999), 84n11.

26. Charles V. Hamilton, *Adam Clayton Powell, Jr.: The Political Biography of an American Dilemma* (New York: Atheneum, 1991), 184; Zora Neale Hurston, "A Negro Voter Sizes Up Taft," *Saturday Evening Post*, December 8, 1957.

27. Bettye Collier-Thomas, *Jesus, Jobs, and Justice: African American Women and Religion* (New York: Knopf, 2010), 295–96; Douglas Flamming, *Bound for Freedom: Black Los Angeles in Jim Crow America* (Berkeley: University of California Press, 2005), 373; Rymph, 83; Jack Greenberg, *Crusaders in the Courts: How a Dedicated Band of Lawyers Fought for the Civil Rights Revolution* (New York: Basic, 1994), 17.

28. McMillen, 214; "Carey the Republican," *New Republic*, October 18, 1948, 10; Church and Church, 81.

29. Roscoe Conkling Simmons, *The Republican Party and American Colored People* (s.n., 1936), 10; Simon Topping, "'Turning Their Pictures of Abraham Lincoln to the Wall': The Republican Party and Black America in the Election of 1936," *Irish Journal of American Studies* 8 (May 2000): 46–48; "Roscoe Conkling Simmons," in George Sewell and Margaret Dwight, *Mississippi Black History Makers* (Jackson: University Press of Mississippi, 1984), 56; Topping, *Lincoln's Lost Legacy*, 41; Manfred Berg, *"The Ticket to Freedom": The NAACP and the Struggle for Black Political Integration* (Gainesville: University Press of Florida, 2005), 65.

30. Thomas Spencer, "The Good Neighbor League Colored Committee and the 1936 Democratic Presidential Campaign," *Journal of Negro History* 63, 4 (October 1978): 313; Sitkoff, *A New Deal for Blacks*, 70; Greenberg, 210; James Kenneally, *A Compassionate Conservative: A Political Biography of Joseph W. Martin, Jr., Speaker of the U.S. House of Representatives* (Lanham, Md.: Lexington, 2003), 23–24.

31. Simmons, *The Republican Party and American Colored People*, 15–18; Robert Mason, *The Republican Party and American Politics from Hoover to Reagan* (New York: Cambridge University Press, 2012), 94; James W. Ford, "The Negro People and the Elections," *Communist* 16 (1937): 65.

32. Edward Benson and Paul Perry, "Analysis of Democratic-Republican Strength by Population Groups," *Public Opinion Quarterly* 4, 3 (September 1940): 467; Weiss, 217.

33. Katherine Tate, *From Protest to Politics: The New Black Voters in American Elections*, enlarged edition (Cambridge, Mass.: Harvard University Press, 1994), 51; Gunnar Myrdal, *An*

American Dilemma: The Negro Problem and Modern Democracy (New York: Harper and Brothers, 1944), 495; Everett Carll Ladd, Jr., with Charles Hadley, *Transformations of the American
Party System: Political Coalitions from the New Deal to the 1970s* (New York: Norton, 1978), 60;
Topping, *Lincoln's Lost Legacy*, 46; Alexander Heard, *A Two-Party South?* (Chapel Hill: University of North Carolina Press, 1952), 231.

34. Samuel Lubell, *White and Black: Test of a Nation* (New York: Harper and Row, 1964), 48;
Taylor, 104-5; Leah Wright, "The Loneliness of the Black Conservative: Black Republicans and
the Grand Old Party, 1964-1980," Ph.D. dissertation (Princeton University, 2009), 21; Tracy
K'Meyer, *Civil Rights in the Gateway to the South: Louisville, Kentucky, 1945-1980* (Lexington:
University Press of Kentucky, 2009), 40; "The Negro Faces November," *New Republic*, August 27,
1944, 243.

35. Benjamin Hooks with Jerry Guess, *The March for Civil Rights: The Benjamin Hooks Story*
(Chicago: American Bar Association, 2003), 345-46; Laurie Green, *Battling the Plantation Men-
tality: Memphis and the Black Freedom Struggle* (Chapel Hill: University of North Carolina Press,
2007), 140; Tucker, 148-49; Vernon E. Jordan with Annette Gordon-Reed, *Vernon Can Read: A
Memoir* (New York: Public Affairs, 2001), 49; Tim S. R. Boyd, *Georgia Democrats, the Civil Rights
Movement, and the Shaping of the New South* (Gainesville: University Press of Florida, 2012), 73;
Clifford Kuhn, Harlon Joye, and E. Bernard West, *Living Atlanta: An Oral History of the City,
1914-1948* (Athens: University of Georgia Press, 2005), 358.

36. Malcolm Moos, *The Republicans: A History of Their Party* (New York: Random House,
1956), 402; "Washington Rhodes," *NYT*, June 25, 1970; "Negro Legislators," *The Crisis*, January
1933, 13; Julius J. Adams, *The Challenge: A Study in Negro Leadership* (New York: Wendell Mal-
liet, 1949), 97; "Willkie Endorses Isaacs and Rivers," *NYT*, October 25, 1943; Greenberg, 210;
Eben Miller, *Born Along the Color Line: The 1933 Amenia Conference and the Rise of a National
Civil Rights Movement* (New York: Oxford University Press, 2012), 253; Russell Davis, *Black
Americans in Cleveland: From George Peake to Carl B. Stokes, 1796-1969* (Washington, D.C.:
Associated Publishers, 1972), 234; "William Walker Dies," *NYT*, October 30, 1981.

37. "Pennsylvania Politics as of the Year 1934," *The Crisis*, July 1934, 212; "The Pennsylvania
Civil Rights Act," *The Crisis*, November 1935, 341; "Meet: Chester K. Gillespie," *Afro-American*,
August 12, 1950; "Along the Color Line," *The Crisis*, March 1933, 63; Andrew E. Kersten, *Race,
Jobs, and the War: The FEPC in the Midwest, 1941-46* (Urbana: University of Illinois Press,
2000), 76; William Wayne Giffin, "The Negro in Ohio, 1914-1939," Ph.D. dissertation (Ohio
State University, 1968), 441-42.

38. Emma Lou Thornbrough, *Indiana Blacks in the Twentieth Century* (Bloomington: Indiana University Press, 2000), 92, 111; Richard B. Pierce, *Polite Protest: The Political Economy of
Race in Indianapolis, 1920-1970* (Bloomington: Indiana University Press, 2005), 29, 35-36;
"Brokenburr, Robert Lee," in David Bodenhamer and Robert Graham Barrows, eds., *The Encyclopedia of Indianapolis* (Bloomington: Indiana University Press, 1994), 357; Erma Brooks Williams, *Political Empowerment of Illinois' African-American State Lawmakers from 1877 to 2005*
(Lanham, Md.: University Press of America, 2008), 11-12; Kersten, 25; "Yesterday in Afro-American History," *Jet*, December 10, 1970, 10.

39. Peter Wallenstein, "Pioneer Black Legislators from Kentucky, 1860-1960s," *Register of
the Kentucky Historical Society* 110, 3 and 4 (Summer/Autumn 2012): 545-46; George C. Wright,
A History of Blacks in Kentucky: In Pursuit of Equality, 1890-1980 (Frankfort: Kentucky Historical Society, 1992), 158-60; John Hardin, *Fifty Years of Segregation: Black Higher Education in
Kentucky, 1904-1954* (Lexington: University Press of Kentucky, 1997), 100; Gerald L. Smith, *A*

Black Educator in the Segregated South: Kentucky's Rufus B. Atwood (Lexington: University Press of Kentucky, 1994), 74; K'Meyer, 10; "Oneth M. Travis," *Pittsburgh Post-Gazette*, August 20, 1991; "Eugene Clayton, Ex-Louisville Alderman, Dies at 66," *Jet*, April 7, 1960, 8.

40. Nicol C. Rae, *The Decline and Fall of the Liberal Republicans: From 1952 to the Present* (New York: Oxford University Press, 1989), 31; Timothy Thurber, *Race and Republicans: The GOP's Frayed Relationship with African Americans, 1945–1974* (Lawrence: University Press of Kansas, 2013), 24; Ellsworth Barnard, *Wendell Willkie: Fighter for Freedom* (Marquette: Northern Michigan University Press, 1966), 340; Joseph Barnes, *Willkie: The Events He Was Part of— The Ideas He Fought For* (New York: Simon and Schuster, 1952), 327; Harvard Sitkoff, *Toward Freedom Land: The Long Struggle for Racial Equality in America* (Lexington: University Press of Kentucky, 2010), 129.

41. Ralph J. Bunche, "Report on the Needs of the Negro (for the Republican Program Committee)," June 10, 1939, Folder 21, Box 60, Bunche Papers; Weiss, 268–70; James Kenneally, "Black Republicans During the New Deal: The Role of Joseph W. Martin, Jr.," *Review of Politics* 55, 1 (Winter 1993): 131; "Republican Platform of 1940," in Kirk Porter and Donald Bruce Johnson, eds., *National Party Platforms, 1840–1960* (Urbana: University of Illinois Press, 1961), 393; Church and Church, 144–45.

42. Republican National Committee, "An Appeal to the Common Sense of Colored Citizens," Frame 0065, Reel 29, NAACP Papers, Part 18; Lawrence Scott and William Womack, Sr., *Double V: The Civil Rights Struggle of the Tuskegee Airmen* (East Lansing: Michigan State University Press, 1994), 124; Sitkoff, *Toward Freedom Land*, 133; Kenneally, "Black Republicans During the New Deal," 132; Weiss, 282.

43. Susan Welch and Lorn Foster, "Class and Conservatism in the Black Community," *American Politics Quarterly* 15, 4 (October 1987): 448; Kenneally, "Black Republicans During the New Deal," 133–34; Ralph J. Bunche, "The Negro in the Political Life of the United States," *Journal of Negro Education* 10, 3 (July 1941): 580.

44. Young, 200; Church and Church, 74–83.

45. "Republican Platform of 1944," in Porter and Johnson, 412; "The Negro Faces November," 242; Church and Church, 83; Topping, *Lincoln's Lost Legacy*, 99.

46. "Negroes Seen for Dewey," *NYT*, April 23, 1944; Topping, *Lincoln's Lost Legacy*, 90; Geoffrey Kabaservice, *Rule and Ruin: The Downfall of Moderation and the Destruction of the Republican Party* (New York: Oxford University Press, 2012), 8.

47. "The Negro Faces November," 241; "The Negro Vote," *Harper's Magazine*, July 1944, 152; "A Declaration by Negro Voters," *The Crisis*, January 1944, 16; Henry Lee Moon, *Balance of Power: The Negro Vote* (Garden City, N.Y.: Doubleday, 1948), 34.

48. Republican American Committee, "Declaration to the Republican Party," August 24–25, 1945, Folder 9, Box 6, Church Collection; Herbert Brownell with John Burke, *Advising Ike: The Memoirs of Attorney General Herbert Brownell* (Lawrence: University Press of Kansas, 1993), 69; Laura Jane Gifford, *The Center Cannot Hold: The 1960 Presidential Election and the Rise of Modern Conservatism* (DeKalb: Northern Illinois University Press, 2009), 70–71; Church and Church, 86, 259–60.

49. Church and Church, v–vi, 76–77, 245–46; Russell Kirk and James McClellan, *The Political Principles of Robert A. Taft* (New York: Fleet Press, 1967), 74.

50. Thomas Sugrue, *Sweet Land of Liberty: The Forgotten Struggle for Civil Rights in the North* (New York: Random House, 2008), 113–15; Anthony S. Chen, "Virtue, Necessity, and Irony in the Politics of Civil Rights: Organized Business and Fair Employment Practices in

Postwar Cleveland," in Kim Phillips-Fein and Julian E. Zelizer, eds., *What's Good for Business: Business and American Politics Since World War II* (New York: Oxford University Press, 2012), 45; Richard Norton Smith, *Thomas E. Dewey and His Times* (New York: Simon and Schuster, 1982), 447; Republican Congressional Committee, "The Republican Party and the Negro: Facts for Party Speakers and Workers," 9, Folder: OF–142-A Negro Matters-Colored Question (3), Box 731, Official File, DDERP-WHCF.

51. Gary W. Reichard, *Politics as Usual: The Age of Truman and Eisenhower* (Arlington Heights, Ill.: Harlan Davidson, 1988), 18; Gary Donaldson, *Truman Defeats Dewey* (Lexington: University Press of Kentucky, 1999), 11; "FDR Independent Voters League Neutral on Childress and Henderson," *Louisville Leader*, November 1, 1947; "Reveals Heavy Colored Ballot in Close Races," *Chicago Tribune*, November 17, 1946; J. Erroll Miller, "The Negro in Present Day Politics," 328–32.

52. "Powell Record Attacked," *NYT*, October 23, 1946; Wil Haygood, *King of the Cats: The Life and Times of Adam Clayton Powell, Jr.* (New York: Amistad, 1993), 135–41; Hamilton, 183.

53. Neil Hickey and Ed Edwin, *Adam Clayton Powell and the Politics of Race* (New York: Fleet, 1965), 104–7; Hamilton, 143–45.

54. Dennis Dickerson, *African American Preachers and Politics: The Careys of Chicago* (Jackson: University Press of Mississippi, 2010), 77–78, 95–96; James Farmer, *Lay Bare the Heart: An Autobiography of the Civil Rights Movement* (New York: Arbor House, 1985), 109; William Grimshaw, *Bitter Fruit: Black Politics and the Chicago Machine, 1931-1991* (Chicago: University of Chicago Press, 1992), 65; William Grimshaw, "Harold Washington: The Enigma of the Black Political Tradition," in Paul Green and Melvin Holli, eds., *The Mayors: The Chicago Political Tradition*, rev. ed. (Carbondale: Southern Illinois University Press, 1995), 181–82; "Carey the Republican," 12.

55. "Minister Follows Path of Three Generations," *Chicago Tribune*, March 31, 1966; Dickerson, 98, 168; "Carey the Republican," 10; Preston H. Smith, II, "The Quest for Racial Democracy: Black Civic Ideology and Housing Interests in Postwar Chicago," *Journal of Urban History* 26, 2 (January 2000): 148; Grimshaw, *Bitter Fruit*, 58.

56. "Asks End to Segregation," *NYT*, July 17, 1948; "Dewey Gets 'Jim Crow' Protest," *NYT*, August 23, 1948; "A Triumph for Civil Disobedience," *The Nation*, August 28, 1948, 228; Phillip McGuire, ed., *Taps for a Jim Crow Army: Letters from Black Soldiers in World War II* (Lexington: University Press of Kentucky, 1993), 248–49; Andrew E. Kersten, *A. Philip Randolph: A Life in the Vanguard* (Lanham, Md.: Rowman and Littlefield, 2007), 79.

57. William Berman, *The Politics of Civil Rights in the Truman Administration* (Columbus: Ohio State University Press, 1970), 59, 87–88; "Committee Forces Senate to Act on Ives FEPC Bill," *NYT*, February 6, 1948.

58. "Negro Group Urges Rights Bill Passage," *NYT*, October 26, 1948; "The Republican American Committee," October 2, 1947, Frame 0218, Reel 29, NAACP Papers, Part 18.

59. Cecelia Van Auken, "The Negro Press in the 1948 Presidential Election," *Journalism Quarterly* 26, 4 (December 1949): 432–33; Topping, *Lincoln's Lost Legacy*, 115; Berman, 103.

60. Harvard Sitkoff, "Harry Truman and the Election of 1948: The Coming of Age of Civil Rights in American Politics," *Journal of Southern History* 37, 4 (November 1971): 613; "Does the Republican Party Want the Negro Vote?," *The Crisis*, December 1949, 366; Topping, *Lincoln's Lost Legacy*, 135–38, 203.

61. "The Twilight of Two Eras," *Ebony*, August 1951, 102; Church and Church, 291.

Chapter 2. Flirting with Republicans: Black Voters in the 1950s

1. "Dixie Negroes Shift to GOP," *Atlanta Journal-Constitution*, November 11, 1956.

2. Herbert Brownell with John Burke, *Advising Ike: The Memoirs of Attorney General Herbert Brownell* (Lawrence: University Press of Kansas, 1993), 98; Simon Topping, *Lincoln's Lost Legacy: The Republican Party and the African American Vote, 1928–1958* (Gainesville: University Press of Florida, 2008), 167; "Political Roundup," *LD*, June 18, 1952; Jennifer Delton, *Rethinking the 1950s: How Anticommunism and the Cold War Made America Liberal* (New York: Cambridge University Press, 2013), 47.

3. Leonard Lurie, *The King Makers* (New York: Coward McCann and Geoghegan, 1971), 182–89; "Republicans Clash on Civil Rights," *NYT*, July 9, 1952; "Republican Platform of 1952," in Kirk Porter and Donald Bruce Johnson, eds., *National Party Platforms, 1840–1960* (Urbana: University of Illinois Press, 1961), 504.

4. George Hart, ed., *Official Report of the Proceedings of the Twenty-Fifth Republican National Convention* (Washington, D.C.: Republican National Committee, 1952), 95–96; Drew Hansen, *The Dream: Martin Luther King, Jr., and the Speech That Inspired a Nation* (New York: HarperPerennial, 2005), 108, 114; John Kilstrom, "The Politics of Principle: A Political Portrait of Archibald J. Carey, Jr.," M.A. thesis (Northern Illinois University, 1969), 25.

5. Dennis Dickerson, *African American Preachers and Politics: The Careys of Chicago* (Jackson: University Press of Mississippi, 2010), 119–20.

6. Nicol C. Rae, *The Decline and Fall of the Liberal Republicans: From 1952 to the Present* (New York: Oxford University Press, 1989), 38, 99; Kevin Yuill, *Richard Nixon and the Rise of Affirmative Action: The Pursuit of Racial Equality in an Era of Limits* (Lanham, Md.: Rowman and Littlefield, 2006), 122; Greg Mitchell, *Tricky Dick and the Pink Lady: Richard Nixon vs. Helen Gahagan Douglas—Sexual Politics and the Red Scare, 1950* (New York: Random House, 1998), 205.

7. "Rep. Powell Blasts Both Parties for Weak Platforms," *LD*, August 6, 1952; "The Democrats Present," *LD*, August 6, 1952; "Sparkman Quoted as Foe of Civil Rights Measures," *Pittsburgh Post-Gazette*, October 20, 1952.

8. Bradley L. Morison to John Cowles, September 3, 1952, Folder: Campaign—Suggestion (3), Box 6, Campaign Series, DDEPP-Whitman File; Frederick Ayer to Sinclair Weeks, October 16, 1952, Folder: Campaign—Suggestions (2), Box 6, Campaign Series, DDEPP-Whitman File; "Dewey Condemns Sparkman Record," *NYT*, October 3, 1952; "Jim Crow Sparkman Would Be One Heartbeat from the White House," *LD*, October 15, 1952.

9. "Carey Reveals Ike's Position on Civil Rights," *Chicago Daily Tribune*, August 27, 1952; Dickerson, 121–24; Kilstrom, 27–28.

10. E. Frederic Morrow, interview by Ed Edwin, January 31, 1968, CUOHP; "Family Motto Was Career Inspiration," *Oakland Post*, September 3, 1970; E. Frederic Morrow, *Forty Years a Guinea Pig* (New York: Pilgrim, 1980), 73–74; "Black Man in the White House," *Ebony*, April 1961, 78; E. Frederic Morrow, *Way Down South Up North* (Philadelphia: United Church Press, 1973), 26.

11. "Two Negro Leaders Criticize Sparkman," *NYT*, July 27, 1952; "Jane Spaulding, Ike Appointee, Dies of a Stroke," *Jet*, September 30, 1965, 56; "Negro Delegation Hails Eisenhower," *NYT*, August 5, 1952; "A.M.E. Bishop for Eisenhower," *Philadelphia Inquirer*, August 7, 1952; "Mrs. Daisy Lampkin," *NYT*, March 12, 1965; Edna McKenzie, "Daisy Lampkin: A Life of Love and Service," *Pennsylvania Heritage* 9, 3 (Summer 1983): 10; Daisy Lampkin to Fellow American, October 23, 1952, Frame 0426, Reel 29, NAACP Papers, Part 18.

12. Manfred Berg, *"The Ticket to Freedom": The NAACP and the Struggle for Black Political Integration* (Gainesville: University Press of Florida, 2005), 193; Archibald Carey, Jr., to Roy Wilkins, November 6, 1952, Frame 0434, Reel 29, NAACP Papers, Part 18.

13. "Ike Will Give Early Address Here Sept. 26," *Charlotte Observer*, September 10, 1952; "Ike Welcomed in South," *LD*, October 1, 1952; "Eisenhower Campaign Statements on Civil Rights and Immigration," Folder: Eisenhower Campaign Statements on Civil Rights and Immigration, 1952, Box 6, Maxwell Rabb Papers; Elizabeth Gritter, *River of Hope: Black Politics and the Memphis Freedom Movement, 1865–1954* (Lexington: University Press of Kentucky, 2014), 206–7; "Eisenhower Special Train Gets New Look in West," *Baltimore Afro-American*, September 23, 1952; "Ike Speaks at Meet Here," *LD*, September 24, 1952.

14. Bart Landry, *The New Black Middle Class* (Berkeley: University of California Press, 1987), 74; E. Frederic Morrow to Sherman Adams, September 20, 1952, Folder: Aboard the Eisenhower Campaign Train, 1952, Box 1, Morrow Papers; Speech delivered by E. Frederic Morrow in Philadelphia, PA, September 19, 1955, Folder: OF–142-A Negro Matters-Colored Question (3), Box 731, Official File, DDERP-WHCF.

15. Tim S. R. Boyd, *Georgia Democrats, the Civil Rights Movement, and the Shaping of the New South* (Gainesville: University Press of Florida, 2012), 82; James Nabrit, Jr., "The Future of the Negro Voter in the South," *Journal of Negro Education* 26, 3 (Summer 1957): 418; Samuel Lubell, *Revolt of the Moderates* (New York: Harper and Brothers, 1956), 217.

16. E. Frederic Morrow to Sherman Adams, December 16, 1955, Folder: Civil Rights–Official Memoranda 1956–1955, Box 10, Morrow Records; Sherman Adams, *Firsthand Report: The Story of The Eisenhower Administration* (New York: Harper, 1961), 333; Beverly Greene Bond, "Roberta Church: Race and the Republican Party in the 1950s," in Nina Mjagkij, ed., *Portraits of American Life Since 1865* (Wilmington, Del.: Scholarly Press, 2003), 189–94; Robert Frederick Burk, *The Eisenhower Administration and Black Civil Rights* (Knoxville: University of Tennessee Press, 1984), 69; Loren Miller, "The Negro Voter in the Far West," *Journal of Negro Education*, 26:3 (Summer 1957), 265; "Ernest Wilkins Backed," *NYT*, March 12, 1954.

17. Edward Clayton, *The Negro Politician: His Success and Failure* (Chicago: Johnson, 1964), 114; Dickerson, 134–37, 145–46; Ronald Huggins, "Eisenhower and Civil Rights," Ph.D. dissertation (University of California at Los Angeles, 1985), 31–32.

18. Morrow, *Forty Years a Guinea Pig*, 89–90; "Whatever Happened to E. Frederic Morrow," *Ebony*, December 1971, 182; Burk, 79.

19. Beverly Washington Jones, *Quest for Equality: The Life and Writings of Mary Eliza Church Terrell* (New York: Carlson, 1990), 72–84.

20. Charles Alexander, *Holding the Line: The Eisenhower Era, 1952–1961* (Bloomington: Indiana University Press, 1976), 116–17; David Nichols, *A Matter of Justice: Eisenhower and the Beginning of the Civil Rights Revolution* (New York: Simon and Schuster, 2007), 43; Adams, 335.

21. Michael Mayer, "Eisenhower's Conditional Crusade: The Eisenhower Administration and Civil Rights, 1953–1957," Ph.D. dissertation (Princeton University, 1984), 6; Brownell with Burke, 183–84; Nichols, 77, 83.

22. Kenneth Robert Janken, *Walter White: Mr. NAACP* (Chapel Hill: University of North Carolina Press, 2003), 356; Arthur Larson, *Eisenhower: The President Nobody Knew* (New York: Scribner's, 1968), 125; Earl Warren, *The Memoirs of Chief Justice Earl Warren* (Lanham, Md.: Madison Books, 2001), 291; Dwight Eisenhower, *Mandate for Change, 1953–1956* (Garden City, N.Y.: Doubleday, 1963), 230; Cross Reference Sheet, June 9, 1954, Folder: White—Walter [NAACP] Only, Box 3330, Alphabetical File, DDERP-WHCF.

23. Speech delivered by E. Frederic Morrow in Philadelphia, Pa., September 19, 1955, Folder: OF-142-A Negro Matters-Colored Question (3), Box 731, Official File, DDERP-WHCF; Val Washington, "On Decision by the Supreme Court on the Ending of Segregation in Education," May 17, 1956, Folder: Washington, Val 1954–26, Box 101, Hall Papers; Burk, 165.

24. Timothy Thurber, *Race and Republicans: The GOP's Frayed Relationship with African Americans, 1945–1974* (Lawrence: University Press of Kansas, 2013), 49; "The Year of the Great Decision: Report of the Executive Secretary," Folder: GF 124-A-2 NAACP(1), Box 922, General File, DDERP-WHCF; Steven F. Lawson, *Black Ballots: Voting Rights in the South, 1944–1969* (New York: Columbia University Press, 1976), 143; Allen Jones, "Equal Rights to All, Special Privileges to None: The Black Press in Iowa, 1882–1985," in Henry Lewis Suggs, ed., *The Black Press in the Middle West, 1865–1985* (Westport, Conn.: Greenwood Press, 1996), 94.

25. Matthew Rees, *From the Deck to the Sea: Blacks and the Republican Party* (Wakefield, N.H.: Longwood Academic, 1991), 197; Pearl Robinson, "Whither the Future of the Republican Party?," *Political Science Quarterly* 97, 2 (Summer 1982): 219; Paul Allen Beck, "Partisan Dealignment in the Postwar South," *American Political Science Review* 71, 2 (June 1997): 481; Clifford Kuhn, Harlon Joye, and E. Bernard West, *Living Atlanta: An Oral History of the City, 1914–1948* (Athens: University of Georgia Press, 2005), 348; "Lee Is Most Effective Negro Republican," *Pittsburgh Courier Magazine*, December 19, 1959.

26. Carl Murphy to Richard Nixon, September 4, 1957, Folder: Afro-American Newspapers, Box 22, Nixon Pre-Presidential Papers, Series 320; C. Fraser Smith, *Here Lies Jim Crow: Civil Rights in Maryland* (Baltimore: Johns Hopkins University Press, 2008), 102; Herbert C. Smith and John T. Willis, *Maryland Politics and Government: Democratic Dominance* (Lincoln: University of Nebraska Press, 2012), 49; "More than Half of Negro Voters Here are Registered Republican," *LD*, August 13, 1952; Richard Clayton Smoot, "John Sherman Cooper: The Paradox of a Liberal Republican in Kentucky Politics," Ph.D. dissertation (University of Kentucky, 1988), 136–37, 198.

27. Ripon Society, *From Disaster to Distinction: A Republican Rebirth* (New York: Pocket Books, 1966), 33; Republican National Committee, "The 1952 Elections: A Statistical Analysis," October 1953, Folder: Political—Republican National Committee Publications, Box 201, Mitchell Papers; G. James Fleming and Christian E. Burckel, eds., *Who's Who in Colored America: An Illustrated Biographical Directory of Notable Living Persons of African Descent in the United States*, 7th ed. (Yonkers-on-Hudson, N.Y.: Christian E. Burckel and Associates, 1950); Henry Lee Moon, "The Negro Vote in the Presidential Election of 1956," *Journal of Negro Education*, 26:3 (Summer 1957), 226; Morrow Diary, "October 1, 1956," Folder 2, Box 2, Morrow Papers; Cross Reference Sheet, March 29, 1954, Folder: Washington, Val (Only) (1), Box 3269, Alphabetical File, DDERP-WHCF.

28. Alton Hornsby, Jr., *Black Power in Dixie: A Political History of African Americans in Atlanta* (Gainesville: University Press of Florida, 2009), 54; Val Washington to Charles McWhorter, December 19, 1957, Folder: Washington, Val, Box 801, PPPRN, Series 320; "Negroes Blame McKeldin," *Baltimore Sun*, October 1, 1951.

29. Charles Wesley, *History of the Improved Benevolent and Protective Order of Elks of the World, 1898–1954* (Washington, D.C.: Association for the Study of Negro Life and History, 1955), 223, 417–18; Theda Skocpol, Ariane Liazos, and Marshall Ganz, *What a Mighty Power We Can Be: African American Fraternal Groups and the Struggle for Racial Equality* (Princeton, N.J.: Princeton University Press, 2006), 172, 178, 190, 207; "Elks Elect Robert Johnson Grand Exalted

Ruler," *Jet*, September 11, 1952, 12; "Will He Revive the Great Antlered Herd?," *NPC*, September 10, 1960.

30. Skocpol, Liazos, and Ganz, 207; Lionel Hampton with James Haskins, *Hamp: An Autobiography* (New York: Amistad, 1993), 96–97; Remarks delivered by Perry Howard in Chicago, September 14, 1950, Frame 0334, Reel 10, Papers of the Republican Party, Part I, Series A; E. Frederic Morrow to George W. Lee, October 15, 1959, Folder 68, Box 3, Lee Collection.

31. Skocpol, Liazo, and Ganz, 181, 195; Wesley, 332, 378–79; Erik Gellman, *Death Blow to Jim Crow: The National Negro Congress and the Rise of Militant Civil Rights* (Chapel Hill: University of North Carolina Press, 2012), 139; "Johnson Asks Elks to Replace NAACP Where It's Outlawed," *Baltimore Afro-American*, September 1, 1956; David Tucker, *Lieutenant Lee of Beale Street* (Nashville, Tenn.: Vanderbilt University Press, 1971), 203–6.

32. Annette Church and Robert Church, *The Robert R. Churches of Memphis: A Father and Son who Achieved in Spite of Race* (Ann Arbor, Mich.: Edwards Brothers, 1974), 193; Bond, 185–87; "Republicans Name J. J. Adams," *NYT*, July 21, 1950; Paul David, Ralph Goldman, and Richard Bain, *The Politics of National Party Conventions* (Washington, D.C.: Brookings Institution Press, 1960), 330; Felecia G. Jones Ross, "Democracy's Textbook: A History of the Black Press in Ohio, 1865–1985," in Suggs, 258–59; "E. Washington Rhodes Named to Pa. Parole Board," *Jet*, October 22, 1953, 5; David L. Wesson, "Black Republicans in Chicago," M.A. thesis (University of Maine, 1973), 51; Arthur Fletcher, interview by Robert Wright, January 21, 1970, MSRC; David Hamilton Golland, "A Mind Is a Terrible Thing to Waste: Arthur Fletcher, Spirituality, and the American Underclass," *Claremont Journal of Religion* 1, 1 (January 2012): 108–9; Mark Peterson, "The Kansas Roots of Arthur Allen Fletcher: Football All-Star to the 'Father of Affirmative Action,'" *Kansas History* 34 (Autumn 2011): 236–37.

33. "One Congressman Who Cannot Be Beaten," *NYT*, November 16, 1952; Otha Richard Sullivan and James Haskins, *African American Millionaires* (Hoboken, N.J.: Wiley, 2005), 80; "Crispus Wright Seeking James Roosevelt Upset," *Los Angeles Times*, April 9, 1958; "Crispus Wright," *Los Angeles Sentinel*, December 19, 2001.

34. Dennis Nordin, *From Edward Brooke to Barack Obama: African American Political Success, 1966–2008* (Columbia: University of Missouri Press, 2012), 11–12.

35. Dickerson, 103–4; "Ticker Tape U.S.A.," *Jet*, March 24, 1955, 15; "Edgar Brown Launches Fight on Rebel Hat," *Jet*, February 28, 1952, 7.

36. P. Bernard Young, "Negro Pastors Boo Dawson," October 20, 1956, Folder: Civil Rights, Box 153, PPPRN, Series 320; David Beito and Linda Royster Beito, *Black Maverick: T.R.M. Howard's Fight for Civil Rights and Economic Power* (Urbana: University of Illinois Press, 2009), xii, 176–87.

37. Samuel Lubell, *White and Black: Test of a Nation* (New York: Harper and Row, 1964), 63; A. James Reichley, *The Art of Government: Reform and Organization Politics in Philadelphia* (New York: Fund for the Republic, 1959), 69–70.

38. Beatrice Lumpkin, *"Always Bring a Crowd!" The Story of Frank Lumpkin, Steelworker* (New York: International Publishers, 1999), 105; "Battle of Negro Wards," *NYT*, September 28, 1956; Ted Watson, "Equal Rental Opportunity Bill Defeated in Illinois," *NPC*, July 1, 1961; Beito and Beito, 174.

39. Quintard Taylor, *The Forging of a Black Community: Seattle's Central District from 1870 Through the Civil Rights Era* (Seattle: University of Washington Press, 1994), 176; Stephanie Stokes Oliver, *Song for My Father: Memoir of an All-American Family* (New York: Atria, 2004),

24; C. Fraser Smith, *Here Lies Jim Crow*, 108; "Vote Registration Drive Slated in Maryland," *Jet*, July 26, 1953, 7; "Maryland's Senate Gets Anti-Bias Bills," *NYT*, January 13, 1957.

40. Archibald Carey, Jr., to Martin Luther King, Jr., June 7, 1955, in Clayborne Carson et al., eds., *The Papers of Martin Luther King, Jr.*, vol. 2, *Rediscovering Precious Values, July 1951–November 1955* (Berkeley: University of California Press, 1992), 560; Martin Luther King, Jr., and E. N. French to Archibald Carey, Jr., December 27, 1955, in Clayborne Carson et al., eds., *The Papers of Martin Luther King, Jr.*, vol. 3: *Birth of a New Age, December 1955–December 1956* (Berkeley: University of California Press, 1992), 93–93, 153; Martin Luther King, Jr., to Archibald Carey, Jr., December 20, 1957, in Clayborne Carson et al., eds., *The Papers of Martin Luther King Jr.*, vol. 4, *Symbol of the Movement, January 1957–December 1958* (Berkeley: University of California Press, 1992), 343; Kilstrom, 39–41.

41. "N.A.A.C.P. Fund Elects Ex-Judge," *NYT*, February 2, 1965; Arthur Fletcher, interview by Robert Wright, January 21, 1970, MSRC; Harold Martin, *Atlanta and Environs: A Chronicle of Its People and Events*, vol. 3 (Athens: University of Georgia Press, 1987), 249, 404; "Bribe Offer Hinted to Foil Negro Suit," *NYT*, January 23, 1959; "Urban League Forms Committee to Seek Solution to Race Problem," *Tri-State Defender*, January 18, 1964; "John Calhoun" *NYT*, May 10, 1988; Hornsby, 95.

42. Roy Wilkins to Archibald Carey, Jr., November 10, 1952, Frame 0436, Reel 29, NAACP Papers, Part 18; Elbert Lee Tatum, *The Changed Political Thought of the Negro, 1915–1940* (New York: Exposition Press, 1951), 182.

43. "The Negro Defection," *Christian Science Monitor*, May 8, 1956; Steven Wagner, *Eisenhower Republicanism: Pursuing the Middle Way* (DeKalb: Northern Illinois University Press, 2006), 77; Alexander, 194–95; Roy Wilkins with Tom Mathews, *Standing Fast: The Autobiography of Roy Wilkins* (Cambridge, Mass.: Da Capo, 1994), 234.

44. "Republican Platform of 1956," in Porter and Johnson, 554; Morrow Diary, "August 14, 1956," Folder 2, Box 2, Morrow Papers; Pero Dagbovie, *African American History Reconsidered* (Champaign: University of Illinois Press, 2010), 122–23; "Washington Merry-Go-Round," *Gadsden Times*, August 26, 1956; Lloyd Harkins, ed., *Official Report of the Proceedings of the Twenty-Sixth Republican National Convention* (Washington, D.C.: Republican National Committee, 1956), 273.

45. Hanes Walton, Jr., and Robert C. Smith, *American Politics and the African American Quest for Universal Freedom*, 2nd ed. (New York: Longman, 2003), 142; "Civil Rights Plank," *The Crisis*, August–September 1956, 419; "Who Gets the Negro Vote?" *Look*, November 13, 1956, 38.

46. Simeon Booker, *Black Man's America* (Englewood Cliffs, N.J.: Prentice-Hall, 1964), 206; "Nixon Will Direct Panel on Job Bias," *NYT*, August 16, 1953; Robert Donovan, *Eisenhower: The Inside Story* (New York: Harper and Brothers, 1956), 160; Adam Fairclough, *Race and Democracy: The Civil Rights Struggle in Louisiana, 1915–1972*, 2nd ed. (Athens: University of Georgia Press, 2008), 150.

47. Morrow, *Forty Years a Guinea Pig*, 187; Julius Adams to Richard Nixon, January 14, 1956, Folder: Adams, Julius, Box 19, PPPRN, Series 320; Mary Feaster to James Byrnes, August 20, 1953, Folder: Nixon, Richard (5), Box 28, Administration Series, DDEPP-Whitman File; James Byrnes to Dwight Eisenhower, August 27, 1953, Folder: Nixon, Richard (5), Box 28, Administration Series, DDEPP-Whitman File; Herbert Parmet, *Richard Nixon and His America* (Boston: Little, Brown, 1990), 268.

48. "Text of Nixon's Address to the Republican Club Dinner Here," *NYT*, February 14, 1956;

"Nixon Asks Tolerance," *NYT*, April 23, 1956; "Sees Racial Harmony," *Milwaukee Journal*, October 19, 1956; "Nixon Says G.O.P. Aids Civil Rights," *NYT*, November 1, 1956.

49. Of the eighty-two representatives to sign the manifesto, two were Republicans: Joel Broyhill and Richard Poff of Virginia. Tennessee Republicans Howard Baker, Sr., and B. Carroll Reece, and Texas Republican Bruce Alger refused to sign the document. "The Southern Manifesto," *Congressional Record*, 84th Cong., 2nd Sess., vol. 102, pt. 4, March 12, 1956 (Washington, D.C.: GPO, 1956), 4459–60; "The Southern Manifesto," *Time*, March 26, 1956.

50. Morrow Diary, "November 8, 1956," Folder 2, Box 2, Morrow Papers; Max Rabb to Bryce Harlow, June 20, 1956, Folder: OF–142-A Negro Matters-Colored Question (4), Box 731, Official File, DDERP-WHCF; Speech delivered by Hugh Scott in San Francisco, June 29, 1956, Frame 0711, Reel 4, NAACP Papers, Supplement to Part 1, 1956–1960.

51. "Grant Reynolds Breaks with Republican Party," *Washington Afro-American*, June 17, 1950; "Many Voters Show Signs of Returning to GOP's Ranks," *Wall Street Journal*, April 13, 1956; "Negroes in Switch to Republicans," *New York Herald Tribune*, March 19, 1956; "State G.O.P. Maps Negro Vote Drive," *NYT*, September 2, 1956; "Negro Leaders Urge Support for Ike Ticket," *Chicago Daily Tribune*, October 20, 1956; Val Washington to Fellow Citizen, n.d., Folder: Civil Rights (2), Box 10, Harlow Records.

52. "The Negro Vote and the Democrats," *The Reporter*, May 31, 1956, 11; "Ticker Tape U.S.A.," *Jet*, January 29, 1959, 11; Val Washington to Helen Edmonds, August 30, 1956, Folder: Correspondence, Republican Nat'l Committee, 1953–1956 expense accounts and itineraries, Box 2, Edmonds Papers; Helen Edmonds to Allen James Lowe, December 15, 1956, Folder: Correspondence, Republican National Committee, Letters from Rank and File Persons During the Following Dr. Edmonds Campaign Tour, 1956, Box 2, Edmonds Papers; Dickerson, 149; Tucker, 167; Bobby Lovett, *The Civil Rights Movement in Tennessee: A Narrative History* (Knoxville: University of Tennessee Press, 2005), 259.

53. Rumors spread that Powell endorsed Eisenhower in return for protection from a potential investigation of his finances by the Internal Revenue Service. There no solid evidence to support the claim, and Powell's praise of Eisenhower as early as 1954 indicates his genuine support for the president, rather than a quid pro quo in 1956. Bernard Shanley, Memorandum Covering Appointment of Congressman Adam Clayton Powell with the President, October 11, 1956, Folder: Oct. '56 Diary-Staff Memos, Box 19, DDE Diary Series, DDEPP-Whitman File; "The President and the Negro," *Reader's Digest*, October 1954, 61–63; Wil Haygood, *King of the Cats: The Life and Times of Adam Clayton Powell, Jr.* (New York: Amistad, 2006), 193, 218–19; Nichols, 138.

54. "Civil Rights," *The Crisis*, January 1956, 34; "The Negro Vote and the Democrats," 10; Taylor Branch, *Parting the Waters: America in the King Years, 1954–63* (New York: Simon and Schuster, 1988), 191; Beito and Beito, 173; Thurber, 75.

55. Moon, 219–25.

56. "Negro Vote Shift Heaviest in South," *NYT*, November 11, 1956; C.G. Gomillion, "The Negro Voter in Alabama," *Journal of Negro Education* 26, 3 (Summer 1957): 286; C. A. Bacote, "The Negro Voter in Georgia Politics, Today," *Journal of Negro Education* 26, 3 (Summer 1957): 317; Moon, 223–28; Beito and Beito, 174; Adam Fairclough, *To Redeem the Soul of America: The Southern Christian Leadership Conference and Martin Luther King Jr.* (Athens: University of Georgia Press, 1987), 41; Donald Strong, *Urban Republicanism in the South* (University: Bureau of Public Administration, University of Alabama, 1960), 12.

57. Research Division, Republican National Committee, "The Negro Vote," August 1957,

Folder: Negro Vote, Box 554, PPPRN, Series 320; Henry McGuinn and Tinsley Spraggins, "Negro in Politics in Virginia," *Journal of Negro Education* 26, 3 (Summer 1957): 383; Moon, 223; Numan V. Bartley and Hugh Davis Graham, *Southern Politics and the Second Reconstruction* (Baltimore: Johns Hopkins University Press, 1975), 87; Philip Klinkner, *The Losing Parties: Out-Party National Committees, 1956-1993* (New Haven, Conn.: Yale University Press, 1995), 34; Lovett, 259.

58. Moon, 220–22; "Negro Vote Switch," *The Crisis*, December 1956, 614.

59. "Negro Vote Switch," 614; McGuinn and Spraggins, 384–85; "The Negro Vote," August 1957, Folder: Negro Vote, Box 554, PPPRN, Series 320.

60. Fairclough, *Race and Democracy*, 222; McGuinn and Spraggins, 384; "Negro Vote Shift Heaviest in South," *NYT*, November 11, 1956; "Many Voters Show Signs of Returning to GOP's Ranks," *Wall Street Journal*, April 13, 1956.

61. "The Negro Vote," August 1957, Folder: Negro Vote, Box 554, PPPRN, Series 320; "The Negro Break-Away from the Democrats," *New Republic*, December 3, 1956, 17; Moon, 228; J. W. Anderson, *Eisenhower, Brownell, and the Congress: The Tangled Origins of the Civil Rights Bill of 1956-1957* (Tuscaloosa: University of Alabama Press, 1964), 138; Moses Rischin, *"Our Own Kind": Voting by Race, Creed, or National Origin* (Santa Barbara, Calif.: Center for the Study of Democratic Institutions, 1960), 16; Charles V. Hamilton, *Adam Clayton Powell, Jr.: The Political Biography of an American Dilemma* (New York: Atheneum, 1991), 274–75.

62. Morrow Diary, "January 19, 20, 21—1957," Folder 3, Box 2, Morrow Papers; "Only 3 New Faces are in His Cabinet," *NYT*, January 21, 1957; Haygood, 221; Branch, 203; "Dixie Negroes Shift to GOP," *Atlanta Journal-Constitution*, November 11, 1956.

Chapter 3. Bit by Bit: Civil Rights and the Eisenhower Administration

1. E. Frederic Morrow, *Forty Years a Guinea Pig* (New York: Pilgrim, 1980), 210; Martin Luther King, Jr., *Why We Can't Wait* (New York: Harper and Row, 1964), 157–58.

2. Charles H. Thompson, "Editorial Comment: The Negro Voter in the South," *Journal of Negro Education* 26, 3 (Summer 1957): 213; Robert Frederick Burk, *The Eisenhower Administration and Black Civil Rights* (Knoxville: University of Tennessee Press, 1984), 219, 237; Roy Wilkins with Tom Mathews, *Standing Fast: The Autobiography of Roy Wilkins* (Cambridge, Mass.: Da Capa, 1994), 234.

3. Burk, 204; David Nichols, *A Matter of Justice: Eisenhower and the Beginning of the Civil Rights Revolution* (New York: Simon and Schuster, 2007), 146–47; Charles Alexander, *Holding the Line: The Eisenhower Era, 1952-1961* (Bloomington: Indiana University Press, 1976), 196.

4. David Goldfield, "Border Men: Truman, Eisenhower, Johnson, and Civil Rights," *Journal of Southern History* 80, 1 (February 2014): 8; "Alcorn Accuses Six of Dam-Rights Deal," *NYT*, June 24, 1957; Steven F. Lawson, *Civil Rights Crossroads: Nation, Community, and the Black Freedom Struggle* (Lexington: University Press of Kentucky, 2003), 58; Alexander, 196.

5. Taylor Branch, *Parting the Waters: America in the King Years, 1954-63* (New York Simon and Schuster, 1988), 221; Stephen Ambrose, *Eisenhower*, vol. 2, *The President* (New York Simon and Schuster, 1984), 408, 411; Karl Campbell, *Senator Sam Ervin: Last of the Founding Fathers* (Chapel Hill: University of North Carolina Press, 2007), 124; Nichols, 161.

6. "Meaning of the Civil Rights Bill," *The Crisis*, August-September 1957, 422; Gilbert Jonas, *Freedom's Sword: The NAACP and the Struggle Against Racism in America, 1909-1969* (New York: Routledge, 2005), 165; Martin Luther King, Jr., to Richard Nixon, August 30, 1957, Folder: King, Martin Luther, Correspondence 1957-1962, Box 22, PPPRN, Series 320; "Citizens Wire

Ike," *Pittsburgh Courier*, August 31, 1957; Morrow Diary, "August 7, 1957," Folder 4, Box 2, E. Morrow Papers; Robert Caro, *The Years of Lyndon Johnson: Master of the Senate* (New York: Random House, 2002), 991.

7. Val Washington to Asa Spaulding, August 13, 1957, Folder: Asa Spaulding Subgroup. Correspondence: Washington, Val J. January 10, 1958–June 14, 1956, Box AC–36, Spaulding Papers; "Citizens Wire Ike," *Pittsburgh Courier*, August 31, 1957; Larry Foster to Dwight Eisenhower, n.d., Folder 22, Box 3, Robinson Papers; Lawson, 58; Julius Adams to Richard Nixon, August 19, 1957, Folder: Adams, Julius, Box 19, PPPRN, Series 320; "Half-Loaf Leaders Spanked," *Pittsburgh Courier*, August 31, 1957; Morrow Diary, "August 7, 1957," Folder 4, Box 2, Morrow Papers.

8. Sherman Adams, *Firsthand Report: The Story of the Eisenhower Administration* (New York: Harper, 1961), 343; Nichols, 159, 167.

9. "How the Senate Passed the Civil-Rights Bill," *The Reporter*, September 5, 1957, 9; Martin Luther King, Jr., to Richard Nixon, August 30, 1957, Folder: Nixon-Vice-President (Corres.) (7) [Jan.–Oct. 1957], Box 50, Rogers Papers; James Nabrit to Richard Nixon, August 28, 1957, Folder: Nabrit, Dr. James M., Jr., Box 543, PPPRN, Series 320; Jackie Robinson to Richard Nixon, August 28, 1957, in Michael Long, ed., *First Class Citizenship: The Civil Rights Letters of Jackie Robinson* (New York: Times Books, 2007), 35.

10. Minutes of Cabinet Meeting, March 23, 1956, Folder; Mar. '56 Miscellaneous, Box 14, DDE Diary Series, DDEPP-Whitman File; E. Frederic Morrow, interview by Ed Edwin, January 31, 1968, CUOHP; Morrow Diary, "January 27, 1959," Folder 5, Box 2, Morrow Papers; "Battle to Woo Negro Vote Is Underway," *Sarasota Herald-Tribune*, August 12, 1956.

11. Simeon Booker, *Black Man's America* (Englewood Cliffs, N.J.: Prentice-Hall, 1964), 208; Alice Allison Dunnigan, *A Black Woman's Experience: From Schoolhouse to White House* (Philadelphia: Dorrance, 1974), 374; Morrow Diary, "January 16, 1957," Folder 3, Box 2, Morrow Papers; Cross Reference Sheet, June 16, 1954, Folder: Morrow, E. Frederic, Box 2167, Alphabetical File, DDERP-WHCF.

12. Morrow, interview by Ed Edwin, January 31, 1968, CUOHP; Andrew Manis, *A Fire You Can't Put Out: The Civil Rights Life of Birmingham's Reverend Fred Shuttlesworth* (Tuscaloosa: University of Alabama Press, 1999), 254; Martin Luther King, Jr., interview by Mike Wallace, June 25, 1958, in Clayborne Carson et al., eds., *The Papers of Martin Luther King, Jr.*, vol. 4, *Symbol of the Movement, January 1957–December 1958* (Berkeley: University of California Press, 1992), 440; Roy Wilkins, "The Future of the Negro Voter in the United States," *Journal of Negro Education* 26, 3 (Summer 1957): 428.

13. Morrow Diary, "December 8, 1955," "December 19, 1955," and "November 9, 1957," Folders 1 and 4, Box 2, Morrow Papers.

14. Morrow, *Forty Years a Guinea Pig*, 101; Cross Reference Sheet, September 29, 1955, Folder: Washington, Val (Only) (2), Box 3269, Alphabetical File, DDERP-WHCF; Herbert Parmet, *Eisenhower and the American Crusades* (New York: Macmillan, 1972), 440.

15. Sara Bullard, ed., *The Ku Klux Klan: A History of Racism and Violence*, 5th ed. (Montgomery, Ala.: Southern Poverty Law Center, 1997), 27; Ben Green, *Before His Time: The Untold Story of Harry T. Moore, America's First Civil Rights Martyr* (New York: Free Press, 1999), 9; Caryl Cooper, "Percy Green and the *Jackson Advocate*," in David Davies, ed., *The Press and Race: Mississippi Journalists Confront the Movement* (Jackson: University Press of Mississippi, 2001), 68; Manis, 108.

16. Morrow Diary, "January 15, 1957" and "December 3, 1958," Folders 3 and 5, Box 2,

Morrow Papers; Roy Wilkins to E. Frederic Morrow, September 4, 1958, Folder: Inter-Racial Affairs—Correspondence and Materials—1958-1957 (1), Box 10, Morrow Records; Martin Luther King, Jr., to Cynthia Bowles, June 12, 1957, in Carson, 221; "Negroes Hold Rally on Rights in Capital," *NYT*, May 18, 1957.

17. Dwight Eisenhower to Roy Wilkins, June 21, 1956, Folder: Civil Rights, Box 3, Fox Records; Morrow Diary, "March 28, 1956," Folder 1, Box 2, Morrow Papers; Speech delivered by George W. Lee in Atlanta, May 16, 1957, Folder 1, Box 4, Lee Collection; Jackie Robinson to Dwight Eisenhower, September 13, 1957, Folder 13, Box 5, Robinson Papers.

18. Morrow Diary, "May 13, 1958," Folder 4, Box 2, Morrow Papers; "Eisenhower Bids Negroes Be Patient About Rights," *NYT*, May 13, 1958; Morrow, *Forty Years a Guinea Pig*, 163–64; E. Frederic Morrow, interview by Thomas Soapes, February 23, 1977, CUOHP.

19. "Eisenhower Bids Negroes Be Patient About Rights," *NYT*, May 13, 1958; Booker, 208–9; Allen Jones, "Equal Rights to All, Special Privileges to None: The Black Press in Iowa, 1882–1985," in Henry Lewis Suggs, ed., *The Black Press in the Middle West, 1865-1985* (Westport, Conn.: Greenwood, 1996), 95; Jackie Robinson to Dwight Eisenhower, May 13, 1956, Folder: OF-142-A Negro Matters-Colored Question (6), Box 731, Official File, DDERP-WHCF.

20. Emmet John Hughes, *The Ordeal of Power: A Political Memoir of the Eisenhower Years* (New York: Dell, 1963), 211; "Transcript of the President's News Conference on Foreign and Domestic Affairs," *NYT*, July 18, 1957; Nichols, 133; Philip Klinkner with Rogers Smith, *The Unsteady March: The Rise and Decline of Racial Equality in America* (Chicago: University of Chicago Press, 1999), 248–49; Jack Bloom, *Class, Race, and the Civil Rights Movement* (Bloomington: Indiana University Press, 1987), 112.

21. Wilkins with Mathews, 250; Helen Edmonds to Val Washington, September 18, 1957, Folder: Correspondence, Republican National Committee, 1957, Box 2, Edmonds Papers; Karen Anderson, *Little Rock: Race and Resistance at Central High School* (Princeton, N.J.: Princeton University Press, 2010), 137; Pete Daniel, *Standing at the Crossroads: Southern Life Since 1900* (New York: Hill and Wang, 1986), 170; Nichols, 197.

22. Philip S. Wilder, Jr., *Meade Alcorn and the 1958 Election* (New York: Holt, 1959), 6–8; Joseph Lowndes, *From the New Deal to the New Right: Race and the Southern Origins of Modern Conservatism* (New Haven, Conn.: Yale University Press, 2008), 47; Daniel Galvin, *Presidential Party Building: Dwight D. Eisenhower to George W. Bush* (Princeton, N.J.: Princeton University Press, 2010), 65.

23. "July-December Budgets," Folder: Minority Groups 1956—32, Box 114, Hall Papers; Morrow Diary, "January 17, 1956," Folder 1, Box 2, Morrow Papers; Timothy Thurber, *Race and Republicans: The GOP's Frayed Relationship with African Americans, 1945-1974* (Lawrence: University Press of Kansas, 2013), 67.

24. Ann Whitman, handwritten note attached to letter, Val Washington to Dwight Eisenhower, July 18, 1957, Folder: Civil Rights Bill, Box 9, Morrow Records; T. R. M. Howard to Richard Nixon, October 20, 1955, Folder: Howard, T. R. M., Box 358, PPPRN; Morrow Diary, "September 10, 1957," Folder 4, Box 2, Morrow Papers.

25. Robert Dallek, *Lyndon B. Johnson: Portrait of a President* (New York: Oxford University Press, 2004), 107; Jere Nash and Andy Taggart, *Mississippi Politics: The Struggle for Power, 1976-2006* (Jackson: University Press of Mississippi, 2006), 39–40; Wirt Yerger, Jr., with Joseph Maxwell, III, *A Courageous Cause: A Personal Story of Modern Republicanism's Birth from 1956 to 1966* (Jackson, Miss.: LifeStory, 2010), 76; Remarks by Lee Potter in Washington, D.C., January 30, 1958, Frame 0256, Reel 16, Papers of the Republican Party, Part I, Series A; Nichols, 205.

26. Earl Black and Merle Black, *The Rise of Southern Republicans* (Cambridge, Mass.: Belknap Press of Harvard University Press, 2002), 23; Bruce Kalk, *The Origins of the Southern Strategy: Two-Party Competition in South Carolina, 1950–1972* (Lanham, Md.: Lexington, 2001), xii–xii.

27. Melvin E. Diggs to Val Washington, November 13, 1956, Folder: Minority Groups 1956—32, Box 114, Hall Papers; Frank Atkinson, *The Dynamic Dominion: Realignment and the Rise of Two-Party Competition in Virginia, 1945–1980*, rev. 2nd. ed. (Lanham, Md.: Rowman and Littlefield, 2006), 93; Geoffrey Kabaservice, *Rule and Ruin: The Downfall of Moderation and the Destruction of the Republican Party* (New York: Oxford University Press, 2012), 282; Helen Edmonds to Val Washington, October 23, 1956, Folder: Correspondence. Republican Nat'l Committee, 1953–1956 expense accounts and itineraries, Box 2, Edmonds Papers; Clarence L. Townes, Jr., interview by author, October 18, 2011, in possession of author; Republican National Committee, "News Release," May 7, 1954, Folder: Minority Groups 1954–32, Box 114, Hall Papers.

28. Tim S. R. Boyd, *Georgia Democrats, the Civil Rights Movement, and the Shaping of the New South* (Gainesville: University Press of Florida, 2012), 105; "Nab 2 Ga. GOP Leaders on Peddling Charges," *Jet*, May 28, 1953, 7; "Southern Fund Is No 'Commy Group,'" *Baltimore Afro-American*, February 20, 1954; "Ike's Action Is Upheld by Georgia Republicans," *Rome News-Tribune*, October 4, 1957; Anne Emanuel, *Elbert Parr Tuttle: Chief Jurist of the Civil Rights Revolution* (Athens: University of Georgia Press, 2011), 88.

29. "Lee is Most Effective Negro Republican," *Pittsburgh Courier Magazine*, December 19, 1959; Elizabeth Gritter, *River of Hope: Black Politics and the Memphis Freedom Movement, 1865–1954* (Lexington: University Press of Kentucky, 2014), 198–200.

30. Gritter, 198–200, 207; Bobby Lovett, *The Civil Rights Movement in Tennessee: A Narrative History* (Knoxville: University of Tennessee Press, 2005), 256; "Resolution Adopted by Unanimous Vote of Shelby County Republican Executive Committee," March 19, 1960, Folder 10, Box 9, Lee Collection.

31. "Negro Quits Big GOP Meet in Jim Crow Row," *Jet*, March 18, 1954, 9; Kalk, 44; Theodore Hemmingway, "South Carolina," in Henry Lewis Suggs, ed., *The Black Press in the South, 1865–1979* (Westport, Conn.: Greenwood, 1983), 294; Cross Reference Sheet, May 7, 1957, Folder: Washington, Val (Only) (3), Box 3269, Alphabetical File, DDERP-WHCF; Earl M. Middleton with Joy Barnes, *Knowing Who I Am: A Black Entrepreneur's Struggle and Success in the American South* (Columbia: University of South Carolina Press, 2008), 85.

32. Oscar W. Adams, Jr., to Val Washington, May 8, 1954, Washington to Adams, May 14, 1954, Leonard Hall to Claude O. Vardaman, May 26, 1954, and Vardaman to Hall, May 31, 1954, Folder: Minority Groups 1954–32, Box 114, Hall Papers; Geraldine Moore, *Behind the Ebony Mask: What American Negroes Really Think* (Birmingham, Ala.: Southern University Press, 1961), 201–2.

33. Meade Alcorn, interview by Ed Edwin, June 5, 1967, CUOHP; Lewis Wade Jones to E. Frederic Morrow, September 25, 1956, Folder: Civil Rights—Official Memoranda 1956–1955, Box 10, Morrow Records; A. M. Walter to Leonard Hall, September 7, 1956, Folder: Civil Rights 1956–9, Box 9, Hall Papers; Glenn Feldman, "Ugly Roots: Race, Emotion, and the Rise of the Modern Republican Party in Alabama and the South," in Glenn Feldman, ed., *Before Brown: Civil Rights and White Backlash in the Modern South* (Tuscaloosa: University of Alabama Press, 2004), 278.

34. "Republicans Warned Against Link with Citizens Council," October 27, 1955, Frame 0526, Reel 29, Papers of the NAACP, Part 18; Yerger with Maxwell, 12; Joseph Crespino, *In*

Search of Another Country: Mississippi and the Conservative Counterrevolution (Princeton, N.J.: Princeton University Press, 2007), 84; Nash and Taggart, 37–40.

35. "Helen G. Edmonds. Durham, North Carolina," n.d., Folder: Correspondence. Republican Nat'l Committee, 1953–1956 expense accounts and itineraries, Box 2, Edmonds Papers; Speech delivered by George W. Lee in Birmingham, Ala., March 20, 1958, Folder 1, Box 4, Lee Collection.

36. Allan Lichtman, *White Protestant Nation: The Rise of the American Conservative Movement* (New York: Atlantic Monthly Press, 2008), 201; Rick Perlstein, *Before the Storm: Barry Goldwater and the Unmaking of the American Consensus* (New York: Hill and Wang, 2001), 27; Yerger with Maxwell, 59; "Goldwater Labels Warren Socialist," *NYT*, April 18, 1959.

37. Edward Carmines and James Stimson, *Issue Evolution: Race and the Transformation of American Politics* (Princeton, N.J.: Princeton University Press, 1989), 63, 69; "Civil Rights Act Urged by Javits," *NYT*, August 10, 1959; "Republicans Plan a Civil Rights Bill to Test New Rule," *NYT*, January 14, 1959.

38. Citizens for Rockefeller-Keating, "Your Key to Equality: Nelson A. Rockefeller for Governor," Folder 411, Box 41, Record Group 4, Series J.1, NARPP; New York Republican State Committee, "Nelson Rockefeller: 'Regular Guy,'" Folder 411, Box 41, Record Group 4, Series J.1, NARPP; Andrew Coleman to "Friend and Neighbor," October 23, 1958, Folder 411, Box 41, Record Group 4, Series J.1, NARPP; Laura Jane Gifford, *The Center Cannot Hold: The 1960 Presidential Election and the Rise of Modern Conservatism* (DeKalb: Northern Illinois University Press, 2009), 66; "Republicans Regard Negro Vote as Important," *Congressional Quarterly Fact Sheet*, January 23, 1959, 117, Folder: Negro Vote 1958, Box 38, RDNC, Series I.

39. "National Election Picture," *NYT*, November 5, 1958; "Senate Vote Hits G.O.P. Right Wing," *NYT*, November 6, 1958.

40. "Republicans Regard Negro Vote as Important," *Congressional Quarterly Fact Sheet*, January 23, 1959, 117, Folder: Negro Vote 1958, Box 38, RDNC; "GOP Gaining Few Negro Voters," *Public Opinion News Service*, May 28, 1958, Folder: Negro Vote 1958, Box 38, RDNC, Series I; E. Frederic Morrow to Richard Nixon, November 10, 1958, Folder: Morrow, Fred, Box 532, PPPRN, Series 320; Theodore Cross, *The Black Power Imperative: Racial Inequality and the Politics of Nonviolence* (New York: Faulkner, 1984), 193; Bloom, 191; William M. McClenahan, Jr., and William H. Becker, *Eisenhower and the Cold War Economy* (Baltimore: Johns Hopkins University Press, 2011), 96.

41. David Reinhard, *The Republican Right Since 1945* (Lexington: University Press of Kentucky, 1983), 157–58; Hughes, 292.

42. "Helen G. Edmonds. Durham, North Carolina," n.d., Folder: Correspondence. Republican Nat'l Committee, 1953–1956 expense accounts and itineraries, Box 2, Edmonds Papers; Morrow Diary, "October 21, 1958" and "November 21, 1958," Folder 5, Box 2, Morrow Papers.

43. "Negro Vote Vital, G.O.P. Women Told," *NYT*, April 15, 1959; Morrow, *Forty Years a Guinea Pig*, 193–96; Thurber, 111.

44. Morrow, *Forty Years a Guinea Pig*, 194–96; Jackie Robinson to E. Frederic Morrow, April 15, 1959, Folder 9, Box 5, Robinson Papers.

Chapter 4. Ye Cannot Serve Both God and Mammon: The 1960 Presidential Election

1. Martin Luther King, Jr., to Earl Mazo, September 2, 1958, in Clayborne Carson et al., eds., *The Papers of Martin Luther King, Jr.*, vol. 4, *Symbol of the Movement, January 1957–December*

1958 (Berkeley: University of California Press, 1992), 482; L. K. Jackson, "An Open Letter," November 14, 1960, Folder: Jackson, Rev. Dr. L.K., Box 374, PPPRN, Series 320.

2. "Exclusive," *Jet*, June 27, 1957, 4–6; Taylor Branch, *Parting the Waters: America in the King Years, 1954–63* (New York: Simon and Schuster, 1988), 218–20; Adam Fairclough, *To Redeem the Soul of America: The Southern Christian Leadership Conference and Martin Luther King, Jr.* (Athens: University of Georgia Press, 1987), 40–41.

3. Timothy Thurber, "Racial Liberalism, Affirmative Action, and the Troubled History of the President's Committee on Government Contracts," *Journal of Policy History* 18, 4 (2006): 458, 466; Robert Frederick Burk, *The Eisenhower Administration and Black Civil Rights* (Knoxville: University of Tennessee Press, 1984), 100; "Job Bias Parley Opens Tomorrow," *NYT*, May 10, 1959; "Fight on Job Bias Spurred by Nixon," *NYT*, May 12, 1959; Dennis Dickerson, *African American Preachers and Politics: The Careys of Chicago* (Jackson: University Press of Mississippi, 2010), 153–54.

4. Steven F. Lawson, "The View from the Nation," in Steven F. Lawson and Charles Payne, eds., *Debating the Civil Rights Movement, 1945–1968*, 2nd ed. (Lanham, Md.: Rowman and Littlefield, 2006), 16; David Nichols, *A Matter of Justice: Eisenhower and the Beginning of the Civil Rights Revolution* (New York: Simon and Schuster, 2007), 255; Charles Alexander, *Holding the Line: The Eisenhower Era, 1952–1961* (Bloomington: Indiana University Press, 1976), 201; Burk, 255.

5. "Spotlight on Nixon," *Industrial Statesman*, June 1960, Folder: Negro Leaders List— Nationwide 1960, Box 3, Campaign 1960 Collection, PPS 57; William Stover, "Memo for Files," August 13, 1959, Folder: Civil Rights, Box 153, PPPRN, Series 320; Virginia Durr to Clark Foreman, December 1959, in Patricia Sullivan, ed., *Freedom Writer: Virginia Foster Durr, Letters from the Civil Rights Years* (New York: Routledge, 2003), 194–95.

6. Todd Purdum, *An Idea Whose Time Has Come: Two Presidents, Two Parties, and the Battle for the Civil Rights Act of 1964* (New York: Holt, 2014), 49; Jeremy D. Mayer, *Running on Race: Racial Politics in Presidential Campaigns, 1960–2000* (New York: Random House, 2002), 14; Victor Lasky, *J.F.K.: The Man and the Myth* (New Rochelle, N.Y.: Arlington House, 1966), 201; Guy Paul Land, "John F. Kennedy's Southern Strategy, 1956–1960," *North Carolina Historical Review* 56, 1 (January 1979): 43; Branch, 313.

7. Mark Stern, *Calculating Visions: Kennedy, Johnson, and Civil Rights* (New Brunswick, N.J.: Rutgers University Press, 1992), 9; "Analysts Hedge on Kennedy's Negro Backing," *Minneapolis Morning Tribune*, August 19, 1960; "Spotlight on Nixon," *Industrial Statesman*, June 1960, PPS 57; "GOP Official Says Democrats Should Tear Up Their Platform," August 12, 1960, Folder 16, Box 2, Lee Collection.

8. "The Civil Rights Plank," *NYT*, July 12, 1960; "Sees Opposition by Negro Voters," *NYT*, July 12, 1960; Stern, 22.

9. Roy Wilkins with Tom Mathews, *Standing Fast: The Autobiography of Roy Wilkins* (Cambridge, Mass.: Da Capa, 1994), 276; "Nominees Appeal for Negro Votes," *NYT*, July 16, 1960; "Lyndon Johnson Tells Homefolks He'll Fight Part of Rights Plank," *Iowa Bystander*, August 11, 1960.

10. Richard Nixon, *Six Crises* (Garden City, N.Y.: Doubleday, 1962), 305, 314; Nicol C. Rae, *The Decline and Fall of the Liberal Republicans: From 1952 to the Present* (New York: Oxford University Press, 1989), 41; "Governor Blunt," *NYT*, June 9, 1960; "Floor Test Looms," *NYT*, July 24, 1960; Branch, 321; "The Platform Statements by Rockefeller and Nixon," *NYT*, July 24, 1960.

11. Laura Jane Gifford, *The Center Cannot Hold: The 1960 Presidential Election and the Rise*

of Modern Conservatism (DeKalb: Northern Illinois University Press, 2009), 76; Theodore White, *The Making of the President 1960: A Narrative History of American Politics in Action* (New York: Atheneum House, 1961; reprint, 1988), 251; "Texts of Republican Planks on Civil Rights, Defense and Education and Conclusion to the Platform," *NYT*, July 27, 1960; Richard Nixon to Clarence Mitchell, September 25, 1960, Folder: Republican Convention and Richard M. Nixon, 1960, Box 29, Wilkins Papers; "Text of Goldwater's Withdrawal Talk," *NYT*, July 28, 1960.

12. "Transcript of Nixon's Address Accepting the Republican Presidential Nomination," *NYT*, July 29, 1960; Morrow Diary, "November 10, 1960," Folder: Diary—E. Frederic Morrow (5), Box 2, Morrow Papers.

13. Morrow Diary, "November 10, 1960," Folder: Diary—E. Frederic Morrow (5), Box 2, Morrow Papers; Henry Cabot Lodge Jr., *The Storm Has Many Eyes: A Personal Narrative* (New York: Norton, 1973), 27; Branch, 323; "GOP'ers Temporarily Put Party Activities Above the Party," *Jet*, August 11, 1960, 40.

14. Hanes Walton, Jr., and Robert C. Smith, *American Politics and the African American Quest for Universal Freedom*, 2nd ed. (New York: Longman, 2003), 142; Jere Nash and Andy Taggart, *Mississippi Politics: The Struggle for Power, 1976-2006* (Jackson: University Press of Mississippi, 2006), 40.

15. David Falkner, *Great Time Coming: The Life of Jackie Robinson, from Baseball to Birmingham* (New York: Simon and Schuster, 1995), 267; Mary Kay Linge, *Jackie Robinson: A Biography* (Westport, Conn.: Greenwood, 2007), 122-23; Edmund F. Kallina, Jr., *Kennedy vs. Nixon: The Presidential Election of 1960* (Gainesville: University Press of Florida, 2010), 139, 145; Jackie Robinson to Chester Bowles, August 26, 1959, in Michael Long, ed., *First Class Citizenship: The Civil Rights Letters of Jackie Robinson* (New York: Times Books, 2007), 70; Jackie Robinson, *I Never Had It Made* (New York: HarperCollins, 1995), 137.

16. Kallina, 144; Jackie Robinson to Richard Nixon, June 25, 1957, in Long, 32; Linge, 125; Jackie Robinson to Ray Robinson, January 4, 1960, Folder 19, Box 5, Robinson Papers.

17. Rose Mary Woods to Richard Nixon, March 30, 1960, Folder: Robinson, Jackie, Box 649, PPPRN, Series 320; Hugh Scott to Jackie Robinson, July 12, 1960, Folder 19, Box 5, Robinson Papers; Richard Nixon to Jackie Robinson, June 3, 1960, in Long, 97-98; Robinson, *I Never Had It Made*, 136-37.

18. Arnold Rampersad, *Jackie Robinson: A Biography* (New York: Knopf, 1997), 324, 340-41; Falkner, 348; Jackie Robinson to Richard Nixon, March 19, 1957, Folder 22, Box 4, Robinson Papers; David Pietrusza, *LBJ vs. JFK vs. Nixon: The Epic Campaign That Forged Three Presidencies* (New York: Union Square Press, 2008), 302.

19. "Jackie Robinson Begins," *Jet*, October 27, 1960, 6; Robinson, *I Never Had It Made*, 138; David Tucker, *Lieutenant Lee of Beale Street* (Nashville, Tenn.: Vanderbilt University Press, 1971), 173-74; "How Nixon Campaigns for the Negro Vote," *Jet*, November 3, 1960, 17; "Jackie Robinson Joins Nixon Campaign Drive," *NYT*, September 1, 1960; Bobby Lovett, *The Civil Rights Movement in Tennessee: A Narrative History* (Knoxville: University of Tennessee Press, 2005), 280; "750 Hear Ex-Dodger Urge Election of Nixon," *Louisville Courier-Journal*, October 18, 1960.

20. "Nixon Goes South, Pleads on Rights," *NYT*, August 17, 1960; "State of the Nations," *Christian Science Monitor*, August 25, 1960; Gifford, 81.

21. G. Wayne Dowdy, *Crusades for Freedom: Memphis and the Political Transformation of the American South* (Jackson: University Press of Mississippi, 2010), 75-76; George W. Lee, "Profile of Two Candidates in a Southern Background," October 5, 1960, Folder 2, Box 4, Lee

Collection; Clay Claiborne to George W. Lee, October 5, 1960, Folder 67, Box 3, Lee Collection.

22. E. Frederic Morrow, *Black Man in the White House* (New York: Coward-McCann, 1963), 293; Pietrusza, 317; Cornelius P. Cotter and Bernard C. Hennessy, *Politics Without Power: The National Party Committees* (New Brunswick, N.J.: Transaction, 1964), 75–76.

23. "The 'Solid South' Moves Closer to a Two-Party System," *NYT*, September 11, 1960; "Republicans," *Time*, August 29, 1960; Nixon, *Six Crises*, 325, 342; "Nixon Making All-Out Drive for South's Vote," *Nashville Banner*, October 6, 1960.

24. "Pledge on Negro Diluted by Lodge," *NYT*, October 14, 1960; Stephanie R. Rolph, "Courting Conservatism: White Resistance and the Ideology of Race in the 1960s," in Laura Jane Gifford and Daniel K. Williams, eds., *The Right Side of the Sixties: Reexamining Conservatism's Decade of Transformation* (New York: Palgrave Macmillan, 2012), 24.

25. "Nixon Renews Bid for South's Votes," *NYT*, October 3, 1960; "A Brand New Jeffersonian is Mr. Nixon," *Louisville Courier-Journal*, October 6, 1960; "The G.O.P. Fumbled Away Its Chances in the South," *Louisville Courier-Journal*, November 14, 1960; "20,000 Hear Vice President," *Nashville Banner*, October 6, 1960.

26. "Nixon Speaks on Rights and Oil in Louisiana-Mississippi Drive," *NYT*, September 24, 1960; Nash and Taggart, 41–42; Telephone Calls, September 25, 1960, Folder: Telephone Calls September 1960, Box 52, DDE Diary Series, DDEPP-Whitman file; "200,000 Welcome Nixon in Atlanta," *NYT*, August 27, 1960; Gifford, 162–63.

27. "The Drama of Issues," *Life*, September 19, 1960, 35; Allen Matusow, *The Unraveling of America: A History of Liberalism in the 1960s* (New York: Harper and Row, 1984), 21; Research Division, Republican National Committee, "Democratic Criticism of Eisenhower Role in Little Rock and Civil Rights in General," June 1963, Folder: Civil Rights GOP Achievements & Programs (3), Box 652, Republican National Committee (Additional Files of) Clip Sheet—1958 Republican News, Dwight D. Eisenhower Presidential Library.

28. Kallina, 147–148; Nick Bryant, *The Bystander: John F. Kennedy and the Struggle for Black Equality* (New York: Basic Books, 2006), 169–71.

29. "Pledge on Negro Diluted by Lodge," *NYT*, October 14, 1960; "Nixon and Lodge Fail to Heal Rift on Naming Negro," *NYT*, October 16, 1960; Pietrusza, 304.

30. "RT" to Robert Finch, June 14, [1960] and "RT" to Stan McCaffrey, August 31, [1960], Folder: Washington, Val, Box 801, PPPRN, Series 320.

31. Burk, 86; "How Nixon Campaigns for the Negro Vote," 16; Gifford, 83; Dickerson, 154–55; "North Carolina," n.a./n.d., Folder: Alphabetical Files. Political Material. Addresses, Reports, Memoranda, etc., of the Republican Nat'l Cmte, 1960-1, Box 1, Edmonds Papers; Helen Edmonds to Val Washington, November 19, 1960, Folder: Correspondence. Republican Party, 1959–60, Box 2, Edmonds Papers.

32. Simeon Booker, *Black Man's America* (Englewood Cliffs, N.J.: Prentice-Hall, 1964), 207; Speech delivered by Grant Reynolds at Oberlin College Young Republican Club, February 12, 1965, Folder 319, Box 51, Hinman Files, Record Group III4 J.2; "Jackie Robinson Blames Nixon Defeat on Advisors," *Young Republican News*, March–April 1961, Folder 9, Box 5, Robinson Papers; L. K. Jackson, "Tell It Like It Is! A Chapter from a Forthcoming Book, 'Give Me This Mountain,'" sent to Richard Nixon, April 7, 1969, Folder 34, Box 1, Jackson Papers.

33. Archibald Carey to Richard Nixon, August 19, 1960, Folder: Carey, Archibald James, Jr., Box 132, PPPRN, Series 320; Fawn Brodie, "Interview with Jim Bassett of the LA Times," March 27, 1975, Folder 2, Box 42, Brodie Papers.

34. Morrow Diary, "November 10, 1960."

35. Morrow Diary, "November 10, 1960"; John H. Calhoun, interview by John Britton, May 23, 1968, MSRC; Dickerson, 155; "Why Nixon Lost the Negro Vote," *The Crisis*, January 1961, 9.

36. A.B. Hermann to Leonard Hall, October 4, 1960, Hermann to Hall and Robert Finch, October 8, 1960, Hermann to Hall, October 11, 1960, Hermann to Finch, October 14, 1960, Folder: Ethnic & Minority Material, Box 39, Morton Collection; Sara Judith Smiley, "The Political Career of Thruston B. Morton: The Senate Years, 1956–1968," Ph.D. dissertation (University of Kentucky, 1975), 86.

37. "Why Nixon Lost the Negro Vote," 8–9; Purdum, 50; Bryant, 153, 165; Kallina, 147–49.

38. Claude Barnett to Herbert Klein, November 28, 1959, Folder: Barnett, Claude A., Box 63, PPPRN, Series 320; Booker, 146.

39. Val Washington to Helen Edmonds, December 6, 1960, Folder: Correspondence. Republican Party, 1959–60, Box 2, Edmonds Papers; Robinson, *I Never Had It Made*, 140; Morrow Diary, "November 10, 1960"; Dickerson, 155; Helen Edmonds to Mrs. Charles Dean, Jr., November 29, 1960, Folder: Correspondence. Republican Party, 1959–60, Box 2, Edmonds Papers; "Report from Lt. Lee," *Tri-State Defender*, May 20, 1961; Tucker, 175.

40. "Georgia Negroes Strong in GOP," *Pittsburgh Courier*, July 30, 1960; "Nine Attend Chicago Convention," *NPC*, July 30, 1960; Calhoun, interview by John Britton, May 23, 1968, MSRC; Alton Hornsby, Jr., *Black Power in Dixie: A Political History of African Americans in Atlanta* (Gainesville: University Press of Florida, 2009), 101; Branch, 349, 373.

41. Christopher Matthews, *Kennedy and Nixon: The Rivalry that Shaped Postwar America* (New York: Simon and Schuster, 1996), 170; Harry Lefever, *Undaunted by the Fight: Spelman College and the Civil Rights Movement, 1957–1967* (Macon, Ga.: Mercer University Press, 2005), 79; John Calhoun, interview in Howell Raines, *My Soul Is Rested: Movement Days in the Deep South Remembered* (New York: Penguin, 1983), 94–95.

42. Clipping, "Lt. Lee Gives Opinion on Why GOP Defeated," unknown newspaper/date, Folder 24, Box 5, Robinson Papers; George W. Lee, "The Selection of New Targets for a New Intellectual, Moral, and Political Climate," October 1972, Folder 21, Box 9, Lee Collection; Morrow Diary, "November 10, 1960"; E. Frederic Morrow, interview by Thomas Soapes, February 23, 1977, OH 376, CUOHP; Rampersad, 351; Tom Wicker, *One of Us: Richard Nixon and the American Dream* (New York: Random House, 1995), 239.

43. Harris Wofford and Coretta Scott King, interviews in Henry Hampton and Steve Fayer, eds., *Voices of the Civil Rights Movement: An Oral History of the Civil Rights Movement from the 1950s through the 1980s* (New York: Bantam Books, 1990), 68–70; Matthews, 171.

44. Wofford in Hampton and Fayer, 70; Kallina, 154; Clifford M. Kuhn, "'There's a Footnote to History!' Memory and the History of Martin Luther King's October 1960 Arrest and Its Aftermath," *Journal of American History* 84, 2 (September 1997), 593.

45. Bryant, 185; "Kennedy will be Great President," *Tri-State Defender*, November 25, 1960; "Two Men and Rev. Martin King," *New York Post*, October 28, 1960.

46. "Negro Unit Charges King Aids Kennedy," *NYT*, November 2, 1960; "King Hails Kennedy and Scores G.O.P.," *NYT*, November 6, 1960; Clayborne Carson, ed., *The Autobiography of Martin Luther King, Jr.* (New York: Warner Books, 1998), 148; Kallina, 155.

47. "King Incident Sparks Kennedy Win in Detroit," *NPC*, November 19, 1960; Matthews, 172–73; Kallina, 155.

48. Charles Evers and Andrew Szanton, *Have No Fear: The Charles Evers Story* (New York: Wiley, 1997), 111; "Negro Vote Held Vital to Kennedy," *NYT*, November 26, 1960; "New Orleans

Strong for Yankee President," *NPC*, November 19, 1960; White, 323; Donald Matthews and James Prothro, "Southern Images of Political Parties: An Analysis of White and Negro Attitudes," *Journal of Politics* 26, 1 (February 1964), 91; Doug McAdam, *Political Process and the Development of Black Insurgency, 1930–1970*, 2nd ed. (Chicago: University of Chicago Press, 1982), 158.

49. Thomas Melton, "The 1960 Presidential Election in Georgia," Ph.D. dissertation (University of Mississippi, 1985), 228; "Kennedy Scores Heavily in South," *NYT*, November 9, 1960; Hugh Davis Graham, *Civil Rights and the Presidency: Race and Gender in American Politics, 1960–1972* (New York: Oxford University Press, 1992), 31; G. Scott Thomas, *A New World to Be Won: John Kennedy, Richard Nixon, and the Tumultuous Year of 1960* (Santa Barbara, Calif.: Praeger, 2011), 178; Rae, 42.

50. Burk, 107–8; Theodore Cross, *The Black Power Imperative: Racial Inequality and the Politics of Nonviolence* (New York: Faulkner, 1984), 193; Matthews and Prothro, 93.

51. Paul Frymer, *Uneasy Alliances: Race and Party Competition in America* (Princeton, N.J.: Princeton University Press, 2010), 101; "Two Million of Negroes in South Registered," *Washington Post*, August 3, 1964; Hazel Gaudet Erskine, "The Polls: Race Relations," *Public Opinion Quarterly* 26, 1 (Spring 1962), 147; "Savannah, Augusta, Columbus for Nixon, Too!," *NPC*, November 19, 1960; Branch, 369.

52. L. K. Jackson, "An Open Letter," November 14, 1960, Folder: Jackson, Rev. Dr. L. K., Box 374, PPPRN, Series 320; Garland Brown, "Personal Report: Young Republican National Federation Minority Resources Conference," April 28–30, 1961, Folder: Alphabetical Files. Political Material. Addresses, Reports, Memoranda, etc., of the Republican Nat'l Cmte, 1960–1961, Box 1, Edmonds Papers; "Civil Rights, A Republican Imperative: Democratic Failure Provides New Opportunity," *Advance: A Journal of Political Thought* 3 (July 1961): 8; "Russell Says Image of Lincoln Is Not Enough," *Baltimore Afro-American*, May 6, 1961.

53. "Jackie Lashes Campaign Tactics," *NPC*, November 26, 1960; Jackie Robinson to A. B. Hermann, November 18, 1960, Folder 19, Box 5, Robinson Papers; George W. Lee to Jackie Robinson, November 19, 1960, Folder 52, Box 3, Lee Collection; L. K. Jackson, "An Open Letter," November 14, 1960, Folder: Jackson, Rev. Dr. L. K., Box 374, PPPRN, Series 320.

54. E. Frederic Morrow, *Forty Years a Guinea Pig* (New York: Pilgrim, 1980), 218–19.

Chapter 5. Somebody Had to Stay and Fight:
Black Republicans and the Rise of the Right

1. "Don't Let It Happen Again," *New York Amsterdam News*, May 27, 1967.

2. Patrick Buchanan, *The Greatest Comeback: How Richard Nixon Rose from Defeat to Create the New Majority* (New York: Crown Forum, 2014), 2; Mary C. Brennan, *Turning Right in the Sixties: The Conservative Capture of the GOP* (Chapel Hill: University of North Carolina Press, 1995), 2, 58–59; Allan Lichtman, *White Protestant Nation: The Rise of the American Conservative Movement* (New York: Atlantic Monthly Press, 2008), 246; Laura Jane Gifford, *The Center Cannot Hold: The 1960 Presidential Election and the Rise of Modern Conservatism* (DeKalb: Northern Illinois University Press, 2009), 200.

3. Timothy Thurber, *Race and Republicans: The GOP's Frayed Relationship with African Americans, 1945–1974* (Lawrence: University Press of Kansas, 2013), 175; Ripon Society and Thomas Petri, *Election '64: A Ripon Society Report* (Cambridge, Mass.: Ripon Society, 1968), 16–18; David Tucker, *Lieutenant Lee of Beale Street* (Nashville, Tenn.: Vanderbilt University Press, 1971), 179–80; Edward Clayton, *The Negro Politician: His Success and Failure* (Chicago: Johnson

Publishing Co., 1964), 192; "G.O.P. Parley Charts Campaign for a 2-Party System in South," *NYT*, November 19, 1961; "The Real Sen. Goldwater of GOP," *NPC*, December 2, 1961; Lichtman, 232.

4. Barry Goldwater, *The Conscience of a Conservative* (Shepherdsville, Ky.: Victor, 1960), 33, 36–37; Democratic National Committee, "A Goldwater Primer," n.d., Folder: Goldwater (1 of 2), Box 32, Office Files of Bill Moyers; "Public Statements of Senator Barry Goldwater," n.d., Folder: Public Statements of Senator Barry Goldwater w/Index, Box 164, RDNC, Series II; Edwin McDowell, *Barry Goldwater: Portrait of an Arizonan* (Chicago: Henry Regnery, 1964), 177; "Paranoid Patriotism," *Atlantic Monthly*, November 1962, 94.

5. William F. Abe to John F. Kennedy, July 31, 1963, Folder: Civil Rights, Box 109, Halleck Mss.; Robert Steamer, "Southern Disaffection with the National Democratic Party," in Allan P. Sindler, ed., *Change in the Contemporary South* (Durham, N.C.: Duke University Press, 1963), 169–70; Wirt Yerger, Jr., with Joseph Maxwell, III, *A Courageous Cause: A Personal Story of Modern Republicanism's Birth from 1956 to 1966 in Mississippi* (Jackson, Miss.: LifeStory, 2010), 115; George W. Lee to Leonard Hall, May 23, 1962, Folder: Lee, George W., Box 444, PPPRN, Series 320; G. Wayne Dowdy, *Crusades for Freedom: Memphis and the Political Transformation of the American South* (Jackson: University Press of Mississippi, 2010), 90–91; "George W. Lee Answers Candidate Robert James," *Tri-State Defender*, June 23, 1962.

6. Philip Klinkner, *The Losing Parties: Out-Party National Committees, 1956–1993* (New Haven, Conn.: Yale University Press, 1995), 55, 69; Chandler Davidson, *Race and Class in Texas Politics* (Princeton, N.J.: Princeton University Press, 1992), 234; William Workman, Jr., *The Case for the South* (New York: Devin-Adair, 1960), 162; Philip Klinkner with Rogers Smith, *The Unsteady March: The Rise and Decline of Racial Equality in America* (Chicago: University of Chicago Press, 1999), 262; Samuel DuBois Cook, "Political Movements and Organizations," in Avery Leiserson, ed., *The American South in the 1960s* (New York: Praeger, 1964), 149.

7. Geoffrey Kabaservice, *Rule and Ruin: The Downfall of Moderation and the Destruction of the Republican Party* (New York: Oxford University Press, 2012), 70; Nicol C. Rae, *The Decline and Fall of the Liberal Republicans: From 1952 to the Present* (New York: Oxford University Press, 1989), 119; Michael Bowen, *The Roots of Modern Conservatism: Dewey, Taft, and the Battle for the Soul of the Republican Party* (Chapel Hill: University of North Carolina Press, 2011), 8–9, 198–99; Yerger with Maxwell, 120; Gifford, 24, 199–200.

8. Helen Edmonds to E. Frederic Morrow, n.d., Folder: Alphabetical Files. Political Material. NC Republican Party, 1951–76, Box 2, Edmonds Papers; George W. Lee to Jackie Robinson, November 19, 1960, Folder 52, Box 3, Lee Collection; George W. Lee to Thruston Morton, January 5, 1961, Folder 24, Box 5, Robinson Papers; "Lautier, Reynolds Fill Two New GOP Posts," *Jet*, September 28, 1961, 5; Republican National Committee, "Clay Claiborne Joins GOP Headquarters," August 24, 1962, Folder: Claiborne, Clay J., Box 154, PPPRN, Series 320.

9. Ripon Society, *From Disaster to Distinction: A Republican Rebirth* (New York: Pocket Books, 1966), 30; Grant Reynolds to George Hinman, "Reactivation of Minorities Division," "Republican Party Platform," and "Operation Dixie," February 7, 1963, Folder 319, Box 51, Hinman Files, Record Group III4 J.2.

10. "G.O.P. Is Attacked for Its Aid to Segregationists in the South," *NYT*, November 26, 1962; Thurber, 252; Ripon Society, *From Disaster to Distinction*, 36; Jacob Javits, *Order of Battle: A Republican's Call to Reason* (New York: Atheneum, 1964), 229–30, 302; Meade Alcorn, interview by Ed Edwin, July 5, 1967, OH 163, CUOHP.

11. C. Clayton Powell to George W. Lee, May 23, 1963, Lee Collection; Robert R. Douglass

to Grant Reynolds' File, April 28, 1961, Hinman Files; Grant Reynolds to George Hinman, "Republican National Committee," February 7, 1963, Hinman Files; George W. Lee to Thruston Morton, January 5, 1961, Folder 24, Box 5, Robinson Papers.

12. Bob Douglass to Bob McManus, Hugh Morrow, and John Deardourff, January 30, 1963, Folder 319, Box 51, Hinman Files; "Senator Goldwater and the Negro," *The Reporter*, October 8, 1964, 27; Klinkner, *The Losing Parties*, 64–65; Ripon Society, *From Disaster to Distinction*, 30; Ripon Society and Petri, *Election '64*, 16–18; "Party Machinery Is Goldwater Geared," *Modesto Bee*, October 11, 1963; Grant Reynolds to William Miller, January 8, 1963, Folder 319, Box 51, Hinman Files; Robert R. Douglass to George Hinman, July 16, 1963, Folder 319, Box 51, Hinman Files; George Gilder and Bruce Chapman, *The Party That Lost Its Head* (New York: Knopf, 1966), 61.

13. Todd Purdum, *An Idea Whose Time Has Come: Two Presidents, Two Parties, and the Battle for the Civil Rights Act of 1964* (New York: Henry Holt, 2014), 18; Hugh Davis Graham, *The Civil Rights Era: Origins and Development of National Policy, 1960-1972* (New York: Oxford University Press, 1990), 31; Nick Bryant, *The Bystander: John F. Kennedy and the Struggle for Black Equality* (New York: Basic, 2006), 286–87; Allen Matusow, *The Unraveling of America: A History of Liberalism in the 1960s* (New York: Harper and Row, 1984), 66.

14. "Kennedy Assailed by Negro on Rights," *NYT*, June 22, 1962; "Kennedy is Accused of Appeasing the South," *NYT*, July 23, 1962; "Report from Lt. Lee," *Tri-State Defender*, May 20, 1961; "Open Letter to Richard Nixon," *Tri-State Defender*, May 11, 1963.

15. "Civil Rights, A Republican Imperative: Democratic Failure Provides New Opportunity," *Advance: A Journal of Political Thought* 3 (July 1961): 6–9; Mark Stern, *Calculating Visions: Kennedy, Johnson and Civil Rights* (New Brunswick, N.J.: Rutgers University Press, 1992), 45, 74; "Civil Rights Plan Offered by G.O.P.," *NYT*, March 29, 1963; Carl Brauer, *John F. Kennedy and the Second Reconstruction* (New York: Columbia University Press, 1977), 223; Meg Greenfield, *Washington* (New York: Public Affairs, 2009), 186; Kabaservice, 81.

16. Paul Beers, *Pennsylvania Politics Today and Yesterday: The Tolerable Accommodation* (University Park: Pennsylvania State University Press, 1980), 310; "Negroes Offer Bill to Crack Ohio Housing Bias," *Jet*, March 7, 1963, 10; Sidney Fine, *"Expanding the Frontiers of Civil Rights": Michigan, 1948-1968* (Detroit: Wayne State University Press, 2000), 219; "Romney Leads NAACP Parade," *Indianapolis Star*, June 30, 1963; Frank Gervasi, *The Real Rockefeller: The Story of the Rise, Decline and Resurgence of the Presidential Aspirations of Nelson Rockefeller* (New York: Atheneum, 1964), 232–33; David Falkner, *Great Time Coming: The Life of Jackie Robinson, from Baseball to Birmingham* (New York: Simon and Schuster, 1995), 292; Nelson Rockefeller to Jackie Robinson, September 19, 1962, Folder 2027, Box 201, Record Group 4, Series L, NARPP; Purdum, 32.

17. "Gov. Scranton Warns of States-Righters Who May Try to Use Republican Party," *NPC*, February 9, 1963; "A Republican Footnote," *Reporter*, May 23, 1963, 14; "2 GOP Senators Blast Any 'Lily White' Move," *Washington Star*, June 29, 1963; Kenneth Keating, letter to the editor, *New York Herald Tribune*, June 28, 1963; "Nixon Says Republicans 'Just Stupid' About Negroes," *Jet*, May 25, 1961, 9; "How Republican Leaders View the Negro," *Ebony*, March 1964, 25.

18. "GOP Runs Strong in City," *LD*, November 10, 1960; Thurber, 178; Joshua D. Farrington, "'*Even I* Voted Republican': African American Voters and Public Accommodations in Louisville, Kentucky, 1960-1961," *Register of the Kentucky Historical Society* 103, 3-4 (Summer/Autumn 2011), 427–29; Brauer, 202–3; Ripon Society, *From Disaster to Distinction*, 30; Kabaservice, 62; Gilder and Chapman, 63.

19. Carl Shipley to Grant Reynolds, September 12, 1961, Folder 319, Box 51, Hinman Files; Russell Davis, *Black Americans in Cleveland: From George Peake to Carl B. Stokes, 1796–1969* (Washington, D.C.: Associated Publishers, 1972), 363; "GOP 'Doomed' in New York Unless Negroes Are Courted," *NPC*, November 21, 1964; Beers, 310; Dennis Dickerson, *Out of the Crucible: Black Steel Workers in Western Pennsylvania, 1875–1980* (Albany: State University of New York Press, 1986), 117, 204; "Pa. Gov. Appoints Negro GOP'er to Top Cabinet Job," *Jet*, January 17, 1963, 8.

20. "Charles M. Stokes, Pioneering Judge, Dies at 93," *Jet*, January 13, 1997, 18; John Henry Cutler, *Ed Brooke: Biography of a Senator* (Indianapolis: Bobbs-Merrill, 1972), 53; Chuck Stone, *Black Political Power in America* (Indianapolis: Bobbs-Merrill, 1968), 102; Edward W. Brooke, III, 95, Senate Pioneer, Is Dead," *NYT*, January 3, 2015.

21. "Six Win Seats in Indiana Elections," *Baltimore Afro-American*, November 29, 1966; Emma Lou Thronbrough, *Indiana Blacks in the Twentieth Century* (Bloomington: Indiana University Press, 2000), 171; Farrington, 428; Edward W. Brooke, *The Challenge of Change: Crisis in Our Two-Party System* (Boston: Little, Brown, 1966), x.

22. Cutler, 41, 49, 124; Peter Wallenstein, "Pioneer Black Legislators from Kentucky, 1860–1960s," *Register of the Kentucky Historical Society* 110, 3 and 4 (Summer/Autumn 2012): 548–49; Thronbrough, 171; "Negroes Offer Bill to Crack Ohio Housing Bias," 10; Russell M. Jones to Paul Jones, July 10, 1972, Folder: Blacks II (1 of 14), Box 23, Malek Papers, Series II; "Micellaneous [sic]," *The Crisis*, October 1961, 505.

23. William T. Coleman, Jr., with Donald Bliss, *Counsel for the Situation: Shaping the Law to Realize America's Promise* (Washington, D.C.: Brookings Institution Press, 2010), 170; "N.A.A.C.P. Fund Elects Ex-Judge," *NYT*, February 2, 1965; "Herman Smith Faces Hawkins in 21st Dist.," *Los Angeles Times*, October 12, 1962; "Services Planned for Lawyer Herman Smith," *Los Angeles Times*, August 22, 1985; "Inquest Ripped on Watts Riot," *NPC*, November 27, 1965; Republican National Committee, press release, May 7, 1954, Folder: Minority Groups 1954–32, Box 114, Hall Papers; "Negroes Threaten to Boycott Other Richmond Stores," *Free Lance-Star* (Fredericksburg, Virginia), March 22, 1960; "Open-Housing Law Sought by NAACP," *Free Lance-Star*, October 23, 1967; Richard C. Fuller, *George Romney and Michigan* (New York: Vantage, 1966), 69; "Black History Month," *Louisville Courier-Journal*, February 13, 2009; "Honorary Commencement and Testimonial Dinner, Dr. L. K. Jackson," September 14, 1973, Folder 36, Box 1, Jackson Papers; "Crusader—Dr. L. K. Jackson," *The Crisis*, February 1962, 116–17; "'Old Prophet' Was New 'Hell Raiser' in Gary," *Post-Tribune* (Indiana), January 14, 1999.

24. Open Letter, L. K. Jackson to William Miller, "Some Reasons Why the Republican Party Which Has Every Historical and Logical Reason to Win the Negro Vote, Is Losing Them," October 29, 1962, Folder 24, Box 5, Robinson Papers; "The President and the Housing Order," *New York Amsterdam News*, December 1, 1962; "Yale University Hears Speech by Lt. Lee," *Yale Daily News*, October 31, 1962, Folder 8, Box 1, Lee Collection; Brooke, *The Challenge of Change*, 13.

25. Charles Randolph to "Friend," n.d., and Letter, Helen Edmonds to William F. Buckley, Jr., November 1, 1957, both in Folder: Correspondence. General 1951–1959, Box 1, Edmonds Papers.

26. Maureen Buckley to Helen Edmonds, November 19, 1957, Folder: Correspondence. General 1951–1959, Box 1, Edmonds Papers; Klinkner, *The Losing Parties*, 64–65; William Miller to George W. Lee, December 18, 1962, Folder 16, Box 2, Lee Collection; "Answers to Questions from Simeon Booker," January 1964, Folder: Box (2), Box 26, 1964 Principal File, DDEPPP.

27. Kabaservice, 67; Robert Novak, *The Agony of the G.O.P. 1964* (New York: Macmillan, 1965), 176–78; Thurber, 180.

28. Taylor Branch, *Pillar of Fire: America in the King Years, 1963–65* (New York: Simon and Schuster, 1998), 77, 108, 137.

29. "Back Rights Bill, Nixon Urges G.O.P.," *NYT*, June 16, 1964; Charles and Barbara Whalen, *The Longest Debate: A Legislative History of the 1964 Civil Rights Act* (New York: Mentor, 1986), 190; Robert Peabody, "The Survivors: The 1965 House Minority Leadership Contest," in Bernard Cosman and Robert Huckshorn, eds., *Republican Politics: The 1964 Campaign and Its Aftermath for the Party* (New York: Praeger, 1968), 163; Branch, 405; Kabaservice, 103; "Thanks for Cloture Vote," *The Crisis*, August–September 1964, 438; Charles Evers and Andrew Szanton, *Have No Fear: The Charles Evers Story* (New York: Wiley, 1997), 163.

30. Stern, 193; Branch, 356–57; Barry Goldwater to Dwight D. Eisenhower, June 13, 1964, Folder: Goldwater, Barry (1), Box 37, 1964 Principal File, DDEPPP.

31. Gary Donaldson, *Liberalism's Last Hurrah: The Presidential Campaign of 1964* (Armonk, N.Y.: M.E. Sharpe, 2003), 111; Cary Reich, *The Life of Nelson A. Rockefeller: Worlds to Conquer, 1908–1958* (New York: Doubleday, 1996), 689; Kabaservice, 84; "Governor Wants to Be Known as Fighter for Rights of Negroes," *Jet*, March 22, 1962, 18; Evers and Szanton, 88; Roy Wilkins with Tom Mathews, *Standing Fast: The Autobiography of Roy Wilkins* (Cambridge, Mass.: Da Capa, 1994), 261–62.

32. David Reinhard, *The Republican Right Since 1945* (Lexington: University Press of Kentucky, 1983), 176; Rockefeller National Campaign Committee, "The Nelson Rockefeller Story," n.d., Folder: Campaign Literature, Box 30, Molitor Papers; "Why Jackie Joined Rocky's Staff," *NPC*, February 8, 1964; Arnold Rampersad, *Jackie Robinson: A Biography* (New York: Knopf, 1997), 385; Mary Kay Linge, *Jackie Robinson: A Biography* (Westport, Conn.: Greenwood, 2007), 136; "In Your Heart, Governor Rockefeller, You Know Senator Goldwater Is Wrong!," n.d., Folder: Ku Klux Klan/John Birch Soc., Box 161, RDNC, Series II; George Young and Rockefeller for President, press release, March 11, 1964, Folder: Civil Rights (2 of 2), Box 10, Hinman Files; Kabaservice, 93, 95; Jonathan Schoenwald, *A Time for Choosing: The Rise of Modern American Conservatism* (New York: Oxford University Press, 2001), 141; Branch, 403.

33. George Gallup, *The Gallup Poll: Public Opinion, 1935–1971*, vol. 3 (New York: Random House, 1972), 1880; Democratic National Committee, "What Scranton Really Thinks of Goldwater," Folder: Ku Klux Klan/John Birch Soc., Box 161, RDNC, Series II.

34. Lichtman, 246; Kabaservice, 62; Tim S. R. Boyd, *Georgia Democrats, the Civil Rights Movement, and the Shaping of the New South* (Gainesville: University Press of Florida, 2012), 107, 137–38; "The Great Purge of Negroes from GOP Hierarchy in Dixie," *Jet*, July 9, 1964, 10–12; "Georgia Is Cool to Goldwater but He Gets 22 of 24 Delegates," *NYT*, May 3, 1964; Branch, 301.

35. Dowdy, 98–99; Tucker, 183–84; "Lee's Convention Lasts 3 Minutes," *Memphis Commercial Appeal*, March 17, 1964; Elizabeth Gritter, *River of Hope: Black Politics and the Memphis Freedom Movement, 1865–1954* (Lexington: University Press of Kentucky, 2014), 214.

36. Tucker, 185; "State GOP Leaders Act to Bar Negro Delegates," *Chattanooga Daily Times*, May 2, 1964; "Lee's Convention Lasts 3 Minutes," *Memphis Commercial Appeal*, March 17, 1964.

37. "State GOP Leaders Act to Bar Negro Delegates," *Chattanooga Daily Times*, May 2, 1964; Tucker, 190; George W. Lee to Jackie Robinson, July 1, 1964, Folder 52, Box 3, Lee Collection; George W. Lee to Jackie Robinson, May 27, 1964, Folder 52, Box 3, Lee Collection; George W. Lee to Richard Nixon, May 29, 1964, Folder 46, Box 3, Lee Collection.

38. Tucker, 189–97; "Negro Gives Scranton an Issue," *Louisville Courier-Journal*, July 12, 1964; "Negroes Debating Role in Goldwater G.O.P.," *Washington Star*, July 14, 1964; Shelby County Republican Executive Committee, "Answer of the Delegates and Alternates to the Republican National Convention from the Ninth Congressional District of Tennessee to a Contest Filed by George W. Lee," June 24, 1964, Folder: 1964 Presidential Campaign: Republican National Convention: Answer of Delegates and Alternates, 9th District, Tennessee, Box 3H508, Shadegg/ Goldwater Collection.

39. "Democrats Snap Race Tradition," *Memphis Commercial Appeal*, April 3, 1964; Branch, 301, 403; Thomas Edsall with Mary Edsall, *Chain Reaction: The Impact of Race, Rights, and Taxes on American Politics* (New York: Norton, 1991), 43; Tucker, 197.

40. Hugh Scott, "Minority Views on Extremism" and "Minority Views on Civil Rights," July 13, 1964, Folder 49, Box 8, Record Group 4, Series G, DNC, NARPP; "Final Platform Hearings," *Congressional Quarterly Weekly Report* 22 (1964): 1488–89; "Standing in the Wings," *Los Angeles Sentinel*, February 25, 1965; Leah Wright, "The Loneliness of the Black Conservative: Black Republicans and the Grand Old Party, 1964–1980," Ph.D. dissertation (Princeton University, 2009), 68.

41. Theodore White, *The Making of the President 1964* (New York: Atheneum, 1965), 202; "Text of Second Half of 1964 Republican Platform," *NYT*, July 13, 1964; Reinhard, 194.

42. Kabaservice, 113; Edward W. Brooke, *Bridging the Divide: My Life* (New Brunswick, N.J.: Rutgers University Press, 2007), 109; Jackie Robinson, *I Never Had It Made* (New York: Harper-Collins, 1995), 169–70; Elaine Brown Jenkins, *Jumping Double Dutch: A New Agenda for Blacks and the Republican Party* (Silver Spring, Md.: Beckham, 1996), 25; Stanley Scott to Alexander Haig and Jerry Jones, August 23, 1973, Folder: Black Appointees (3), Box 3, Scott Papers; John Ehrlichman, *Witness to Power: The Nixon Years* (New York: Simon and Schuster, 1982), 36; Cutler, 139.

43. Tucker, 194; "Agnew Resigns," *Jet*, October 25, 1973, 6; Belva Davis with Vicki Haddock, *Never in My Wildest Dreams: A Black Woman's Life in Journalism* (Sausalito, Calif.: PoliPoint Press, 2001), 4; "Goldwater Show Is Jolting," *NPC*, July 25, 1964; Joseph Lowndes, *From the New Deal to the New Right: Race and the Southern Origins of Modern Conservatism* (New Haven, Conn.: Yale University Press, 2008), 73.

44. Brooke, *The Challenge of Change*, 16; Jonathan Martin Kolkey, *The New Right, 1960–1968. With Epilogue, 1969–1980* (Washington, D.C.: University Press of America, 1983), 210; "Senator's Rise Is Compared to the Upshoot of Adolph Hitler," *Jet*, July 30, 1964, 22–27; Robinson, *I Never Had It Made*, 169.

45. Reinhard, 192–94; Klinkner, *The Losing Parties*, 69; Hanes Walton, Jr., and Robert C. Smith, *American Politics and the African American Quest for Universal Freedom*, 2nd ed. (New York: Longman, 2003), 142.

46. "Transcript of Goldwater's Speech Accepting Republican Presidential Nomination," *NYT*, July 17, 1964; Doug McAdam, *Freedom Summer* (New York: Oxford University Press, 1990), 96; Reinhard, 195.

47. "Top Negro Delegates Unite Like Never Before at Confab," *Jet*, July 30, 1964, 19–20; Thurber, 189; Leah Wright, "Conscience of a Black Conservative: The 1964 Election and the Rise of the National Negro Republican Assembly," *Federal History Journal Online* 1 (January 2009): 35–36; Wright, "The Loneliness of the Black Conservative," 71–72; "Negro Republicans Challenge Goldwater's Fitness to Enforce Civil Rights Law," *NYT*, July 15, 1964.

48. "Top Negro Delegates Unite Like Never Before at Confab," 19–21; "Negro Republicans

Challenge Goldwater's Fitness to Enforce Civil Rights Law," *NYT*, July 15, 1964; "Senator's Rise is Compared to the Upshoot of Adolph Hitler," 24; "A Choice—Not an Echo," *Newsweek*, July 27, 1964, 21; Branch, 403–4.

49. "Tie to Democrats Weakens Negroes," *Des Moines Register*, June 24, 1964; "Remarks of Jackie Robinson—NY State GOP Fund-Raising Dinner," January 29, 1964, Folder 1, Box 13, Robinson Papers; George W. Lee to Richard Nixon, May 29, 1964, Folder 46, Box 3, Lee Collection.

50. "Senator's Rise Is Compared to Upshoot of Adolph Hitler," 24–25; George W. Lee, interview by Clayton Braddock, November 1968, MSRC; Clarence L. Townes, Jr., interview by Robert Wright, July 7, 1970, MSRC.

Chapter 6. Fighting the Enemy Within:
Black Republicans in the Wake of Goldwater

1. "Delegates Disconsolate," *NYT*, July 17, 1964; "Minutes of the General Session. National Negro Republican Convention Workshop," August 23, 1964, Folder: Attorney General, 1964 National Negro Republican Assembly, Box 619, Brooke Papers; Leah Wright, "The Loneliness of the Black Conservative: Black Republicans and the Grand Old Party, 1964–1980," Ph.D. dissertation (Princeton University, 2009), 73.

2. "Minutes of the General Session. National Negro Republican Convention Workshop," August 23, 1964, Folder: Attorney General, 1964 National Negro Republican Assembly, Box 619, Brooke Papers; speech by George Fleming in Philadelphia, August 22, 1964, Folder: Attorney General, 1964 National Negro Republican Assembly, Box 619, Brooke Papers.

3. Grant Reynolds to "Fellow Republican," October 15, 1964, Townes Papers; John H. Clay to "Republican Leaders," n.d., Folder: Attorney General, 1964 National Negro Republican Assembly, Box 619, Brooke Papers; National Negro Republican Assembly, "Senators Keating, Scott and Republican Governors and Congressmen Endorsed by National Negro Republican Assembly for Civil Rights Achievements," November 1, 1964, Townes Papers; Wright, "The Loneliness of the Black Conservative," 78–79.

4. "Negro Republicans in 5 Major Cities Are Turning to Johnson," *NYT*, September 27, 1964; "End to Marches Urged," *NYT*, July 22, 1964; "Urge Republicans to Excommunicate Sen. Goldwater," *Jet*, July 9, 1964, 12; John Henry Cutler, *Ed Brooke: Biography of a Senator* (Indianapolis: Bobbs-Merrill, 1972), 139; "Negro GOP Officer 'Can't Back Nominee,' " *Los Angeles Times*, July 23, 1964; "Negro Republicans Feeling Big Squeeze," *Charleston Gazette*, July 13, 1964; Geoffrey Kabaservice, *Rule and Ruin: The Downfall of Moderation and the Destruction of the Republican Party* (New York: Oxford University Press, 2012), 118.

5. "Negro Units Urge Lull in Rights Fight," *Des Moines Register*, July 30, 1964; "Goldwater Views Rapped as Urban League Convenes," *Washington Star*, August 3, 1964; "Why NAACP Opposes Goldwater," *The Crisis*, August–September 1964; Ripon Society and Thomas Petri, *Election '64: A Ripon Society Report* (Cambridge, Mass.: Ripon Society, 1968), 16; David Levering Lewis, *King: A Biography*, 3rd ed. (Urbana: University of Illinois Press, 2013), 250; Adam Fairclough, *To Redeem the Soul of America: The Southern Christian Leadership Conference and Martin Luther King, Jr.* (Athens: University of Georgia Press, 1987), 206.

6. "G.O.P. in Harlem Favors Scranton," *NYT*, July 9, 1964; L. K. Jackson to Lyndon Johnson, March 12, 1965, Folder 5, Box 1, Jackson Papers; "Johnson to Make Issue of Rights," *NPC*, August 1, 1964; Jackie Robinson, *I Never Had It Made* (New York: HarperCollins, 1995), 174; "Jackie Robinson Says," *Tri-State Defender*, July 11, 1964.

7. Dennis Dickerson, *African American Preachers and Politics: The Careys of Chicago* (Jackson: University Press of Mississippi, 2010), 158–60; James Nabrit, interview by Stephen Goodell, March 28, 1969, AC 74–54, Oral Histories, Lyndon B. Johnson Presidential Library; Benjamin Hooks with Jerry Guess, *The March for Civil Rights: The Benjamin Hooks Story* (Chicago: American Bar Association, 2003), 346.

8. "Goldwater's GOP Ousts Negro," *Jet*, September 17, 1964, 6; Karl Lamb, "Under One Roof: Barry Goldwater's Campaign Staff," in Bernard Cosman and Robert Huckshorn, eds., *Republican Politics: The 1964 Campaign and Its Aftermath for the Party* (New York: Praeger, 1968), 33; "Oops, What Goldwater Really Meant Was," *Jet*, October 22, 1964, 5; Ripon Society, *From Disaster to Distinction: A Republican Rebirth* (New York: Pocket Books, 1966), 31.

9. "Claiborne Indicted for King Election Pamphlets," *NPC*, November 28, 1964; Jeremy Mayer, *Running on Race: Racial Politics in Presidential Campaigns, 1960–2000* (New York: Random House, 2002), 64–65; "The Negro Who Can Help Save the GOP," *Jet*, December 3, 1964, 17; "Clay Claiborne Freed in Vote Write-In Case," *Baltimore Afro-American*, June 7, 1966.

10. Oscar Williams, *George S. Schuyler: Portrait of a Black Conservative* (Knoxville: University of Tennessee Press, 2004), 143–44; Maria Diedrich, "George S. Schuyler's *Black No More*—The Black Conservative's Socialist Past," *Western Journal of Black Studies* 12, 1 (1988), 55; George Schuyler, *Black and Conservative: The Autobiography of George S. Schuyler* (New Rochelle, N.Y.: Arlington House, 1966), 348; Clipping, "Negro Weekly Supports Goldwater," Folder 8, Box 1, Lee Collection; Justine Priestly, *By Gertrude Wilson: Dispatches of the 1960s, From a White Writer in a Black World* (Edgartown, Mass.: Vineyard Stories, 2005), 123; "Negroes Cancel Goldwater Talk," *NYT*, September 11, 1964; "Barry's Most Ardent Negro," *Jet*, November 27, 1964, 4–5.

11. Timothy Thurber, *Race and Republicans: The GOP's Frayed Relationship with African Americans, 1945–1974* (Lawrence: University Press of Kansas, 2013), 194, 197, 201; George C. Roberts, "The 1964 Presidential Election in Arkansas," in John M. Claunch, ed., *The 1964 Presidential Election in the Southwest* (Dallas: Arnold Foundation, Southern Methodist University, 1966), 85; Clipping, "GOP Leader Won't Reject Klan Support," n.d., Folder: Ku Klux Klan/John Birch Society, Box 161, RDNC, Series II; "Klan Leader Blasts Civil Rights Act," *New York Herald*, July 23, 1964; "Welcome Disavowal of the Klan," *Louisville Times*, August 8, 1964; Edward W. Brooke, *The Challenge of Change: Crisis in Our Two-Party System* (Boston: Little, Brown, 1966), 17.

12. Robert Donovan, *The Future of the Republican Party* (New York: New American Library of World Literature, 1964), 15–16; Brooke, *The Challenge of Change*, 6; Thurber, *Race and Republicans*, 202; Jere Nash and Andy Taggart, *Mississippi Politics: The Struggle for Power, 1976–2006* (Jackson: University Press of Mississippi, 2006), 45; Hugh Davis Graham, *Civil Rights and the Presidency: Race and Gender in American Politics, 1960–1972* (New York: Oxford University Press, 1992), 90; Wayne Greenhaw, *Elephants in the Cottonfields: Ronald Reagan and the New Republican South* (New York: Macmillan, 1982), 60.

13. Timothy Thurber, "Goldwaterism Triumphant? Race and the Republican Party, 1965–1968," *Journal of the Historical Society* 7, 3 (September 2007): 354; Hugh Scott, *Come to the Party* (Englewood Cliffs, N.J.: Prentice-Hall, 1968), 222; Edward W. Brooke, *Bridging the Divide: My Life* (New Brunswick, N.J.: Rutgers University Press, 2007), 109; "The Kennedy Victory," *NYT*, November 4, 1964; "Taft Will Not Seek Ohio Vote Recount," *NYT*, December 2, 1964; "Percy Lashes Anti-Righters Joining GOP," *Chicago Tribune*, December 5, 1964.

14. Thomas Edsall with Mary Edsall, *Chain Reaction: The Impact of Race, Rights, and Taxes*

on American Politics (New York: Norton, 1991), 35–36; Ripon Society, *From Disaster to Distinction*, 32; Donovan, 88; Thurber, *Race and Republicans*, 255; John R. Petrocik, *Party Coalitions: Realignments and the Decline of the New Deal Party System* (Chicago: University of Chicago Press, 1981), 89.

15. "Edward Brooke Counsels," *NPC*, March 6, 1965; "G.O.P. Negroes Map Drive," *NYT*, November 13, 1964; Andrew Hacker, "Is There a New Republican Majority?," in Louise Kapp Howe, ed., *The White Majority: Between Poverty and Affluence* (New York: Random House, 1970), 266; Lee W. Huebner and Thomas Petri, *The Ripon Papers 1963–1968* (Washington, D.C.: National Press, 1968), 20, 34–38; "Bliss and the Negroes," *Ripon Forum*, June 1966, Folder: Ripon Society, Box 79, RDNC, Series II; "Moderates Form New G.O.P. Group," *NYT*, February 4, 1965; Thurber, "Goldwaterism Triumphant?," 359; Kabaservice, 128; Marvin Caplan to Grant Reynolds, November 22, 1966, Folder: Council of Republican Organizations 1966, Box I:61, LCCRR.

16. Thurber, "Goldwaterism Triumphant?," 357; "Bliss and the Negroes"; Leah Wright, "'The Challenge of Change: Edward Brooke, The Republican Party, and the Struggle for Redemption," *Souls: A Critical Journal of Black Politics, Culture, and Society* 13, 100; "G.O.P. Aide 'Starts from Scratch' in Drive to Win Negroes," *NYT*, May 31, 1966; Clarence L. Townes, Jr., interview by Robert Wright, June 11, 1970, MSRC; Frank Atkinson, *The Dynamic Dominion: Realignment and the Rise of Two-Party Competition in Virginia, 1945–1980*, rev. 2nd ed. (Lanham, Md.: Rowman and Littlefield, 2006), 167; Julian Bond, *Black Candidates: Southern Campaign Experiences* (Atlanta: Voter Education Project, Southern Regional Council, 1969), 35–36.

17. "Bliss and the Negroes"; Clarence Townes to Barry Goldwater, December 20, 1964, Townes Papers; Wright, "The Loneliness of the Black Conservative," 68–69; Clarence Townes, interview by Robert Wright; Clarence Townes, interview by author, October 18, 2011, in possession of author.

18. Alfred Duckett Associates, "National Committee Charged with Attempt to Dictate to Negro Republican Assembly," n.d., Townes Papers; "National Negro Republican Assembly," December 3, 1965, Townes Papers; "Bliss and the Negroes"; Kabaservice, 176.

19. Alfred Duckett Associates, "National Committee Charged with Attempt to Dictate to Negro Republican Assembly," n.d., Townes Papers; "National Negro Republican Assembly," December 3, 1965, Townes Papers; "Bliss and the Negroes".

20. Alfred Duckett Associates, "National Committee Charged with Attempt to Dictate to Negro Republican Assembly," n.d., Townes Papers; "Keep Parties Guessing," *Jet*, June 16, 1966, 4; "Bliss and the Negroes"; Michael Long, ed., *First Class Citizenship: The Civil Rights Letters of Jackie Robinson* (New York: Times Books, 2007), 230–31.

21. "Lindsay Woos Negroes in N.Y. Mayor Race," *Jet*, June 17, 1965, 6; "Rev. Walker Endorses Lindsay," *Pittsburgh Courier*, October 30, 1965; Thurber, "Goldwaterism Triumphant?," 358; Kabaservice, 158; "Cities," *Time*, November 12, 1965; Richard Keiser, *Subordination or Empowerment? African American Leadership and the Struggle for Urban Political Power* (New York: Oxford University Press, 1997), 98.

22. "Negro Republicans Issue 82 National Endorsements," November 7, 1966, Folder: Natl. Negro Republican Assembly 1966, Box 173, LCCRR; "Negro Republicans Support Governor," *NYT*, October 15, 1966; Grant Reynolds to Nelson Rockefeller, May 12, 1967, Folder 319, Box 51, Hinman Files, Record Group III4 J.2; Nelson Rockefeller to Grant Reynolds, December 1, 1964, Folder 319, Box 51, Hinman Files; George Hinman to Grant Reynolds, April 14, 1967, Folder 319, Box 51, Hinman Files.

23. National Negro Republican Assembly, "The Executive Committee Meeting," October 15, 1965, Townes Papers; George Hinman to George Fowler, March 22, 1965, Folder 319, Box 51, Hinman Files.

24. "The Dilemma of a GOP Presidential Candidate and the Negro Voter," n.a./n.d., Townes Papers; Clarence Townes, interview by Robert Wright; "GOP Seeks Blacks in Nixon Camp," *Jet*, February 6, 1964, 52; Clarence Townes, interview by author; Republican National Committee, "Republicans Improve their Image," *St. Louis Sentinel*, March 16, 1968; "Proposed Plan of Action for the Kansas City Area," n.d., Townes Papers; "A Suggested Outline for Jackson County Republican Committee Minorities Program," n.d., Townes Papers; Frank Kent, "Proposal," n.d., Townes Papers; Catherine Rymph, "The Republican Party and the Problem of Diversity, 1968–1975," in Robert Mason and Iwan Morgan, eds., *Seeking a New Majority: The Republican Party and American Politics, 1960–1980* (Nashville, Tenn.: Vanderbilt University Press, 2013), 78.

25. Wright, "The Challenge of Change," 107; "GOP Must 'Walk in Negro's Shoes,'" *Jet*, July 14, 1966, 7–9; Kabaservice, 177, 214–15.

26. Speech delivered by Clarence Townes in New Orleans, January 24, 1967, Townes Papers; Clarence Townes, interview by Robert Wright.

27. William Brink and Louis Harris, *Black and White: A Study of U.S. Racial Attitudes Today* (New York: Simon and Schuster, 1967), 75–77; Mark Levy and Michael Kramer, *The Ethnic Factor: How America's Minorities Decide Elections* (New York: Simon and Schuster, 1972), 55, 63; Wright, "The Challenge of Change," 106; Nick Thimmesch, *The Condition of Republicanism* (New York: Norton, 1968), 68; Greenhaw, 208.

28. John Kirk, *Redefining the Color Line: Black Activism in Little Rock, Arkansas, 1940–1970* (Gainesville: University Press of Florida, 2002), 166–67; John Kirk, "A Southern Road Less Traveled: The 1966 Gubernatorial Election and (Winthrop) Rockefeller Republicanism in Arkansas," in Glenn Feldmann, ed., *Painting Dixie Red: When, Where, Why, and How the South Became Republican* (Gainesville: University Press of Florida, 2011), 187; Grif Stockley, *Ruled by Race: Black/White Relations in Arkansas from Slavery to the Present* (Fayetteville: University of Arkansas Press, 2009), 354–55; Cathy Kunzinger Urwin, *Agenda for Reform: Winthrop Rockefeller as Governor of Arkansas, 1967–71* (Fayetteville: University of Arkansas Press, 1991), 56.

29. Chuck Stone, *Black Political Power in America* (Indianapolis: Bobbs-Merrill Co., 1968), 202; Cutler, 118; Levy and Kramer, 64; "Republican Resurgence," *Time*, November 18, 1966.

30. Kabaservice, 184; Cutler, 64, 175; John Becker and Eugene Heaton, Jr., "The Election of Senator Edward W. Brooke," *Public Opinion Quarterly*, 31, 3 (Autumn 1967): 352; "Edward Brooke Sounds Off," *Jet*, August 18, 1966, 8; "A Man We Can Be Proud Off [sic]," *New York Amsterdam News*, November 26, 1966; "Senator-Elect Edward W. Brooke," *The Crisis*, November 1966, 472.

31. Brooke, *Bridging the Divide*, 153; Theodore Cross, *The Black Power Imperative: Racial Inequality and the Politics of Nonviolence* (New York: Faulkner, 1984), 309; Cutler, 164; "Elections, 1970," *The Crisis*, December 1970, 393; "'I'm a Soul Brother,'" *Ebony*, April 1967, 150.

32. Speech by Edward W. Brooke in Los Angeles, July 28, 1963, Folder: Urban League Keynote Address July 28, 1963, Box 566, Brooke Papers; Cutler, 4–5, 339; "Edward Brooke Addresses Democratic Black Caucus," *Bay State Banner*, October 18, 1973; Charles Rangel to Edward Brooke, November 10, 1975, Folder: Rangel, Charles B., Box 189, Brooke Papers; Shirley Chisholm to Julian Goodman, November 20, 1975, Folder: Chisholm, Shirley, Box 178, Brooke Papers.

33. Brooke, *Bridging the Divide*, 172; Cutler, 246; National Advisory Commission on Civil

Disorders, *The Kerner Report: The 1968 Report of the National Advisory Commission on Civil Disorders* (New York: Pantheon, 1988), xxii, 1.

34. Brooke, *Bridging the Divide*, 173; "Congress Chiefs Ask Riot Inquiry," *NYT*, July 26, 1967; Thurber, "Goldwaterism Triumphant?," 370; "Sen. Brooke Has His 'Day,'" *Jet*, August 17, 1967, 6.

35. Brooke, *Bridging the Divide*, 175–77; "Senate Approves Civil Rights Bill by 71-to-20 Vote," *NYT*, March 12, 1968; "Brooke Saves Rights Bill from Filibuster," *Baltimore Afro-American*, March 5, 1968; Transcript, *Face the Nation* (CBS), April 7, 1968, Folder: PR 12 4-6-68—5-20-68, Box 280, Gen PR 12, WHCF, Johnson Library.

36. Thurber, *Race and Republicans*, 264; "Political Notes," *Time*, January 14, 1966; "Negro Mayor Highlights Urban League Banquet," *Bay State Banner*, April 23, 1966; "Memorial Service Held for Dr. Paul P. Boswell," *Jet*, March 22, 1982, 6; "State Representatives," *Ebony*, April 1965, 194; "Dems Reject Open Housing Compromise," *Chicago Tribune*, June 10, 1965; "Racial Bias Hot Issue," *Jet*, July 14, 1966, 54; "Rites Held for Cleveland RTA Atty. John W. Kellogg," *Jet*, January 7, 1982, 9; "Claimants of Civil Equality Help Fight," *Life*, September 19, 1960, 38–39.

37. Georgia Davis Powers, *I Shared the Dream: The Pride, Passion and Politics of the First Black Woman Senator from Kentucky* (Far Hills, N.J.: New Horizon Press, 1995), 132–33; Anthony Newberry, "Civil Rights Act of 1966," in John Kleber, ed., *The Kentucky Encyclopedia* (Lexington: University Press of Kentucky, 1992), 191; "Remove These Relics," *Washington Afro-American*, April 5, 1966; Luther Adams, *Way Up North in Louisville: African American Migration in the Urban South, 1930–1970* (Chapel Hill: University of North Carolina Press, 2010), 145, 175, 181.

38. Stone, 76; "Republicans Improve their Image," *St. Louis Sentinel*, March 16, 1968; Arnold Rampersad, *Jackie Robinson: A Biography* (New York: Knopf, 1997), 405–6; Mary Kay Linge, *Jackie Robinson: A Biography* (Westport, Conn.: Greenwood, 2007), 139; "Bergen Democrats Depose Chairman and Elect Andora," *NYT*, June 10, 1965; "First Negro in High GOP State Post," *Detroit News*, December 5, 1965; Ethel Payne to Louis E. Martin, October 1, 1965, Folder: Memorandums, Box 79, RDNC, Series II; "Black Political Leader Warders, Dead at 63," *Louisville Defender*, July 9, 1981.

39. Philip E. Converse, "A Major Political Realignment in the South?," in Allan P. Sindler, ed., *Change in the Contemporary South* (Durham, N.C.: Duke University Press, 1963), 215; Petrocik, 88; Pearl Robinson, "Whither the Future of Blacks in the Republican Party?," *Political Science Quarterly* 97, 2 (Summer 1982): 211; Paul Allen Beck, "Partisan Dealignment in the Postwar South," *American Political Science Review* 71, 2 (June 1977): 481.

40. Nick Kotz, *Judgment Days: Lyndon Baines Johnson, Martin Luther King, Jr., and the Laws That Changed America* (New York: Houghton Mifflin, 2005), 416, 424; Transcript, *Face the Nation* (CBS), April 7, 1968.

41. Joseph Lowndes, *From the New Deal to the New Right: Race and the Southern Origins of Modern Conservatism* (New Haven, Conn.: Yale University Press, 2008), 73; Thurber, *Race and Republicans*, 254; Thurber, "Goldwaterism Triumphant?," 356; "Ford's Natchez Boycott Symbolic," *Clarion Ledger*, November 20, 1965; William Link, *Righteous Warrior: Jesse Helms and the Rise of Modern Conservatism* (New York: St. Martin's, 2008), 79.

42. Kabaservice, 161; "Goldwater's GOP Ousts Negro," 7; D.J. Bond to George Romney, March 12, 1965, Folder: Civil Rights 1965. A-F, Box 116, Romney Papers; Stephen Grant Meyer, *As Long as They Don't Move Next Door: Segregation and Racial Conflict in American Neighborhoods* (Lanham, Md.: Rowman and Littlefield, 2000), 179–81; Taylor Branch, *Pillar of Fire:*

America in the King Years, 1963–65 (New York: Simon and Schuster, 1998), 494; Hazel Erskine, "The Polls: Speed of Racial Integration," *Public Opinion Quarterly* 32, 3 (Autumn 1968): 523–24.

43. Matthew Dallek, *The Right Moment: Ronald Reagan's First Victory and the Decisive Turning Point in American Politics* (New York: Free Press, 2000), 188; Taylor Branch, *At Canaan's Edge: America in the King Years, 1965–68* (New York: Simon and Schuster, 2006), 543; Lisa Mc-Girr, *Suburban Warriors: The Origins of the New American Right* (Princeton, N.J.: Princeton University Press, 2001), 205; "Reagan Keeps Silent," *Sumter Daily Item*, August 8, 1966.

44. "Reagan Storms from Meeting of Negro GOP Unit," *Los Angeles Times*, March 6, 1966; Dallek, 200; Lee Edwards, *The Conservative Revolution: The Movement that Remade America* (New York: Free Press, 1999), 157; Lyn Nofziger, *Nofziger* (Washington, D.C.: Regnery Gateway, 1992), 38; NNRA/Wolverine State Republican Organization, "NNRA Convention," n.d., Townes Papers.

45. Samuel Lubell, *White and Black: Test of a Nation* (New York: Harper and Row, 1964), 171; Herman Smith, "Politics and Policies of the Negro Community," in Eugene Dvorin and Arthur Misner, eds., *California Politics and Policies* (Reading, Mass.: Addison-Wesley, 1966), 333–34; Bayard Rustin, *Strategies for Freedom: The Changing Patterns of Black Protest* (New York: Columbia University Press, 1976), 52.

46. "Republican Party," *Time*, November 18, 1966; Cutler, 94; "The Senate," *Time*, February 17, 1967; Brooke, *Bridging the Divide*, 55; "Lt. George W. Lee...Replies to Dr. Martin Luther King's Charge of Hypocrisy in the Republican Party," n.d., Folder 11, Box 4, Lee Collection; George W. Lee to Jackie Robinson, November 19, Folder 52, Box 3, Lee Collection; Speech delivered by Junius Griffin in Nashville, Tenn., March 25, 1967, Townes Papers; Long, 154–55; L. K. Jackson to Roy Wilkins, June 14, 1963, Folder 5, Box 1, Jackson Papers.

47. Edward W. Brooke, "Negroes and the Open Society," *Congressional Record* 12, 13 (August 2, 1966), 17865; Brooke, *Bridging the Divide*, 177.

48. Clarence Taylor, *The Black Churches of Brooklyn* (New York: Columbia University Press, 1996), 118; David Falkner, *Great Time Coming: The Life of Jackie Robinson, from Baseball to Birmingham* (New York: Simon and Schuster, 1995), 177; Clarence Taylor, "Voices of the Black Religious Community of Brooklyn, New York," in Tony Carnes and Anna Karpathakis, eds., *New York Glory: Religions in the City* (New York: New York University Press, 2001), 358; Taylor Branch, *Parting the Waters: America in the King Years, 1954–63* (New York: Simon and Schuster, 1988), 356; "Negro Minister Applauds Lindsay's Courage Before Conference in Harlem," *NYT*, April 8, 1968; Lionel Hampton with James Haskins, *Hamp: An Autobiography* (New York: Amistad, 1993), 155–56; Rampersad, 406.

49. Long, 228; "Jackie Robinson Says," *Tri-State Defender*, December 7, 1963; Brooke, *Bridging the Divide*, 55, 107; "Tell It Like It Is! A Chapter from a Forthcoming Book, 'Give Me This Mountain,'" sent to Richard M. Nixon, April 7, 1969, Folder 34, Box 1, Jackson Papers.

50. Kabaservice, 142; "Romney Leads a Protest," *NYT*, March 10, 1965; Thurber, "Goldwaterism Triumphant?," 364–66; Quintard Taylor, *The Forging of a Black Community: Seattle's Central District from 1870 Through the Civil Rights Era* (Seattle: University of Washington Press, 1994), 208; Wright, "The Loneliness of the Black Conservative," 157; Justin P. Coffey, "Spiro T. Agnew: The Decline of Moderates and Rise of the Republican Right," in Laura Jane Gifford and Daniel K. Williams, eds., *The Right Side of the Sixties: Reexamining Conservatism's Decade of Transformation* (New York: Palgrave Macmillan, 2012), 243; Charles Evers and Andrew Szanton, *Have No Fear: The Charles Evers Story* (New York: Wiley, 1997), 88; "Agnew Ups Draft Board

Race Members," *Baltimore Afro-American*, September 30, 1967; John L. Ward, *The Arkansas Rockefeller* (Baton Rouge: Louisiana State University Press, 1978), 175–76; Urwin, 197–98.

51. Grant Reynolds, Jackie Robinson, and John D. Silvera, press release, May 12, 1967, Folder 319, Box 51, Hinman Files; "Jackie Robinson Says," *NPC*, December 11, 1965; Speech delivered by Clarence Townes in Louisville, Ky., March 11, 1967, Townes Papers; Clarence L. Townes, Jr., interview by Robert Wright; Brooke, *The Challenge of Change*, xii; George W. Lee, "The Selection of New Targets for a New Intellectual, Moral, and Political Climate," October 1972, Folder 21, Box 9, Lee Collection.

52. "Political Patience Is One Trait of Republican Negro Women," *NYT*, August 18, 1969; "Cora Walker Pushing Bid for 21st Senatorial Seat," *Pittsburgh Courier*, April 18, 1964; "Top GOP Post to Ex-Aide of King," *Chicago Sun-Times*, January 10, 1967; Radio address delivered by L. K. Jackson, "What Can We Believe of What Congressman Adam Clayton Powell and the Democratic Bosses of Gary Say?," Gary, Indiana, October 22, 1960, Folder: Alphabetical Files, Political Material, Addresses, Reports, Memoranda, etc., of the Republican Nat'l Cmte, 1960–1961, Box 1, Edmonds Papers.

53. "Dawson's Foe Named to County President's Team," *Jet*, December 22, 1966, 10; Speech delivered by David Reed in Washington, D.C., October 6, 1966, Townes Papers; Kabaservice, 178–82, 187; "Table of Votes for the House of Representatives in the Elections Last Tuesday," *NYT*, November 13, 1966.

54. "Reflections on the November Elections," *The Crisis*, November 1965, 552; Branch, *At Canaan's Edge*, 283; William Brink and Louis Harris, *The Negro Revolution in America* (New York: Simon and Schuster, 1964), 87; Ralph David Abernathy, *And the Walls Came Tumbling Down: An Autobiography* (New York: Harper and Row, 1989), 590; "Meredith to Run Against Powell as a Republican," *NYT*, March 8, 1967; "G.O.P. Names James Farmer for Brooklyn Race for Congress," *NYT*, May 20, 1968.

55. Grant Reynolds, Jackie Robinson, and John D. Silvera, press release, May 12, 1967, Folder 319, Box 51, Hinman Files; "Revolt of Negro Democrats in Hinted," *Evening Star* (Washington, D.C.), October 2, 1967; Everett Carll Ladd, "Negro Politics in the South: An Overview," in Harry A. Bailey, Jr., ed., *Negro Politics in America* (Columbus, Ohio: Merrill, 1967), 250–51; "Negro Democrats Organizing for LBJ," *New York Post*, June 1, 1967; "What Republican Victory Means to the Negro," *Ebony*, February 1967, 92.

56. Thurber, *Race and Republicans*, 259.

Chapter 7. A Piece of the Action:
Black Capitalism and the Nixon Administration

1. "Wright Speaks to Alpha Phi Alpha," *Bay State Banner*, August 14, 1969; Nathan Wright, Jr., "The Social Arena of Black Political Action," in Nathan Wright, Jr., ed., *What Black Politicians Are Saying* (New York: Hawthorn, 1972), 200–202.

2. Peniel Joseph, *Waiting 'Til the Midnight Hour: A Narrative History of Black Power in America* (New York: Henry Holt, 2006), 133–43.

3. Peniel Joseph, "Introduction: Toward a Historiography of the Black Power Movement," in Peniel Joseph, ed., *The Black Power Movement: Rethinking the Civil Rights-Black Power Era* (New York: Routledge, 2006), 3; Manning Marable and Leith Mullings, eds., *Let Nobody Turn Us Around: Voices of Resistance, Reform, and Renewal* (Lanham, Md.: Rowman and Littlefield, 2000), 373; U.S. Department of Commerce, "A System to Develop Minority Businessmen," September 1970, Folder 6129, McKissick Papers.

4. Christopher Alan Bracey, *Saviors or Sellouts: The Promise and Peril of Black Conservatism, from Booker T. Washington to Condoleezza Rice* (Boston: Beacon, 2008), 110; "T. R. M. Howard, Noted Physician, Dies at 68," *Jet*, May 20, 1976, 14; David Beito and Linda Royster Beito, "T. R. M. Howard: Pragmatism over Strict Integrationist Ideology in the Mississippi Delta, 1942–1954," in Glenn Feldman, ed., *Before Brown: Civil Rights and White Backlash in the Modern South* (Tuscaloosa: University of Alabama Press, 2004), 70; David Tucker, *Lieutenant Lee of Beale Street* (Nashville, Tenn.: Vanderbilt University Press, 1971), 50; George W. Lee, interview by Clayton Braddock, November 1968, MSRC; Matthew J. Countryman, *Up South: Civil Rights and Black Power in Philadelphia* (Philadelphia: University of Pennsylvania Press, 2007), 110, 119.

5. Congressional Quarterly Service, *The Presidential Nominating Conventions 1968* (Washington, D.C.: Congressional Quarterly Service, 1968), 69; Edward W. Brooke to Thruston Morton, April 12, 1968, Folder: Civil Rights, 1967–1968, Box 119, Morton Collection; Nathan Wright, Jr., *Let's Work Together* (New York: Hawthorn, 1968), 151; Speech delivered by Clarence Townes in Washington, D.C., March 23, 1968, Townes Papers; Clarence Townes, "1968 Minorities Division Report," February 1966 [*sic* 1968], Townes Papers.

6. Clarence L. Townes, Jr., interview by Robert Wright, July 7, 1970, MSRC; "The Senate," *Time*, February 17, 1967; "A Negro Leader's Advice to Republicans," *U.S. News and World Report*, February 1, 1965; William T. Coleman, Jr., with Donald Bliss, *Counsel for the Situation: Shaping the Law to Realize America's Promise* (Washington, D.C.: Brookings Institution), 2, 360.

7. Edward Brooke, "Where I Stand," *Atlantic Monthly*, March 1966, 62; Coleman with Bliss, 363; Arthur Fletcher, *The Silent Sell-Out: Government Betrayal to Blacks to the Craft Unions* (New York: Third Press, 1974), 17.

8. Republican National Committee, "Republicans Improve Their Image," *St. Louis Sentinel*, March 16, 1968; "The Birth Pangs of Black Capitalism," *Time*, October 18, 1968, 99; Leah Wright, "'The Challenge of Change': Edward Brooke, The Republican Party, and the Struggle for Redemption," *Souls: A Critical Journal of Black Politics, Culture, and Society* 13, 107; "Black Republican State Conference and Dinner," April 26, 1969, Folder: Minorities, 1962–73, Box 46, Republican Party (Michigan State Central Committee Records).

9. "A Great and Mighty Walk for Cora Walker," *New York Amsterdam News*, February 11, 1999; "Cora Walker, 84, Dies," *NYT*, July 20, 2006; "Buckley Is Named as G.O.P. Delegate," *NYT*, April 12, 1972; "Residents of Harlem Open Their Own Supermarket," *NYT*, June 5, 1968; "Harlem Market Thrives as Co-Op," *NYT*, August 11, 1968.

10. David Hamilton Golland, *Constructing Affirmative Action: The Struggle for Equal Employment Opportunity* (Lexington: University Press of Kentucky, 2011), 125–26; "Art Fletcher," *Sepia*, March 1970, 62; "Art Fletcher," *Ellensburg Daily Record*, August 6, 1968; Leah Wright, "The Black Cabinet: Economic Civil Rights in the Nixon Administration," in Glenn Feldman, ed., *Painting Dixie Red: When, Where, Why, and How the South Became Republican* (Gainesville: University Press of Florida, 2011), 253–54.

11. Clarence E. Jones, "From Protest to Black Conservatism: The Demise of the Congress of Racial Equality," in Ollie A. Johnson, III, and Karin Stanford, eds., *Black Political Organizations in the Post-Civil Rights Era* (New Brunswick, N.J.: Rutgers University Press, 2002), 87–88; Roger Biles, "The Rise and Fall of Soul City: Planning Politics and Race in Recent America," *Journal of Planning History* 4, 1 (February 2005): 58; Robert H. Brisbane, *Black Activism: Racial Revolution in the United States, 1954–1970* (Valley Forge, Pa.: Judson Press, 1974), 144–45, 265; William L. Van Deburg, *New Day in Babylon: The Black Power Movement and American Culture, 1965–1975*

(Chicago: University of Chicago Press, 1992), 133–34; August Meier and Elliott Rudwick, *CORE: A Study in the Civil Rights Movement* (New York: Oxford University Press, 1973), 416.

12. Dean Kotlowski, *Nixon's Civil Rights: Politics, Principle, and Policy* (Cambridge, Mass.: Harvard University Press, 2001), 132; Devin Fergus, "Black Power, Soft Power: Floyd McKissick, Soul City, and the Death of Moderate Black Republicanism," *Journal of Policy History* 22, 2 (2010): 152; Michael O. West, "Whose Black Power? The Business of Black Power and Black Power's Business," in Laura Warren Hill and Julia Rabig, eds., *The Business of Black Power: Community Development, Capitalism, and Corporate Responsibility in Postwar America* (Rochester, N.Y.: University of Rochester Press, 2012), 289; Deburg, 134–35; "F. B. McKissick Enterprises, Inc. Purpose and Potential," n.a./n.d., Folder 6443, McKissick Papers; "McKissick Is Succeeding Although Not 'Supposed To,' " *NYT*, December 22, 1974.

13. "Roy Innis," *Ebony*, October 1969, 170, 176; Roy Innis, "Truth, Lies, and Consequences," in Jeffrey M. Elliot, ed., *Black Voices in American Politics* (New York: Harcourt Brace, 1986), 241, 244; Deburg, 137; Clarence Long, *Grassroots at the Gateway: Class Politics and Black Freedom Struggle in St. Louis, 1936–75* (Ann Arbor: University of Michigan Press, 2009), 234; Kenneth Jolly, *Black Liberation in the Midwest: The Struggle in St. Louis, Missouri, 1964–1970* (New York: Routledge, 2006), 138.

14. "Nathan Wright Jr., Black Power Advocate, Dies at 81," *NYT*, February 24, 2005; "Nathan Wright Jr.," *Los Angeles Sentinel*, March 24–30, 2005; "Dr. Nathan Wright Quits Episcopal Church Post," *Jet*, April 17, 1969, 4; Wright, *Let's Work Together*, 94–95, 217; Wright, "The Social Arena of Black Political Activism," 200–202.

15. Robert L. Allen, *Black Awakening in Capitalist America: An Analytic History* (Garden City, N.Y.: Doubleday, 1969), 133, 138; Manning Marable, *Race, Reform, and Rebellion: The Second Reconstruction and Beyond in Black America, 1945–2006*, 3rd ed. (Jackson: University of Mississippi Press, 2007), 95–96; "Black Power Workshop Underway," *Star-News* (Wilmington, N.C.), July 22, 1967; "Newark Meeting on Black Power Attended by 400," *NYT*, July 21, 1967; West, 277; Marcus Pohlmann, *Black Politics in Conservative America*, 2nd ed. (New York: Longman, 1999), 270.

16. Ernie Allen, "Black Nationalism on the Right," *Soulbook* 1, 1 (Winter 1964): 8, 13; "Black Panthers See Violence," *Spokane Daily Chronicle*, February 24, 1970; "Eldridge Cleaver Discusses Revolution: An Interview from Exile," October 1969, in Philip Fonder, ed., *The Black Panthers Speak* (New York: Da Capo, 1995), 108–9; Henry Winston, *Class, Race, and Black Liberation* (New York: International Publishers, 1977), 145.

17. Donna Jean Murch, *Living for the City: Migration, Education, and the Rise of the Black Panther Party in Oakland, California* (Chapel Hill: University of North Carolina Press, 2010), 10, 169; Rhonday Williams, "Black Women, Urban Politics, and Engendering Black Power," in Joseph, *The Black Power Movement*, 95; Joseph, *Waiting 'Til the Midnight Hour*, 218–19.

18. Ibram H. Rogers, "Acquiring 'A Piece of the Action': The Rise and Fall of the Black Capitalism Movement," in Michael Ezra, ed., *The Economic Civil Rights Movement: African Americans and the Struggle for Economic Power* (New York: Routledge, 2012), 137; Molly Michelmore, *Tax and Spend: The Welfare State, Tax Politicians, and the Limits of American Liberalism* (Philadelphia: University of Pennsylvania Press, 2011), 68; Bayard Rustin, *Down the Line: The Collected Writings of Bayard Rustin* (Chicago: Quadrangle, 1971), 251; "Stans to Promote a Minority Business Enterprise," *NYT*, March 6, 1969; "Nixon's Black Capitalism... Dead," *Sacramento Observer*, July 17, 1969.

19. Joseph E. Persico, *The Imperial Rockefeller: A Biography of Nelson A. Rockefeller* (New

York: Simon and Schuster, 1982), 65; "Poll Shows Rockefeller Strong Among Negroes in 6 Big Cities," *NYT*, July 18, 1968; "Negro Publishers Hear Rockefeller," *NYT*, June 24, 1968; Press release, Rockefeller for President, April 11, 1968, Folder: Rockefeller for President: J. Irwin Miller, Box 110, Morton Collection; "Rockefeller Given Support by Artists and Entertainers," *NYT*, July 17, 1968; "Mules of the Poor Protest Elephant," *Daily Iowan*, August 7, 1968; Richard Nathan to Alton Marshall, July 2, 1968, Folder 63, Box 9, Record Group 4, Series G, DNA, NARPP.

20. Earl Mazo and Stephen Hess, *Nixon: A Political Portrait* (New York: Harper and Row, 1968), 316; Timothy Thurber, "Goldwaterism Triumphant? Race and the Republican Party, 1965–1968," *Journal of the Historical Society* 7, 3 (September 2007): 371; Nicol C. Rae, *The Decline and Fall of the Liberal Republicans: From 1952 to the Present* (New York: Oxford University Press, 1989), 120–21.

21. Speech delivered by Richard Nixon in Boston, February 15, 1968, Folder: Nixon, Richard M., 1968 (1), Box 14, Special Names Series, DDEPPP; Jules Witcover, *The Resurrection of Richard Nixon* (New York: Putnam's, 1970), 129–30.

22. Jeremy Mayer, "Reagan and Race: Prophet of Color Blindness, Baiter of the Backlash," in Kyle Longley et al., *Deconstructing Reagan: Conservative Mythology and America's Fortieth President* (Armonk, N.Y.: M.E. Sharpe, 2007), 76; Thurber, 371–73; Witcover, 343–44.

23. Hanes Walton, Jr., and Robert C. Smith, *American Politics and the African American Quest for Universal Freedom*, 2nd ed. (New York: Longman, 2003), 142; "Nixon Seeks No Wallace Rapprochement," *Toledo Blade*, June 14, 1968; "Dixie Influence Big Factor in Miami," *Washington Afro-American*, August 13, 1968; "Spotlight on Political Conventions," *The Crisis*, October 1968, 277; Justine Priestly, *By Gertrude Wilson: Dispatches of the 1960s, From a White Writer in a Black World* (Edgartown, Mass.: Vineyard Stories, 2005), 180–82; Garry Wills, *Nixon Agonistes: The Crisis of a Self-Made Man* (Boston: Houghton Mifflin, 1970), 296.

24. Edward Carmines and James Stimson, *Issue Evolution: Race and the Transformation of American Politics* (Princeton, N.J.: Princeton University Press, 1989), 53; "The Public Records of Richard M. Nixon and Spiro T. Agnew," *Congressional Quarterly Weekly Report*, August 16, 1968, 2169–71.

25. "Jackie Robinson Rejects Support for Nixon-Agnew," *Toledo Blade*, August 12, 1968; John Henry Cutler, *Ed Brooke: Biography of a Senator* (Indianapolis: Bobbs-Merrill, 1972), 312; "G.O.P. Distresses Negro Delegates," *NYT*, August 11, 1968; "Hard Job Selling Nixon to Negro Voters," *Toledo Blade*, August 12, 1968; "English Authors Note GOP 'Southern Strategy,'" *Jet*, July 16, 1970, 45.

26. Matthew Rees, *From the Deck to the Sea: Blacks and the Republican Party* (Wakefield, N.H.: Longwood Academic, 1991), 270; "Vote Results," *Jet*, November 21, 1968, 9; Clarence Townes, "1968 Minorities Division Report," February 1966 [*sic* 1968], Townes Papers; Clarence Townes to James Howard, October 4, 1968, and Clarence Townes to Leonard Garment, October 21, 1968, Folder: Nixon/Agnew Presidential Campaign, 1968. Brooke Participation Oct. 1968 and undated, Box 640, Brooke Papers; "Down the Big Road," *Call and Post* (Cleveland), November 2, 1968; Allen Jones, "Equal Rights to All, Special Privileges to None: The Black Press in Iowa, 1882–1985," in Henry Lewis Suggs, ed., *The Black Press in the Middle West, 1865–1985* (Westport, Conn.: Greenwood, 1996), 96; "Ticker Tape USA," *Jet*, August 22, 1968, 14; "The Negro—Tough Challenge to the GOP," *Washington Star*, August 11, 1968.

27. Hubert Humphrey to Asa Spaulding, May 31, 1968, Folder: Asa Spaulding Subgroup Correspondence. General Correspondence: Hubert Humphrey, Box AC–15, Spaulding Papers; "Jackie Robinson Rejects Support for Nixon-Agnew," *Toledo Blade*, August 12, 1968; Jackie

Robinson, *I Never Had It Made* (New York: HarperCollins, 1995), 207–8; Dorsey Miller, interview by author, October 27, 2012, in possession of author; "Billy Rowe's Note Book," *Chicago Metro News*, April 17, 1976.

28. Garth Pauley, *The Modern Presidency and Civil Rights: Rhetoric on Race from Roosevelt to Nixon* (College Station: Texas A&M University Press, 2001), 201–2; Lewis Killian, *White Southerners* (Amherst: University of Massachusetts Press, 1985), 54; Kevin Kruse, *White Flight: Atlanta and the Making of Modern Conservatism* (Princeton, N.J.: Princeton University Press, 2005), 6; Tali Mendelberg, *The Race Card: Campaign Strategy, Implicit Messages, and the Norm of Equality* (Princeton, N.J.: Princeton University Press, 2001), 97; Kenneth O'Reilly, *Nixon's Piano: Presidents and Racial Politics from Washington to Clinton* (New York: Free Press, 1995), 327; Ian Haney Lopez, *Dog Whistle Politics: How Coded Racial Appeals Have Reinvented Racism and Wrecked the Middle Class* (New York: Oxford University Press, 2013), 24.

29. Matthew Lassiter, *The Silent Majority: Suburban Politics in the Sunbelt South* (Princeton, N.J.: Princeton University Press, 2006), 1–9; Kruse, 253.

30. "Nixon Gives Views on Aid to Negroes and the Poor," *NYT*, December 20, 1967; Thurber, 372; Terry H. Anderson, *The Pursuit of Fairness: A History of Affirmative Action* (New York: Oxford University Press, 2004), 119.

31. Thomas Sugrue, *Sweet Land of Liberty: The Forgotten Struggle for Civil Rights in the North* (New York: Random House, 2008), 442; Gerald and Deborah Strober, *Nixon: An Oral History of His Presidency* (New York: HarperCollins, 1994), 112; Thurber, 370; Speech delivered by Richard Nixon in Boston, February 15, 1968, Folder: Nixon, Richard M., 1968 (1), Box 14, DDEPPP; Marable, *Race, Reform, and Rebellion*, 95–96; "Black Power and Private Enterprise," *Wall Street Journal*, May 21, 1968; George H. Nash, *The Conservative Intellectual Movement in America Since 1945* (New York: Basic, 1976), 282.

32. Nixon for President Committee, "'Bridges to Human Dignity': An Address by Richard M. Nixon on the CBS Radio Network," April 25, 1968, Folder: Nixon, Richard M., 1968 (1), Box 14, Special Names Series, DDEPPP; Speech delivered by Richard Nixon, "Bridges to Human Dignity: II," on NBC Radio, May 2, 1968, Folder: Civil Rights, Box 22, Molitor Papers; Rees, 268.

33. Stephanie Dyer, "Progress Plaza: Leon Sullivan, Zion Investment Associates, and Black Power in a Philadelphia Shopping Center," in Ezra, 147; Wright, "The Black Cabinet," 272; "Nixon Gets First Big Race Turnout," *Oakland Post*, October 23, 1968.

34. Theodore Brown to Clarence Townes, September 24, 1968, and Clarence Townes to Leonard Garment, October 21, 1968, Folder: Nixon/Agnew Presidential Campaign, 1968. Brooke Participation Oct. 1968 and undated, Box 640, Brooke Papers; "This Time, Vote Like Homer Pitts' Whole World Depended on It," *Jet*, November 7, 1968.

35. John McClaughry to John Conyers, October 29, 1968, Folder 6199, McKissick Papers; Congressional Quarterly Service, 62.

36. Robert Weems with Lewis A. Randolph, *Business in Black and White: American Presidents and Black Entrepreneurs in the Twentieth Century* (New York: New York University Press, 2009), 119; "Blacks Have Mixed Reaction to Nixon," *New York Amsterdam News*, November 16, 1968; Robert L. Allen, *A Guide to Black Power in America: An Historical Analysis* (London: Gollancz, 1970), 194.

37. Hugh Davis Graham, *Civil Rights and the Presidency: Race and Gender in American Politics, 1960–1972* (New York: Oxford University Press, 1992), 135; Kruse, 253; Rae, 196–97; "Reveal Big Black Vote for President-Elect," *Jet*, November 21, 1968, 10; Edward Ashbee, "The Republican Party and the African-American Vote Since 1964," in Peter Eisenstadt, ed., *Black*

Conservatism: Essays in Intellectual and Political History (New York: Garland, 1999), 235; Ripon Society, *Lessons of Victory* (New York: Dial, 1969), 176.

38. Wright, "The Black Cabinet," 247–49; "Changing of the Guard," *Ebony*, March 1969, 29–32.

39. Herbert Parmet, *Richard Nixon and His America* (Boston: Little, Brown, 1990), 600; Graham, 137; Patrick Buchanan, *The Greatest Comeback: How Richard Nixon Rose from Defeat to Create the New Majority* (New York: Crown Forum, 2014), 39; Daniel Patrick Moynihan to Richard Nixon, January 16, 1970, Folder: Civil Rights History, Box 1, WHCF, Staff Member and Office Files, Patterson Files; Melvin Small, *The Presidency of Richard Nixon* (Lawrence: University Press of Kansas, 1999), 162; Marable, *Race, Reform, and Rebellion*, 110.

40. Allen Matusow, *The Unraveling of America: A History of Liberalism in the 1960s* (New York: Harper and Row, 1984), 233–34; Kotlowski, 44–45, 55–61; Robert Mason, *Richard Nixon and the Quest for a New Majority* (Chapel Hill: University of North Carolina Press, 2004), 149.

41. "Changes in Nixon's Political Tactics?," *U.S. News and World Report*, August 3, 1970; A. James Reichley, *Conservatives in an Age of Change: The Nixon and Ford Administration* (Washington, D.C.: Brookings Institution, 1981), 184, 189; Small, 162, 164; Monroe Lee Billington, *The Political South in the Twentieth Century* (New York: Scribner's, 1975), 150–51; John David Skrentny, *The Ironies of Affirmative Action: Politics, Culture, and Justice in America* (Chicago: University of Chicago Press, 1996), 189–90; Kevin Yuill, *Richard Nixon and the Rise of Affirmative Action: The Pursuit of Racial Equality in an Era of Limits* (Lanham, Md.: Rowman and Littlefield, 2006), 117.

42. Kevin J. McMahon, *Nixon's Court: His Challenge to Judicial Liberalism and Its Political Consequences* (Chicago: University of Chicago Press, 2011), 114, 122–23, 127, 136; Theodore Cross, *The Black Power Imperative: Racial Inequality and the Politics of Nonviolence* (New York: Faulkner, 1984), 309; "The Carswell Defeat," *The Crisis*, April 1970, 148; "New Look at an Old Memo Casts More Doubt on Rehnquist," *NYT*, March 19, 2012.

43. "Minorities Get Business Plan," *St. Petersburg Times*, March 6, 1969; "Nixon Sets Up Agency to Help Blacks Own, Manage Businesses," *Jet*, March 20, 1969, 21; Maurice Stans, "A Balance Sheet," in Kenneth Thompson, ed., *The Nixon Presidency: Twenty-Two Intimate Perspectives of Richard M. Nixon* (Lanham, Md.: University Press of America, 1987), 38; Maurice Stans, "A Piece of the Action: Report to the President on Minority Business Enterprise," June 30, 1970, Folder: Commerce Dept. Minority Business Enterprise 1969–1971, Box 130, John Sherman Cooper Collection; Richard Nixon, *The Memoirs of Richard Nixon* (New York: Grosset and Dunlap), 438; Joan Hoff, *Nixon Reconsidered* (New York: BasicBooks, 1994), 97; Sean Dennis Cashman, *African-Americans and the Quest for Civil Rights, 1900–1990* (New York: New York University Press, 1991), 229.

44. John David Skrentny, *The Minority Rights Revolution* (Cambridge, Mass.: Belknap Press of Harvard University Press, 2002), 148; Yuill, 163; "Federal Contracts Go to Negro Firms," *Atlanta Daily World*, December 30, 1971; Wright, "The Black Cabinet," 261; Robert Brown, "Nixon," *American Visions* 10, 1 (February/March 1995): 45; Maurice Stans, "A Piece of the Action," June 30, 1970, Folder: Commerce Dept. Minority Business Enterprise 1969–1971, Box 130, Cooper Collection; Cross, 171; Kotlowski, 145.

45. "Nixon Blasted by Rights Leader," *Philadelphia Tribune*, July 20, 1968; Yuill, 117; Wright, "The Black Cabinet," 243, 271n18; Cutler, 7, 315.

46. Harry Dent, *The Prodigal South Returns to Power* (New York: John Wiley and Sons, 1978), 176; Robert C. Smith, *We Have No Leaders: African Americans in the Post-Civil Rights Era*

(Albany: State University of New York Press, 1996), 140; Robert Turner, *Up to the Front of the Line: Blacks in the American Political System* (Port Washington, N.Y.: Kennikat Press, 1975), 127; "Jewel Lafontant-Mankarious," *NYT*, June 3, 1997; Cross, 345; Benjamin Hooks with Jerry Guess, *The March for Civil Rights: The Benjamin Hooks Story* (Chicago: American Bar Association, 2003), 95.

47. "Robert Brown, Man in the News," *Sacramento Observer*, January 9, 1969; Floyd McKissick to Jack Ford, August 1, 1972, Folder 7732, McKissick Papers; Clarence Townes, interview by author, October 18, 2011, in possession of author; Kotlowski, 141.

48. Robert Brown to John Ehrlichman and Leonard Garment, July 2, 1970, Folder: Black College Presidents and Black Colleges [2 of 3], Box 49, WHCF, Staff Member and Office Files, Garment Files; Bradley Patterson to Leonard Garment, January 30, 1973, Folder: Black Colleges/University Associates [CFOA 1373], Box 14, Patterson Files; Wright, "The Black Cabinet," 259–60; Kotlowski, 152–55.

49. "Romney Appoints 2 Negroes to Fill Major Positions," *NYT*, January 26, 1969; "Ticker Tape USA," *Jet*, July 31, 1969, 12; "Blacks Entitled to Role in Construction," *Bay State Banner*, July 8, 1971; "Black Policy-Makers," *Life*, July 24, 1970, 61; "Homecoming for Sam Jackson," *Ebony*, July 1971, 61–68; Speech delivered by Samuel C. Jackson in St. Louis, August 10, 1970, in *Vital Speeches of the Day* 36, 23 (September 15, 1970): 708.

50. James Farmer, *Lay Bare the Heart: An Autobiography of the Civil Rights Movement* (New York: Arbor House, 1985), 318–33.

51. "Arthur Fletcher, 'The Father of Affirmative Action,' Dies at 80," *Jet*, August 1, 2005, 18; Graham, 161; "Contract Compliance," *Sacramento Observer*, November 25, 1971; "In the Nation's Press," *The Crisis*, February 1970, 67; Thomas Sugrue, "Affirmative Action from Below: Civil Rights, the Building Trades, and the Politics of Racial Equality in the Urban North, 1945–1969," *Journal of American History* 91, 1 (June 2004): 172; Kotlowski, 103–4; "Labor," *Time*, August 17, 1970; Fletcher, 120; "Art Fletcher," *Sepia*, 61; Anderson, 116.

52. Smith, *We Have No Leaders*, 145–46; Kotlowski, 106–7, 113; Skrentny, *The Ironies of Affirmative Action*, 177, 194, 198.

53. Rustin, 251; "Labor and Blacks Part Company," *NYT*, December 28, 1969; Edward W. Brooke, "Negroes and the Open Society," *Congressional Record* 12, 13 (August 2, 1966): 17867.

54. "Negro Aides Find Gain Under Nixon," *NYT*, September 29, 1969; "The Blacks Who Work for Nixon," *NYT*, November 29, 1970; "Robert Brown, Man in the News," *Sacramento Observer*, January 9, 1969; "The 100 Most Influential Black Americans," *Ebony*, April 1971, 34–36.

55. "U.S. to Start Plan Giving Minorities Jobs in Building," *NYT*, September 24, 1969.

Chapter 8. Not a Silent Minority: Black Republicans in the 1970s

1. "The Nixon Inauguration," *Ebony*, March 1973, 156–58.

2. "Agnew Resigns," *Jet*, October 25, 1973, 7; "Ticker Tape U.S.A.," *Jet*, March 27, 1969, 12; Speech delivered by Clarence Townes at Southern State Republican Campaign Management Seminar, April 25, 1969, Townes Papers; Minorities Division, Republican National Committee, *Election Analysis: 1968 and the Black American Voter* (Washington, D.C.: Republican National Committee, 1969), 53; "The Blacks Who Work for Nixon," *NYT*, November 29, 1970.

3. "Agnew Resigns," 7; Geoffrey Kabaservice, *Rule and Ruin: The Downfall of Moderation and the Destruction of the Republican Party* (New York: Oxford University Press, 2012), 283, 295, 323; "GOP Launches Project to Study Ghetto Problems," *Times-News* (Hendersonville, N.C.), June 30, 1969.

4. "Black GOP Forming on Peninsula," *San Mateo Times*, February 12, 1969; Clarence Townes to Leonard Garment, October 21, 1968, Folder: Nixon/Agnew Presidential Campaign, 1968. Brooke Participation Oct. 1968 and undated, Box 640, Brooke Papers; "GOP Opens Voter Drive in Harlem," *New Directions '68*, 1:3, Folder: Civil Rights. Publications, Box 12, Campaign 1968 Collection, Research Files (PPS 500, 501); Lee Bostic to "Fellow Republicans," n.d., and "By-Laws of the New York State Conference of Black Republicans," May 8, 1976, Folder 12, DuBard Papers; "Statement by Black Elected Republican Officials, Washington, D.C.," March 20, 1970 and John W. Kellogg to Rogers Morton, March 21, 1970, Folder: Black Elected Republicans 1970, Box I: 107, LCCRR.

5. Leah Wright Riguer, *The Loneliness of the Black Republican: Pragmatic Politics and the Pursuit of Power* (Princeton, N.J.: Princeton University Press, 2015), 93; "Negroes Appeal to Nixon to Act," *NYT*, November 7, 1968; "Minorities Seek Political Gains," *NYT*, July 3, 1968; Curtis T. Perkins to The Committee for the Re-Election of the President, October 27, 1972, Folder: Blacks III (3 of 20), Box 23, Malek Papers, Series II; "Lodge Terms Comic Books Public Insult," *Hartford Courant*, October 29, 1950; "The Black Boycott," *The Crisis*, May 1966, 254; "Open Meeting: Afro-American Republicans," n.d., Townes Papers; Congressional Quarterly Service, *The Presidential Nominating Conventions 1968* (Washington, D.C.: Congressional Quarterly Service, 1968), 23, 33.

6. Curtis T. Perkins to Tom Evans, March 15, 1971, and Curtis Perkins, "Can Black Republicans Work Together for National & Local Respect by the Republican Party," n.d., both in Folder: Black Republican Project—Curtis T. Perkins, Box 37, Hartmann Papers; Curtis T. Perkins, "Some Urgent Goals for All Black Republicans-Nationwide," n.d., Folder: Black Vote in 1972—General (1), Box 6, Scott Papers; "Quo Vadis Mr. President?," *Afro-American Voter*, May-June 1969, Folder: Civil Rights/Minorities, Box 177, Morton Papers; "Join Your National Council Afro-American Republicans, Inc.," Folder: Blacks III (6 of 20), Box 24, Malek Papers, Series II.

7. "BSMC Swells to 6,336 Members," *The Black National Silent Majority Committee Newsletter*, January 1971, Folder: Civil Rights/Minorities. Althouse-Lund, Box 219, Morton Papers; "Today in Washington," *Sumter Daily Item*, July 6, 1970; "'Silent Majority' of Blacks Formed," *NYT*, July 12, 1970.

8. "Black Silent Majority Plans Crusade" *Evening Star* (Washington, D.C.), May 13, 1971; "'Silent Majority' of Blacks Formed," *NYT*, July 12, 1970; Black Silent Majority Committee, "What is the Black Silent Majority?," Folder: National Black Silent Majority Committee, Box 9, WHCF, Staff Member and Office Files, Finch Files ; "'Silent Majority' Promotes Nixon," *Sacramento Observer*, August 12, 1971; Richard Nixon to Clay Claiborne, October 7, 1970, Folder: Civil Rights/Minorities, Althouse-Lund, Box 219, Morton Papers; Bob Wilson to Edward Brooke, February 25, 1972, Folder: Civil Rights. Nixon Administration, 1968–72, Box 422, Brooke Papers; Clay Claiborne to Ollie Atkins, October 16, 1972, Folder: Blacks III (4 of 20), Box 23, Malek Papers, Series II.

9. "Black Unit Asks 'Common Sense,'" *Palm Beach Post*, October 11, 1970; "Black Silent Majority Meet," *Sacramento Observer*, October 22, 1970; Black Silent Majority Committee, "What Is the Black Silent Majority?," n.d., and Clay Claiborne to "Fellow American," n.d., Folder: National Black Silent Majority Committee, Box 9, Finch Files; Black Silent Majority Committee, "'Right On'...to What? Handbook for Blacks on Being a Patriotic American," n.d. , Folder: Black Silent Majority Committee, Box 5, Scott Papers.

10. Jonathan Bean, *Big Government and Affirmative Action: The Scandalous History of the*

Small Business Administration (Lexington: University Press of Kentucky, 2001), 61–62; Berkeley Burrell, interview by Robert Wright, August 6, 1970, MSRC; "The National Business League," *Black Enterprise*, June 1972, 38, 41; Paul Jones to Curt Herge, July 10, 1972, Folder: Blacks II (1 of 14), Box 23, Malek Papers, Series II; "Black Publishers to Honor Berkeley Burrell at S.F. Confab," *Sun Reporter* (San Francisco), June 7, 1975.

    11. Floyd B. McKissick, "A Proposal for Planning Funds to Develop Soul City," August 24, 1969, Townes Papers; William L. Van Deburg, *New Day in Babylon: The Black Power Movement and American Culture, 1965–1975* (Chicago: University of Chicago Press, 1992), 135; Devin Fergus, *Liberalism, Black Power, and the Making of American Politics, 1965–1980* (Athens: University of Georgia Press, 2009), 197; Christopher Strain, "Soul City, North Carolina and the Business of Black Power," in Michael Ezra, ed., *The Economic Civil Rights Movement: African Americans and the Struggle for Economic Power* (New York: Routledge, 2013), 195.

    12. "A Proposal for Planning Funds to Develop Soul City," Townes Papers; Fergus, *Liberalism, Black Power, and the Making of American Politics*, 197, 228; Floyd McKissick, "Black Business Development with Social Commitment to Black Communities," in John H. Bracey, Jr., August Meier, and Elliot Rudwick, eds., *Black Nationalism in America* (Indianapolis: Bobbs-Merrill Co., 1970), 492–93; John Jenkins to Floyd McKissick, September 28, 1971, Folder 6129, McKissick Papers; Leonard Garment to Mel Laird, June 21, 1973, Folder: Soul City [2 of 3], Box 64, Patterson Files.

    13. Floyd B. McKissick, "Making Black Capitalism Work," in Jeffrey Elliot, ed., *Black Voices in American Politics* (New York: Harcourt Brace Jovanovich, 1986), 282; Roger Biles, "The Rise and Fall of Soul City: Planning, Politics, and Race in Recent America," *Journal of Planning History*, 4:1 (February 2005), 58, 63; "Blacks," *Newsweek*, August 14, 1972, 24; Timothy Minchin, "'A Brand New Shining City': Floyd B. McKissick, Sr., and the Struggle to Build Soul City, North Carolina," *North Carolina Historical Review* 82, 2 (April 2005), 126; Strain, 194; Speech delivered by Robert Brown in Soul City, N.C., July 21, 1972, Folder: 7/21/72—Soul City (Brown, Robert J.), Box 25, Scott Papers; "Homecoming for Sam Jackson," *Ebony*, July 1971, 66; Fergus, *Liberalism, Black Power, and the Making of American Politics*, 214; Devin Fergus, "Black Power, Soft Power: Floyd McKissick, Soul City, and the Death of Moderate Black Republicanism," *Journal of Policy History*, 22:2 (2010), 172, 180; Harold Woodard, "Floyd McKissick: Portrait of a Leader," M.A. thesis (University of North Carolina at Chapel Hill, 1981), 41.

    14. Harry Dent to Rogers Morton, April 1, 1969, Folder: WHSF, SMOF, Harry Dent: 1969 Southern GOP 2/3, Box 5, Nixon Presidential Materials Collection: White House Special Files: Contested Materials, Richard Nixon Presidential Library; Harry Dent, *The Prodigal South Returns to Power* (New York: Wiley, 1978), 177, 180–83; John Ehrlichman, *Witness to Power: The Nixon Years* (New York: Simon and Schuster, 1982), 235–36.

    15. "Blacks for Nixon Stress Equality," *Chicago Tribune*, August 23, 1972; "The Joint Center for Political Studies' Guide to Black Politics '72, Part II: The Republican Convention," August 1, 1972, Folder: Black Elected Officials, Box 14, Patterson Files; Paul Jones, "Black Convention Participation," August 8, 1972, Folder: Blacks II (3 of 14), Box 23, Malek Papers, Series II; Jackson R. Champion, *Blacks in the Republican Party? The Story of a Revolutionary, Conservative Black Republican* (Washington, D.C.: LenChamps, 1976), 25–26; "Blacks at GOP Convention Hard to Get Together for Special Caucus Sessions," *Jet*, September 7, 1972, 10; "Black Woman Is GOP Vice Chairman in Missouri," *Jet*, October 1, 1970, 7; "Sammy Davis, College President to Testify Before GOP Platform Committee," *Jet*, August 24, 1972, 7.

    16. Dent, 184; Memo, Henry Cashen II to Charles Colson, April 28, 1971, Folder: The Black

Vote [4 of 5], Box 12, Magruder Papers; "Instead of Fighting for a Place on It, Sammy Davis, Jr., Has Bought the Bus," *NYT*, October 15, 1972; Jason Killian Meath, *Hollywood on the Potomac* (Charleston, S.C.: Arcadia, 2009), 52; Alan Schroeder, *Celebrity-in-Chief: How Show Business Took Over the White House* (Boulder, Colo.: Westview Press, 2004), 101.

17. "Jubilant G.O.P. Delegates Show Mood of Confidence," *NYT*, August 22, 1972; Gary Fishgall, *Gonna Do Great Things: The Life of Sammy Davis, Jr.* (New York: Scribner, 2003), 281–82.

18. "GOP Blacks Not Typical of All Blacks," *Long Island Press*, August 24, 1972; "Sammy Davis, College President to Testify before GOP Platform Committee," 6; "Statement of the Council of Black Appointees Before the Platform Committee of the Republican Party," August 16, 1972, Folder 7711, McKissick Papers; Clipping, "Roy Innis Calls for a Two-Party System," n.d., Folder 7671, McKissick Papers; Henry Lucas, Wendell Handy, and James Woods to John Mitchell, June 30, 1972, Folder: Citizens—Black II (1 of 7), Box 25, Malek Papers, Series II; "Blacks Decry Role in Republican Party Activities," *Chicago Tribune*, August 22, 1972; "Blacks at GOP Convention Hard to Get Together for Special Caucus Sessions," 7–8.

19. "Black Republican Group to Fight for Convention Representation," *Chicago South Suburban News*, August 19, 1972; National Council of Afro-American Republicans Inc., "National Black Republicans Convocation '72," June 9–10, 1972, Folder: Blacks III (6 of 20), Box 24, Malek Papers, Series II; Clipping, "Blames Top Republicans for Lack of Black Participation," September 3–5, 1972, Folder: Blacks III (6 of 20), Box 24, Malek Papers, Series II; Matthew Rees, *From the Deck to the Sea: Blacks and the Republican Party* (Wakefield, N.H.: Longwood Academic, 1991), 295.

20. Norman Mailer, *St. George and the Godfather* (New York: Signet Special, 1972), 152, 210; Pat Buchanan to Richard Nixon, August 2, 1972, Folder: WHSF: SMOF: H.R. Haldeman [Campaign Strategy Memos from Buchanan 2 of 2], Box 21, Nixon Presidential Materials Collection: White House Special Files: Contested Materials; "Rules Panel Approves '76 Delegate Plan Retaining Small-State Advantage Intact," *NYT*, August 22, 1972; Warren E. Miller and M. Kent Jennings, *Parties in Transition: A Longitudinal Study of Party Elites and Party Supporters* (New York: Russell Sage, 1986), 68; "Blacks at GOP Convention Hard to Get Together for Special Caucus Sessions," 9–10; "Blacks Decry Role in Republican Party Activities," *Chicago Tribune*, August 22, 1972.

21. "Criticism Mounts Over Entertainers for Richard Nixon," *Jet*, November 2, 1972, 6; Henry Cashen II to Charles Colson, April 28, 1971, Folder: The Black Vote [4 of 5], Box 12, Magruder Papers; "F. McKissick Lauds Nixon," *Tri-State Defender*, June 24, 1972; Dean Kotlowski, *Nixon's Civil Rights: Politics, Principle, and Policy* (Cambridge, Mass.: Harvard University Press, 2001), 184; Stanley Scott, "Memorandum for the President's File," August 10, 1972, Folder: Presidential Meeting, 1971–72, Box 18, Scott Papers; "Brown Urges Nixon to Help Blacks and Endorses President," *Jet*, November 2, 1972, 9.

22. Cynthia Griggs Fleming, *Yes We Did? From King's Dream to Obama's Promise* (Lexington: University Press of Kentucky, 2009), 121; Paul Jones to Fred Malek and Frank Herringer, September 22, 1972, Folder: Blacks III (12 of 20), Box 24, Malek Papers, Series II; Frank Herringer to Paul Jones, October 4, 1972, Folder: Blacks III (9 of 20), Box 24, Malek Papers, Series II; "Evers Predicts Nixon Will Get Large Black Vote," *Washington Post*, September 28, 1972; "Robinson Jumps Parties," *Bay State Banner*, September 14, 1972; "Blacks Here Take a Wary Look at the Politicians," *Capital Times* (Madison, Wis.), July 27, 1972; "Mrs. Maier's Role Disturbs Knowles," *Milwaukee Sentinel*, August 22, 1972; "New Republican Pitts Gets Job of Wooing Angry Blacks," *Milwaukee Journal*, August 21, 1972.

23. "Black Caucus, Republicans Plan $100-A-Plate Dinners," *Jet*, May 11, 1972, 9; "Nixon Begins Drive to Woo Black Voters," *Jet*, August 24, 1972, 25; Frank Carpenter, "Minutes of Black Surrogate's Briefing Meetings," September 7, 1972, Folder 7553, McKissick Papers; Fergus, "Black Power, Soft Power," 158; "Statement–F. B. McKissick," September 1, 1972, Folder 7638, McKissick Papers; "McKissick Is Succeeding Although 'Not Supposed To,'" *NYT*, December 22, 1974; "Black Parleys in Capital Hail Nixon and Thurmond," *NYT*, June 12, 1972; "Blacks Meet in D.C.," *Cincinnati Herald*, June 24, 1972; "F. McKissick Lauds Nixon," *Tri-State Defender*, June 24, 1972; Dent, 184; "Some Nixon Jazz," *Atlanta Daily World*, June 2, 1972; "McKissick: It's Time to Give Up the Sugar Tit," *Black Advocate*, August 1972, Folder: Blacks II (14 of 14), Box 23, Malek Papers, Series II.

24. George Berkner, *Black Capitalism and the Urban Negro* (Tempe: Arizona State University, 1970); Abraham Venable, *Building Black Business: An Analysis and a Plan* (New York: Earl G. Graves Publishing Co., 1972); Kotlowski, 151; "Statement – F. B. McKissick" September 1, 1972, Folder 7638, McKissick Papers; "Blacks Getting Serious About 1972 Election," *Rome News-Tribune*, October 26, 1972; "Jones: Nixon's Work for Blacks Outstanding, But Overlooked," *The Black Advance*, August 1972, Folder: Blacks II (14 of 14), Box 23, Malek Papers, Series II; "Nixon Begins Drive to Woo Black Voters," 23; "Stanley S. Scott Dies in New Orleans," *Washington Informer*, April 22, 1992; Stan Scott to Herb Klein and Ken Clawson, November 10 1972, Folder: Black Vote in 1972–General (5), Box 6, Scott Papers.

25. Thomas Sugrue, *Sweet Land of Liberty: The Forgotten Struggle for Civil Rights in the North* (New York: Random House, 2008), 499; "Gary's Political Review: Souvenir Edition, Welcome First National Black Caucus," March 12, 1972, Folder: Newspaper Black National Political Convention, 1972, Box 24, City of Gary Collection; "The National Black Political Agenda," April 24, 1972, Folder 160, Box 10a, City of Gary Collection; Robert C. Smith, *We Have No Leaders: African Americans in the Post-Civil Rights Era* (Albany: State University of New York Press, 1996), 303n81; Komozi Woodard, *A Nation Within a Nation: Amiri Baraka (LeRoi Jones) and Black Power Politics* (Chapel Hill: University of North Carolina Press, 1999), 205–6; John D. Ehrlichman to Paul Jones, April 13, 1972, Folder: Citizens–Blacks II (6 of 7), Box 26, Malek Papers, Series II; "Republican Group Issues Demands for Greater Role," *Washington Afro-American*, August 22, 1972; Robert Brown to John Ehrlichman, July 17, 1972, Folder: Blacks II (2 of 14), Box 23, Malek Papers, Series II.

26. Paul Jones to Fred Malek and Frank Herringer, September 13, 1972, Folder: Blacks III (16 of 20), Box 24, Malek Papers, Series II; "Jesse Jackson," *NYT*, July 9, 1972; Fergus, "Black Power, Soft Power," 157; Herbert Parmet, *Richard Nixon and His America* (Boston: Little, Brown, 1990), 601; Richard Whalen, *Taking Sides: A Personal View of America from Kennedy to Nixon to Kennedy* (Boston: Houghton Mifflin, 1974), 176; "Edward Brooke Addresses Democratic Black Caucus," *Bay State Banner*, October 18, 1973; Jesse Jackson, letter to the editor, *NYT*, November 6, 1972; "Brooke Cites Economics as Basis to Woo Blacks," *Jet*, March 16, 1978, 6.

27. "Blacks for Nixon Queried," *Jet*, July 20, 1972, 4; Schroeder, 102; Timothy Thurber, *Race and Republicans: The GOP's Frayed Relationship with African Americans, 1945–1974* (Lawrence: University Press of Kansas, 2013), 357; Paul Jones to Fred Malek, July 18, 1972, Folder: Blacks II (1 of 14), Box 23, Malek Papers, Series II; Frank Carpenter, "Minutes of Black Surrogate's Briefing Meetings," September 7, 1972, Folder 7553, McKissick Papers.

28. "Blacks for Nixon Sharply Rebuked," *NYT*, August 3, 1972; Speech delivered by Robert Brown in Soul City, N.C., July 21, 1972, Folder: 7/21/72—Soul City (Brown, Robert J.), Box 25, Scott Papers; "Homecoming for Sam Jackson," 66; Charles Evers with Andrew Szanton, *Have No*

Fear: The Charles Evers Story (New York: Wiley, 1997), 251; Fleming, 121; Robert J. Norrell, *Reaping the Whirlwind: The Civil Rights Movement in Tuskegee* (Chapel Hill: University of North Carolina Press, 1998), 205–6.

29. Fred Malek to John Mitchell, June 26, 1972, Folder: Blacks II (1 of 14), Box 23, Malek Papers, Series II; Paul Jones to Fred Malek, April 18, 1972, Folder: Citizens—Blacks II (6 of 7), Box 26, Malek Papers, Series II; "Aid to Minority Business a Lever for Nixon in '72," *NYT*, November 18, 1973.

30. Nathan Wright, Jr., "The Social Arena of Black Political Action," in Nathan Wright, Jr., ed., *What Black Politicians Are Saying* (New York: Hawthorn, 1972), 202; "Young Negroes Say Nixon is 'The Man' for Them," *Atlanta Daily World*, October 10, 1972.

31. "Hopes Flimsy for Dakotan," *Lawrence Journal-World*, October 28, 1972; "Nixon and McGovern Battle for Black Votes," *Jet*, November 2, 1972, 25; Nick Aaron Ford, *Black Studies: Threat-or-Challenge* (Port Washington, N.Y.: Kennikat, 1973), 71; "Dr. Charles Hurst," *Ebony*, March 1970, 34–38; "Black Educator Says He'll Vote for Nixon," *Free Lance-Star* (Fredericksburg, Va.), September 20, 1972; "Blacks at GOP Convention Hard to Get Together for Special Caucus Sessions," 8.

32. Kotlowski, 184; Fred Malek to John Mitchell, April 24, 1972, Folder: Citizens–Blacks II (6 of 7), Box 26, Malek Papers, Series II; Curtis T. Perkins to The Committee for the Re-Election of the President, October 27, 1972, Folder: Blacks III (3 of 20), Box 23, Malek Papers, Series II; Frank Herringer to Robert Brown, September 14, 1972, Folder: Blacks II (1 of 14), Box 23, Malek Papers, Series II; Bob Brown to Fred Malek, July 19, 1972, Folder: Blacks II (3 of 14), Box 23, Malek Papers, Series II; Paul Jones to Fred Malek, September 5, 1972, Folder: Citizens–Blacks I (2 of 2), Box 25, Malek Papers, Series II.

33. Kabaservice, 296; Thomas Edsall with Mary Edsall, *Chain Reaction: The Impact of Race, Rights, and Taxes on American Politics* (New York: Norton, 1991), 97; Robert Mason, *Richard Nixon and the Quest for a New Majority* (Chapel Hill: University of North Carolina Press, 2004), 181.

34. George H. Gallup, *The Gallup Poll: Public Opinion 1935–1971*, vol. 3 (New York: Random House, 1972), 2243, 2323; C. Vann Woodward, *The Strange Career of Jim Crow*, 3rd rev. ed. (New York: Oxford University Press, 2002), 214; Edward W. Brooke, *Bridging the Divide: My Life* (New Brunswick, N.J.: Rutgers University Press, 2007), 200; "Today in Washington," *Sumter Daily Item*, July 6, 1970; "A True Alternative to Segregation—A Proposal for Community School Districts," February 1970, Folder: Desegregation–Innis Plan [CFOA 5019], Box 76, WHCF, Staff Member and Office Files, Garment Files; Wright, 204; McKissick, interview by Bass and Devries, December 6, 1973.

35. Floyd McKissick to Robert Brown, November 29, 1972, Folder 7602, McKissick Papers; "The National Committee for a Two-Party System, Inc.: A Third Force," Folder: Blacks III (1 of 20), Box 23, Malek Papers, Series II; "McKissick Forms New Group to Help the Republican Party," *NYT*, October 15, 1972; Johnny Ford to "Concerned Citizen," n.d., Folder 7628, McKissick Papers; Floyd McKissick to George Bush, May 22, 1973, Folder: Soul City [2 of 3], Box 64, Patterson Files; "Minutes of the Meeting of The National Committee for a Two Party System," May 12, 1973, Folder 7635, McKissick Papers.

36. "The National Committee for a Two-Party System, Inc. Board of Directors," n.d., Folder 7599, McKissick Papers; Speech delivered by Kwame McDonald at Shaw University, November 16, 1972, Folder 7638, McKissick Papers; "What the National Committee for a Two-Party System, Inc., Does Not Believe," May 16, 1973, Folder: Soul City [2 of 3], Box 64, Patterson Files; "McKissick Tells Blacks Forget OEO Dismantling," *Jet*, May 31, 1973, 5.

37. "Conference Notes for Meeting with Mr. George Bush," March 30, 1973, Folder 7703, McKissick Papers; George Bush to Floyd McKissick, April 12, 1973, Folder 7703, McKissick Papers; Champion, 26–27.

38. "Cummings COPs Black Republican Chair Nod," *Jet*, September 2, 1976, 10–11; "Washington Notebook," *Ebony*, January 1977, 26; "Blacks and the Grand Old Party," *Black Enterprise*, August 1978, 19; Karen Hawkins, " 'From a Militant Civil Rights Activist to Another Stand Altogether': James H. Meredith's Embrace of Modern Conservatism, 1968–1992," conference paper presented at the New Perspectives in African American History and Culture Conference at the University of North Carolina at Chapel Hill, February 18, 2011; James Cummings, Jr., to "State Chairman," April 19, 1977, Folder: N.B.R.C. 1976-'77, Box 38, Republican Party (Michigan State Central Committee).

39. Curtis T. Perkins, "Blacks and the Republican Party," June 3, 1974, Folder: National Black Republican Council, Box 118, Gerald R. Ford Vice Presidential Papers; Rees, 309; "Black G.O.P. Seeks Congress Seats," *NYT*, November 19, 1975; Elaine Brown Jenkins, *Jumping Double Dutch: A New Agenda for Blacks and the Republican Party* (Silver Spring, Md.: Beckham House, 1996), 70; "Senator Pledges Help," *Oakland Post*, April 6, 1975; Kotlowski, 38.

40. Kenneth Blackwell was elected on a third-party ticket, but had become a fixture of the city and state's GOP establishment by the early 1980s. Eddie N. Williams, "Black Political Progress in the 1970s: The Electoral Arena," in Michael B. Preston, Lenneal J. Henderson, Jr., and Paul Puryear, eds., *The New Black Politics: The Search for Political Power* (New York: Longman, 1982), 74–75; "Yesterday in Afro-American History," *Jet*, January 8, 1970, 11; "Robert Blackwell, One of a Kind," *Michigan Chronicle*, December 31–January 6, 2008–2009; Robert Blackwell to Stanley Scott, September 5, 1974, Folder: Black Republicans (2), Box 5, Scott Papers; "Bivens First Black Mayor of Inkster in Close Vote," *Windsor Star*, May 19, 1970; "New Mayors, and Some Old Ones, to Run Big Cities," *NYT*, November 8, 1973; "The Changing Color of U.S. Politics," *Ebony*, August 1991, 30; "Cincinnati City Council Candidates," *Cincinnati Magazine*, October 1987, 125.

41. "Statement by Black Elected Republican Officials, Washington, D.C.," March 20, 1970, Folder: Black Elected Republicans 1970, Box I:107, LCCRR; Robert Turner, *Up to the Front of the Line: Blacks on the American Political System* (Port Washington, N.Y.: Kennikat Press, 1975), 129; David Wesson, "Black Republicans in Chicago," M.A. thesis (University of Maine, 1973), 10; "John Calhoun," *NYT*, May 10, 1988; "Blacks and the GOP," *Congressional Quarterly Weekly Report*, April 29, 1978, 1051; "Dr. Ethel Allen," *Philadelphia Tribune*, February 18, 2003; "I've Learned to Survive," *Philadelphia Inquirer, Today*, January 1976; "Dr. Allen's Newest Patient," *Ebony*, May 1973, 126; "Two States Choose Black Women as Secretaries," *Ebony*, October 1979, 78.

42. "Resolutions Adopted by the Sixty-Ninth Annual Convention of the NAACP at Portland, Oregon," *The Crisis*, April 1979, 3; "Dr. Ethel Allen," *Philadelphia Tribune*, February 18, 2003; "Michigan's 1st Black Mayor Robert Blackwell Succumbs," *Los Angeles Sentinel*, January 8, 2009; "The Rev. Lyman Parks," *Grand Rapids Press*, November 5, 2009.

43. Betty Friedan, *"It Changed My Life": Writings on the Women's Movement* (Cambridge, Mass.: Harvard University Press, 1998), 212; Fergus, *Liberalism, Black Power, and the Making of American Politics*, 226; Clipping, "Blames Top Republicans for Lack of Black Participation," September 3–5, 1972, Folder: Blacks III (6 of 20), Box 24, Malek Papers, Series II; Justin Coffey, "Spiro T. Agnew: The Decline of Moderates and Rise of the Republican Right," in Laura Jane Gifford and Daniel K. Williams, eds., *The Right Side of the Sixties: Reexamining Conservatism's*

Decade of Transformation (New York: Palgrave Macmillan, 2012), 243; Alec MacGillis, *The Cynic: The Political Education of Mitch McConnell* (New York: Simon and Schuster, 2014), 14; "Draft Abortion-Reform Plank Being Written at White House," *NYT*, August 6, 1972; "Dr. Allen's Newest Patient," *Ebony*, May 1973, 126.

44. Paul Frymer, *Uneasy Alliances: Race and Party Competition in America* (Princeton, N.J.: Princeton University Press, 2010), 102; Charles S. Rooks, *Southern Black Representation at National Party Conventions* (Atlanta: Voter Education Project, [1972]), 9; David Lublin, *The Republican South: Democratization and Partisan Change* (Princeton, N.J.: Princeton University Press, 2004), 43; David Goldfield, *Black, White, and Southern: Race Relations and Southern Culture, 1940 to Present* (Baton Rouge: Louisiana State University Press, 1990), 196.

45. Pearl Robinson, "Whither the Future of Blacks in the Republican Party?," *Political Science Quarterly* 97, 2 (Summer 1982), 220–21; Champion, 236; Hanes Walton, Jr., and Robert C. Smith, *American Politics and the African American Quest for Universal Freedom*, 2nd ed. (New York: Longman, 2003), 142.

46. Mary Pottillo-McCoy, *Black Picket Fences: Privilege and Peril Among the Black Middle Class* (Chicago: University of Chicago Press, 2000), 21; Burrell, interview by Wright, August 6, 1970; "What the National Committee for a Two-Party System, Inc. Does Not Believe," May 16, 1973, Folder: Soul City [2 of 3], Box 64, Patterson Files; "McKissick Tells Blacks Forget OEO Dismantling," 5.

47. Theodore Cross, *The Black Power Imperative: Racial Inequality and the Politics of Nonviolence* (New York: Faulkner, 1984), 334; Stan Scott to John D. Ehrlichman, March 2, 1973, Folder: Scott, Stanley (1), Box A152, Laird Papers; "Nixon is Expected to Appoint Blacks," *NYT*, February 25, 1973; Stan Scott to Jerry Jones, October 23, 1973, Folder: Scott, Stanley (4), Box A152, Laird Papers; Thurber, 362.

48. Kenneth O'Reilly, *Nixon's Piano: Presidents and Racial Politics from Washington to Clinton* (New York: Free Press, 1995), 333; Timothy Minchin and John Salmond, *After the Dream: Black and White Southerners Since 1965* (Lexington: University Press of Kentucky), 145; "Blacks Remember Gerald Ford Fondly," *Afro-American Red Star*, January 6, 2007; William T. Coleman, Jr., with Donald Bliss, *Counsel for the Situation: Shaping the Law to Realize America's Promise* (Washington, D.C.: Brookings Institution Press, 2010), 256; "Equality—Not Yet," *NYT*, July 13, 1981.

49. Roy Wilkins with Tom Mathews, *Standing Fast: The Autobiography of Roy Wilkins* (Cambridge, Mass.: Da Capa, 1994), 339; "Whatever Happened to Black Capitalism," *Black Enterprise*, August 1990, 164–66; Ibram H. Rogers, "Acquiring 'A Piece of the Action': The Rise and Fall of the Black Capitalism Movement," in Ezra, 140; Manning Marable, *Race, Reform, and Rebellion: The Second Reconstruction and Beyond in Black America, 1945–2006*, 3rd ed. (Jackson: University of Mississippi Press, 2007), 169.

50. See also N. D. B. Connolly, *A World More Concrete: Real Estate and the Remaking of Jim Crow South Florida* (Chicago: University of Chicago Press, 2014) for the complicity of some black businessmen and black capitalism in maintaining structural racism and failing to solve black economic woes. Sean Dennis Cashman, *African-Americans and the Quest for Civil Rights 1900–1990* (New York: New York University Press, 1991), 229; Peter Carroll, *It Seemed like Nothing Happened: The Tragedy and Promise of America in the 1970s* (New York: Holt, Rinehart, 1982), 47–48; Cross, 125, 171, 270; Robert E. Weems, Jr., "Where Did All Our Customers Go? Historic Black Owned Business and the African American Consumer Market," in Alustine Jalloh and Toyin Falola, eds., *Black Business and Economic Power* (Rochester, N.Y.: University of

Rochester Press, 2002), 417; Fergus, *Liberalism, Black Power, and the Making of American Politics*, 227; "Black Businesses Are Hard Pressed," *NYT*, February 10, 1975.

51. Jason Sokol, *There Goes My Everything: White Southerners in the Age of Civil Rights, 1945–1975* (New York: Knopf, 2006), 334; Ronald Walters, *White Nationalism, Black Interests: Conservative Public Policy and the Black Community* (Detroit: Wayne State University Press, 2003), 28; William Link, *Righteous Warrior: Jesse Helms and the Rise of Modern Conservatism* (New York: St. Martin's, 2008), 79, 259–61.

52. Fergus, *Liberalism, Black Power, and the Making of American Politics*, 215; Fergus, "Black Power, Soft Power," 165–68.

53. Fergus, "Black Power, Soft Power," 165, 175; Minchin, "A Brand New Shining City," 129, 148; Minchin and Salmond, *After the Dream*, 190.

54. Floyd McKissick to Robert Morgan, August 22, 1979, Folder 7729, McKissick Papers; "Washington Notebook," *Ebony*, January 1977, 26.

55. "Statement of Purposes of 'The National Committee for a Two-Party System, Inc.,'" September 1, 1972, Folder 7596, McKissick Papers.

Epilogue. Black Republicans in the Shadow of Reagan

1. Bernard Anderson et al., *The Fairmont Papers: Black Alternatives Conference, 1980* (San Francisco: Institute for Contemporary Studies, 1980), xi–xii; Christopher Alan Bracey, *Saviors or Sellouts: The Promise and Peril of Black Conservatism, from Booker T. Washington to Condoleezza Rice* (Boston: Beacon, 2008), xvii–xviii, 123–24.

2. Peter Eisenstadt, "Introduction," in Peter Eisenstadt, ed., *Black Conservatism: Essays in Intellectual and Political History* (New York: Garland, 1999), xxii; George Schuyler, *Black and Conservative: The Autobiography of George Schuyler* (New Rochelle, N.Y.: Arlington House, 1966), 348.

3. Paul Glover, "The Socialization, Recruitment, and Selection of Black Political Elites: A Comparative Analysis of Black Republicans and Democrats Delegates to the 1976 National Party Conventions," Ph.D. dissertation (Southern Illinois University, 1979), 74, 119, 122; Katherine Tate, *From Protest to Politics: The New Black Voters in American Elections*, enlarged ed. (Cambridge, Mass.: Harvard University Press, 1994), 63.

4. Robert C. Smith, *We Have No Leaders: African Americans in the Post-Civil Rights Era* (Albany: State University of New York Press, 1996), 122–23, 135; Lewis A. Randolph, "Black Neoconservatives in the United States: Responding with Progressive Coalitions," in James Jennings, ed., *Race and Politics: New Challenges and Responses for Black Activism* (London: Verso, 1997), 151–53; "GOP Makes 'Top Priority' of Converting Black Voters," *Washington Post*, December 25, 2003; "'Black and Conservative' Takes Many Different Tones," *NYT*, December 22, 1991.

5. Angela Dillard, "The Civil Rights Movement and the Rise of Modern Black Conservatism: Re-Thinking Alliances, Allegiances and the Complexities of Political Culture," presented at annual meeting of the Southern Historical Association, November 3, 2012, Mobile, Alabama; Manning Marable, *Race, Reform, and Rebellion: The Second Reconstruction and Beyond in Black America, 1945–2006*, 3rd ed. (Jackson: University of Mississippi Press, 2007), 198; Deborah Toler, "Black Conservatives," in Chip Berlet, ed., *Eyes Right! Challenging the Right Wing Backlash* (Somerville, Mass.: Political Research Associates, 1995), 294; Paul Hendrickson, *Sons of Mississippi: A Story of Race and Its Legacy* (New York: Knopf, 2003), 169–71; William Link, *Righteous Warrior: Jesse Helms and the Rise of Modern Conservatism* (New York: St. Martin's, 2008), 371.

6. Manning Marable, *How Capitalism Underdeveloped Black America: Problems in Race, Political Economy and Society* (Boston: South End Press, 1983), 175; Anderson et al., 117–18; Charles Evers with Andrew Szanton, *Have No Fear: The Charles Evers Story* (New York: Wiley, 1997), 289–94; Ralph David Abernathy, *And the Walls Come Tumbling Down: An Autobiography* (New York: Harper and Row, 1989), 589–90, 602–3; "Driving with Hosey," *Atlanta*, November 2004, 234; "Chicago Mayor Supports Jesse Jackson's Candidacy," *Jet*, March 5, 1984, 6.

7. Stephen Tuck, *We Ain't What We Ought to Be: The Black Freedom Struggle from Emancipation to Obama* (Cambridge, Mass.: Belknap Press of Harvard University Press, 2010), 373; "Transcript of Ronald Reagan's 1980 Neshoba County Fair Speech," *Neshoba Democrat*, November 15, 2007; Lou Cannon, *President Reagan: The Role of a Lifetime* (New York: Public Affairs, 2000), 458; Earl Black and Merle Black, *The Rise of Southern Republicans* (Cambridge, Mass.: Belknap Press of Harvard University Press, 2002), 218–19; Matthew Rees, *From the Deck to the Sea: Blacks and the Republican Party* (Wakefield, N.H.: Longwood Academic, 1991), 331; Thomas E. Cavanagh, *Inside Black America: The Message of the Black Vote in the 1984 Elections* (Washington, D.C.: Joint Center for Political Studies, 1985), 39.

8. "Reagan Sends Mixed Signals on Civil Rights," *NYT*, July 16, 1981; Raymond Wolters, *Right Turn: William Bradford Reynolds, the Reagan Administration, and Black Civil Rights* (New Brunswick, N.J.: Transaction, 1996), 219; "Black Leaders Draw Charge of 'New Racism,'" *Los Angeles Times*, March 5, 1985; Dennis Deslippe, *Protesting Affirmative Action: The Struggle over Equality After the Civil Rights Revolution* (Baltimore: Johns Hopkins University Press, 2012), 211; Theodore Rueter, "The New Black Conservative," in Theodore Rueter, ed., *The Politics of Race: African Americans and the Political System* (Armonk, N.Y.: M.E. Sharpe, 1995), 86; John Karaagac, *Between Promise and Policy: Ronald Reagan and Conservative Reformism* (Lanham, Md.: Lexington, 2000), 140; "Cabinet Aide Greeted by Reagan as 'Mayor,'" *NYT*, June 19, 1981.

9. "Leading Black Republicans Assail Reagan Aide," *NYT*, July 9, 1984; "Whatever Happened to Black Capitalism?," *Black Enterprise*, August 1990, 166; Robert Weisbrot, *Freedom Bound: A History of America's Civil Rights Movement* (New York: Plume, 1991), 304; Dan T. Carter, *From George Wallace to Newt Gingrich: Race in the Conservative Counterrevolution, 1963–1994* (Baton Rouge: Louisiana State University Press, 1996), 56.

10. Ian Haney-Lopez, *Dog Whistle Politics: How Coded Racial Appeals Have Wrecked the Middle Class* (New York: Oxford University Press, 2014), 58–59.

11. Alexander P. Lamis, "The Two-Party South: From the 1960s to the 1990s," in Alexander P. Lamis, ed., *Southern Politics in the 1990s* (Baton Rouge: Louisiana State University Press, 1999), 7–8.

12. Cannon, 455–56; Carter, 62–63.

13. "A Message to Americans," *Ebony*, July 1991, 20; "Ticker Tape U.S.A.," *Jet*, March 1, 1982, 11; "Leading Black Republicans Assail Reagan Aide," *NYT*, July 9, 1984; J. Clay Smith, "A Black Lawyer's Response to the Fairmont Papers," *Howard Law Journal* 26 (1983): 223; Ronald W. Walters, *Black Presidential Politics in America: A Strategic Approach* (Albany: State University of New York Press, 1988), 186; Ethan Bronner, *Battle for Justice: How the Bork Nomination Shook America* (New York: Norton, 1989), 227; "How Resolute Is Reagan on Civil Rights?," *NYT*, October 10, 1982; Wolters, 481.

14. Michael Fauntroy, *Republicans and the Black Vote* (Boulder, Colo.: Lynne Rienner Publishers, 2007), 5; Colin Powell with Joseph E. Persico, *My American Journey* (New York: Random House, 1995), 400; "Colin Powell: GOP Holds 'Dark Vein of Intolerance,'" *Huffington Post*, January 13, 2013.

15. Rueter, 96; "President Vetoes Bill on Job Rights," *NYT*, October 23, 1990; Carter, 106.

16. "Jack Kemp," *Time*, May 8, 2009; "Note to Republicans," *NYT*, April 5, 2014; "RNC Chief to Say it Was 'Wrong' to Exploit Racial Conflict for Votes," *Washington Post*, July 14, 2005; "Rand Paul Stands Out in Courting Black Voters," *NYT*, July 25, 2014; "Paul: African-American Leaders May Not Yet Embrace GOP," *Politico*, October 17, 2014; "Paul to Republicans: Broaden GOP Appeal," *The Hill*, November 2, 2014.

17. Pearl Robinson, "Whither the Future of Blacks in the Republican Party?," *Political Science Quarterly*, 97:2 (Summer 1982), 226; "Coretta King, in New Jersey, Backs Kean as He Seeks the Support of Blacks," *NYT*, October 26, 1985; "Black Republican Renaissance," *Washington Afro-American*, September 16, 1986; Ralph Reiland, "Black Republicanism," *American Enterprise* (January/February 1996), 8; David Bositis, *Blacks and the 2008 Republican National Convention* (Washington, D.C.: Joint Center for Political and Economic Studies, 2008), 13.

18. Manning Marable, *The Great Wells of Democracy: The Meaning of Race in American Life* (New York: BasicCivitas Books, 2002), 178; "Supreme Court Invalidates Key Part of Voting Rights Act," *NYT*, June 25, 2013; "A Black Congressional Hope in Connecticut," *NYT*, August 9, 1990; Rees, 388; "News and Views," *Journal of Blacks in Higher Education*, April 30, 2000, 18.

19. "Did Herman Cain's Fizzle Exacerbate GOP's 'Black Problem'?," *Christian Science Monitor*, December 5, 2011; "Will the New Black Republicans in Congress Be Lawmakers—or Talk Show Hosts?," *The Root*, November 17, 2014.

20. "On Marriage Equality, Clarence Thomas is Right About Dignity," *Slate*, July 8, 2015; "Meet Mia Love," *Washington Post*, November 5, 2014; "Congressman J. C. Watts," *Headway*, April 30, 1997; Angela Dillard, *Guess Who's Coming to Dinner Now? Multicultural Conservatism in America* (New York: New York University Press, 2001), 9; "Are Black Republicans Like Runaway Slaves?," *The Root*, February 13, 2012; "Ben Carson: Abortion is the No. 1 Killer of Black People," *Mother Jones*, August 14, 2015; "Marco Rubio, Tim Scott Talk About Jesus, Christian Faith, and Miracles at Conservative Political Summit," *Christian Post*, October 11, 2013.

21. "Mr. Bush, Meet Mr. Lincoln," *NYT*, June 26, 1988; "Judge Tells U.S. to Make Political Parties Comply with Rights Law," *NYT*, April 8, 1992; "Fighting for the Party of Lincoln," *Focus*, 22:10 (October 1994), 3; David Bositis, *Blacks and the 1992 Republican National Convention* (Washington, DC: Joint Center for Political and Economic Studies, 1992), 17–18; Bositis, *Blacks and the 2008 Republican National Convention*, 7.

22. Clarence Thomas, "No Room at the Inn: The Loneliness of the Black Conservative," in Stan Faryna, Brad Stetson, and Joseph Conti, eds., *Black and Right: The Bold New Voice of Black Conservatives in America* (Westport, Conn.: Praeger, 1997), 8–9; J. C. Watts with Chriss Winston, *What Color is a Conservative? My Life and Politics* (New York: HarperCollins, 2002), 206–8; "Public Lives," *NYT*, February 21, 2000; "Oklahoma Sooner," *The Crisis*, November–December 2002, 37–38; "New Chairman Boos G.O.P. When He's Not Cheerleading," *NYT*, March 8, 2009; "Michael Steele: Voter ID Rhetoric Is 'Irresponsible,' Party Needs New Approach to Black Voters," *Huffington Post*, August 31, 2012; Timothy Thurber, *Race and Republicans: The GOP's Frayed Relationship with African Americans, 1945-1974* (Lawrence: University Press of Kansas, 2013), 386.

23. "Equality—Not Yet," *NYT*, July 13, 1981; Clarence L. Townes, Jr., interview by author, October 18, 2011, in possession of author; "The GOP Task of Welcoming New 'Diners,'" *Chicago Tribune*, December 18, 1987; "Rights Bill," *Black Enterprise*, February 1991, 29; "Arthur Fletcher Returns to Political Forefront as a Republican Presidential Candidate," *Jet*, July 31, 1995, 11.

24. "Affirmative Action Pioneer Advised GOP Presidents," *Washington Post*, July 14, 2005;

Fear of a Black Republican, DVD, dir. Kevin J. Williams (Trenton, N.J.: Shamrock Stine Productions, 2011); Brooke, 181.

25. George W. Lee to Kapel Kirkendol, April 29, 1976, Folder 10, Box 9, Lee Collection; George W. Lee, "The Real Republicans of Memphis and Shelby County," n.d., Folder 16, Box 2, Lee Collection.

26. "GOP Leaders Warn Party to Meet Negro Demands," *Chicago Defender*, February 19, 1944; Speech delivered by George G. Fleming at the 1964 NNRA Convention, August 22, 1964, Townes Papers.

27. Abraham Lincoln, "Second Annual Message to Congress," December 1, 1862, in Roy P. Basler, ed., *The Collected Works of Abraham Lincoln*, vol. 5 (New Brunswick, N.J.: Rutgers University Press, 1953), 537.

INDEX

Hays, Will H., 16
Head Start, 164, 191
Helms, Jesse, 220–21, 225, 228
Henderson, Dennis, 31
Henry, Edward, 17
Henry, Robert C., 159, 215
Hermann, A. B., 106, 114
Hicks, Al, 173
Hicks, James, 38, 66
Hill, Betty, 21
Hill, Charles, 39
Hills, Carla, 221
Hobby, Oveta Culp, 71
Hodges, Norman, 173
Holder, Eric, 229
Holshouser, Jim, 202–3, 217, 221
Holton, Linwood, 80, 217
Hooks, Benjamin, 2, 25, 44, 81, 99, 132, 144, 189
Hoover, Herbert, 18–19
Hoover Institution, 223–24
Horton, Willie, 228
House Un-American Activities Committee, 98
Housing. See open housing; public housing
Howard, Perry W., 14, 16, 22–23, 51, 84–85, 96, 121
Howard, T. R. M., 54–55, 61, 78, 95, 171
Howard University, 27, 229
Huckabee, Mike, 230
Hughes, Emmet John, 76, 87
Humphrey, Hubert, 69, 97, 106, 181
Hurd, William, 230
Hurst, Charles, 209–11, 213, 215
Hurston, Zora Neale, 21, 32

Illinois, 36, 109, 111, 168, 190, 209; black Republicans in, 52, 216. See also Allen, Leo; Anderson, John; Chicago, Illinois; Douglas, Paul; Kerner, Otto; Percy, Charles; Stevenson, Adlai
Improved Benevolent and Protective Order of Elks of the World (IBPOEW), 50–52, 70, 81, 119, 130, 143, 184, 224
Independent Citizens for Rockefeller, 130
Independent Democrats for Eisenhower, 62

Indiana, 44, 64, 208; black Republicans in, 26, 125–26, 214. See also Halleck, Charles; Jackson, L. K.; Willkie, Wendell
Industrial Statesman, 92–93
Innis, Roy, 175, 177, 184–85, 195, 212
Iowa, 49. See also Hoover, Herbert; Miller, Jack
Iowa Bystander, 76, 181
Ives, Irving, 31, 34, 87

Jackson, Andrew, 102
Jackson, Jesse, 208–9
Jackson, L. K., 2, 90, 104, 113–14, 126, 164–65, 167
Jackson, Mahalia, 204
Jackson, Maynard, 215
Jackson, Samuel C., 2, 152, 190, 194, 199, 203, 205, 207–8, 214–15
Javits, Jacob, 1, 34, 65, 69, 86, 89, 120, 124, 139, 165
"Jeannette Weiss Principle," 205–6
The Jeffersons, 208
Jenkins, Charles, 26
Jenkins, Elaine, 135
Jet, 59, 72, 95, 107, 130, 139, 167, 185, 208
John Birch Society, 117, 132–33, 138, 145
Johnson, Frank M., 48
Johnson, Henry Lincoln, 13, 16, 51
Johnson, James Weldon, 15–16
Johnson, Lyndon B., 60, 69–71, 91, 93–95, 102–3, 112, 117, 218; presidency of, 128, 141, 143–47, 152, 157–58, 160, 189, 194
Johnson, Robert H., 51, 70
Jones, Paul, 207–11
Jones, Russell M., 126
Jones, Scipio, 13
Jordan, Vernon, 25
Jourdain, Edward, 29

Kansas, 19; black Republicans from, 53, 57, 152, 190. See also Hall, Fred; Landon, Alf
Karenga, Maulana, 176
Kean, Thomas, 229
Keating, Kenneth, 52, 86–87, 92, 124, 139, 146
Kefauver, Estes, 58, 60, 62

Church, Robert R., Jr.; Church, Roberta; Dunn, Winfield; Hooks, Benjamin; Kefauver, Estes; Lee, George W.; *Tri-State Defender*

Terrell, Mary Church, 46

Texas, 40, 67, 71, 94, 112, 117–18, 145; black Republicans in, 173, 230. *See also* Black-and-Tans

Third World Republicans, 197

Thomas, Clarence, 224, 226, 230–31

Thomas, Thalia, 45, 61

Thompson, William, 33

Thrower, Randolph, 65

Thurmond, Strom, 161, 163, 179–80, 200, 215

Till, Emmett, 54, 72–73

Time, 155, 164

Tobin, Richard, 48

Toomer, L. B., 45, 80

Tower, John, 117

Townes, Clarence, Jr., 80, 135–36, 141, 148–50, 152–53, 166, 172, 180–81, 189, 197, 232

Townsend, Prentice, 53

Travis, Oneth M., 27

Tri-State Bank, 171

Tri-State Defender, 110

Truman, Harry S., 34, 36, 41, 43, 45, 47, 163, 219

Tucker, Amelia, 125

Tucker, Bishop C. Ewbank, 186

Tucker, Charles M., 126

Turnage, Elliot, 83

Tuttle, Elbert, 25, 48

Unions: black Republicans and, 6, 22, 56, 125, 174, 202; black voters and, 22, 53, 55, 78, 221; and civil rights, 70; discrimination within, 56, 123, 125, 207. *See also* Philadelphia Plan

United Nations, 95, 189

United Negro College Fund, 232

United Republican Club of Harlem, 143

Universal Life Insurance Company, 171

Universal Negro Improvement Association, 171

University of Alabama, 62

University of Georgia, 93

University of Mississippi, 168, 220, 225

University of South Carolina, 92

Urban unrest, 153, 157–58, 162, 179–80, 199

U.S. Civil Rights Commission, 190, 226

U.S. News and World Report, 110

Utah, 86, 230

Vandiver, Ernest, 110

Vann, Robert, 18–19, 28

Vardaman, Claude O., 83

Vermont, 146

Vietnam, 166, 178

Virgin Islands, 175, 231

Virginia, 47, 101, 135, 182; black Republicans in, 79–80, 126, 142, 204, 216; black voters in, 63–64, 146, 217

Virginia Union University, 65

Voinovich, George, 229

Volpe, John, 154

Voter Education Project, 120, 154, 189

Voting Rights Act of 1965, 147, 161–62, 166, 215, 219–20, 226, 230

Walker, Cora, 167, 173–74

Walker, William O., 26, 52, 76, 124, 180

Walker, Wyatt Tee, 151, 160

Wall Street Journal, 183

Wallace, George, 179, 182, 185, 212

Wallace, Henry, 36

War on Poverty, 6, 218. *See also* Great Society

Warders, Jesse, 159–60, 199

Warren, Earl, 21, 48, 59, 85, 118, 165, 187, 232

Washington, 17, 24, 174, 208. *See also* Evans, Daniel; Magnuson, Warren; Stokes, Charles

Washington, Booker T., 17, 20, 171, 200

Washington, D.C., 59, 65, 153, 162, 196; black Republicans in, 15, 29, 46, 124, 134–35, 164, 198

Washington, Genoa, 2

Washington, George, 150

Washington Post, 98, 113, 123

Washington, Roy, 33

Washington Star, 99

ACKNOWLEDGMENTS

Thurgood Marshall said, in reference to the conservative Clarence Thomas, "None of us got where we are solely by pulling ourselves up by our bootstraps. We got here because somebody—a parent, a teacher, an Ivy League crony or a few nuns—bent down and helped us pick up our boots." And while I am not a nominee to the Supreme Court, nor do I have many cronies (Ivy League or otherwise), I have had many individuals who bent down and helped me pick up, put on, and tie my scholarly boots.

At the University of Kentucky, Gerald Smith's innumerable hours spent reading and critiquing the pages of this book made them demonstrably better. At all times during my career he has had my back, helping secure needed funding and employment. Gerald, there is nothing that I can say to properly express my gratitude for the past ten years so I will leave it at this: Thank You.

Also at Kentucky, Ronald Eller's kindness and warmth was unmatched, and his scholarship on Appalachia convinced me to write with passion about that which is important to me, not what's historiographically fashionable. Similarly, Tracy Campbell's advice not to "hide behind footnotes" and to think and write in ways that challenge traditions has given me the courage to think outside the confines of our historical "boxes."

I could not have asked for a better editor than Robert Lockhart at the University of Pennsylvania Press. From the first day we spoke, Bob embraced my vision of this book, challenged me to live up to that vision, and provided the resources and guidance to make our shared vision a reality. I would not have met Bob had it not been for Michael Kazin, who endorsed and subtly nudged this book along at pivotal stages in its development. Karen Ferguson and an anonymous reviewer both provided key analytical insights that pushed me to strengthen and clarify my arguments. Indeed, there was not a single person who contributed to this project at Penn Press who did not provide valuable assistance.

Over the past five years, other historians—all with important books to write and busy schedules of their own—have provided commentary on my research and opened doors of opportunity that shaped this book in meaningful ways. A special thank you to Marsha Barrett, N. D. B. Connolly, Angela Dillard, Devin Fergus, Ron Formisano, Nishani Frazier, Laura Jane Gifford, Karen Hawkins, Ibram X. Kendi, Anna von der Goltz, Britta Waldschmidt-Nelson, Juliet E. K. Walker, Robert E. Weems, Jr., and Daniel K. Williams. The strengths of this book are a reflection of the dozens of intellectual giants who provided me with guidance along the way; its weaknesses are all mine.

Thanks must also go to those who made history, and were willing to talk to me about their experiences, especially Clarence Townes, Dorsey Miller, Stephanie Stokes, and Timothy Jenkins. Though he was unable to conduct an interview before his death because of his declining health, Edward W. Brooke graciously granted unfettered access to his restricted papers at the Library of Congress.

Because of the national scope of this project, research could not have been completed without significant funding. David Hamilton played a central role in helping me obtain significant funding from the University of Kentucky. Additional funding was provided by the Harry Middleton Fellowship in Presidential Studies from the Lyndon Baines Johnson Foundation, and travel grants from the Dwight D. Eisenhower Foundation, Rockefeller Archive Center, and Gerald R. Ford Foundation.

Throughout my travels, I had the pleasure of working with archivists who found documents in collections that had never even crossed my mind. Among those who devoted unwarranted time and attention to my ceaseless inquiries were Valoise Armstrong at the Dwight D. Eisenhower Presidential Library, William McNitt at the Gerald R. Ford Presidential Library, Meghan Lee at the Richard M. Nixon Presidential Library, Tom Rosenbaum at the Rockefeller Archive Center, and Matt Harris at the University of Kentucky. Ray Bonis at Virginia Commonwealth University was particularly generous in providing a digitized copy of the entire unprocessed papers of Clarence Townes.

Special recognition must also be given to Kathy Carter. As my advisor at High Point University over a decade ago, she was responsible for instilling in me the confidence to pursue an academic career in history. Her intelligence, down-to-earth insight, humor, and grace are rare combinations. At Kentucky, though they would probably note that I rarely ventured out of my house to participate in any social functions, it has been a pleasure to spend what time I did with those I am proud to call friends: Lori Whitmire, Stephen Pickering,

Danielle Dodson, Jill Abney, and my "teammate" at the Kentucky African American Encyclopedia Project, Sallie Powell.

My parents deserve acknowledgment as much as anyone else involved in this project. As my personal editor, Mom read every page everything I've ever written—including a wearisome Hegelian analysis of the U.S. Revolution. Dad, on the other hand, tried to read the first chapter of this book, but fell asleep by page ten. He has, however, been my proudest supporter. Financially, he made the life of a poor scholar a little easier, but, more important, his belief in me has never waned. This work is dedicated to his unwavering support and love.

My wife had to bear the biggest burden during the duration of this project. Even after the birth of our two children (Hi, Cassidy and Norman!), she never said a word of complaint during any of my extended absences researching across the country or during my hours spent writing and rewriting the same sentence. To Katie: I want no world (for beautiful you are my world).

Lightning Source UK Ltd.
Milton Keynes UK
UKOW01n1459111016

285017UK00002B/34/P

9 780812 248524